i-NET +
CERTIFICATION
TRAINING GUIDE

Copyright 2001 MARCRAFT International Corporation

Trademark Acknowledgments

All brand and product names are trademarks or registered trademarks of their respective companies. All terms mentioned in this book that are known to be trademarks or service marks are listed below. MARCRAFT cannot attest to the accuracy of this information. Use of a term in this book should not be regarded as affecting the validity of any trademark or service mark.

Windows 95/98/NT/2000 are registered trademarks of Microsoft Corporation.

Apple and Macintosh are registered trademarks of Apple Computer, Incorporated.

NetWare is a registered trademark of Novell, Incorporated.

AT&T is a registered trademark of AT&T.

MCI and WorldCOM are registered trademarks of MCI WorldCOM.

Sprintlink is a registered trademark of Sprint, Incorporated.

Netscape and Netscape Navigator and Communicator are registered trademarks of Netscape/AOL.

Shockwave is a registered trademark of Macromedia.

RealPlayer is a registered trademark of RealPlayer Networks.

Adobe Acrobat is registered trademark of Adobe.

IBM is a registered trademark of International Business Machines.

Written by Randy L. Ratliff
Original graphics created by Michael R. Hall and Cathy J. Boulay

ISBN: 0-13-033452-9

P/N DC-700
Printed in the United States of America
1-11/00

Preface

Marcraft International has been producing certification courseware for different facets of the electronic, computer architecture, computer repair, and IT industry since 1988. This book has been designed to prepare students for the CompTIA i-Net+ Certification exam and prepare them with the necessary tools for grasping the complex technologies of the Internet.

i-Net+ Certification

The i-Net+ Certification exam represents a standard benchmark from which companies, professionals, and students of the Internet can measure their knowledge of the rapidly changing Internet.

Key Features

The pedagogical features of this book were carefully developed to provide readers with key content information, as well as review and testing opportunities. Each chapter begins with a list of learning objectives that establishes a foundation and systematic preview of the chapter. Each chapter concludes with a chapter summary of the points and objectives that should have been accomplished. A complete i-Net+ objective map has been used to provide content directly related to the i-Net+ Certification exam. Key terms are presented in bold or italics throughout the text. Backgound Info sections appear throughout the chapters to add in-depth discussions, which can be used as background information.

Appendices

Appendix A is the OSI Reference Model, which provides supplemental information. Appendix B provides the i-Net+ Objective Map for the i-Net+ Certification exam. Appendix C is a comprehensive glossary of words and meanings to provide quick, easy access to key term definitions that appear in each chapter.

Evaluation and Test Material

There is an abundance of test materials available with this course. Each chapter contains an open-ended Review Questions section and a Multiple-Choice Questions section. The review questions are designed to test critical thinking while the multiple-choice questions reflect the real i-Net+ Certification exam. Additional i-Net+ test material in the form of multiple-choice questions can be found on the companion CD-ROM.

Lab Guide Exercises

The i-Net+ Certification Lab Guide provides an excellent hands-on component to emphasize the theoretical materials from the i-Net+ Certification Training Guide. Applying the concepts of each chapter in the textbook to the lab exercises is crucial in preparing for a successful career as a Web site administrator. There are twenty-seven lab procedures, which are divided into the following seven lab groups:

Lab Group 1 provides an introduction to the Internet and covers such topics as URLs and multimedia file formats, as well as cache and cookie management.

Lab Group 2 covers Web site construction and publishing using MS FrontPage. Topics include: HTML, using FrontPage, ActiveX controls and page objects, basic programming, and Web-based database construction.

Lab Group 3 covers the TCP/IP utilities.

Lab Group 4 provides instruction on Telnet, FTP, e-mail clients, and client workstation management.

Lab Group 5 consists of labs covering Windows NT Server setup including topics such as: proxy servers, firewalls, SMTP servers, and intruder detection and auditing.

Lab Group 6 covers system security issues and investigates topics such as: Web server setup, anti-virus software for networks, Remote Access Services/Virtual Private Networks, and domain name registration.

Lab Group 7 provides an introduction to Web site management including copyrighting your Web site and multiple-language Web publishing.

Interactive CD-ROM

The i-Net+ Certification Training Guide is accompanied by a comprehensive additional test bank, which is sealed on the back cover of the book. This CD testing material was developed to simulate the i-Net+ Certification Exam testing process and to allow students to complete mock tests, determine their weak points, and study more strategically. The accompanying CD provides two styles of testing:

- Study Mode

- Practice Exam

In the Study Mode, the correct answer is presented on the screen along with the reference heading where the material can be found in the text. A single mouse click takes you quickly to the corresponding section of the electronic text book for a more detailed explanation of the answer.

ORGANIZATION

In general, it is not necessary to move through this text in the same order that it is presented. Also, it is not necessary to teach any specific portion of the material to its extreme. Where you begin depends on your knowledge of networking in general, and the Internet in particular. Instead, the material can be adjusted to fit the length of your course.

Chapter 1—Internet Infrastructure describes the basic architecture of the global Internet. Basic terminology is introduced and explained. Common hardware devices are presented with a slant for their specific purpose in accessing the Internet, or for making the Internet work. The technologies used to work with hardware applied on the Internet are also described in detail.

Chapter 2—Web Site Development is a conglomeration of the many software tools associated with the Internet. The intent of this chapter is to provide an overview of the function and applications of the tools that are commonly used to create a Web site.

Chapter 3—Internet Protocols is a comprehensive description of the protocols—or rules—that define how information moves across the Internet. Particular emphasis is placed on TCP/IP, which is the common protocol that has made the Internet possible. Several diagnostic tools, which can be used for troubleshooting Internet connections, are presented in this chapter.

Chapter 4—Internet Clients is focused on the user side of an Internet connection. Topics such as client protocols, client configuration, and types of Internet clients are discussed.

Chapter 5—Internet Servers is devoted to the servers on the Internet. The many types of servers used on the Internet are discussed along with typical applications. Finally, this chapter includes information on how to test a Web server as well as typical problem spots.

Chapter 6—Internet Security details the significant importance of security on the Internet. Methods of controlling access to a Web server, as well as methods of detecting an intruder to a Web site are discussed. Common Web server attacks—which could cripple or disable a Web site—are described along with measures for thwarting the attacks. For sites that sell goods to consumers, the specific methods of ensuring privacy and protecting consumer data are detailed.

Chapter 7—Business On The Internet contains practical information about running an Internet-based business. From copyrighting the content of a Web site, to dealing with foreign currencies and defining the business model of a Web site, this chapter lists many characteristics that make the difference between whether a site will be a "major force" or a footnote in Internet history.

Teacher Support

An Instructor's Guide is available for the course. Answers for all of the end-of-chapter review questions and multiple-choice questions are included along with a paragraph reference in the chapter where that item is covered. Sample schedules are included as guidelines for possible course implementations. Answers to all Lab Review Questions are provided so that there is an indication of what the expected outcomes should be. A sample test of 20 multiple-choice questions with answers given is also provided for each chapter. Instructors can use these sample tests as chapter tests or combine them into a midterm or final test.

Test Taking Tips

Due to the breadth of the i-Net+ exam, and the complexity of the Internet, the i-Net+ Certification exam is difficult. To prepare for the i-Net+ Certification exam, be sure to do the following:

- Experience the Internet. If you're not connected, then do so.

- Answer the questions at the end of each chapter in this book. If you can't remember the correct answer, read back through the chapter until you have absorbed enough to accurately answer the question.

- Try the techniques and practices described in the book. There are many free downloads on the Internet. Find them and try them out. Many companies that sell Internet software provide free demo downloads.

- Quiz yourself by using the CD-ROM that accompanies this book. If you get an answer wrong, go to the referenced chapter and study the material. Then, try again.

- Study the glossary at the end of the book. If there are terms that you're not familiar with, use the Index, locate the correct section of the book where the term is described, and study it.

- Make sure that words or phrases that have been highlighted in the margins of each page are familiar to you. These words and phrases are often key terminology that is used on the exam.

- Good luck.

ACKNOWLEDGMENTS

The author wishes to thank the following in appreciation for their help in the preparation of this book:

Cathy Boulay for her extensive editing expertise that brought this book to a high level of professionalism. To Mike Hall for smooth and it-looks-so-easy graphics that were anything but that. To the e-commerce folks at Ameritech who gave me the low-down on Web site security and commercial encryption schemes. To the engineering staff at onemain.com/Zoomnet. To the patient Help Desk at VeriSign. To Whitney Freeman—who wasn't actively involved in this book—but nevertheless I sensed him looking over my shoulder, frowning when the words were bad and smiling when they were good. Special thanks to Nancy Warner for detailed line editing and suggestions that make the book a much better reading and learning experience. To Phoebe Ratliff for sharp and precise research (and, by extension, to the Dawson-Bryant School District in Ohio for creating a learning atmosphere that at once fosters personal growth and Internet contributions). To countless corporations who provide ready access to white papers on their Web sites, and to Internet-based organizations and groups that actively collect and distribute tutorials about Internet technology.

To CompTIA for once again braving inevitable criticism for their efforts to bring order from chaos; an effort that will challenge all of us to look a bit closer at what we do and how we do it.

To Chuck Brooks who was with me a long time ago in a distant place—and is proof that the discourse of ideas and creativity knows no time nor distance.

To my wife, Jan; daughter, Phoebe; and son, Nick. And, of course, Paris.

This book is for Phoebe—
Who plunged into the Internet
Not knowing north or south
Or east or west
But wasn't afraid

Table of Contents

Chapter 1—Internet Infrastructure

Chapter 2—Web Site Development

Chapter 3—Internet Protocols

Chapter 4—Internet Clients

Chapter 5—Internet Servers

Chapter 6—Internet Security

Chapter 7—Business on the Internet

Appendix A—OSI Reference Model

Appendix B—i-Net+ Objective Map

Appendix C—Glossary

Index

CHAPTER
1

INTERNET INFRASTRUCTURE

LEARNING
OBJECTIVES

U pon completion of this chapter and its related lab procedures, you should be able to perform the following tasks:

1. (4.1) Describe the core components of the current Internet infrastructure and how they relate to each other. Content may include:

    - Network access points

    - Backbone

2. (5.6) Describe the differences between the following:

    - Internet

    - Intranet

    - Extranet

3. (4.8) Describe hardware connection devices and their uses. Content could include the following:

    - Network interface card

    - Various types of modems including analog, ISDN, DSL, and cable

    - Adapter

    - Bridge

    - Hub

    - Router

    - Switch

    - Gateway

4. (4.9) Describe the various types of Internet bandwidth technologies. Content could include the following:

    - T1/E1

    - T3/E3

    - Frame Relay

    - X.25

    - ATM

5. (1.1) Describe a URL, its function and components, different types of URLs, and use of the appropriate type of URL to access a given type of server. Content may include the following:

    - Protocol

    - Address

    - Port

CHAPTER 1

Internet Infrastructure

INTRODUCTION

The Internet is a collaborative effort of thousands of individuals from all parts of the world. It began as a small, interconnected network between four sites in 1969. Today, there are thousands of sites and millions of machines connected to the Internet.

The Internet grows and evolves each day. This chapter attempts to describe the current state of the Internet infrastructure as it is today, and according to objectives defined for the i-Net+ Certification exam.

In addition to the material presented in this chapter, study papers on the Internet about the Internet. Experience the Internet personally. Use several of the URLs presented in this chapter to develop a hands-on sense of when each is appropriate and how to use the URLs.

ORGANIZATION OF THE INTERNET

The **Internet** is organized according to high-speed access points and a complex network of backbones that carry high-speed traffic. The Internet is also organized by protocols that define how data is sent and received on the Internet.

Internet

This section examines the physical infrastructure of the Internet. The protocols that may be found on the Internet vary with specific technologies used to transport data, but there's one set of protocols that tends to bind all other protocols. This set of protocols is called the **TCP/IP** (Transmission Control Protocol/ Internet Protocol) **stack** and is briefly discussed in this chapter and described in detail in Chapter 3. TCP/IP is a protocol requirement for accessing the Internet. TCP/IP must be installed on any computer that will be using the Internet.

TCP/IP stack

Network Access Points

Originally, the National Science Foundation created four **Network Access Points (NAP)** to provide voice and data switching centers in the United States. A NAP provides high-speed interconnectivity to the Internet. The NAPs were created to provide a transition from a US government-sponsored Internet to a commercially operated Internet.

Network Access Points (NAP)

Today, there are six major NAPs in the United States and all of them are commercially owned and operated. The NAPs are:

- New York, operated by Sprint

- New York (Big East), operated by ICS Network systems

- Washington D.C. (MAE East), operated by MCI WorldCom

- Chicago, operated by Ameritech

- San Francisco, operated by Pacific Bell

- San Jose (MAE West), operated by MCI WorldCom

mesh network

Figure 1-1 shows a map of the United States and the locations of all six NAPs. Notice that all NAPs are connected together into a **mesh network**. A mesh network consists of multiple paths to all connection points. In addition to providing interconnectivity in the United States, NAPs provide connections to the rest of the world.

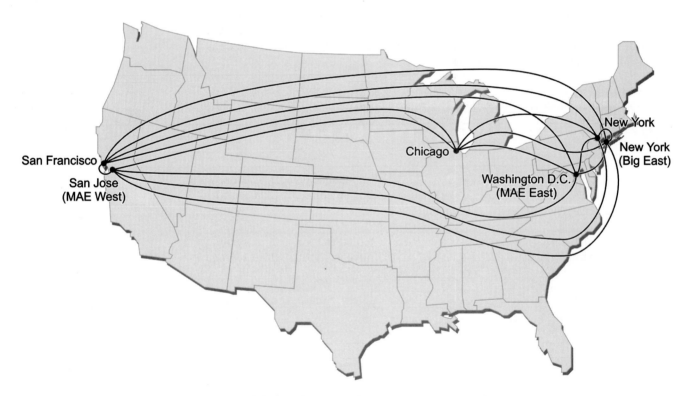

Figure 1-1 Major Internet Network Access Points

The Internet is a global network. There are similar access points in Europe, Africa, Asia, South America, and the Middle East. Since there are connections that tie the NAPs together around the world, we're able to use the NAPs to access a server that's located anywhere on the Internet.

An Internet NAP is a busy switching center. It's not uncommon for each NAP to process 100,000,000 packets of data each day. The lines that feed a NAP are high-speed digital lines such as a 44.736 Mbps T3 line, or fiber optic lines running at 622.08 Mbps and higher. (See the Bandwidth Technology section later in this chapter for a discussion of the T-carrier system.)

NAP operators charge a fee for the use of their switching facilities. Many NAP operators have complex arrangements with traditional long-distance carriers such as AT&T. In some cases, the NAP is owned by a long distance carrier. For example, MCI WorldCom owns the Washington D.C. and San Jose NAPs. MCI WorldCom provides long distance connections to their own NAPs, as well as leases the connections to other NAP operators.

Internet Backbone

Each of the network access points may be accessed from the United States commercial backbone. A **backbone** is a common channel that allows networks to be connected together. The Internet commercial backbone provides voice and data lines across the United States. Other parts of the world have similar backbones used to provide voice and data communications along with access to NAPs.

backbone

The commercial backbone feeding the NAPs is large, fast, and complicated. The backbone communicates with NAPs on T3 or OC3 lines. Many backbones include tributaries that link cities to network access points on slower T1 (1.544 Mbps) or OC1 (54.84 Mbps) lines.

Companies that contribute to the backbone include:

- AT&T Network Systems

- Cable and Wireless, USA

- Sprintlink

- MCI WorldCom

- BBN Planet

Figure 1-2 shows the AT&T IP Backbone for the United States. Notice that the backbone intersects NAPs in New York, Washington D.C., Chicago, and San Francisco. It's possible that when a packet of data is sent across the Internet, the packet will never use the NAP facilities. Instead, the packet will only travel on the backbone to the destination server. For example, an Internet user in Dallas can access a server in Los Angeles on the AT&T backbone without accessing a NAP.

The physical wiring used on the backbone may be owned by a backbone operator, or it may be leased from a regional carrier such as Pacific Bell, Bell South, or Ameritech. The actual direction, or path, that a packet travels across the Internet backbone wiring is determined by **routers**. A router is a device that stores the locations of other network devices and uses that information to plot a path to a remote network. For more information on routers, refer to the Router section later in this chapter.

routers

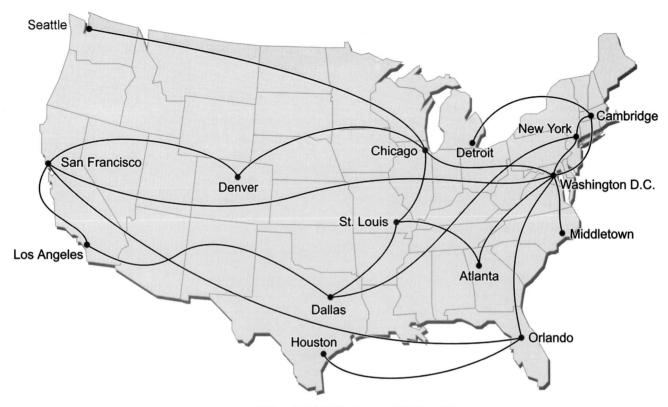

Figure 1-2 The AT&T Internet IP Backbone

In addition to using routers to map a path across the Internet, backbone operators engage in "peer arrangements" with other backbone operators, regional carriers, or large **Internet Service Providers (ISP)**. A **peer arrangement** is an agreement between providers to use one another's facilities for switching data and voice packets. For example, AT&T may reach an agreement with Ameritech to use Ameritech's wiring infrastructure in the Midwest in exchange for switching Ameritech packets to the Washington D.C. NAP.

Internet Service Providers

An Internet Service Provider (ISP) provides user access to the Internet infrastructure. The ISP is said to have an Internet **point-of-presence** since the ISP maintains the equipment necessary to access a commercial backbone provider. Typically, the ISP is directly connected to the commercial backbone with equipment such as routers, switches, and servers. The commercial backbone operator—through peer arrangements or NAP access—ensures that packets are deliverable to any Internet address in the world.

An ISP may also be a backbone operator or a NAP provider. Ameritech, for example, is a regional telecommunications company that also acts as an ISP, leases its wiring infrastructure to backbone operators, and maintains a NAP in Chicago.

An ISP may be regional such as Ameritech, or NEARNet in New England. Or, an ISP may be local and serve a small town or community.

In addition to offering Internet access, an ISP may offer other services such as e-mail, Web site hosting and development, e-commerce using secure servers for monetary transactions over the Internet, or dedicated switching facilities to companies that use the Internet as part of their own network.

TYPES OF NETWORKS

A network is a collection of **nodes** (servers or workstations, for example) that can directly send and receive data. While there are many types of networks, and many ways to describe and classify a network, the i-Net+ exam focuses on types of networks that use protocols or services that may be found on the Internet.

nodes

A **protocol** is the set of rules that govern data transactions between devices on a network. The most common protocol used with the Internet is TCP/IP. The services that may be found on the Internet include e-mail, file transfers, or Web-based documents. This section defines three basic network types that use TCP/IP as well as make use of some Internet services.

protocol

Internet

The Internet is a network consisting of thousands of networks. It's a global, public network that uses an infrastructure consisting of network access points, a commercial backbone, and Internet service providers.

Background Info

Internet vs. internet

An **internet** (without the capital I) is a general reference to any interconnected network that uses protocols that are used with the Internet. The most common Internet protocol is TCP/IP. The i-Net+ exam doesn't make a distinction between *internet* and *Internet*. Instead, the exam is focused on the more accurate and precise terms as described in this section.

internet

The topology used on the Internet is a physical and logical mesh. Since the NAPs are interconnected, and they are intersected by the commercial backbone providers (which are also interconnected), it's fair to say that all machines connected to the Internet are physically connected. It's not a simple topology. The physical connections are extremely complex and convoluted.

IP (Internet Protocol)

The Internet is a logical mesh because of the TCP/IP protocol used with the Internet. **IP** (**Internet Protocol**) provides a logical addressing mechanism in which routers, servers, or workstations have a unique address. Since all of the IP addresses are unique, any router, server, or workstation can be located anywhere on the Internet through a process that involves converting the IP address to a particular machine name (Host or domain name) or physical address (MAC address). IP addressing is detailed in Chapter 3, while MAC addressing is discussed in the Hardware Connection Devices section of this chapter.

Due to the size of the Internet, and the lack of inherent security controls in the TCP/IP protocols, the lack of security on the Internet is notorious. Network administrators must work diligently to ensure that connections to the Internet will thwart intruders, as well as detect intruders. It's a constant challenge because once a remedy is put in place, an intruder tends to find another hole in the system. Chapter 6 describes security practices common to protecting network and server resources for Internet devices.

Intranet

intranet

An **intranet** is a private network that supports Internet applications and doesn't use the public telecommunications system to connect users. Examples of Internet applications include e-mail, FTP, Web browsing, and telnet.

server farm

An example of an intranet is a network in which several smaller networks are connected together as shown in Figure 1-3. Notice that an intranet uses a private wiring infrastructure to connect users. The network has TCP/IP running on all nodes. The **server farm** includes an e-mail server so that users at all workstations can send and receive e-mail internally. A server farm is a collection of servers that are typically housed in a single location and used by many users. A Web server is also included.

With TCP/IP (or an equivalent protocol such as SPX/IPX) running on the intranet, data packets will be sent and received between the smaller networks.

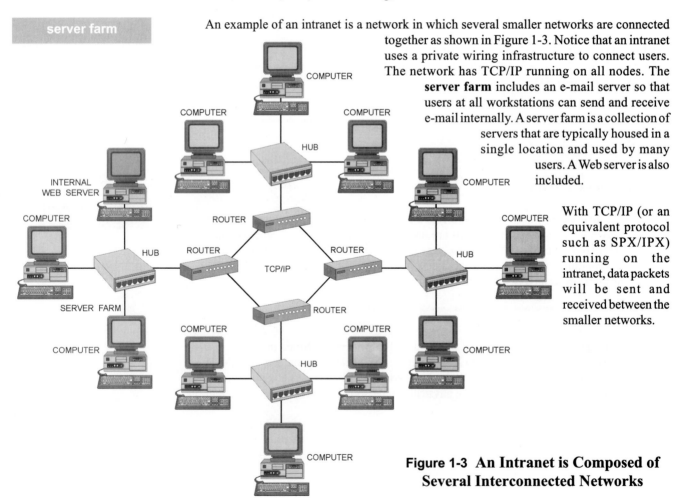

Figure 1-3 An Intranet is Composed of Several Interconnected Networks

The Web server may be used only for an internal Web site that isn't accessible from the public Internet. A company often uses an internal Web site to post company telephone books, documentation such as standard operating procedures, various software tools such as WinZip or QuickTime, and to store frequently used forms such as employee W4 forms and address changes.

An intranet offers the best in terms of security. The reason is that an intranet isn't connected to the Internet, so outside intruders have no way of hacking into the network resources. An increasing challenge of network administrators, however, is to prevent employees from violating security practices by opening an unsecured port for intruders. Many network literate employees are finding that they can "beat the system" and connect to the Internet without the immediate knowledge of information technology personnel.

Extranet

An **extranet** is a private network that supports Internet applications and uses the public telecommunications system to share company information with users, customers, and partners. Essentially, an extranet extends an intranet to the public Internet. Parts of an extranet remain private and separate from the Internet, while other parts of it are accessible from the Internet.

Figure 1-4 shows an example of an extranet. In the figure, a customer Web server is connected to the Internet. The server authenticates customers by prompting them for an assigned password. When the customer enters the correct password, they are able to access the contents of the server.

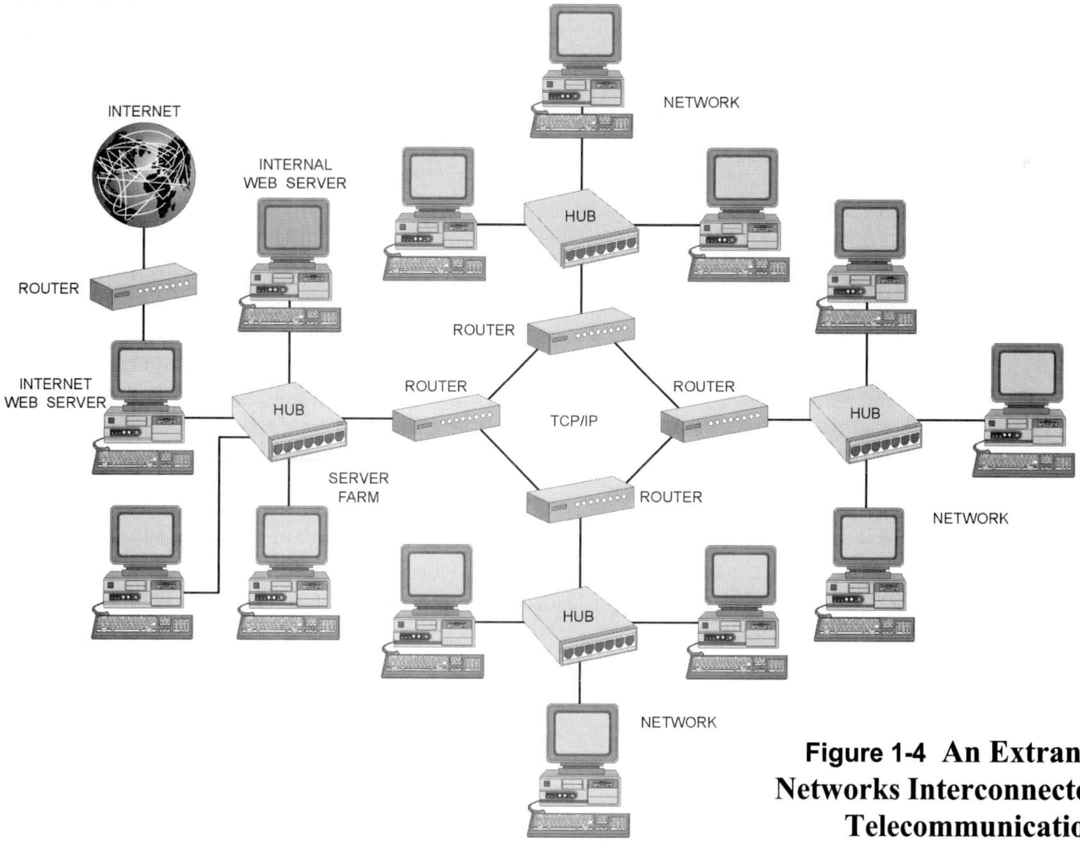

Figure 1-4 An Extranet Consists of Networks Interconnected by the Public Telecommunications System

A business partner of a company can also use an extranet for jointly developing a product. For example, a company may need specialized work to be performed by a contractor while a product is in the development stage. The contractor will need specific drawings and documentation of the developing product to ensure the work is done to specification. Since the Internet is a global network, the company can provide the information to a contractor located anywhere.

Many e-commerce Web sites utilize an extranet. When a customer purchases a product on the Internet with a credit card, the buyer's card number is validated on a secure server of the card issuer. The secured server isn't available to the general public; only those companies that have been authorized to check the balance and status of the card.

In terms of security, an extranet is a security risk that falls between the Internet and an intranet. Since an extranet is typically password-protected, or includes other mechanisms for determining that access to a network server has been authorized, an extranet will deter the majority of casual intruders.

Virtual Private Network

virtual private network (VPN)

A **virtual private network**, or VPN, is similar to an intranet. A VPN, however, uses the Internet infrastructure as the communication medium between different network sites. Recall that an intranet is private, and doesn't directly connect to the Internet; rather, the intranet infrastructure consists of private cabling.

A VPN, on the other hand, allows users to exchange data packets (such as e-mail, or access to remote servers) across the Internet using any of the common Network layer protocols such as IP, NetBEUI, or IPX.

Point-to-Point Tunneling Protocol (PPTP)

Data packets sent over the VPN are encapsulated in a protocol that provides for data encapsulation as well as encryption of the user data. The most common protocol used with a VPN in **Point-to-Point Tunneling Protocol** (**PPTP**). PPTP includes enhanced security features such as encryption for protecting data sent across the public Internet.

A VPN represents a specialized application of the network types found on the Internet. The i-Net+ exam contains specific objectives related to VPNs. For detailed information on VPNs, including a discussion of common protocols used with VPNs, refer to Chapter 6.

HARDWARE CONNECTION DEVICES

hardware connection device

The types of networks described in the previous section are constructed from hardware connection devices. A **hardware connection device**, as far as the i-Net+ exam is concerned, includes equipment that's commonly used at the server and workstation port level, equipment that allows a network to be extended, or equipment that's used to interconnect different networks.

NIC

A **network interface card** (**NIC**), also called a network adapter, is a printed circuit card used to access the network resources. A NIC contains electronic circuitry that organizes data into unique frames so that the data can be sent, and received, on the network.

A NIC is specialized to the access protocol running on the network. The most common NICs are for Ethernet and Token Ring access protocols. Since the application for a NIC is specialized, you must know the access protocol running on the network before you install the NIC.

A NIC slips into the expansion slot of a server or workstation. Data to be sent onto the network is transferred to the NIC on the parallel bus within the computer. The NIC converts the parallel data to serial data, packages the data into a frame, and sends it to the network.

network interface card (NIC)

Background Info

Serial Data and Parallel Data

Parallel data refers to sending data bits simultaneously along multiple paths. The data bus in a computer is parallel. The principal advantage of a parallel bus is that data can be transferred very quickly. The disadvantage of parallel transmission is that it requires a greater number of wires (or channels) than serial transmission.

Serial data refers to sending data bits one-at-a-time along a single path. Data sent along a network wire is serial data. The advantage of a serial bus is that fewer wires (or channels) are needed to transfer information. The disadvantage of serial transmission is that it's slow compared to parallel transmission.

Parallel data

Serial data

frame headers

When a NIC receives data from the network, it removes the **frame headers** (the portion of a frame that doesn't contain user data), and converts the received serial data to parallel. Refer to the Bridge section later in this chapter for more information on frames.

Figure 1-5 illustrates the different bus styles used in the majority of NICs.

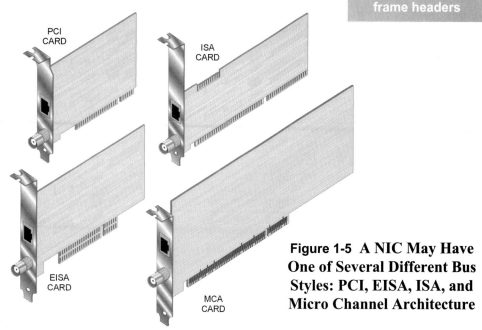

Figure 1-5 A NIC May Have One of Several Different Bus Styles: PCI, EISA, ISA, and Micro Channel Architecture

The following are several different bus styles:

peripheral component
interconnect (PCI)

Extended Industry
Standard Architecture
(EISA)

Industry Standard
Architecture (ISA)

Micro Channel
Architecture (MCA)

- The **peripheral component interconnect (PCI)** style is the most common bus style in use. It supports a 32-bit parallel bus. PCI NICs should be used in Pentium and Power PC-based computers, and later architectures. It provides the fastest transfer rates of all bus styles.

- The **Extended Industry Standard Architecture (EISA)** style supports a 32-bit bus. Adapted from the earlier Industry Standard Architecture bus, it's backwards compatible with the original ISA standard, meaning that an EISA NIC can also be used in computers with a 16-bit bus. While an EISA card transfers data along a bus the same size as a PCI card, it may not have the performance enhancements of PCI (such as RAM buffers or an on-board microprocessor).

- The **Industry Standard Architecture (ISA)** originally supported an 8-bit bus architecture, and was later extended to 16-bits. An ISA NIC will be found in older servers and workstations.

- The **Micro Channel Architecture (MCA)** style bus was developed by IBM. A Micro Channel Architecture bus will support a 16- or 32-bit bus. But since the bus is electrically different than the ISA standard, it can only be used in computers that use the Micro Channel Architecture bus such as an IBM PS/2.

The NIC that you install must use the same type of bus as the server or workstation that it's installed in. Most computers will support more than one bus, such as expansion slots for PCI or EISA.

RJ45 connector

unshielded twisted
pair (UTP)

BNC (British Navel
Connector)

The serial port of a NIC may be one of two basic types. The first is an **RJ45 connector**, which resembles an oversized telephone connector (an RJ11 connector, "RJ" stands for registered jack). RJ45 connectors contain eight pins and connect to **unshielded twisted pair (UTP)** cabling.

The second type of NIC serial port is a **BNC (British Navel Connector)**. A BNC connector is used with coaxial cable. NICs may have a BNC connector, an RJ45 connector, or both types of connectors.

A NIC is installed in a computer by slipping it into one of the expansion slots of the computer. Once installed, the card must be configured. There are a couple of ways to configure a NIC.

Plug-and-Play (PNP)

Most workstations running Windows operating systems, and some servers (Windows 2000, for example), support Microsoft's **Plug-and-Play (PNP)** functionality. A PNP-compliant device such as a NIC is automatically configured by the operating system. The idea is that you install the card, turn-on power to the computer, and PNP handles the configuration details. PNP may not always work if the device being installed partially supports PNP. Or, it may not support it at all. For example, non-Windows operating systems such as Unix may not automatically configure hardware devices.

For a NIC that can't be configured with PNP, you must manually configure the card. There are two ways to do so. The first is accomplished using a software configuration. The second requires you to manually position jumper or DIP switches.

Regardless of the method used to configure the NIC, there are three settings that you should be aware of:

- **Interrupt Request (IRQ)**: The IRQ is a signal sent to the system microprocessor indicating that a device requires the attention of the microprocessor. All peripherals in a computer (mouse, keyboard, CD-ROM) are assigned a unique IRQ so that the microprocessor will know which device it's communicating with. Any unused IRQ numbers will work for a NIC, but IRQ 10 has become a de facto standard.

- **Base Input/Output (I/O) Port**: The base I/O port is a hexadecimal number used by the system microprocessor to identify the destination of data sent to a peripheral device. Because the bus in a computer is shared by all peripherals, the base I/O port identifies where data is to be sent within the computer. The base I/O port for all devices must be unique. Common 32-bit base I/O ports are 0300 and 031F.

- **Base Memory Address**: The base memory address is a unique area of the computer RAM where data is temporarily stored. Since data is moving very quickly on the computer parallel bus, it needs to be stored while the slower serial data is moved out of the NIC and onto the network wire. As with the IRQ and base I/O port, the base memory address must be unique for the NIC. A common base memory address is the hexadecimal address D8000.

Data that's sent to a workstation (or server) is placed on the network by the NIC. In an Ethernet network, all data is placed on a common bus (not at the same time, though). To ensure that data placed on the bus is received by the correct workstation, each NIC has an address used to distinguish it from all other workstations. The address is called the **MAC (Media Access Control)** sub-layer of the Data Link layer of the OSI Model, or physical address. See the Appendix for an overview of the OSI Model.

A **MAC address** is a 48-bit number expressed as six hexadecimal numbers. All devices (such as servers and workstations) that will be sending and receiving data frames will have a MAC address. Each MAC address must be unique for all devices on the network. An example of a MAC address is 00-60-08-71-C7-B2. The MAC address isn't user configurable; that is, it ships from a manufacturer with the address "burned" into the card.

Hub

A **hub** is a device used to provide centralized access to the network. Hubs are used in a physical star topology as shown in Figure 1-6. The network nodes connect to ports in the hub via a cable such as UTP or coaxial. One end of the cable plugs into the node NIC card while the other end plugs into a port on a hub.

The advantage of a hub is that it can be located at a central point in the network. The alternative to using a hub is to daisy-chain the nodes with cable segments. In a network in which the nodes aren't likely to change location, this is fine. But in a more dynamic setting, physical changes in location can create a wiring nightmare since each time a node is moved, the cable segment linking the node to its neighbors must be replaced. A hub simplifies changes because, if a node is moved, all that's needed is to run a cable from the new location to an available port on the hub.

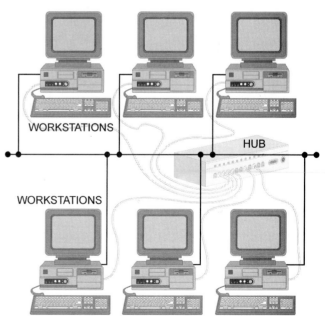

WORKSTATIONS

HUB

WORKSTATIONS

Figure 1-6 A Hub is Used in a Physical Star Topology

Interrupt Request (IRQ)

Base Input/Output (I/O) Port

Base Memory Address

MAC (Media Access Control)

MAC Address

hub

Most **local area networks (LAN)** use hubs in a star topology due to the relative ease of installation of connecting servers and workstations.

Hubs may be classified as either passive or active. A **passive hub** is nothing more than a pass-through for data. A passive hub doesn't alter the data signal in any way; it receives its power from the connected computers. If a data signal becomes noisy, a passive hub will pass along the noise with the data signal.

An **active hub** operates under its own power supply. Data signals may be amplified in an active hub to restore signal losses, or to remove noise from the data signal. Active hubs are also called **repeaters**.

In addition to being placed in a **physical topology** such as a star, a hub participates in a logical topology. A **logical topology** refers to the specific method a server or workstation accesses the network. Ethernet, for example, is a bus technology. A hub in an Ethernet network includes an internal bus that nodes compete for before they are able to use the network resources.

A Token Ring network, on the other hand, may also be implemented in a physical star. The Token Ring "hub" is actually called a **Multi-station Access Unit (MSAU or MAU)**. Within the MSAU is a logical ring topology. Nodes are connected to each port in the hub ring. When a node is connected to the ring, it may send or receive data.

Bridge

A **bridge** is used to reduce network traffic by filtering Data Link layer **frames**. A frame is the unit of measure of data that's sent between nodes. Frames contain headers that may specify source and destination addresses as well as a header for error checking. A bridge examines MAC addresses to determine if the frame should be sent on to another portion of a network, or if it should remain in the portion of the network where it originated.

For example, a LAN may grow over the years to the point that it slows due to the large number of workstations sending and receiving data. Network traffic congestion can be reduced by separating workstations into groups, particularly groups that tend to exchange information frequently. The separated groups are called segments. A **segment** is a portion of a network in which any node on that portion of the network can sense whether any other node is transmitting data frames.

Bridges use two basic methods for bridging network segments. The bridging methods are called **transparent bridging** and **source-route bridging**.

In a transparent bridge, the bridge collects MAC addresses of all nodes on the network. It then compares the source and destination addresses of received frames to the addresses in its table. Based on the result of the comparison, the bridge will determine if a frame is destined for the same segment it originated from, or if it's to be forwarded to another segment. Transparent bridges are used with Ethernet LANs.

Figure 1-7 shows an example of transparent bridging. In the figure, an Ethernet LAN has been separated into two segments. The workstations will send frames that contain a source and destination MAC address (the MAC address that's burned into the NIC). When workstation A-1 sends a message to workstation A-2, the frame is first sent to the bridge. The bridge examines the destination address in the frame and compares it to MAC addresses in its tables. Since the destination address is on the same segment as the source address in the frame, the bridge ignores the frame. If, however, A-1 sends a frame of data to workstation B-2 on segment B, the bridge will forward the frame to segment B.

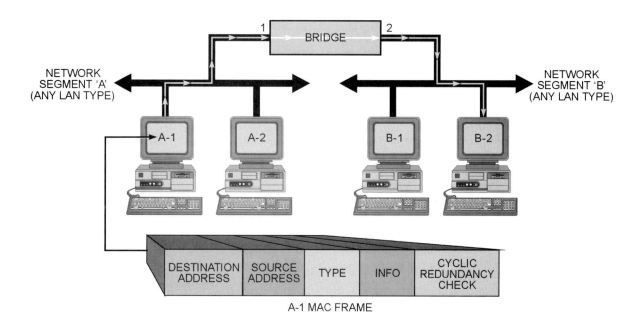

Figure 1-7 A Transparent Bridge Examines MAC Addresses Of Data Frames

If a transparent bridge doesn't recognize the destination address of a frame, it broadcasts the frame to all segments except the segment that the frame originated from. (A **broadcast** message is a message sent to all nodes on a network.)

In a source-routing bridge, each workstation provides path information to the destination node. Used in Token Ring networks, a source-routing bridge is used only to transfer the frame to the destination segment. The workstation does the majority of the work because it dictates to the bridge the route that the frame is to take.

An advantage of source-routing over transparent bridging is that frames may be transferred faster. The source-routing bridge will store the path information when it's delivered from the workstation and use that same path each time a frame arrives that's to be sent to the same destination address. Transparent bridges, on the other hand, examine each frame and compare the address to information in their address tables, which takes time and slows the network.

Because a bridge is a Data Link layer device, it can be used to connect networks with different access protocols. For example, a bridge may connect Token Ring and Ethernet segments. A **translation bridge** is used to connect segments that utilize different access protocols.

Figure 1-8 shows an example of a translation bridge. The network is composed of Ethernet, Token Bus, and Token Ring segments. A workstation on the Ethernet segment sends a frame to the Token Ring segment. When the first bridge receives the frame, it examines the MAC address and determines the frame that is to be sent on. Before sending the frame, it converts the frame headers from Ethernet to Token Bus. When bridge 2 receives the frame, it also examines the destination address, determines the frame is destined for a workstation on the Token Ring segment, and converts the frame format from Token Bus to Token Ring. The frame is then placed on the Token Ring segment and delivered to the destination workstation.

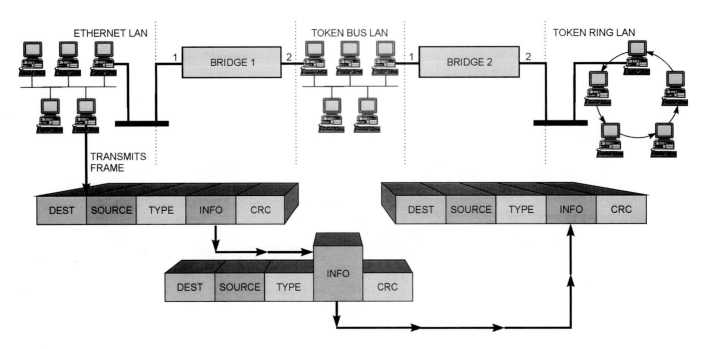

Figure 1-8 A Translation Bridge is Used to Connect Network Segments That Use Different Access Protocols

A translation bridge is noted for interoperability among LAN access protocols. As described in Figure 1-8, it's used to bridge data frames across different segment types such as Ethernet and Token Ring. Transparent and source-route bridging will only connect segments that use the same access protocols such as Ethernet or Token Ring—but not both in the same network.

Router

router

A **router** is used to connect different networks and, occasionally, different network segments. A "network" in this context, refers to a group of nodes that share the same network portion of an IP address. If two groups of nodes don't have the same network portion of an IP address, they are located on different networks.

Routers operate at the Network layer of the OSI model. A router isn't concerned if the data it receives originated from a Token Ring LAN or an Ethernet LAN. To the router, its only concern is getting the data to the correct destination network.

A router may be used to connect network segments by examining MAC addresses in a manner that's similar to a bridge. Both devices use MAC addresses at the Data Link layer to forward data. A router; however, goes a step further by also looking at IP addresses to locate remote networks. There are a couple of differences between the two devices, as well. A bridge will forward any unknown destination MAC addresses. A router will discard any unknown MAC addresses. A bridge will forward broadcast messages to all network segments. A router will discard broadcast messages. A bridge will forward a message if the destination address is known, even if the frame is corrupted. A router will discard a corrupted frame.

In some situations, a router may be more effective than a bridge for linking segments on a network. For example, if several access protocols are used on portions of a network, the router can be used to decrease traffic congestion by filtering all broadcast messages as well as all corrupted frames.

To directly connect network workstations to the Internet, a router is used at the interface of the local network (where the workstations reside) and the Internet. The router will locate a remote network (such as a Web site server) so that the workstation user can connect to the remote site and download the content of that site to the local workstation.

To directly connect network workstations to the Internet, a router is used at the interface of the local network (where the workstations reside) and the Internet. The router will locate a remote network (such as a Web site server) so that the workstation user can connect to the remote site and download the content of that site to the local workstation.

logical addresses

IP address

To successfully transfer data across networks, a router relies on **logical addresses**. The most common logical address used by routers is an **IP address**. An IP address is a 32-bit address that's composed of a network portion and a host portion. The network portion of the address identifies the source or destination network, while the host portion of the address identifies the specific source or destination node on a network. (For details on IP addresses, see Chapter 3, TCP/IP.)

Figure 1-9 illustrates the method routers use to locate a node on a remote network. The router interconnects data packets across a network running TCP/IP. The network consists of an Ethernet, a Token Ring, and a Token Bus LAN. Notice the router allows computers on all three LANs to communicate regardless of the topology and access protocols. The LAN hardware used with the computers may be from diverse vendors and operate at different bandwidths. The router, because it is basically concerned only with network addresses, is involved in a limited capacity at the Physical layer and the Data Link layer. This is the reason why the LAN hardware, cabling medium, and access protocols may all be different, but the networks can still communicate.

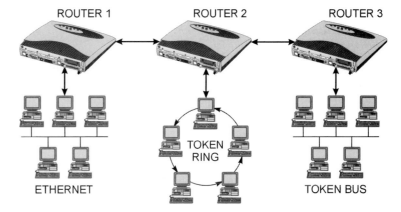

MAC DESTINATION	MAC SOURCE	IP SOURCE	IP DESTINATION	DATA	CRC
ROUTER 1	ETHERNET NODE	ETHERNET NODE	TOKEN BUS NODE	XXX	XXX
ROUTER 2	ROUTER 1	ETHERNET NODE	TOKEN BUS NODE	XXX	XXX
ROUTER 3	ROUTER 2	ETHERNET NODE	TOKEN BUS NODE	XXX	XXX

Figure 1-9 A Router Transfers Data Packets Between Different Networks

Assume that a workstation on the Ethernet LAN sends a message to a workstation on the remote Token Bus LAN. The table shown with the figure includes generic MAC addresses of the IP packets, along with generic IP addresses. The first two columns contain destination and source MAC addresses of the router and respective LAN nodes. Initially, the MAC source address is the address of the node on the Ethernet LAN, and the destination address is the MAC for router 1. When the frame arrives at the router, the physical addressing fields of the MAC frame are removed, leaving only the IP addresses, user data, and error checking fields (shown in the figure as **CRC**, which stands for **Cyclic Redundancy Check**).

Notice that the IP addresses never change. This is because they are the only indication of where the frames are going as they move from router to router. At each router hop, the router will compare its list of MAC addresses to the destination IP address. If they aren't the same, it will reframe the MAC addresses and pass it on.

Since router 1 isn't the destination for the frame, router 1 reframes the message with new MAC address fields. Router 1 is now the source of the message and the destination address is the MAC address of router 2.

Router 2 compares its list of IP addresses to the destination IP address in the received frame. Since the destination IP address isn't located on the Token Bus network, router 3 reframes the message. Now the source MAC address will be the MAC address of router 2 and the destination MAC address will be the MAC address of router 3.

Router 3 will strip the MAC addresses and examine the destination IP address in the frame. It will match the destination IP address to the list of IP addresses in its tables and correctly determine that the message is destined for the Token Ring network. The message will now be delivered to the node on the Token Ring network whose IP address matches the MAC address that the router has in its tables.

The process of locating specific nodes on a large network such as the Internet is a bit more involved. Typically, a user won't know the IP address of a remote node or network. However, the user will likely know the Internet **domain name** of the remote node, or the host name of the node. An Internet domain name is a name preceding a suffix such as com, edu, or net. For example, the domain name of Microsoft is microsoft.com. Host names follow a similar convention. Before a router can begin to route a message to a remote network, it must know the IP address of the remote node. The process used to convert domain or host names to IP addresses is called the **Domain Name Service** or **System (DNS)**. For routers used to interconnect networks on the Internet, the process of reconciling domain names to IP addresses must be performed before a message is sent to a router.

A router is used to connect network users to the Internet. Even if a home-based user connects to an ISP via a modem, the ISP will have routers installed at the intersection to the Internet. If the router isn't working properly, it's impossible to access the Internet. If the router is down, network users will not be able to access the Internet at all. But note that if the routers used at an ISP are down, a user will likely be able to connect to the ISP site, but won't be able to go beyond it.

One of two types of routers can be used to gather information about the networks the router is connected to. The first type of router is called a **static router**. A static router receives IP addressing information manually. That is, a network administrator will periodically update addressing tables in a static router. The update is required any time a node address changes.

The second type of router is called a **dynamic router**. A dynamic router learns addressing information automatically, without intervention from the network administrator. Dynamic routers broadcast the addressing information in their tables in the form of advertisements. For example, a dynamic router may send (or advertise) its list of IP addresses to adjacent routers once every thirty seconds. The adjacent routers compare their list of IP addresses, and if there's a difference, update their table with the new information.

Router advertisements tend to increase network congestion. But the alternative is to update addressing information manually. The time spent manually updating router tables far exceeds the disadvantage of increased router traffic due to advertisements.

Routers route data packets across the Internet by using routing protocols. The most common routing protocol used on the Internet is called **Border Gateway Protocol (BGP)**. BGP runs on routers that are installed at the interface of a local network to the Internet. BGP contains dynamic characteristics that make it an excellent choice for Internet applications. These include the use of a 30 second "keep-alive" message sent between routers that's used to detect failed routers, or routes that aren't operational. The efficiency of a router running BGP is very good since it initially receives a complete route table update when it's first connected to the Internet. After the initial update, changes in the router are incremental, which means that the information in the routing table reflects only changes—not a complete table update for any change.

Other common routing protocols include **RIP (Routing Information Protocol)**, **OSPF (Open Shortest Path First)**, **IGRP (Interior Gateway Routing Protocol)**, and **EIGRP (Enhanced Interior Gateway Routing Protocol)**. The difference between these protocols and BGP is they are "interior" routing protocols. An **interior routing protocol** is used to interconnect network segments, or networks on an intranet. An interior routing protocol isn't normally used at the interface of the local network and the Internet, whereas BGP runs data packets across the local network and Internet interface.

Switch

A **switch** allows each connected node to be dynamically connected to any other node port. The connections established between ports in a switch are handled with software. The connection is a virtual circuit that is built-up and torn-down each time a node connects to a different port. In effect, a switch provides a direct and dedicated connection between two nodes.

Physically, a switch resembles a conventional hub. It has ports to which nodes are connected via the cabling infrastructure. In a conventional 10BaseT hub, each node listens for traffic on the bus (located in the hub). When a message is sent from a workstation, it arrives at the hub and is placed on the bus. The message is then repeated to all nodes connected to the hub. If the destination MAC address matches the MAC address of one of the workstations, that workstation receives the message. All other workstations ignore the message. Notice that each time a frame is sent, the total bandwidth of the network (10 Mbps in a 10baseT network) is divided among all nodes since each message is sent to all nodes.

A switch avoids dividing the available bandwidth by providing a direct connection between two ports. Rather than using a logical bus or ring topology, a switch uses a logical mesh topology. A switch implements a logical mesh with a backplane. A backplane allows any port to be connected to any other port. During the time two ports are connected, data is sent at the full bandwidth that's available since no other nodes are connected to the two ports. The effect is a dramatic increase in the time required to send a packet from one node to another.

Since a switch automatically connects two nodes, there's no reason that other nodes must wait to send or receive data. The connections occur between two nodes only. And, since the nodes are directly connected, a data message can be immediately forwarded onto the destination node, even before the complete frame has arrived at the switch. This process is called cut-through. A **cut-through** switch is noted for high speeds and throughput. Throughput, in the context of a switch, refers to the time required to process data at the switch. The less time the switch spends with the frame, the higher the throughput.

A switch may also process data using a method called **store-and-forward**. In a store-and-forward switch, the complete data message is received and buffered (stored) by the switch before the message is sent to the destination node. Because the switch is in possession of the complete message, it may check the message for errors, provide filtering between network segments, or reframe the message so that it can be sent to a segment that uses a different access protocol than the source segment.

The advantage of a switch over conventional hubs is that each port offers the connected nodes the full bandwidth that's available on the network.

Gateway

A **gateway** is a device used to convert from one incompatible protocol to another protocol. A gateway may operate at any one of the layers of the OSI model, or at several layers of the model. For example, a gateway would be used to convert from TCP/IP to Novell SPX/IPX.

The processing power required to convert from one incompatible protocol to another is considerable. If possible, the conversion should be avoided. Instead, plan to use common protocols on a network. This will save time and money.

MODEMS AND ADAPTERS

A **modem** is used as an interface to the public telephone network. An analog modem is used to interface a computer to the analog portion of the telephone system, primarily to connect to an Internet Service Provider. A cable modem is used to connect a computer to the coaxial and fiber optic-based cable television system for Internet access.

An **ISDN adapter** is used to connect to the digital ISDN telephone network. An ISDN adapter (sometimes incorrectly called an ISDN modem) provides access to a complete digital channel. ISDN is faster than its analog cousin, but requires specialized equipment at the interface.

DSL is a technology that can use existing twisted-pair cabling used for voice communication to send and receive digital data at high data rates.

DSL

Modems can be generally classified as **asynchronous** and **synchronous**. An asynchronous modem makes use of start and stop bits to separate 7- or 8-bit bytes. The stop and start bits are used between end devices to keep track of each data word. Since each byte contains stop and start bit overhead, asynchronous data is routinely compressed to increase the speed of data transfers. The most common data compression method is the ITU V.42 protocol.

asynchronous

synchronous

A synchronous modem uses discrete bits to keep track of data words. Rather than send start and stop bits with each byte, a synchronizing bit (or bit pattern) is inserted following a number of data bits. ISDN and T-carrier are technologies that utilize terminal adapters for synchronous communication.

Analog Modem

An **analog modem** is used to access the analog portion of the dial-up telephone system. The dial-up telephone system is the same system used for voice communication. An analog modem converts the digital data in a computer to an analog format so that the data can be sent across the analog portion of the telephone system. At the opposite end of the connection, another analog modem converts the received analog data back to digital.

analog modem

An analog modem may be an internal modem or an external modem. An internal modem slips into the expansion slot of a computer. An external modem connects to one of the serial ports located on the back of the computer. Neither has a particular advantage over the other. Internal modems cost slightly less since they don't have a case to house the modem. An external modem can be moved easily to another computer by disconnecting the cable between the modem and computer port.

Analog modems are frequently used to access the Internet through an Internet Service Provider (ISP). Figure 1-10 shows a typical application. A modem is connected to a computer. The modem has a telephone jack (**RJ11**) that's used to connect to the 4-wire telephone line. (Although a standard telephone cable contains four wires, only two of the wires are needed for analog modem or voice communication. Data to be sent to the ISP from the computer is first converted to analog by the modem. This is necessary because the analog portion of the telephone network (called the local loop) won't accept digital formatted data. Once the data is passed beyond the local loop, it's converted back to digital by the **public switched telephone network (PSTN)**. The PSTN is nearly all digital. The PSTN is connected to an ISP. The ISP accepts the message from the remote computer for access to the Internet.

RJ11

public switched telephone network (PSTN)

Data that's received from the Internet is first delivered to the ISP as digital information. It's then passed to the PSTN and converted back to analog before being sent to the computer across the local loop. The modem converts the received analog data to digital and passes it to the computer.

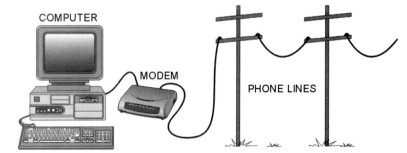

Figure 1-10 Analog Modems are Used as an Interface Between a Computer and the Analog Telephone System

You may see references to a **virtual modem**. A virtual modem uses software to interface data in a computer to another computer that's typically remote. The most common applications for virtual modems are for a telnet or FTP connection. (Telnet utilizes a command line interface that allows you to use the services of a remote computer. FTP allows you to transfer files. See Chapter 3 for more information on telnet and FTP.)

Since a virtual modem is specialized for particular tasks, it's not appropriate for accessing the World Wide Web portion of the Internet. The Web requires a connection in which multiple protocols must be run and this is difficult to achieve with a virtual modem.

Most modems used today are software configured using the **Hayes AT Command Set**. The modem manufacturer uses AT commands to provide the functionality that's found in a modem such as auto dial, auto answer, and a host of commands used to test the operation of the modem. When a modem is installed and configured in a computer, the dialog boxes used to enter dialing information represent a graphical interface to the Hayes AT commands.

Modem standards are administered by the **International Telecommunication Union (ITU)**. The ITU standards related to modems are covered in the V-series standards.

The **V-series standards** describe communication over the telephone network and include specifics concerning the highest data rate of a modem, the type of modulation used in a modem (such as Quadrature Amplitude Modulation), the type of communication that two modems will engage in (simplex, half-duplex, or full-duplex), and the type of telephone system connection between the two modems (standard 2-wire or switched).

Table 1-1 lists common ITU V-series standards for modems.

Table 1-1 The ITU V-series Standards for Modems

V-SERIES STANDARD	DESCRIPTION
V.2	Specifies power levels for data transmission.
V.17	Two-wire fax modem with data rates up to 14.4 Kbps.
V.21	300 bps standard.
V.22	1200 bps standard for point-to-point leased line.
V.22bis	2400 bps standard for point-to-point leased line.
V.23	600/1200 bps standard.
V.24	Defines the interchange circuits used between DTEs and DCEs.
V.25bis	Synchronous and asynchronous auto-dialing procedures used on switched networks.
V.26bis	2400/1200 bps standard.
V.27bis	4800/2400 bps standard.
V.29	9600 bps standard for use on four-wire leased lines.
V.32bis	9600 bps full-duplex standard for use on leased lines.
V.33	14.4 Kbps.
V.34V	33.6 Kbps standard.
V.42bis	Data compression standard.

Cable Modem

A **cable modem** uploads and downloads data using the existing cable television (CATV) wiring infrastructure. The wiring infrastructure consists of coaxial or, more likely, fiber optic cabling. Because coaxial and fiber optic cable have wider bandwidth capabilities than the wiring used in the analog telephone loop, data will travel at faster rates than over the CATV system.

Data rates can vary widely for a cable modem. The maximum rate is close to 38 Mbps, while typical rates will fall in the range of 1 Mbps to about 10 Mbps.

A cable modem uses the wide bandwidth that's available on the CATV cable to transfer data at very high speeds. Typical applications include Internet access, distance learning, or medical diagnoses to rural areas. The obstacle to implementing access to computers is that the current system is primarily simplex in nature. That is, data travels in only one direction over the CATV cable. At the cable headend, cable television is piped to homes and business via a point-to-multi-point configuration. The multi-point cables lead to boxes that attach to television sets. A television receives information; it doesn't transmit back any information, so there hasn't been much of a need to incorporate transceivers at the headend that can send as well as receive data.

But in order to access and communicate with a distant network such as the Internet, full-duplex communication is a requirement. While there are a couple of methods used to implement full-duplex operation with cable modems, Figure 1-11 shows the fastest method. A cable modem is placed at the user site. A CAT 5 UTP cable is connected between the cable modem and a NIC card in the computer. The NIC is a 10BaseT card at the subscriber site. The cable modem has a BNC used to attach the coaxial cable from the CATV plant to the cable modem.

A cable modem uses TCP/IP as the internetworking protocol. This is a requirement since the Internet identifies nodes with an IP address.

An alternative to the method shown in Figure 1-11 is to use a V.34 modem (33.6 Kbps data rate) for uploads from the computer to the ISP. Downloads are received from the CATV cable as described above. But when data is sent to the ISP, it's transferred across the analog telephone network. This system alleviates the cable operator from installing expensive transceivers at the cable plant. The effect on the user is minimal since uploads mainly consist of mouse clicks on Internet sites.

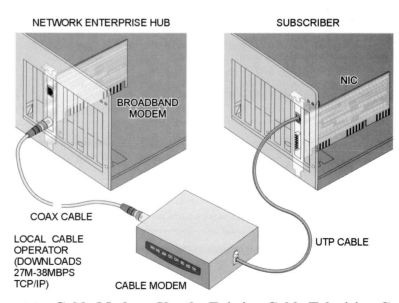

Figure 1-11 Cable Modems Use the Existing Cable Television Coaxial and Fiber Optic Cabling Infrastructure for Transferring Data

Data Over Cable
Service Interface
Specification
(DOCSIS)

Multimedia Cable
Network Systems
(MCNS)

Downstream

Upstream

Subscriber Interface

Network Interface

The cable television network uses a bus topology. Each cable subscriber is attached to the bus with a segment of coaxial or fiber optic cable. All subscribers share the bandwidth. Potentially, data rates used for Internet access will slow with the number of connected subscribers. While a cable modem may be able to receive data at 38 Mbps, don't expect downloads at this rate. Still, cable modems are very fast when compared to competing technologies. An analog V.90 modem downloads at rates slightly lower than 53 Kbps, while an ISDN connection provides a maximum data rate of 128 Kbps.

The standard currently governing cable modems is called the **Data Over Cable Service Interface Specification (DOCSIS)**, which was established by the **Multimedia Cable Network Systems (MCNS)**, a consortium of cable companies. This is a consortium within the cable television industry that sets cable-based standards. The DOCSIS standard was approved by the ITU in March of 1998.

Pertinent specifications of the DOCSIS standard are:

Downstream

- Modulation: 64 and 256 QAM

- Carrier Rate: 6 MHz

- Data Rate: 27 or 36 Mbps

Upstream

- Modulation: QPSK or 16 QAM

- Carrier Rate: Variable, 200 KHz to 3.2 MHz

- Data Rate: 320 Kbps to 10 Mbps

Subscriber Interface

- 10BaseT

Network Interface

- 10BaseT

- 100BaseT

- ATM

- FDDI

A competing standard is the IEEE 802.14 (not approved at the time of this writing). The IEEE standard specifies ATM at the user interface, rather than 10BaseT. All data formatted to the ATM protocol is separated into 53 byte frames, or cells, as they're called. The cell size is fixed and predictable.

The huge advantage of using ATM is that the small cells can be passed through nearly any type of network on their way to a final destination. This makes ATM very routable across nearly all network types. Because of the almost guaranteed routability of ATM, it's used for multimedia applications such as video, voice, and graphics.

While cable operators have included ATM in the DOCSIS standard, don't expect to see it widely implemented for some time to come; the operators feel it adds an unnecessary level of complexity to the system and increases the time to market for cable modems. The IEEE would specifically require that subscribers interface to the operator using ATM.

The **IEEE 802.14 standard** is the better standard because it looks to the future and anticipates bandwidth demands on the coaxial cable that the DOCSIS standard won't be able to address. Unfortunately, it also increases the cost of implementing cable modems.

If the user is accessing the cable operator through a network, there are more options available—100 Mbps Ethernet, FDDI at 100 Mbps, or ATM. In this configuration, a single cable modem at the subscriber site will be used to connect the network users (which can range in number from four to a maximum of sixteen). The cable modem connects to a hub via CAT 5 UTP cable.

ISDN Adapter

Integrated Services Digital Network (ISDN) is a set of digital services that are available over telephone lines. ISDN is a complete digital solution from end-user to end-user. Because the connection is all digital, data rates can be much higher than an analog telephone connection. With ISDN, data rates can be as high as 128 Kbps.

ISDN is an alternative to conventional telephone connections for Internet access or for wide area connections in a multi-user environment. ISDN competes with fractional T-1, cable modems, and to a lesser degree, Frame Relay.

Users are charged a monthly fee to use ISDN. The equipment needed to interface and use the service is specialized and limited to ISDN technology. Due to geographical limits of ISDN, it may not be available in all areas, or if it is, it may not be cost effective. The end user site must be within 18,000 feet (3.4 miles) of the local loop central office to receive an ISDN line. (A central office is a local telephone switching center. It's designated by the first three digits of a local, seven-digit telephone number.) The distance limitation may be exceeded if a wide bandwidth repeater is installed. The cost of the repeater is passed-on to customers and may offset cost advantages of ISDN over a competing technology.

As ISDN frame carries data in a **Bearer channel (B channel)** that has a 64 Kbps bandwidth. On older telephone systems, B channels may drop to 56 Kbps. A **Data channel (D channel)** carries supervisor and signaling information at 16 Kbps (and sometimes at 64 Kbps).

There are two types of ISDN connections, a **Basic Rate Interface (BRI)** and a **Primary Rate Interface (PRI)**. A BRI connection is composed of two 64 Kbps B channels and one 16 Kbps D channel. It's normally referred to as BRI 2B+D. A PRI channel has twenty-three 64 Kbps B channels and one 64 Kbps D channel. It's normally called PRI 23B+D.

Channel information in an ISDN line is sent one byte after another. For example, if two devices are connected to the line, the first device will send a byte of data, then the next device will send a byte, then the first device will send a byte. The bearer channels are then routinely multiplexed. A single facility may have many ISDN lines with the channels multiplexed onto a single channel. When B channels are multiplexed, the connection is described by including an H suffix. Typical transmission rates are:

- BRI H0=6 B channels (384 Kbps)

- PRI H10=23 B channels (1472 Kbps)

- PRI H11=24 B channels (1536 Kbps)

- BRI+PRI H12=30 B channels (1929 Kbps)

ISDN Interfaces

ISDN comes with its own equipment and interfaces that are needed to establish a physical connection. Refer to Figure 1-12 to link the definitions described below to their place in the physical layout.

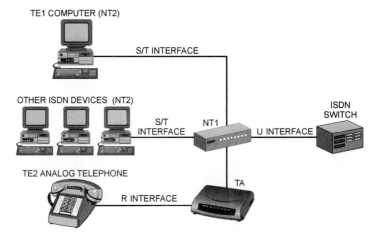

Figure 1-12 An ISDN Connection is Described Using Interface References

ISDN Terminals

- TE1: Terminal Equipment Type 1. A subscriber-side device that is specialized for ISDN. This may include a computer connection or an ISDN telephone. These are shown in the figure as TE1 Computer and Other ISDN Devices.

- TE2: Terminal Equipment Type 2. Also a subscriber-side device but one that predates the ISDN standard such as the analog telephone shown in the figure.

Terminal Adapter (TA)

A terminal adapter is needed only to connect older-style equipment to an ISDN line. The analog telephone is shown with a TA because it's not ISDN-ready. TAs are sometimes, incorrectly, called ISDN modems. A TA may be either a standalone device or a printed circuit board inside the TE2 device. If it's an external device, it connects to the TE2 via a standard physical interface such as EIA/TIA-232 or V.35.

Network Termination

- (NT1) Network Termination Type 1: An NT1 is a device at the ISDN switch side (in Europe—but at the customer site in North America) of the connection that performs a 2-wire to 4-wire conversion. Four physical wires are used at the subscriber side for full duplex transmission. Two of the wires are used for transmit and two for receiving. Many ISDN devices have an NT1 built into them that makes installations quicker and easier.

- (NT2) Network Termination Type 2: An NT2 handles layer 2 and 3 ISDN protocols. Because these are included in all ISDN devices, they are shown in the figure in parentheses with TE1 devices.

Reference Interface

ISDN specifies several reference points that define logical interfaces between terminals and network termination points.

- **S Interface**: The reference point between subscriber-side ISDN equipment and NT2.

- **T Interface**: The reference point between NT1 and NT2. Notice in the figure that the S and T interfaces are shown on the same line. First, they're electrically identical; second, an S reference is inside the subscriber device.

- **R Interface**: The reference point between non-ISDN devices and a TA. The analog telephone has an R interface because it's not ISDN equipment.

- **U Interface**: The reference between the carrier switch and the ISDN device (NT1) at the subscriber site. Keep in mind, ISDN is intended to provide digital connections using a 2-wire local loop. The U interface refers to this 2-to-4 wire hybrid.

Figure 1-13 shows a typical application of ISDN. A small LAN is arranged in a star topology with a hub. One of the hub ports is connected to a router. The router contains an ISDN adapter. The adapter is likely to be a circuit card or module that plugs into the router and contains all electronics needed for the NT1 at the U interface. The NT1 contains an RJ45 connector. UTP cable terminated with RJ45 connectors (using straight-through pinning) is used to connect the NT1 U interface to an ISDN line terminated at a wall plate near the router.

The ISDN line connects to an ISDN switch at the central office. If the network in Figure 1-13 is to be used for Internet access, the connection will continue from the ISDN switch to an ISP. The ISP must also have an ISDN switch.

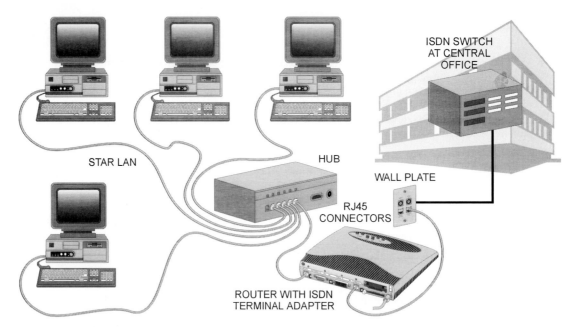

STAR LAN

HUB

ISDN SWITCH
AT CENTRAL
OFFICE

WALL PLATE

RJ45
CONNECTORS

ROUTER WITH ISDN
TERMINAL ADAPTER

Figure 1-13 Users Connect to an ISDN Line Through a Hub that Connects to a Router that May Contain an ISDN Terminal Adapter

Digital Subscriber Line

Digital Subscriber
Line (DSL)

Digital Subscriber Line, or **DSL**, is a connection technology that uses standard twisted-pair telephone wires to send and receive data at high data rates. The absolute maximum data rate available with DSL is 8.445 Mbps, but a more typical data rate varies from 512 Kbps to 1.544 Mbps for downloads. The upload data rate ranges from 128 Kbps to less than 1 Mbps.

DSL takes full advantage of the available bandwidth of copper wire. With DSL, voice and data can be sent on the same wire, along with complex graphics such as 3D animation and other multimedia files.

Like ISDN, DSL is a complete end-to-end digital connection. Because a data signal doesn't need to be converted in the analog portion of the local loop, data rates aren't hampered with analog and digital conversion that ultimately limit the maximum data rates of analog modems. Also like ISDN, DSL users must be located within 18,000 feet of the central office where the phone company's DSL equipment is located. (Although, some phone companies have extended the range beyond 18,000 feet by using fiber optic cabling rather than copper twisted-pairs.)

Because a DSL line is dedicated to a user, the user has access to the full bandwidth that the channel offers. (DSL bandwidth varies with the distance a user is located from the central office. The closer you are, the higher the data rate.) No matter how many of your neighbors are subscribing to DSL, your data rates won't change. But recall that with a cable modem, data rates drop as more users subscribe to the service.

One of the attractive features of DSL is that existing telephones can use the DSL line at the same time as computers. But to share the line with analog telephones, a splitter must be installed at the subscriber site. A splitter is used to provide a separate, narrow-bandwidth channel for voice communications.

In a typical application, a business will subscribe to a DSL line and offer users access through a hub connected to a router that's connected to a DSL modem. The DSL modem connects to a terminated DSL line.

There are many versions of DSL. The following summarizes several of the most common versions:

- **Asymmetric Digital Subscriber Line** (**ADSL**): An ADSL modem reserves most of the bandwidth for downloads, particularly downloads from the Internet. A small amount of the available bandwidth is made available for uploads from the user to the Internet. Maximum ADSL data rates are 6.1 Mbps upstream and 640 Kbps downstream.

- **DSL Lite**, also called **G.Lite**, was developed by Microsoft, Compaq, and Intel. It allows the line to be split at the central office rather than at the subscriber site. This makes DSL Lite easier to install. It also reduces data rates to between 6 Mbps and 1.544 Mbps for downloads, and to between 128 Kbps and 384 Kbps for uploads. DSL Lite is an approved ITU-T standard and is expected to be widely deployed.

- **Rate Adaptive DSL**, or **RADSL**, is an ADSL technology that was developed by Westfall. With RADSL, software at the central office is used to determine the best rate to send and receive data signals. The software then adjusts the data rate accordingly. Downstream data rates vary from 640 Kbps to about 2 Mbps. Upstream data rates vary from 272 Kbps to about 1 Mbps.

Asymmetric Digital Subscriber Line (ADSL)

DSL Lite

G.Lite

Rate Adaptive DSL (RADSL)

BANDWIDTH TECHNOLOGY

Bandwidth technology refers to methods used to interconnect wide area networks. **Bandwidth**, when used with networks, refers to the bit rate of the network. The higher the bandwidth, the more bits that can be sent or received.

Before discussing the specific i-Net+ bandwidth technologies, there are several terms common to internetworking that need to be defined.

- **Circuit Switching** A circuit switched network is one in which a path is set up and maintained between two devices for the duration of the transmission.

- **Packet Switching** A packet switched network is one in which data may travel across many paths between two devices.

- **Virtual Circuit** A virtual circuit (also called a permanent virtual circuit) refers to a specified amount of bandwidth that's guaranteed for the duration of a transmission between two devices. Packet switched networks use virtual circuits.

- **Connection-oriented** A connection-oriented network, when applied to wide area networks (WANs), refers to the guarantee of a transmission path or bandwidth. A virtual circuit is an example of a connection-oriented network. The most common connection-oriented protocol is TCP. The most common connection-oriented protocol is TCP.

Bandwidth technology

Bandwidth

Circuit Switching

Packet Switching

Virtual Circuit

Connection-oriented

- **Connectionless** A connectionless network is one in which there is no guarantee of a path between two end-devices, or that the bandwidth will be available for the two devices to communicate. This type of connection is often called "best-effort." Connectionless protocols such as UDP (User Defined Protocol) and HTTP (Hyper-Text Transfer Protocol) use a best-effort strategy for sending data packets. This type of connection is often called "best-effort". Connectionless protocols such as UDP (User Defined Protocol) and HTTP (Hyper-Text Transfer Protocol) use a best-effort strategy for sending data packets.

- **Frequency Division Multiple Access (FDMA)** FDMA is a multiplexing technique in which the channel bandwidth is divided into discrete units that are permanently made available to all users. Broadcast AM, FM, and television are examples of FDMA.

- **Time Division Multiple Access (TDMA)** TDMA is a multiplexing technique in which the full channel bandwidth is available to each user for specific time periods. All of the bandwidth technology types described in this section use TDMA.

Digital T-carrier

The **T-carrier system** is a digital transmission method that has been in use for over thirty years. In that time, it has evolved from a transmission method used only to connect large volumes of voice calls between common carrier switching centers, to a complete digital transmission method used for voice, data, and video between networks.

T-carrier uses circuit switching to dedicate a path between devices attached to the ends of the connection. Because the connection is connection-oriented, upper layer protocols aren't required to maintain the connection or to recover from errors. However, a T-carrier channel frequently carries IP packets so that end-device messages can be accurately routed across the Internet or private internetwork.

Because the T-carrier system is digital, there are no analog portions of the system from source to destination. The effect is a very reliable, low-distortion link between networks.

T-carrier data is transmitted at 64 Kbps (or 56 Kbps in older T-carrier systems) simultaneously in both directions. Compare the T-carrier data rate to the maximum data rates available in the analog local loop. Data rates in the analog local loop are fixed at a maximum of 35 Kbps for uploads, while download rates (using V.90 modems) won't exceed 53 Kbps.

The T-carrier system is composed of a number of 8-bit digital signals. (Referred to as DS0. **DS** is actually short for **digital service**, while the 0 represents the lowest level of the T-carrier hierarchy.) Before being formatted for a T-carrier frame, each digital signal has a maximum bandwidth of 4 KHz. The 4 KHz signals are sampled before transmitting using a technique called **Pulse Code Modulation (PCM)**. Each DS0 is sampled 8,000 times a second. Because there are 8 bits in each signal, and because each signal is sampled 8,000 times a seconds, the data rate of each DS0 is 8 bits X 8,000 samples = 64,000 bps.

The sampled digital signals are organized into a frame before being transmitted. The smallest T-carrier frame contains 24 DS0 signals, and is called a **T-1 frame**. Twenty-four 8-bit signals represents 24 X 8 = 192 bits. A single **framing bit** (used to keep the sending and receiving equipment synchronized) is added so that the total frame length is 193 bits. A T1 frame is transmitted at 1.544 Mbps. The T1 data rate is derived as follows:

- With a sampling rate of 8,000 times each second, the frame is sampled 1/8,000 = 125 S. In other words, the frame is sampled once every 125 S.

- With a frame sample rate of 125 S, and with 193 bits in each frame, the time of each bit in the frame is 125 S/193 bits = .647 S.

- For a bit time of .647 S, the frequency rate of the bits is 1/.647 S = 1.544 Mbps.

T-carrier Hierarchy

The T-carrier system is organized in a hierarchical format beginning with T1. Within each level of the hierarchy, each channel has a bandwidth of 4,000 Hz and is transmitted at 64 Kbps. A **T1 carrier** is composed of 24 4,000 Hz channels. The data rate of a T1 channel is 1.544 Mbps. Likewise, a **T2 carrier** contains 96 channels (DS2 signals) that are transmitted at 6.312 Mbps. A **T3 carrier** contains 672 channels (DS3 signals) that are transmitted at 44.736 Mbps. Finally, a **T4 carrier** contains 4032 channels (DS4 signals) that are transmitted at 274.174 Mbps.

Table 1-2 summarizes the hierarchy. Notice that there are sub-divisions at T1c and T3c. These occur due to advances in channel bank technology. A **channel bank** is the terminating equipment used to format each channel. As the technology improved over the years, more channels could be framed within a channel bank. This resulted in filling some wide gaps in the number of channels that could be transmitted from T1 to T2 and from T3 to T4. In practice, T1 and T3 are the normal carrier implementations.

T-CARRIER	DIGITAL SIGNAL	DATA RATE	CHANNEL CAPACITY
	DS0	64 Kbps	1 channel
T1	DS1	1.544 Mbps	24 channels
T1c	DS1c	3.152 Mbps	48 channels
T2	DS2	6.312 Mbps	96 channels
T3	DS3	44.736 Mbps	672 channels
T3c	DS3c	89.472 Mbps	1344 channels
T4	DS4	274.176 Mbps	4032 channels

Table 1-2 T-carrier Common Carrier Hierarchy

T-carrier Frame Format

The basic data unit used with T-carrier is a frame. The **frame format** of T1 is shown in Figure 1-14. Twenty-four PCM encoded channels of 8-bits/channel are carried in the frame. The 192 data bits in the frame are preceded by a single framing bit to give a total frame length of 193 bits. The frame is transmitted at 1.544 Mbps.

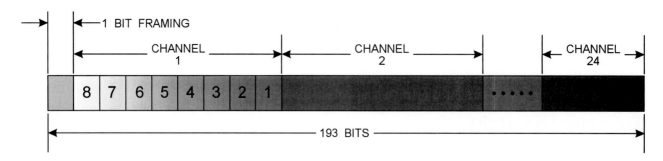

Figure 1-14 T1 Carrier Frame Format

The framing bit serves as a marker to identify the beginning of the frame. As the frame is transferred through various switching facilities, and at the final receiver, it allows the equipment to synchronize to small differences in bit times so that the frame won't be lost.

The frame format shown in the figure is only for T1. All higher order carrier facilities frame the channels a bit differently and treat a T1 frame as nothing more than a series of bits. This is why a T1c carrier with 48 channels transmits at 3.152 Mbps rather than the expected 2 X 1.544 Mbps.

T-carrier framing has been through numerous changes. With each change, more data was sent faster. The changes are the direct results of chip technology and channel bank advances. A channel bank is equipment responsible for combining the channels at the T-carrier facility. There are five different channel banks in the system and they are referred to as D1, D2, D3, D4, and DCT (Digital Carrier Trunk, also called D5, which is only used between T-carrier facilities and therefore is not available to subscribers.).

Table 1-3 shows the frame format used with a D4 channel bank, called a **superframe**. A superframe contains twelve T1 frames. Each frame has 193 bits. Except for the sixth and twelfth frames, all eight bits contain user data. In the sixth and twelfth frames, one bit is designated for carrying signaling information that contains the status of the connection.

Table 1-3 T-carrier Superframe Format

FRAME NUMBER	TERMINAL SYNC BIT	SUPERFRAME SYNC BIT	INFORMATION BITS	SIGNALING BIT
1	1	-	1 through 8	-
2	-	0	1 through 8	-
3	0	-	1 through 8	-
4	-	1	1 through 8	-
5	1	-	1 through 8	-
6	-	1	1 through 7	8
7	0	-	1 through 8	-
8	-	1	1 through 8	-
9	1	-	1 through 8	-
10	-	1	1 through 8	-
11	0	-	1 through 8	-
12	-	0	1 through 7	8

The 193rd bit in each frame is still used for synchronization of each frame. Beginning with D2 technology, synchronization was divided between terminal framing and superframe synchronization. Terminal synchronization is used by the terminal equipment at the ends of the link to ensure channel synchronization, while superframe synchronization ensures the full twelve T1 frames are tracked through each switching facility along the route to the destination.

Each synchronization technique uses a specific 6-bit code that's interleaved within the superframe. **Interleaving** is the process of alternating the terminal and superframe bits. The bit codes are as follows:

Terminal: 101010
Superframe: 011110

Beginning with the terminal bit, 1, the two codes are interleaved at bit position 193 in each of the T1 frames. This produces the following 12-bit code:

100011011100

As you can see in the figure, the terminal synchronization bits are placed in each of the odd numbered frames, while the superframe synchronization bits are placed in each of the even numbered frames. With this code, the transmit and receive stations will know if a frame is lost and will be able to correctly track channel data within +/- two frames.

T-carrier frame formats grew in size with the advent of AT&T's **Extended Superframe Format (ESF)**. The format is illustrated in Table 1-4. The ESF contains twenty-four 24-channel T1 frames (576 total channels). Bit 193 is multiplexed to serve three distinct purposes:

Fe bit

Data Link (DL) bit

CRC-6

- The **Fe bit** provides frame synchronization at every fourth frame using the bit pattern 001011. Fe serves the same purpose as the S and T bits in the D4 format.

- The **Data Link (DL) bit** carries line performance information at every other frame.

- The **CRC-6** is a 6-bit cyclic redundancy check that inspects all 4,632 bits of the frame for errors.

Table 1-4 T-carrier Extended Superframe Format

FRAME NUMBER	Fe BIT	DATA LINK BIT	CRC-6	INFORMATION BITS	SIGNALING BIT
1	-	m	-	1 through 8	-
2	-	-	C1	1 through 8	-
3	-	m	-	1 through 8	-
4	0	-	-	1 through 8	-
5	-	m	-	1 through 8	-
6	-	-	C2	1 through 7	8
7	-	m	-	1 through 8	-
8	0	-	-	1 through 8	-
9	-	m	-	1 through 8	-
10	-	-	C3	1 through 8	-
11	-	m	-	1 through 8	-
12	1	-	-	1 through 7	8
13	-	m	-	1 through 8	-
14	-	-	C4	1 through 8	-
15	-	m	-	1 through 8	-
16	0	-	-	1 through 8	-
17	-	m	-	1 through 8	-
18	-	-	C5	1 through 7	8
19	-	m	-	1 through 8	-
20	1	-	-	1 through 8	-
21	-	m	-	1 through 8	-
22	-	-	C6	1 through 8	-
23	-	m	-	1 through 8	-
24	1	-	-	1 through 7	8

Signaling data is retained at every sixth frame as it is for a D4 superframe. The data rate for both D4 and ESF approaches 64 Kbps. Due to the sixth frame signaling bits (sometimes called the **robbed bit**, or **7 5/6 coding** because 5 of 6 frames contain eight user bits and one frame contains seven user bits), the data rate (user information rate) will never reach a full 64 Kbps.

T-carrier Application

Before deciding that a T1 line (and, by extension, a T3 line) is right for your organization, consider the following rules of thumb for T1:

- Make sure it's available in your area. Call your local telephone company and ask them. If T-carrier isn't available, there may be equally good alternatives such as ISDN or Frame Relay.

- Decide if a full T1 line is needed. Generally, if 30 or more users need to connect for either voice or data, a full T1 will make sense when compared to the cost of 30 discrete telephone lines.

- If a full T1 line isn't needed, check to see if a fractional T1 is available in your area. Fractional T1 is some portion of a full T1 line, and is based upon the customer's needs. For example, you can lease 12 channels, instead of the complete 24 channels, using fractional T1. Make the determination based upon the cost and speed of discrete phone lines.

- Determine the level of support your organization can provide for the T-carrier line. Telephone companies market various levels of service with wide area connections such as T1. The level of service ranges from full support from the telephone company (the most expensive), to a level in which the customer controls all configurations for the line (the least expensive).

Before a T-carrier line is installed, a **CSU/DSU (Channel Service Unit/ Digital Service Unit)** must be installed at the customer site. The CSU is responsible for recovering data that's multiplexed in the frame, while the DSU is responsible for removing coding that was used to package the data.

Figure 1-15 shows a typical application. In the figure, a local Ethernet LAN is used to communicate with a remote Ethernet LAN. As each workstation gains access to the Ethernet bus in the hub, the Ethernet frame is transferred to the router and packaged into a packet. The router packets are transferred to the CSU/DSU for T1 frame formatting and encoding. The data is then sent to the remote LAN where another CSU/DSU removes the T1 frame format and coding, before transferring the data to the router. The router then sends frames to the Ethernet bus in the hub, and the workstation whose MAC address matches the address of the received frame accepts the frame.

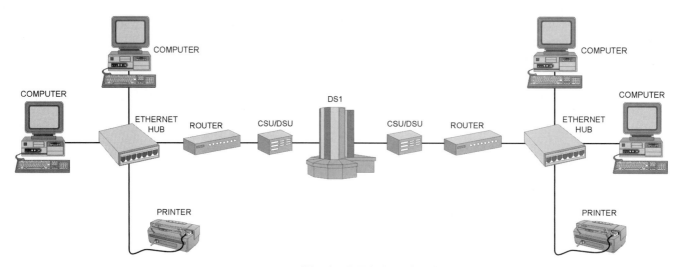

Figure 1-15 Typical T1 Application

If you install a T1 connection today, expect to use D4 channel banks. Your data will be sent using the D4 superframe, or it may use the Extended Superframe Format. With ESF, more information will be sent quicker because fewer overhead bits will be sent.

Table 1-5 summarizes characteristics of T-carrier.

Table 1-5 Summary of T-carrier Characteristics

Application:	Voice, data, video
Data Rate:	DS0 Channel: 64 Kbps
	T1: 1.544 Mbps
	T1c: 3.152 Mbp
	T2: 6.312 Mbps
	T3: 44.736 Mbps
	T3c: 44.736 Mbp
	T4: 274.176 Mbps
	E1: 2.048 Mbps
Switching Technique:	Circuit/frame
Connection Type:	Connection-oriented
Data Unit Length:	193 bits (24 channel T1 frame)

European and Optical Carriers

Europe and some other parts of the world outside of North America have adopted a **multiplexed digital carrier system** that is a bit different than the T-carrier system.

The basic signaling rate is a DS0 signal that's transmitted at 64 Kbps. The signal is developed using a modified form of **PCM-encoding** (PCM is Pulse Code Modulation, a digital technique for superimposing data onto a stream of square waves) that allows a DS0 signal to have better noise immunity at small signal levels. (The T-carrier system provides better noise immunity for idle channels, or channels in which data or voice is sent intermittently.)

multiplexed digital carrier system

PCM-encoding

The basic E-carrier frame, called an E1, contains 30 64 Kbps channels. The frame contains 256 bits.

The European carrier hierarchy is shown in Table 1-6.

E-CARRIER	DIGITAL SIGNAL	LINE SPEED	CHANNEL CAPACITY
	DS0	64 Kbps	1 Channel
E1	DS1	2.048 Mbps	20 Channel
E2	DS2	8.448 Mbps	120 Channel
E3	DS3	34.368 Mbps	480 Channel
E4	DS4	139.268 Mbps	1920 Channel
E5	DS5	565.148 Mbps	7680 Channel

Table 1-6 European Carrier Hierarchy

SONET (Synchronous Optical Network) is a carrier technology that uses optical signals. SONET describes the Physical layer data rates, cabling media, and physical connectors. The standard relies on other technologies such as ATM to transport the data.

The basic SONET frame is called an **optical carrier (OC)**. At the lowest level of the SONET hierarchy, an OC1 frame contains 6,480 bits and propagates through fiber optic cabling at 51.84 Mbps.

The ITU has included a copper cable-based version of SONET in the SONET standard (called **Synchronous Digital Hierarchy**). The electrical signal is called **Synchronous Transport Signal (STS)**, and is equivalent to the OC optical signaling rates.

SONET (Synchronous Optical Network)

optical carrier (OC)

Synchronous Digital Hierarchy

Synchronous Transport Signal (STS)

Table 1-7 lists OC carrier rates for the SONET standard.

Table 1-7 SONET Data Rates

SONET SIGNAL	DATA RATE
OC-1	51.840 Mbps
OC-3	155.52 Mbps
OC-9	466.560 Mbps
OC-12	622.080 Mbps
OC-18	933.120 Mbps
OC-24	1244.160 Mbps
OC-36	1866.240 Mbps
OC-48	2488.320 Mbps

X.25 Packet Switching

X.25 packet
switching

data-terminal
equipment (DTE)

data-communication
equipment (DCE)

X.25 packet switching is an older transport protocol used in WANs, and is modeled after the public telephone system. Data in an X.25 network travels at either 56 or 64 Kbps.

The concept of packet switching is embodied in the recommendation of ITU (CCITT) X.25. X.25 is an interface standard that describes the connection of DTEs (**data-terminal equipment**) and DCEs (**data-communication equipment**) to public switching networks. Essentially, the recommendation is a technology limited to the ports of the DTE, and ports of the DCE. It is a time-tested technology that's been used successfully since the 1970s.

Background Info

DTE and DCE

A WAN typically connects data-terminal equipment (DTE) from one area to a DTE in another area. A DTE is just about any programmable device—a computer, a network of computers, a front-end processor, or controller. The DTE gains access to the WAN through data-communication (circuit terminating) equipment (DCE). The most common DCE is a modem.

bis

The objective of X.25 is to provide a complete communications system for transferring data. X.25 uses packet switching to transfer data. The data is broken into packets that are sent across many paths between sending and receiving nodes. Therefore, it's a connectionless protocol.

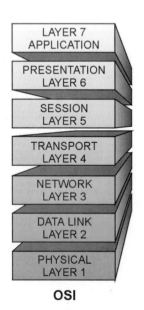

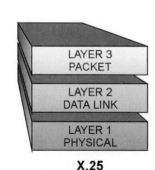

The X.25 protocol adopted a layered approach to data flow that parallels the OSI model. As you can see in Figure 1-16, the X.25 protocol uses a layered approach that parallels the lower three layers of the OSI model. The first three layers of the OSI and X.25 are the same.

At layer 1, the Physical layer, the X.25 interface specifications are contained in the X.21 recommendations. X.21 describes physical, electrical, and functional characteristics of layer 1. The recommendation specifies a 15-pin synchronous interface that's widely used in Europe, but hasn't gained much of a following in the U.S., due to the prevalence of EIA/TIA-232 (RS-232). The ITU has approved an interface functionally equivalent to EIA/TIA-232 in the X.21bis recommendation. (The word **bis** is a Swiss term for alternate.)

Figure 1-16 X.25 Protocol and the OSI Model

The Data Link layer describes the procedures used by the DTE and DCE for synchronization, control, and error detection. X.25 uses a subset of HDLC, known as **Link-Access Procedure-Balanced (LAPB)**. The LAPB protocol is operated in the **Asynchronous Balanced Mode (ABM)**. In this mode, each station on the network can initiate a transmission or terminate the connection.

You shouldn't be misled by the "asynchronous" in the LAPB asynchronous balanced mode. Data flow through an X.25 network is synchronous; the sending and receiving stations use timing parameters to track frames and bits. Instead, "asynchronous" is describing the autonomy of the stations. Each station can transmit a packet of data onto the network whenever it chooses to do so.

Layer three, the **Packet layer**, describes the format of packets, and includes a control field header that governs packet exchanges between DTE and DCE.

Link-Access
Procedure-Balanced
(LAPB)

Asynchronous
Balanced Mode
(ABM)

Packet Layer

X.25 packet

X.25 Packet Format

X.25 uses a variable-size packet to communicate between two devices. The **X.25 packet** is shown in Figure 1-17.

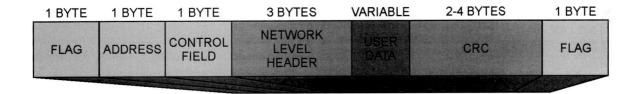

Figure 1-17 X.25 Frame Format

The beginning flag serves to synchronize DTE and DCE. The flag is 8 bits with a value of 01111110. The end flag signals the end of the frame and also has a bit-pattern of 01111110.

The one-byte address identifies the DTE and DCE. It is a fixed bit pattern whose assignment to the DTE and DCE depends upon the usage. The address follows a command/response scheme. In a command/response scheme, a transmitting station will issue a command and the receiving station will reply with a response. In the case of X.25, only two devices are involved, and the address will only be one of two values: 10000000 or 11000000. When a station (DTE or DCE) sends a command, the address specifies the receiver (DTE or DCE). When a station makes a response, the address specifies the station responding. The specific type of command or response is contained in the control field.

Background Info

LAPB Command/Response Assignments

X.25 uses the Link Access Protocol-B as the basis for link communication at the Data Link layer.

The LAPB command address assignments are:

- 10000000, when the DTE sends a command to the DCE. The address is specifying the DCE.

- 1100000, when the DCE sends a command to the DTE. Now, the address specifies the DTE.

The LAPB response address assignments are:

- 11000000, when the DTE responds to a command from the DCE. The address is specifying the DTE.

- 10000000, when the DCE responds to a command from the DTE. Now, the address specifies the DCE.

information

supervisory

unnumbered

Number Sent (NS)

Number Received (NR)

The control field specifies the type of data that's in the packet. There are three types of control fields: **information**, **supervisory**, and **unnumbered**.

The information field indicates that the packet contains user data. An information packet is also used to track the sequence of packets between communication stations. It does so by using two sets of bits called **Number Sent (NS)** and **Number Received (NR)**. Both NS and NR contain three bits. A station can send seven information packets containing user data before being sent a response from the receiver. For each packet sent, the NS will indicate the sequence of the packet. For example, if four packets have been sent, then the fifth packet will have NS=5.

NR is set to the value that the transmitting station expects to receive from the receiving station. The receiving station returns a packet with NR set to the value of the next expected packet. So, the transmitting station will have NS=5 and NR=6 because it expects the receiving station to respond with a value that indicates the next packet, six in this example.

The supervisory field manages control of the link between DTE and DCE by indicating that a receiver is ready to receive, or not ready to receive. Much of the exchange between DTE and DCE consists of commands and responses carried by supervisory packets. Supervisory packets do not carry user data.

The unnumbered field deals with specialized network management functions. For example, when a transmitting station has no more data to send, it will use an unnumbered packet to tell the receiving data to disconnect the link between the stations.

The unnumbered field has commands and responses unique to LAPB. **Set Asynchronous Response Mode (SARM)** is a request by a station to set up the link for data transfer. The proper response to a SARM is an **Unnumbered Acknowledgment (UA)**. The link initiator then sends a **Set Asynchronous Balance Mode (SABM)**, which sets the receive and send counters (NS and NR) in the stations to zero. These counters track the sequencing of data packets. Again, the appropriate response is UA. A **Command Reject (CMDR)** is sent in response to a frame that was received carrying a prohibited command. For example, if a Receive Ready packet is sent before the SARM, the response would be CMDR. A **Frame Reject (FRMR)** would be sent in similar circumstances.

Table 1-8 lists several commands and responses used with each type of control field.

<table>
<tr><td>**Set Asynchronous Response Mode (SARM)**</td></tr>
<tr><td>**Unnumbered Acknowledgment (UA)**</td></tr>
<tr><td>**Set Asynchronous Balance Mode (SABM)**</td></tr>
</table>

Table 1-8 X.25 Control Field Types and Command/Response

Command Reject (CMDR)

Frame Reject (FRMR)

CONTROL FIELD	COMMANDS	RESPONSES
Information	I (information, user data)	
Supervisory	RR (receive ready) RNR (receive not ready) REJ (reject)	RR (receive ready) RNR (receive not ready) REJ (reject)
Unnumbered	SARM (set asynchronous response mode) SABM (set asynchronous balanced mode) DISC (disconnect)	DM (disconnect mode) UA (unnumbered acknowledgment) CMDR (command reject) FRMR (frame reject)

The user data field is a minimum of 24 bits long and a maximum of 1024.

The network field is generally 24 bits (3 bytes) and comprises the minimum bit length of the packet. Figure 1-18 illustrates the network-level header field. The field is responsible for packet format and for directing an orderly data flow between DTE and DCE.

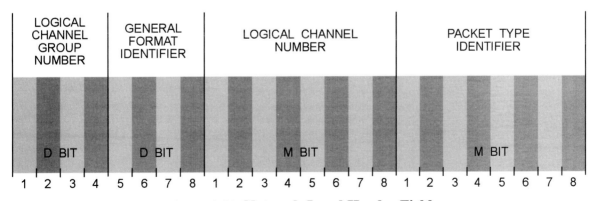

Figure 1-18 Network-Level Header Field

logical channel group

The **logical channel group** identifies the group of which the channel is a part. The X.25 router connecting the DEC to a packet network contains 16 group channels.

256 logical channels

Each group channel contains **256 logical channels**. As an example, a header may be identified as group channel 7, and logical channel 150. A single router may support 40 or more simultaneous, full-duplex channels.

General Format Identifier (GFI)

The **General Format Identifier (GFI)** describes the type of packet as information, supervisory, or unnumbered. For example, 0001 is the data packet format (information). Other bit patterns describe diagnostics and flow control such as Receive Ready (RR), Receive Not Ready (RNR), or reset indications (supervisory) and connection setups such as call request, call accepted, or incoming call (unnumbered).

D-bit

X.25 networks installed since 1984 have a **D-bit** option in the general format identifier. The D-bit is used when a station requires confirmation that data was received at the other end of the connection. D-bit =1 when the calling station requests delivery confirmation from the called station. When D-bit=0, it's ignored.

Packet Type Identifier (PTI)

The **Packet Type Identifier (PTI)** describes the specific function of the packet. For example, the general format identifier may indicate the packet is a call setup packet if the DCE is sending an incoming call to the DTE. The bit pattern for incoming calls is 00001011. Whereas the format identifier is a general indicator of the packet's function, the packet-type identifier is a specific indicator of the function.

M-bit

The **M-bit** contained in the packet type field stands for more data. The M-bit is used to tell the receiving station that more data will follow receipt of the packet. When the bit is set to 1, additional packets have been transmitted and should be considered a part of a unit. If the M-bit is set to 0, there are no more packets.

The users of packet networks find them to be an advantage for short, bursty traffic such as order-entry keystrokes. An exchange of small files among field offices several times a day wouldn't cost-justify a dedicated phone line between the users. X.25 networks route packets dynamically. Routers in the network select the path offering the least amount of congestion. Efficiency and costs, using the network, are thereby kept at a minimum. Packet networks also have the advantage of offering a variety of services to users that are similar to services offered to phone subscribers. These include call-forwarding or reverse charges.

Table 1-9 summarizes the characteristics of X.25.

Table 1-9 Summary of X.25 Characteristics

Application:	Data
Data Rate:	56/64 Kbps
Switching Technique:	Packet/packet
Connection Type:	Connectionless
Data Unit Length:	Variable

Frame Relay

Frame Relay is a variable-bandwidth packet switched technology that utilizes Data Link layer concepts to send data. Its operation is similar to X.25.

Frame Relay is an interface with a variable-length data field that was designed for the **Integrated Services Digital Network (ISDN)**. It uses a TDMA multiplexer for sending messages from many sources over a **Permanent Virtual Circuit (PVC)** to the destination. Because data travels across a virtual circuit, Frame Relay is a connection-oriented protocol.

A Frame Relay network is illustrated in Figure 1-19.

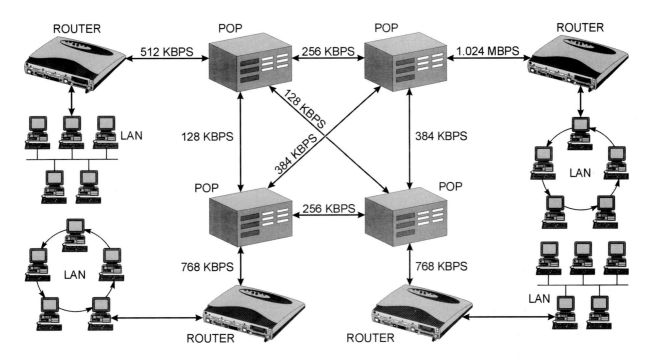

In Figure 1-19, four LANs are connected in a WAN using frame-relay switching. The LANs communicate over a permanent virtual circuit. This is set up and maintained by a common carrier, such as AT&T, MCI, etc.

Figure 1-19 Typical Frame Relay Network

The network administrator specifies which nodes on the LANs will be communicating across the Frame Relay network, and uses this information to determine the size and number of PVCs. The Frame Relay switch stores the PVC and will use it when the nodes transmit.

The LANs gain access to the PVC at the carrier **Point Of Presence (POP)**. The POP is the physical connection at which the carrier assumes control of the frames.

The carriers offer PVCs at varying data rates. The data rate corresponds to channel bandwidth. A network administrator specifies the PVC rates based on a best-estimate of node usage. From this estimate, a **Committed Information Rate (CIR)** is derived. The CIR is the sum of the PVC bandwidths for each LAN. The network administrator specifies the CIR bandwidth, and the Frame Relay switch multiplexes the LAN nodes onto the assigned PVCs.

The advantage of Frame Relay networks is that bandwidth is made variable, and can be matched to the bandwidth needs of the user. This may range from 4 Kbps, to a full T1 line at 1.544 Mbps, or up to a T3 line at 44.736 Mbps.

Frame Relay networks work particularly well with mildly bursty data; the intermittent keystrokes associated with order entries, for example. They are capable of exceeding the CIR for brief periods, because the switch incorporates a statistical multiplexer. A statistical multiplexer contains buffer pools that allow the data rate from nodes to exceed the line rate (the CIR) for short periods.

The reason that Frame Relay transports data so much faster than X.25 is that it only uses the first two layers of the OSI Model, the Physical and Data Link layers. The significance of this is that a Frame Relay network has less frame overhead (fields in the frame that don't contain actual user data) so the frames can be transported very quickly. Frame Relay relies on upper layer protocols such as TCP/IP to provide reliability.

The Data Link layer protocol used by Frame Relay is the **Link-Access Procedure-Frame (LAPF)**. LAPF is a subset of LAPD. The main difference between LAPF and LAPD is that the control field in LAPF doesn't contain sequencing bits (NS and NR) and the complex commands used to manage a link. Like X.25, Frame Relay is a packet-switched technology, but the data unit used with Frame Relay is called a frame, rather than a packet.

Frame Relay transports data at higher rates than X.25, and it is usually implemented at a lower cost than leased lines. Like X.25, users are offered variable amounts of bandwidth. The weakness of Frame Relay is that it is restricted to data traffic and can't be used for voice communications. In addition, Frame Relay packets are prone to being lost when multiplexer buffers approach the overflow point. Remember, Frame Relay doesn't incorporate reliability in the technology. Due to the flow-control capabilities of multiplexers, data from the LAN nodes must be slowed to avoid losing the packets.

Table 1-10 summarizes the characteristics of Frame Relay.

Table 1-10 Summary of Frame Relay Characteristics

Application:	Data
Data Rate:	T1, T3, E1, E3
Switching Technique:	Packet/Frame
Connection Type:	Connection-oriented

Asynchronous Transfer Mode

Asynchronous Transfer Mode is a cell relay standard that uses 53-byte cells for transporting text, voice, video, music, or graphic messages. The typical speed that ATN cells is transferred is 155 Mbps. But read on, because due to the flexibility that the small cell sizes offer, the data rates can easily be extended to 650 Mbps using optical carriers.

ATM was developed by AT&T in 1980 as a technique for transmitting voice and data in a packet format. In 1988, the ITU (CCITT) selected ATM as a standard to use with **Broadband ISDN (BISDN)**. ATM is the standard that describes cell relay technology.

The strength of ATM, and the reason many believe it will be the transport service of the future for both WANs and LANs, is its ability to support large-bandwidth connections that are scalable to the users' needs. **Bandwidth scalability** refers to a channel that is bandwidth-flexible, such as Frame Relay and X.25. ATM is also noted for providing **bit-level service**. Bit-level service refers to transmissions at the Data Link layer; ATM uses only the first two levels of the OSI model.

Since ATM is more scalable than all other bandwidth technologies, it's often used by ISPs to support small to medium customer bases. Most of the cost in implementing ATM resides with the local telephone company. Consequently, a small ISP can support users for multimedia-rich Internet access with a relatively small investment. Keep in mind that in addition to the linked capabilities of the Internet, there are thousands of sites with voice and music files, high-resolution graphics, and video files.

The ability of a protocol to address individual bits is important to transmitting video. Not only does video require large-bandwidth channels, but the channels must also be of high quality because the user is much more sensitive to video distortion than noise distortion; that is, our eyes are more sensitive to distortion than are our ears.

Table 1-11 shows the ATM layered model. Three ATM layers are defined in the model: the Physical layer, the ATM layer, and the ATM Adaption layer. These three layers are roughly analogous to the first two layers of the OSI model. Note, however, that a Network layer is not described. This allows ATM cells to be switched rapidly because the header will not include routing protocols. This can be accomplished directly with upper layer protocols such as TCP/IP.

ATM LAYERED MODEL	
ATM Adaption Layer	Convergence Sublayer
	Segmentation and Reassembly
ATM Layer	Cell Formatting
ATM Physical Layer	Physical Interface and Channel Media

Table 1-11 ATM Layered Model

The Physical layer describes how the ATM cells are transported, and includes the physical interface, channel media, and data rates. Unlike other technologies, ATM can be operated over many physical media types (UTP or fiber optic, for example), and through many physical interfaces. Currently, ATM transports cells through user interfaces (such as an RJ45 connector) at the following data rates:

- 100 Mbps Multimode Fiber Optic (FDDI)

- OC1, OC3, OC4 SONET

- DS1/2/3, E1/3

The DS and E interface is targeted to telecommunications carriers, which typically use coaxial or fiber optic cable at the interconnect level, but use twisted-pair connections to LANs. The 100 Mbps fiber connection is targeted to LANs, and specifically to FDDI LANs running UTP cables. The SONET specification reflects the status of current technology, and will no doubt include the higher rates such as OC24 (1.2 Gbps) and OC48 (2.5 Gbps) as the need arises.

cell format

General Flow Control (GFC)

The ATM layer of the model describes the **cell format** of ATM. ATM uses small, fixed-size cells, 53 bytes long. The header occupies 5 bytes, while the information field (containing user data) is 48 bytes. The cell format of ATM is pictured in Figure 1-20. The **General Flow Control (GFC)** field provides a method for multiple workstations to use the same interface. ATM cells are multiplexed. The GFC indicates to the multiplexer that more than one station is feeding a single port. The GFC also indicates to the multiplexer that the time slot given to the port will contain data from multiple users.

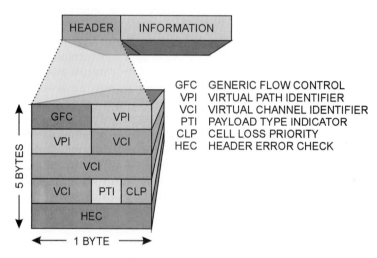

GFC   GENERIC FLOW CONTROL
VPI   VIRTUAL PATH IDENTIFIER
VCI   VIRTUAL CHANNEL IDENTIFIER
PTI   PAYLOAD TYPE INDICATOR
CLP   CELL LOSS PRIORITY
HEC   HEADER ERROR CHECK

Figure 1-20 ATM Cell Format

Virtual Path Identifier (VPI)

Virtual Channel Identifier (VCI)

The three **Virtual Path Identifier (VPI)** fields, and two **Virtual Channel Identifier (VCI)** fields serve as an addressing mechanism used by the ATM switches. A virtual channel represents a guaranteed link from source switch to destination switch. The ATM header contains more than one virtual path and channel because it's assumed that more than one user will be simultaneously accessing an ATM network.

The use of a virtual path means that ATM is a connection-oriented technology. Each port on an ATM switch that is connected to a user workstation has a virtual channel to a destination switch. This is illustrated in Figure 1-21.

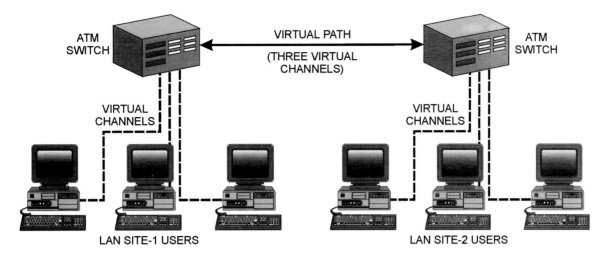

Figure 1-21 ATM Cells Use Virtual Paths and Channels to Connect Users

In Figure 1-21, LAN Site-1 users are connected to LAN Site-2 users through a virtual path. A virtual path is a single cable carrying a number of virtual channels. The VCI, or VPI, indicates the address of ATM switches. Once the cell arrives at the destination switch, connection tables are used to send the cell to the ultimate user destination. The use of **virtual switch addresses** allows ATM to be independent of the Network layer routing protocols.

The **Payload Type Indicator (PTI)** identifies the contents of the information field such as user data, link management information, or control signals.

The **Cell Loss Priority (CLP)** contains instruction for dropping cells if the channel becomes congested and the network is on the verge of crashing.

Error detection and correction of single-bit errors is accomplished in the **Header Error Check (HEC)** field.

Nearly ten percent of an ATM cell is reserved for the header. This constitutes a considerable amount of relative overhead, and is considered a significant weakness.

The ATM Adaption layer prepares higher-layer data such as **Switched Multi-Megabit Data (SMDS)** for conversion to cells. SMDS is a cell-based transmission service that provides for a wide variety of access speeds and destination addressing. It is connectionless, which means it doesn't use acknowledgments to verify the receipt of frames. Being cell based, it has been widely associated with complex ATM networks.

Because ATM supports several different types of applications, the ITU developed several types of services provided by the ATM Adaption layer. Each type responds to the varying characteristics of the ATM application such as voice, data, or video. The classes are summarized in Table 1-12.

> virtual switch addresses
>
> Payload Type Indicator (PTI)
>
> Cell Loss Priority (CLP)
>
> Header Error Check (HEC)
>
> Switched Multi-Megabit Data (SMDS)

Table 1-12
ATM Adaption Layer
Service Types

SERVICE TYPE	APPLICATION
1	Voice communication.
2	Video transfers.
3	Connection-oriented traffic using TCP/IP.
4	Connectionless traffic such as LAN protocols.
5	Connection-oriented traffic using TCP/IP, but with less overhead than Service Type 3.

ATM is being described as the basis for network technology for the future. The reason for this is its capability to process multimedia data over any physical network. This means ATM is compatible with all LAN and WAN technologies. Futurists speculate ATM networks will provide users voice, data, and video services at the same time on a workstation, while the workstation is connected to a conventional LAN such as Ethernet or Token Ring.

Table 1-13 summarizes the characteristics of ATM.

Table 1-13 Summary of
ATM Characteristics

Application:	Voice, data, video
Data Rate:	DS1, DS2, DS3, DS4 E1, E3 OC1, OC4, and higher 100 Mbps FDDI
Switching Technique:	Packet/cell
Connection Type:	Connection-oriented
Data Unit Length:	53 bytes

Uniform Resource Locators

The Internet is constructed of resources, or services, offered to users. The range of services is broad and includes file transfers, database access, e-mail, or access to linked documents on the World Wide Web.

A **uniform resource locator** (**URL**) is used to access services on the Internet.

uniform resource
locator (URL)

A URL is composed of two parts. The first part specifies an Internet resource that's to be accessed. HTTP or FTP are examples of an Internet resource. Frequently, the resource is the name of a particular protocol. For example, both FTP and HTTP are well-established protocols used on the Internet.

The second part of a URL lists the name of the server. The server name is followed by the directory path and file name of a particular document.

For example, consider the URL **HTTP:\\help.com/documents/security.txt**. The URL consists of the following parts:

- HTTP: The protocol, or service, that will be accessed.

- help.com: The **server name** (also called the host name or domain name) that is accessed for files.

- /documents/: The **directory path** from which one, or many specific files may be accessed.

- security.txt: The name of the **file** to be accessed. Note that a typical Web site may have many directories and file names.

Other common ways of referring to an Internet name is to call it a **Web address**, **Internet address**, or **Web site**. This is a reference to the static IP addresses assigned to the server name.

A **host name** is also used to identify the name of a server. The host name and the domain name may or may not be the same. Frequently, the host name is differentiated from the domain name. A domain name points to a specific IP address on the Internet. However, a company with a large Internet presence may need to subdivide its Web site. It does so by appending a host name to the domain name. For example, a Web site called internet.com can include host names such as information.internet.com and products.internet.com. "Information" and "products" are host names, while "internet.com" is the domain name.

When a company has subdivided its domain name, as described in the preceding paragraph, the name is a **Fully Qualified Domain Name (FQDN)**. A FQDN includes all hosts that are attached to the domain name. For example, information.internet.com is a FQDN for the **information host**. And internet.com is a FQDN for the **internet host**. Note that a FQDN is an attempt to tie a particular host name to the URL that it's attached to.

In order to standardize Internet applications, each Internet resource has been assigned a number called a **well-known port number**. A well-known port corresponds to an Internet resource. For example, to begin a session using HTTP, you must initiate the HTTP application by its well-known port number, which is 80. A well-known port number identifies an Internet resource. A URL allows you to specify the resource, launch the application, and begin a session with the application. Typically, all that's required on your part is a single mouse-click.

Well-known port numbers are standardized up to 1024 (out of a total of about 65,000 numbers). Some companies use a standard URL in combination with a specialized, and proprietary, port number that is in the range over 1024. An example is the URL http://www.internet.com:1202. The "1202" portion of the URL may initiate a specialized application on the Web server. Many companies use this practice to specify that TCP (on port number 81) be run between a client Web browser and the Web server.

| server name |
| directory path |
| file |
| Web address |
| Internet address |
| Web site |
| host name |

| Fully Qualified Domain Name (FQDN) |
| Information host |
| Internet host |
| well-known port number |

There are numerous resources available on the Internet.

HyperText Transfer Protocol (HTTP)

HyperText Markup Language (HTML)

HyperText Transfer Protocol Secure (HTTPS)

File Transfer Protocol (FTP)

mailto

news

gopher

telnet

Simple Mail Transfer Protocol (SMTP)

file

- The **HyperText Transfer Protocol (HTTP)** is used to access linked documents on the World Wide Web. The documents are prepared with the **HyperText Markup Language (HTML)**.

- The **HyperText Transfer Protocol Secure (HTTPS)** is used to access linked documents on the World Wide Web that are located on a secure server. A secure server typically requires that a password be entered before access is granted. In some applications, https:// means that documents are encrypted (using the Secure Socket Layer protocol as described in detail in Chapter 6) before sending them to a user that connects to the secure site.

- The **File Transfer Protocol (FTP)** is used to copy files to and from a remote server. When a URL has the ftp:// prefix, it means that the user is accessing a site from which files can be downloaded, or uploaded.

- The **mailto**: prefix is used to access an e-mail server. Once the e-mail server is accessed (usually after entering a username and password), the e-mail application is started and the user can read or write e-mail.

- The **news**: prefix starts the Newsgroup application on the Internet. A newsgroup is a bulletin board arranged by specific discussion group titles such as the Internet, Networking, or Computers. There are thousands of Newsgroups on the Internet.

- The **gopher**:// prefix is used to access the database area of the Internet. Largely replaced by the World Wide Web, Gopher consists of a series of linked menu items.

- The **telnet**:// prefix is used to connect a user to a remote server. Once the connection is established, the user has access to software or tools located on the server. When telnet is specified, a separate telnet application begins on the user's workstation. Like Gopher, telnet is being used less and less. Network operating systems like Windows NT and Novell NetWare contain remote access services that have largely replaced telnet.

- The **Simple Mail Transfer Protocol (SMTP)** is used to send e-mail across the Internet. E-mail uses conventions that are somewhat different than those used with other services.

- The **file**:// prefix is used to access a file on a local server that supports Internet applications. For example, assume the URL http://inet.com/document/help.txt is accessed. Once the help.txt file is open, it may include references to other documents on the inet.com server. The file:// prefix can be used to directly connect to one of the other documents.

Table 1-14 summarizes common URLs and includes the well-known port number for each resource.

Table 1-14 Common Uniform Resource Locators and Well-known Port Numbers

URL PREFIX	DESCRIPTION	PORT NUMBER
http://	Specifies an address on the World Wide Web.	80
https://	Specifies a secure address on the World Wide Web.	443
ftp://	Specifies file transfers.	20/21
mailto:	Initiates e-mail.	24
news:	Initiates access to newsgroups.	144
gopher://	Initiates access to database information.	70
telnet://	Initiates direct access to a remote compuer.	23
SMTP:	Initiates e-mail over the Internet.	25
file://	Initiates access to a file on a local server.	59

Internet Knowledge Resources

One of the many incredible characteristics of the Internet is the vast amount of information that is available. The information ranges from the inane to the critical. Some of the information is useful, some has no apparent value, some is right, some is wrong. The trick, in many cases, is locating what you want, then deciding if what you found is correct. Most of the time, tools are available to help, but you need to know how to use the tools.

This book offers various tools for your use. But thousands more are available on the Internet, and on the computer you use to connect to the Internet. The following lists several options available to you:

- Request For Comments (RFC): An RFC contains technical specifications related to Internet uses, applications, and technologies. There are entire Web sites devoted to listing the many RFCs that have been published. In many cases, an RFC is written, then becomes a standard. An example of an RFC is RFC 1034, which discusses domain names and the terminology associated with the domain name system.

- Browser Help Files: A help file is included with all Web browsers. The help file contains specific instructions on how to operate and configure the browser. As with many operating systems, the help file is an electronic version of the user manual.

- Web Server Help Files: A Web server help file contains instructions on how to perform certain activities at the server. For example, it may have directions that show you how to download files, or how to operate the shopping cart of an e-commerce site.

- Frequently Asked Questions (FAQ): An FAQ is a question-and-answer session. The FAQ may be found on a computer, or it may be found on many Web sites. Companies that offer products usually have a FAQ section on their Web site. The FAQ includes questions that, historically, have been asked by many users or customers. It's a good resource because, chances are, if you have a question, many before you have asked the same question, and you'll find the answer on the FAQ.

- Call Centers: Most ISPs offer technical assistance via the telephone. If you are having problems and can't resolve them using one of the techniques described above, try calling.

- Web Sites: As mentioned, there are thousands of sites that offer help. Using a search engine, enter a key word or phrase, and begin by choosing one of the responses.

KEY POINTS REVIEW

This chapter has presented an exploration of the infrastructure of the Internet.

- The basic infrastructure of the Internet consists of network access points (NAP) and a complex network of commercial backbones that carry high-speed traffic.

- A NAP is fed data packets from the commercial backbone.

- The Internet is a global, public network that uses an infrastructure consisting of network access points, a commercial backbone, and Internet service providers. The Internet provides services to networks that run TCP/IP.

- An intranet is a private network that supports Internet applications and doesn't use the public telecommunications system to connect users.

- An extranet is a private network that supports Internet applications and uses the public telecommunications system to share company information with users, customers, and partners.

- A NIC contains electronic circuitry that organizes data into unique frames so that the data can be sent, and received, on the network. All NICs have a 48-bit MAC address that is unique for each card.

- A hub is a device used to provide centralized access to network resources. Hubs are used in a physical star topology.

- A bridge is a Data Link layer device used to segment networks.

- A router is used to connect different networks and, occasionally, different network segments.

- A switch allows each connected node to be dynamically connected to any other node port. During the time that two nodes are connected, data travels between the two devices at the full bandwidth of the network.

- A gateway is a device used to convert from one incompatible protocol to another protocol.

- Analog modems are used as an interface between a computer and the analog telephone system.

- Cable modems use the existing cable television coaxial and fiber optic cabling infrastructure for transferring data at high data rates.

- ISDN is a complete digital solution from end-user to end-user over digital telephone lines. An ISDN line requires an ISDN adapter at the subscriber site in order to access the line.

- Digital Subscriber Line, or DSL, is a connection technology that uses standard twisted-pair telephone wires to send and receive data at high data rates.

- The T-carrier system is composed of a DS0 signal that has a 64 Kbps data rate. Twenty-four DS0 signals are combined into a T1 frame. The data rate of T1 is 1.544 Mbps.

- A T3 line contains 672 DS0 channels and has a data rate of 44.732 Mbps.

- The European equivalent of the North American T-carrier system uses an E1 line at a data rate of 2.084 Mbps, and an E3 line at a data rate of 34.368 Mbps.

- The Synchronous Optical Network (SONET) uses fiber optic cable to transfer data. Examples of SONET data rates are OC1 at 51.840 Mbps, and OC12 at 622.080 Mbps.

- X.25 is a connectionless protocol that uses packet switching to transfer data at 56 Kbps or 64 Kbps.

- Frame Relay is a variable-bandwidth, packet-switched technology used to transport data.

- Asynchronous Transfer Mode is a cell relay standard that uses 53-byte cells for transporting text, voice, video, music, or graphic messages.

- A uniform resource locator (URL) is used to access services on the Internet. A URL is composed of two parts. The first part specifies the resource that's to be accessed. The second part consists of the path to a resource (or the address of the resource).

- A FQDN refers to extensions that are frequently used with URLs.

- A knowledge resource, such as an RFC, FAQ, or help file, is used to provide in-depth technical information.

REVIEW QUESTIONS

The following questions test your knowledge of the material presented in this chapter:

1. What type of topology is used between network access points?

2. What is the purpose of the commercial backbone?

3. What type of network is described below?
   A private network that includes a Web server that's connected to the Internet.

4. What network device uses MAC addresses to link portions of a network that use different access protocols?

5. Which network devices allow a user access to the full bandwidth of a network?

6. Which type of modem is used to connect a workstation to coaxial or fiber optic cabling for high-speed Internet access?

7. How many DS0 signals are in a T1 frame?

8. Why is X.25 a connectionless protocol?

9. What is the length of an ATM cell?

10. Consider the URL http://inet.com. Which portion of the URL specifies an Internet service?

11. What protocol is used to access a secured Web site?

12. What is the well-known port number for HTTP?

13. What does it means when a protocol uses a "best-effort" strategy when sending data packets?

14. Which device is used to translate between incompatible protocols?

15. Which network type is not directly connected to the Internet?

MULTIPLE CHOICE QUESTIONS

1. The data rate of an E3 line is:
   a. 1.544 Mbps
   b. 34.368 Mbps
   c. 44.736 Mbps
   d. 155.52 Mbps

2. A private network that uses Internet resources but doesn't interconnect with public telecommunications lines is an _____ .

   a. Intranet

   b. Extranet

   c. Internet

   d. NAP

3. What type of device is used to connect to an ISDN line?

   a. Cable Modem

   b. Terminal Adapter

   c. Analog Modem

   d. DSL Modem

4. To receive data at rates in the 1 to 2 Mbps range over standard telephone wiring, what type of device would be used?

   a. Cable Modem

   b. Terminal Adapter

   c. Analog Modem

   d. DSL Modem

5. What is the data rate of a DS0 signal?

   a. 128 Kbps

   b. 4,000 Kbps

   c. 64 Kbps

   d. 256 Kbps

6. Which of the following is a variable-bandwidth technology?

   a. T1

   b. ATM

   c. E3

   d. Frame Relay

7. An Internet application is accessed at port 443. What resource is being accessed?

   a. https

   b. http

   c. Gopher

   d. Telnet

8. The following URL is entered into a Web browser: http://myinternet.org. What is the address of the site?

   a. http

   b. http://

   c. myinternet.org

   d. Http://myinternet.org

9. Which one of the following devices is used to transfer data between networks?

   a. Bridge

   b. Router

   c. Hub

   d. NIC

10. Which of the following technologies would be the best choice for a network that sends and receives multimedia data? Choose all that apply.

    a. ATM

    b. X.25

    c. Frame Relay

    d. T1

11. What is the most common routing protocol used on the Internet?

    a. IGRP

    b. EIGRP

    c. BGP

    d. RIP

12. Consider the following URL:*http://sales.products.com*. Which part of the URL is the host name and which part is the domain name?

    a. Sales is the domain name, products.com is the host name.

    b. Sales is the host name, and product.com is the domain name.

    c. Http is the domain name, and sales is the host name.

    d. Http:// is the host name, and sales.products.com is the domain name.

13. Consider the following URL: *https://finance.com/history.htm*. Which part of the URL represents the server name?

    a. https

    b. finance.com

    c. history.htm

    d. /history.htm

14. Which of the following is used to connect different networks?

    a. Bridge

    b. Hub

    c. DSL

    d. Router

15. To provide the fastest data rates, which of the following should be used?

    a. OC3

    b. T1

    c. DS0

    d. E1

CHAPTER

2

WEB SITE DEVELOPMENT

LEARNING OBJECTIVES

LEARNING OBJECTIVES

Upon completion of this chapter and its related lab procedures, you should be able to perform the following tasks:

1. (3.1) Define programming-related terms. Content could include the following:

   - API
   - ISAPI
   - SQL
   - Active server pages
   - CGI
   - NSAPI
   - DLL

2. (3.5) Demonstrate the ability to create HTML pages. Content could include the following:

   - HTML document structure.
   - Coding simple tables, headings, forms.
   - Compatibility between different browsers.
   - Difference between text editors and GUI editors.

3. (3.2) Describe the differences between popular client-side and server-side programming languages. Examples could include the following:

   - Java
   - XML
   - C
   - Jscript
   - JavaScript
   - VBScript
   - C++
   - Visual Basic
   - Perl
   - VRML

4. (3.6) Identify popular multimedia extensions or plug-ins. Examples could include the following:

   - RealPlayer
   - Windows Media Player
   - Shockwave
   - Flash
   - QTVR (quick time)

5. (3.3) Describe the differences between a relational and a non-relational database.

6. (3.4) Identify when to integrate a database with a Web site and the technologies used to connect the two.

7. (1.4) Describe different types of search indexes—static index/site map, keyword index, full text index. Examples could include the following:

   - Searching your site
   - Indexing your site for a search
   - Searching content

8. (3.7) Describe the use and benefits of various multimedia file formats. Examples could include the following:

   - GIF
   - PNG
   - BMP
   - TIFF
   - GIF89a
   - PDF
   - MOV
   - PostScript
   - JPEG
   - RTF
   - MPEG
   - EPS
   - AVI

CHAPTER 2

Web Site Development

INTRODUCTION

In order to develop a Web site, you must have a thorough understanding of one, and usually more than one, programming language. A Web site is composed of software. The i-Net+ exam doesn't expect you to have any more than a solid understanding of HTML; but, you are expected to be able to generally describe the other languages and applications described in this chapter. Specifically, you should have a sense of which language to use for a given application.

HTML is described in detail in the following sections. Note that this book doesn't cover all aspects of the current version of HTML (Version 4). The programming languages that are discussed, such as Java and C++, are merely described. A complete tutorial on any language other than HTML is beyond the scope of this book and the i-Net+ exam.

It's simply not typical for a single individual to have a thorough understanding of all of the programming languages used on the Internet. This is one of the reasons that the Internet is a collaborative effort. The extent of Web site development and the tools available to develop content on Web sites changes daily. From the topics described in this chapter, consider choosing an area of expertise, and then remain current with the latest technologies.

INTRODUCTION TO WEB PROGRAMMING

The World Wide Web is rich with interactive experiences, such as the search engines that scan sites for particular information. This section provides introductory background information related to common Internet programming.

API

API is an acronym for **Application Programming Interface**. An API consists of a set of functions provided by an operating system or a hardware device that allows software to use it. For example, the Windows operating systems provide APIs (inside dynamic link library files) that permit any software package running on a Windows computer to print to a printer. The creator of the software package need only know the correct API that initiates printing, then incorporate that particular API into the software package.

Application Programming Interface (API)

The specifics of how the API is incorporated depend on the source code of the software package. For example, software written with C++ will automatically link to an API.

An API speeds the development of software that will be using an operating system or a hardware device. For example, the manufacturer of a video card can use the API provided by Windows to write installation software for the card. If Windows didn't have APIs, a unique set of hardware drivers would have to be provided for all possible configurations of the card.

CGI

CGI, which stands for **Common Gateway Interface**, is a program that runs on a server and is typically used to execute some other program. For example, when a user inputs information in a form at a Web site, then presses the submit button, the information is sent to a Web server along with the CGI information. The server may then return information back to the user's browser that's based on the instructions contained in the CGI program.

The CGI program information is called a CGI script. The script may actually launch another program at the server, which is then downloaded to the user's browser. In addition to executing server programs, a CGI may also be used to:

- Load graphics, audio, or video on a browser.

- Reference another Web server so that the content of the server is displayed on the browser.

- Gather information about a Web site, such as the number of visitors.

- Initiate searches on a large database. The user-customized properties of Yahoo!, for example, are written using CGIs.

Note that a CGI executes on the server. You may see this process referred to as **parsing**. Complex code is parsed by breaking the code into smaller units so that it can be translated into a code that a machine can understand. For example, some languages are parsed in order to translate (or compile) them into binary numbers that the computer can directly understand.

A CGI is written with a Web programming language. The most common language used to write CGIs is Perl. The script is written in Perl and stored on a Web server with a filename that's accessed from the user's browser. When the user performs some function, such as pressing a submit button on a form, a request containing the CGI reference and the filename is sent to the server. Because the request contains the CGI reference, the server knows that a CGI will be initiated. The CGI is then initiated on the filename specified in the request.

For example, the following is a typical CGI request that is generated from some user action on a Web browser (such as pressing a button or checking a box):

Http://www.internet.com/cgi-bin/result

When the button is pressed, the server located at www.internet.com is accessed. The server will see the cgi-bin instruction in the URL. The cgi-bin is not a path name, but is an indication to the server that the filename that follows must be called and a response must be returned to the browser that generated the URL. In this case, the filename is the result, so the server will look for a result filename and initiate whatever action is contained in the file.

If the server can't find the file result within a couple of minutes, it will send an error message back to the browser. Note that cgi-bin is a directive to the server to do:

- Whatever is stipulated in the file.

- Send an HTML response to the originating browser.

CGIs are the most common method used to transfer executable information residing on a server to a browser. Notice that each time a server receives a URL containing cgi-bin, the server resources are diverted to handling the activity associated with it. This is a disadvantage of CGI—it may cause a performance loss on a busy server.

Another disadvantage of CGI is that it can't be shared simultaneously between client browsers. If more than one browser sends a request to the same cgi-bin/filename, a new instance for each request is generated.

SQL

SQL, or **Structured Query Language**, is used to manipulate data in a database as well as to define the data that a user wants to see. For example, a database may contain tables containing sales data for various customers. SQL queries can be written that will selectively display specific amounts of information about the customers.

SQL is an **ANSI (American National Standard Interchange)** standardized software tool incorporated into most sophisticated database software systems. Oracle, Sybase, Informix, Microsoft SQL Server, and Access are packages that can be customized using SQL.

A well-designed database will list a single entity in each table in the database. The database may consist of hundreds of tables, each of which contains a single entity. In order to capture comprehensive data from any or all of the tables, SQL allows you to customize search criteria, then presents the information in a single table. For example, consider Tables 2-1 and 2-2.

Table 2-1 Sample Table 1

COMPANY ID	COMPANY NAME
001	Bill's Bean Shop
002	Gail's Coffee Shop

Table 2-2 Sample Table 2

ITEM ID	ITEM NAME
021	Table
022	Chair
023	Lamp

In Table 2-1, all companies are assigned a unique ID number. In the second table, Table 2-2, all items sold are assigned a unique ID number. To determine which companies are purchasing which items, a SQL query can be written that joins the data in the first two tables into a third table. Now, a business manager can tell at a glance which companies are buying, what items, and which companies are not buying.

A typical return for a SQL query that provides information as described above is shown in Table 2-3.

Table 2-3 Result of SQL Query

COMPANY ID	ITEM ID	COMPANY NAME	ITEM NAME
003	021	Harold's Book Store	Table
001	023	Bill's Bean Shop	Lamp
003	022	Harold's Book Store	Chair

The advantage of using SQL is that it's a standardized tool and will work with most databases. This is particularly helpful for databases used on Internet sites where the data that a user wants to see can be spread among many databases originating from many vendors.

NSAPI

Netscape Server Application Programming Interface (NSAPI)

Server Application Functions (SAF)

The **NSAPI (Netscape Server Application Programming Interface)** was developed to provide a set of commonly used server functions to handle HTTP requests and responses.

An NSAPI relies on **Server Application Functions (SAF)** that are built into an enterprise server (such as a Web server). The NSAPI allows the built-in SAFs to be extended or customized for a specific server need. The SAFs are typically request-response driven so that when a browser causes a function to be initiated (such as a graphic to load), the server will attempt to locate the file, and if it's successful, return the graphic along with a status coding indicating that the request can be met. The status code for a successful HTTP request is 200.

If the request can't be filled because the requested server application won't run or a file can't be found, the server must notify the browser. The HTTP status code sent to a browser indicating that the request failed is 404 (file not found).

In essence, an NSAPI—like an ISAPI, described next—allows a Web developer to summarize the core functions of a server to suit the needs of a Web site. Like a CGI, ISAPI cannot respond to multiple instances with a single server function. If more than one client browser initiates a request for the same function, ISAPI will generate a unique response for each. The time required to return multiple responses is less than the time it takes to do so with a CGI.

ISAPI

ISAPI is short for **Internet Server Application Programming Interface**. ISAPI is a proprietary software tool created by Microsoft and designed to run on servers with Microsoft Internet Information Server (IIS) installed.

ISAPI allows Web developers to extend the functionality of a server running IIS. IIS comes with a set of core functions for the server that may not meet the specific needs of a Web site developer. ISAPI lets the developer customize the server functions by using ISAPI.

ISAPI relies on dynamic link libraries (DLL) to initiate the request from a client Web browser. When a browser sends the request to the server, the server will link to the appropriate DLL to initiate the response to the client. The advantage to using DLLs is that performance of the server increases because a program doesn't have to be executed in order to meet the HTTP requirement for sending a response to the client browser.

Note that a CGI can be used to return a client response that such a program is to be executed at the client. But the time required to execute the program that's attached to the CGI lowers server performance. However, like CGI, only a single entity can be launched for each request. If more than one browser sends a request to the server, NSAPI will generate a unique response for each. The time to do so, however, is normally less than when a CGI is used.

Internet Server Application Programming Interface (ISAPI)

DLL

A **DLL**, or **Dynamic Link Library**, is used to access the functions of an operating system. The functions of a DLL refer to communication with a serial port, access to the Internet, or to performing various functions on an operating system such as Microsoft Windows. On a Web server, a DLL is often used as an interface to applications residing on the server.

A DLL may be specific to a particular application software package, such as routines performed on a specialized Web site. If a site developer needs to run customized software on a server, a DLL may need to be created to do so when the client browser sends an HTTP request to the server.

DLLs are written with a server-side programming language such as C. Once the DLL is written, the program is compiled into the machine language of the machine that the DLL will be running on. Once the DLL is compiled, it's ready to be run. What's needed at this point is an interface program that can access the DLL, such as C++, that links to an API that contains the DLL.

A DLL causes the server software to directly access hardware on the server. The server hardware will then perform the function of the DLL. This may mean that a video file will be fetched from memory and sent to a client browser, or a series of files will be fetched and returned to the browser. Note that accessing a DLL has the same effect as a CGI. The advantage of using DLLs to invoke a response to a browser is one of speed and efficiency. DLLs will return responses quicker than a CGI. However, the DLL that's written must be written specifically for the machine that it will be run on, whereas a CGI is not machine dependent.

Dynamic Link Library (DLL)

A DLL is associated with an application or function through binding. There are two ways to bind a DLL to an application: **load time binding** and **on call binding**. Load time binding means that the DLL is made available to the application that needs it at the time the application is loaded on the machine. On call binding means that the DLL is loaded only when the application requires it. For Web-based applications, on call binding is the most efficient because the DLL only uses the server's resources at the time they're actually required, and won't hold the resources when they're not needed.

Active Server Pages

Active Server Pages (ASP) is a proprietary server-side scripting language developed by Microsoft. ASP runs on Windows operating systems, primarily Windows NT/2000 with Internet Information Server software installed on the server. ASP allows dynamic Web documents to be displayed on the client browser.

Examples of the capability of ASP include customized HTTP responses, such as those required on an e-commerce site, or the personalized search engines used to present database information.

When the browser sends a request to a server running ASP, the request will include a reference to a file with an .asp extension. The server will open the asp file and perform the activity described in the file by generating standard HTML that's sent back to the browser. Notice that the browser has very little involvement or responsibility in generating the dynamic activity. The burden of producing HTML that will be displayed on the browser is placed on the server.

ASP is more efficient that CGIs since it relies on including simple instructions in the HTML that's downloaded to the client. Extensive programming experience isn't needed to create simple ASP scripts. Because the information that's returned to the client is also HTML, ASP may speed the performance of database searches on large and complex Web sites.

The disadvantage to ASP is that it can only be run on Microsoft operating systems, although there is some limited third-party support for other operating systems.

HTML

HTML is an abbreviation for **HyperText Markup Language**. It provides a way to code a document so that it can be displayed on the World Wide Web area of the Internet.

The Web operates independently of the type of computer connected to it. For example, a Web document generally looks the same no matter if it's viewed from an IBM computer or an Apple computer. The TCP/IP protocol suite allows for machine independence on the Internet, while HTML allows for document independence on the Web.

Many of the files you may have viewed on the Internet have been encoded with HTML. Newer versions of commercial word processors such as Microsoft Word and Corel WordPerfect include HTML translators so that you can create a document using Word or WordPerfect, and save it as an HTML file. The codes are added during the save. Then, if you open it in a Web browser, it will appear as if you had added all the HTML codes.

An HTML file is essentially a **plaintext** (ASCII file format) document with specific commands added so that it can be viewed on the Web. Windows Notepad is an example of a plaintext editor. You can use Notepad on a Windows computer to create relatively sophisticated Web documents. However, keep in mind that Notepad is a text editor only; you still must know the HTML tags to use.

Tags

Markup tags are used to HTML encode a document. A **tag** specifies the structure, or look, of a document. There are tags indicating the start of a paragraph, for headings, for creating items in a list, for linking to other documents, and so on.

All of the tags used with HTML are enclosed in angle brackets. Angle brackets are an HTML requirement and are used to let the browser know that the command within the brackets contains information on how to display text.

A simple HTML file is shown in Figure 2-1. The first tag used in an HTML document is <html>. (HTML is not case sensitive. You may encode using either upper or lower case letters.) This tag is used when beginning an HTML file and notifies the Web browser that the information to follow is to be displayed according to HTML commands. Many Web documents begin with the <html> tag.

```
<html>
<head><title>HTML Tags </title></head>
<body  text="#000000" link="#0000ff" vlink="#551a8b" alink="#ff0000"
bgcolor="#c0c0c0"

<h1>Create Web Pages Using HTML</h1>

<p>HTML is a method of encoding plain text so that it can be displayed in a Web
browser on the Internet.

<p>HTML tags are identified by placing the coding script in angle brackets.
</body>
</html>
```

Figure 2-1 Basic HTML Tags

The next tag is <head>. It's used to identify the header of the document. You may have noticed that some documents printed from the Internet contain a name in either the top left or right corner. The name is created by using the <head> tag.

Conventionally, the <head> tag is also used for specifying the title of the Web page. In Figure 2-1, the browser is instructed to display it as a title with the <title> command. Now, when the page is printed, the title—the name given to the document with the <head> tag—will be displayed at the top of the page.

Notice that following the title is the tag </title>. And following this is the tag </head>. The backslash used with the command marks the end of an instruction to the browser.

The <body> tag specifies the beginning of the Web page. Notice that a </body> tag doesn't occur until the end of the document. In other words, the <body> and </body> tags bound the content that will appear when the page is opened in a browser.

In the Figure, there are several text commands immediately following the <body> tag. These specify the colors of the text, background, links, and so forth. We'll take a closer look at these later in this section.

The page begins with a heading, marked by the <h1> tag. The <h> tag will be displayed as large, usually bold, text by the browser. There are six heading fonts available with HTML: h1, h2, h3, h4, h5, and h6. The font will be smaller as each number increments, but all are normally displayed in bold. It's acceptable to repeat numerical values in the heading tag, but don't skip any since this may confuse the browser and the heading may be displayed like the rest of the text. Figure 2-2 illustrates the method used to vary the font size of heading tags. The first "Create Web Pages Using HTML" was created with an <h1> tag, while the last heading was created with an <h6> tag. The end of the heading is marked by the </h1> tag.

A paragraph of text is marked with a <p> tag, as shown in Figure 2-2. The tag tells the browser to indent the first line (usually five spaces) and to begin the next line at a left-justified margin. The right margin may wrap to the next line regardless of where it ends in a word—in some older Web browsers. There are HTML commands to avoid this, but most browsers automatically wrap lines. Newer versions of Web browsers wrap at the end of a word.

Figure 2-2 Using Header Tags

```
<html><head><title> HTML Tags </title></head><body text="#000000"
link="#0000ff" vlink="#551a8b" alink="#ff0000" bgcolor="#c0c0c0"><h1>Create
Web Pages Using HTML</h1><h2>Create Web Pages Using HTML</h2><h3>Create
Web Pages Using HTML</h3>

<h4>Create Web Pages Using HTML</h4>

<h5>Create Web Pages Using HTML</h5>

<h6>Create Web Pages Using HTML</h6>

<p>HTML is a method of encoding plain text so that it can be displayed in a Web
browser on the Internet.

<p>HTML tags are identified by placing the coding script in angle brackets.

</body>
</html>
```

In earlier versions of HTML, a paragraph was ended by including a </p> tag. Beginning with version 2 of HTML, this requirement was dropped.

You may, however, include the </p> tag if it helps you keep track of each paragraph. It has no effect on how the file is displayed. When you need to start another paragraph, simply begin the first line with <p>.

Table 2-4 summarizes the basic HTML tags described in the preceding paragraphs.

Table 2-4 Document Tag Summary

HTML DOCUMENT HEADER TAGS	
<html>	Signifies the beginning of a document to be displayed in a browser.
<head>	The beginning of a header. Typically, this is the title of the document.
<title>	The file name of the document.
<body>	Marks the beginning of text or other content that will appear in the browser.
<h1> <h2> <h3> <h4> <h5> <h6>	Heading tags that will be displayed in a font size that inversely corresponds to the number following "h"; an h1 heading is larger than an h2 heading.
<p>	The beginning of a new paragraph.

You may wonder why it's necessary to master basic HTML encoding when there are many commercial products available that do much of the work for you. First, use off-the-shelf HTML editors wherever you can. It saves time and reduces errors since HTML encoding is particularly meticulous. Once you have prepared the basic document, open it in an ASCII text editor (Notepad) so you can revise or massage it to suit your specifications. And, undoubtedly, you will want to make changes in backgrounds, font colors, or link paths to other parts of the page.

Formatting

In order for HTML to be successful as a document, you may need to provide the Web browser with instructions on how to present words or phrases on the screen. These directions are called **formatting tags**. The portion of a document that is tagged is referred to as an **element**. The sentences within a paragraph are elements. A heading is an element. The title of a document is an element. Any part of a HTML document bound with tags is an element.

formatting tags

element

There may be elements within an element. Consider the following sentence:

<p>I love creating HTML documents.

This sentence is a brief paragraph bound by <p>. It's an element. However, the paragraph contains another element, "love", bound by <b> and </b>. The <b> tag (for bold) is an HTML markup command that will cause a word or phrase to appear as bold print.

There are no restrictions to adding elements inside of elements, other than the effect they may have on the reader of a Web document. Usually, keeping it simple is best.

Creating elements is a key factor to writing effective HTML code. Formatting provides you with an array of tools to enliven and enrich a Web page; keep in mind that when formatting is used inappropriately or excessively, the reader of your page might become confused and cruise to another site.

Figure 2-3 shows an HTML file in which the text has been manipulated using several formatting tags. The HTML codes for the document are included in Figure 2-4. The first tag to be used is <b>, which causes an element to appear in a Web browser as bold text. The word "displayed" is bound by the <em> tag that may either bold an element, or cause it to appear in italic text. In this example, the effect is to italicize the text. <cite> is another command that causes the text to appear in italics, as does the tag <i>, for italics.

Background Info

The particular interpretation of HTML tags is determined by the Web browser. Not all browsers will interpret the same tags in the same way. Before posting an HTML document to the Internet, make sure you test it using several browsers including earlier versions of the same browser. Remember your audience.

Figure 2-3 The Effects of Formatting

> **Create Web Pages Using HTML**
> HTML is a method of **encoding** plain text so that it can be *displayed in a Web browser on the Internet.*
> HTML tags are ***identified*** by placing the coding script in <u>angle brackets</u>.

Figure 2-4 HTML Codes for the Document

```
<html><head><title> HTML Tags </title></head><body text="#000000"
link="#0000ff" vlink="#551a8b" alink="#ff0000" bgcolor="#c0c0c0">

<h1>Create Web Pages Using HTML</h1>

<p>HTML is a method of <b>encoding </b>plain text so that it can be <cite>displayed
in a Web browser on the Internet</cite>.

<p>HTML <kbd>tags</kbd> are <strong>identified</strong> by placing the <i>
coding</i> script in <u>angle brackets</u>.

</body>
</html>
```

An interesting tag is keyboard <kbd>, which makes text have an appearance like computer generated, ASCII text. It's typically used to indicate the response a computer makes to a keyboard input and looks similar to the font used in older DOS and UNIX machines. Sometimes, keyboard is used to indicate, in a series of Web-based instructions, the text or commands an operator is to enter with the keyboard.

The <strong> tag is used to emphasize a word or phrase and it is usually interpreted by a browser as a bold command. As you can see in the figure, <strong> had the same effect as <b>.

The <u> tag causes an element to be displayed as underlined text. In the Figure, the phrase "angle brackets" is underlined because it was bound by <u> and </u>.

You may encounter the <br> tag, which stands for **break**. A <br> tag is used to add white space between two paragraphs. Consider the following two paragraphs:

I like creating HTML documents.

HTML is used on the World Wide Web.

In order to tell the browser that there's a space between the two paragraphs, you would add the <br> tag:

```
<p>I like creating HTML documents.</p>
<br>
<p>HTML is used on the World Wide Web.</p>
```

Most browsers will automatically skip a line to add the white space when the next <p> tag is encountered. But if you want to show more than a single line of white space, use the <br> tag to create it.

Table 2-5 summarizes common formatting tags.

HTML FORMATTING TAGS	
<b>	Bold. Appears as **Bold.**
<em>	Emphasis. Appears as **Emphasis.**
<cite>	Cite. Appears as *Cite.*
<kbd>	Keyboard. Appears as Keyboard.
<strong>	Strong. Appears as **Strong.**
<i>	Italic. Appears as *Italic.*
<u>	Underline. Appears as <u>Underline.</u>

Table 2-5 Summary of Common Formatting Tags

Lists

Information is what the Internet is all about. In order to get the information, it must be presented in a manner that makes it easy for the viewer to read. A common technique used to do so is to present the information as a series of lists.

Think of a list on the Internet as a table of contents. Typically, the items in a list are linked to other documents, or they may contain links to sections within a document. Of course, a list may also be used to simply list items without using links.

There are three common types of lists used with HTML: **unordered**, **ordered**, and **definition** lists.

An unordered list displays items with a bullet. To begin an unordered list, start the list with the markup <ul>, which stands for unordered list. Each item in the list is preceded with the tag <li>, for list item. When the list is complete, add the tag </ul> to let the browser know the list has ended.

An example of an unordered list is shown in Figure 2-5. In this simple example, the three types of HTML lists have been placed in an unordered list. As you can see, each item is prefaced with a bullet. Figure 2-6 shows the HTML tags used to create the list. The browser is told that an unordered list follows with the tag <ul>. Next, each item in the list is indicated with the <li> tag. The browser is told the list is completed by adding the </ul> tag at the end of the list.

- Unordered List

- Ordered List

- Definition List

Figure 2-5 Example of an Unordered List

```
<html><head><title> HTML Tags </title>
</head>
<body text="#000000" link="#0000ff" vlink="#551a8b" alink="#ff0000"
bgcolor="#c0c0c0">

<ul>
<li>Unordered List
<li>Ordered List
<li>Definition List
</ul>

</body>
</html>
```

Figure 2-6 Unordered List Tags

An ordered list allows you to number each item in the list. For this reason, you may see references to ordered lists as **numbered** lists.

The tag for an ordered list is <ol>. Each item in the list is proceeded with the tag <li>. Once the list is complete, it ends with the tag </ol>.

An example of an ordered list is shown in Figure 2-7. By making a simple change in the list tag, all items are displayed in numerical order. Look at Figure 2-8. Notice that in the coding, the list items aren't numbered. If numbers had been added to the coded version of this list, they would be duplicated when the document was viewed in a browser.

1. Unordered List

2. Ordered List

3. Definition List

Figure 2-7 Example of an Ordered List

```
<html><head><title> HTML Tags </title></head><body text="#000000"
link="#0000ff" vlink="#551a8b" alink="#ff0000" bgcolor="#c0c0c0">

<ol>
<li>Unordered List
<li>Ordered List
<li>Definition List
</ol>

</body>
</html>
```

Figure 2-8 Ordered List Tags

A definition list contains a term and a description of the term. It begins with the markup <dl>, for definition list. The term to be described is tagged with <dt>, for definition term. The description of the term is tagged with <dd>, for definition description. Once the list is finished, it ends with </dl>.

An example of a definition list is shown in Figure 2-9. The tags used for definition lists are shown in Figure 2-10. Notice that the convention followed is similar to the other list types.

Definition List
    A definition list contains a term and a description of the term.

Figure 2-9 Example of a Definition List

```
<html><head><title> HTML Tags </title></head><body text="#000000"
link="#0000ff" vlink="#551a8b" alink="#ff0000" bgcolor="#c0c0c0">
<dl><dt>Definition List
<dd>A definition list contains a term and a description of the term.
</dl>

</body>
</html>
```

Figure 2-10 Definition List Tags

A definition list contains a term and a description of the term. More than one term may be defined within a single set of definition tags by alternating <dt>, <dd>; <dt>, <dd>; <dt>, <dd>; and so on before ending the list with </dl>.

Table 2-6 contains a summary of all tags associated with unordered, ordered, and definition lists.

Table 2-6 Summary of List Tags

HTML LIST TAGS	
Unordered List Tags	**Appears in Browser As**

`<ul>`
`<li> Item 1`
`<li> Item 2`
`<li> Item X`
`</ul>`
	• Item 1
	
	• Item 2
	
	• Item X

Ordered List Tags	**Appears in Browser As**

`<ol>`
`<li> Item 1`
`<li> Item 2`
`<li> Item X`
`</ol>`
	1. Item 1
	
	2. Item 2
	
	3. Item X

Definition List Tags	**Appears in Browser As**

`<dl>`
`<dt> Term 1`
`<dd> Definition of Term 1`
`<dt> Term 2`
`<dd> Definition of Term 2`
`<dt> Term X`
`<dd> Definition of Term X`
`</dl>`
	Term 1
	    Definition of Term 1
	Term 2
	    Definition of Term 2
	Term x
	    Definition of Term X

Tables

Tables are very easy to build. In fact, many Web sites are set up completely using tables. Tables are commonly used for organizing related information. Figure 2-11 is an example of a basic table that consists of two rows and two columns. Table data is placed in a cell. There are four cells shown in the example.

Figure 2-11 Simple HTML Table

Cell A	Cell C
Cell B	Cell D

Figure 2-12 is the HTML used to create this table.

```
<table border="8">
<tr>
<td>Cell A</td>
<td>Cell C</td>
</tr>
<tr>
<td>Cell B</td>
<td>Cell D</td>
</tr>
</table>
```

Figure 2-12 HTML Table Tags

The purpose of the tags used in the table are:

<table border></table>
or
<table></table>

Either of these attributes will work. The border attribute creates a border around the table and the individual cells. The "8" following the border attribute indicates the width of the border being used. Some browsers may disregard the border attribute.

<TR></TR>

The TR tag, which stands for "Table Row", is used to specify the beginning of each row in the table.

<TD></TD>

The TD tag is "Table Data". The data that you place between the TD and /TD tags is what will appear inside the cells. You must be consistent in the number of cells placed in each row. For example, if the first row has two cells, the second row must also have two cells. If the numbers do not match, the browser will add cells to even them out. In other words, you must have an equal number of cells in each row of the table.

There are other options available with tables such as adding column and row headers and aligning text within the table cells. Some of the more common options are:

<TH></TH>

TH stands for "Table Header". In the example shown previously, you can substitute TH for TD. As the default, the Table Header will appear bold and centered. You can use the align attribute to move the text right or left. You may also use the valign attribute to move the header to the top, middle, or bottom.

<caption></caption>

The caption element is optional. It contains one attribute, which is align. You can align at either the top or bottom. If you do not use the caption attribute, it will revert to the default, which is at the top.

Relative Links

The most valuable aspect of HTML is the ability to link documents. On a Web browser, a word or phrase that's highlighted and/or underlined represents a link. Links may be established to any address on the Internet.

indirect links

Direct links

Web pages primarily use two types of links—URLs (also called **indirect links**) and direct links (also called direct addressing). A URL link, when activated, will take you to another Web site, probably on another server. **Direct links** may be made to other documents on the same server and in the same directory.

Direct Links

Direct links are quite valuable when initially setting up a Web site, and for organizing a large number of files on a site. Assume you develop a series of networking standard operating procedures that will be placed on an intranet server. A direct link will be set up between the procedures that allows a user to go from one to the other simply by clicking a linked procedure title or number. Internet Web sites are created using direct links as well. The site may have many separate pages along with several graphics. When the files are uploaded to an ISP, they're directly linked by the site creator. The ISP administrator will place all files in the same directory on the ISP server. In this way, the administrator will not have to manipulate the tags the creator placed in the documents. Recall from Chapter 1 that URLs (universal resource locators) are used to identify specific addresses of documents on the World Wide Web. Because the addresses are maintained in the files of servers and routers on the Internet, they are used as reference points for navigating the Web. In other words, a URL (along with a corresponding IP address) is as close as you get to a reference anchor on the Internet.

href (hypertext reference)

Each URL link is tagged with the <a> markup, for "anchor". There are several ways to initiate a link in HTML but the <a> tag will notify the browser that a link is to follow. Immediately following the <a> tag is the **href (hypertext reference)** tag. Next comes the URL address, which is the reference for the link.

The browser must also be told how the link will be initiated—by highlighting some text, by inserting an image, and so on. This action is stated in the anchor, as well.

This is an example of a link to the Marcraft homepage:

Let's go to the <a href="http://www.mic-inc.com">Marcraft homepage.</a>

The <a> tag identifies the markup as a link. The href= indicates a hypertext reference to a URL. The complete URL is bound by quotes. It's important to include the beginning and ending quotes, and good form to include the forward slash at the end of the address. Following the address is the section of text that will initiate the link, *Marcraft homepage*. When a user clicks on *Marcraft homepage*, the browser will navigate to the Marcraft Web site. Notice that the text rests between angle brackets. The markup ends with </a>.

The href tag can be placed anywhere on an HTML document. This includes within lists, within a paragraph, or a stand-alone paragraph. **Direct link anchors** are also used to directly link documents. A direct link is used to connect documents with unique file names that reside on the same server and in the same directory. The files that comprise a Web site are typically placed in a single directory and directly linked within the directory. To link files on the same server in the same directory, all that's required is to include the file name in the link anchor. For example, let's assume two files, *file-a.htm* and *file-b.htm*. At a key word in *file-a*, we want to link it to *file-b*. The HTML coding in *file-a* would appear as:

For more information, go to <a href="file-b.htm">file-B.</a>

Notice that the syntax used is identical to that used for a URL link. However, the file name is used in place of the URL. If you create files for a Web site, the ISP that will be hosting your site will require that you use direct links between all files on your site. The name of the page that will open when a visitors first views your site should be named *home.htm.* The tags used with direct and indirect links are summarized in Table 2-7.

Direct Link	Indirect Link
<a href="file-b.htm">file-B.</a>	<a href="http://www.oneworld.owt.com/marcraft/">Marcraft homepage.</a>

Table 2-7 Link Tags

Images

Images can add appeal as well as enhance the functionality of a Web page. They can also overwhelm the user if overused or if they are used inappropriately. How much is too much?

If text can do the job more efficiently, then use text; if an image saves the user time, use it. Web surfers expect a certain amount of graphics due to the graphical appeal of the Web in general. There are some images that users expect to see on a Web site such as buttons, scroll bars, and so on. File formats for graphics used on the Internet vary widely, but GIF and JPEG extensions predominate. Refer to Chapter 1 for a description of the many types of graphical file formats that may be encountered on the Internet. Images are added with the *img* (for image) tag. This is followed by the *src* (source) tag, which is followed by the name of the image. For example, to add an image of a blue ball, the tag looks like:

<img src=blueball.gif>

It's one thing to insert an image in an HTML document and another to put it where you want it to be. This can be tricky but the image markup can be combined with an align tag that helps in the placement. By default, an image will be aligned with the bottom of a line of text. In the example shown above, the bottom of the blue ball will align with the bottom of any text surrounding the ball.

You indicate the location of an image by specifying the alignment. Options available with the align tag are shown in Table 2-8.

Table 2-8 Summary of Image Tags

HTML IMAGE AND ALIGNMENT TAGS	
Tags	**Appears in a Browser As**
Image Tag <img src= file name of the image>	An image tag written in this manner defaults to the bottom of the line of text.
Alignment Tags <img src= image.jpg align=bottom>	Bottom: The bottom of the image aligns with the bottom of the line of text. This is the default specification and needn't be specified.
<img src=image.jpg align=top>	Top: The top of the image aligns with the top of the line of text.
<img src=image.jpg align=middle>	Middle: The middle of the image aligns with the bottom of the next line of text.
<img src=image.jpg align=left>	Left: The image is on the left margin and text flows around it.
<img src=image.jpg align=right>	Right: The image is placed on the right margin and text flows around it.

For example, to align an image so that the top of the image is aligned with the top of the line of text, the markup looks like:

<img src=image.gif align=top>

In addition to specifying the placement of the image, you should also tell the browser the size of the image. This will aid in the loading of a Web page that contains text and graphics. If the browser is told the size and placement of the graphic, the text will be positioned around the portion of the page where the graphic will be placed. Consequently, the page will load faster since the browser doesn't have to decide where to place text and graphical files. Image size is specified according to the width and height in pixels. Typically, if you specify a size other than the actual size of an image, it will be scaled by the browser to fit your dimensions. However, be sure to experiment a bit before placing an extraordinarily large image on a Web site.

The image size attribute looks like:

<img src=image.gif width=50 height=25>

You may also include placement tags in the container. For example, to align the above image to the right margin, the tag is written as:

<img src=image.gif align=right width=50 height=25>

Images are frequently used as links to other sites. The effect is that when you click on a linked image, you're taken to another server, or the link may lead to another document on the same server or directory.

Image links are used to connect to a different URL, as well as to link to documents on the same server/ directory. When you go to a Web site, you begin at the homepage of the site. It will include links to other areas of the site and, at times, these will be represented with a graphic that's descriptive of the area. For example, to send an e-mail to the site, you may be required to click a mailbox.

An example of an image used as a link to another URL is:

<p>This is an image link <a href="http://www.netscape.com/"><img src=image.gif></a> to another site address.

When viewed in a Web browser, the sentence contains a graphic that, when clicked, connects to the Netscape homepage.

Notice that the technique is to include the image element within the <a> tag. Size and placement attributes of the image can also be specified in the image element.

An interesting application of images are **image maps**. An image map consists of a graphic—or text—that links to another file. A typical example is the use of a circle on a Web page. At first glance, the circle appears to be a single color but when a mouse pointer is passed over it, text appears. If the text is clicked, you're whisked off to another page on the site. The single graphic can include multiple links to other URLs or to other sections of a Web site.

image maps

Image maps can be run on a Web server or on the client browser. Increasingly, they are run on client browsers using a CGI script that references a cgi-bin file on the server. A script, such as a JavaScript, is then run on the client browser.

Colors

You may have noticed that some simpler Web pages use standard colors for the background, text, and links. The standard colors used are:

- Background: gray

- Links: blue

- Visited link: purple

- Text: black

These are default colors used with HTML. Unless another color is specified in the code, these same colors will always appear in your browser.

What if you don't like these colors? Then change them. But first, you'll need to know what colors are available. There are several good sites on the Internet that list the colors that can be used with HTML. The charts will be called RGB Color Charts (Typically, an RGB chart will present 256 different colors, but this varies widely with software running on the Web browser.) and will show the actual colors along with the hexadecimal numbers that are used to represent the colors. The various tones, or shades, of each color are obtained by mixing the colors red, green, and blue. The colors are "mixed" by combining six hexadecimal numbers. The six hex numbers that must be used are: 00, 33, 66, 99, CC, and FF.

For example: Orange is specified with the combination FF6600.

Colors are specified in the rigid order of: red, green, and blue. In the example for the color orange, FF (decimal 255) is red, 66 (decimal 102) is green, and 00 (decimal 0) is blue. This produces a color with a heavy red component, medium green component (nearly yellow), and no blue value.

Table 2-9 lists several other examples.

To change the color of text within a paragraph, use the <font color= xxxxxx> tag preceding the text that you want to change. End the tag with </font>. These tags are typically placed immediately following the <body> tag, but can be inserted anywhere in the document.

Table 2-9 Examples of RGB Colors

EXAMPLES OF RGB HEX COLORS		
Hex Number	Decimal	Color
FF0000	(255,0,0)	RED
00FF00	(0,255,0)	GREEN
0000FF	(0,0,255)	BLUE
FF00FF	(255,0,255)	PURPLE
FF6600	(255,102,0)	ORANGE

Examples of using colors in the text of a paragraph are:

<p>While I like <font color=FF0000> red </font>, my favorite color is <font color=0000FF> blue </font> instead.

<p>On occasion, I may give up <font color=0000FF> blue </font> for <font color=00FF00> green </font> unless I decide I like <font color=CCCCFF> mauve </font> instead.

<p> There is, of course, a range of colors in between such as <font color=FF6600> orange </font>, <font color=CCFF00> purple </font>, and <font color=66FF00> greenish-yellow </font>.

You can use the font color markup with other text tags such as <strong>, <cite>, or <underline>. Include the color tag within the format markup. For example, <cite color=FF0000> will change the color of text in italics to red.

The font tag is normally used for small sections of text within a document. It adds emphasis to an area of text. To change the color of all the text in a document, or for links, color tags are placed in the <body> markup. HTML default colors are a gray background, black text, and blue links. When a link has been visited, it changes to purple. A gray, black, and blue screen isn't particularly colorful. Many of the Web pages you've seen contain much brighter color schemes.

If no colors are specified in the <body> tag, HTML defaults to gray, black, and blue. Keep in mind that the <body> tag is inclusive of the entire HTML file; if a markup is placed with the body tag, the complete file will be affected.

To change the color of the background, specify the color in the body tag using the hexadecimal color scheme.

Background colors are specified using the <bgcolor=xxxxxx> tag.

For example:

<body bgcolor=FF6600>

This will change the color of the background to orange. Text color may also be changed by specifying a color in the body markup. However, some care must be taken when specifying the background and text colors. For example, don't make them the same color or too close in value. If you do, you won't be able to read the text.

Specify the text color by using the <text=xxxxxx> tag in the body markup. For example:

<body text=0000CC> will produce blue text.

All links within the document are also specified in the body tag. HTML provides several options, and we'll concentrate on two that are commonly used. The first is the color of a link. This is done with a link tag. For example:

<body link=110000>

This will display links as a dark red. It's normally a good idea to also specify the color of a link that has been visited. This helps the reader keep track of followed links.

A visited link uses a **vlink** tag. For example:

<body link=110000 vlink=FF0000>

This will display links as dark red, but once the link has been clicked, the color will change to a bright red.

Typically, the colors of the background, text, links, and visited links are stipulated in a body element, as in:

<body bgcolor=FF6600 text=6666FF link=33FF00 vlink=FFFFFF>

Table 2-10 summarizes the tags used for specifying colors.

TAG	DESCRIPTION
bgcolor=xxxxxx	Changes the color of the background.
text=xxxxxx	Changes the color of the text.
link=xxxxxx	Changes the color of links.
vlink=xxxxxx	Changes the color of visited links.

Table 2-10 Color Tag Summary

Style Sheets

Style sheets are used with HTML in order to produce documents that are consistently displayed on a Web site. The use of a style sheets allows Web authors the flexibility to specify the formatting tags used on a Web site. Not all browsers interpret a HTML document in the same way, but a style sheet guarantees that the formatting that the author originally intended will be displayed the same way no matter what browser is used.

There is a drawback, of course. The browser must support style sheets. Currently, the following browser versions will support style sheets:

- Internet Explorer 5.0

- Internet Explorer 4.0 (but not with as many style elements as version 5.0)

- Netscape Communicator 4.0

If a Web file containing style sheet elements is displayed on a browser that doesn't support style sheets, only the HTML code will be displayed and the style sheet elements will be ignored.

Table 2-11 Common Style Sheet Elements

ELEMENT	ATTRIBUTE
Text-align	Center, left, right, or justify
Text-indent	Xpt (such as 10 pt, or 12 pt)
Letter-spacing	Xem (such as .75em)
Background	Green, red, blue, etc.
Font-style	Normal, italic, oblique (slanted)
Line-height	N (such as 1, 2, etc.)
Text-case	Lowercase, uppercase, capitalize
Font-weight	Normal, bold, light
Color	Green, red, blue, etc.

Typically, Web designers use style sheets to standardize HTML formatting tags (see the Formatting section in this chapter for more information on HTML formatting tags). Style attributes can be applied to HTML headings, paragraphs, text or background colors. Table 2-11 lists common style sheet elements.

Style sheets are developed by placing the tags <style> </style> within the tags of a HTML document. A typical use of a the <style> tag is:

```
<Head>
<style>
h1 {font-style: Ariel; color: blue, align: center}
</style>
</head>
```

This example will make all h1 headers in the document be Ariel font, be blue, and be aligned on the center of the page. Each time that the h1 header tag is used in the document, the header will be displayed the same way. It's not necessary to repeat the attributes more than once since the <style> tag tells the browser to duplicate the attributes.

Note the use of brackets to bound the specified attributes. The brackets are used when more than one attribute is listed.

Style sheets may also be cascaded. A cascaded style sheet (CSS) is a link placed within the HTML that points to an external style sheet. The external style sheet is a template containing style sheet elements that will be applied to an entire Web site. The advantage of CSS is that if the background color of a large Web site is to be changed, the new color can be specified in the template and the entire Web site will be updated immediately. Note that without CSS, each page on the site must be edited for the background color change.

To implement CSS on two or more Web pages, create a text file using the style sheet elements and desired attribute, and save the file with the "css" file extension. For example, if we wanted to apply the h1 header described in the previous example to all headers, across multiple HTML pages, we would create a file with the following:

h1 {font-style: Ariel; color: blue, align: center}

Save the file as *header.css*. Note that the <style> elements are not used in the text file.

A link to the *header.css* file must now be placed in the HTML document. Place the link in the <head> tag as follows:

<Head>
<link rel="stylesheet" type="text/class" href=*header.css*>
</head>

CSS offers significant time savings for Web page designers, as well as ensures that a site is displayed consistently for all visitors.

Browser Compatibility

Earlier versions of Web browsers didn't support the full range of HTML that browsers today support. An HTML document may appear to look better in one browser than it does in another browser. Today, the distinction isn't as clear since Netscape Navigator and Microsoft Internet Explorer are both mature products. However, neither supports the same range of Web file types. Before placing a Web document that you have created on the Internet, be sure to open it in all of the common Web browsers, including earlier versions of the browsers to ensure the tags used in your Web page are compatible with the widest range of browsers.

Text Editors and GUI Editors

HTML can be written using any ASCII-based text editor. All of the examples shown in the HTML section of this chapter could be written in Notepad, opened in each browser, then saved with an .htm file extension. When opened in the browser, the HTML file will appear as a Web document.

The problem with HTML tags is that mistakes aren't forgiven. If a single tag is incorrect or inexact, the file won't display correctly. Enter GUI (graphical user interface; i.e., Windows) HTML editors. A good example of a GUI HTML editor is Microsoft FrontPage.

FrontPage relieves you of having to enter the tags used with HTML. You enter the text in a manner that's nearly identical to entering it in a word processor, and FrontPage inserts the tags for you. If you want to include graphics, buttons, or other page enhancements, FrontPage allows you to indicate where you want to insert the file, and then does it for you.

Another widely used HTML editor is Dreamweaver from Macromedia (see www.macromedia.com). Dreamweaver is an HTML editor that is the preferred tool for developers creating Web sites that will run on UNIX servers. While FrontPage will run on UNIX servers, it requires some manipulation at the ISP level. FrontPage, being a Microsoft product, runs best on Windows NT or 2000 servers.

So, why bother with learning HTML in the first place if a GUI-based editor does the hard work? Because, after using a GUI editor for a while, you're likely to discover that it won't always do exactly what you want it to do. Or, you may want to make subtle changes in the layout not supported by the GUI editor. The only way to specify exactly how you want the page laid out is to modify the HTML tags used by the GUI editor.

No GUI-based editors free you from having to learn basic HTML syntax. They do, however, free you from having to enter the most common tags and relieve you from the meticulous syntax checking required with HTML.

INTERNET PROGRAMMING LANGUAGES

Internet programming languages are languages that have come to be associated with much of the content you see on complex Web sites. There are two broad categories of languages described in this section:

- Server-side Languages

- Client-side Languages

A server-side language runs on a Web server. The results that are generated after the software runs are downloaded to a client Web browser. An example of a server-side programming language is C or C++. A client-side language runs on a client machine. Typically, the client must be able to support the language that will be run when a small unit of code is sent from the server to the browser. JavaScript is an example of a client-side programming language. Before a JavaScript can be run on the browser, the browser must have JavaScript installed.

Java

Java

Java is a server-side programming language that was developed to avoid the use of CGI and to relieve some of the complexities of C and C++ (described in the next section). Java is used to develop simple as well as complex Web applications.

Java is a machine-independent language and is frequently described as "write once, run anywhere." This means that once a programmer writes Java software, it will run on any machine Web browser that supports Java. Browsers that currently support Java include:

- Sun Microsystems HotJava

- Netscape Navigator version 2.0 and greater

- Microsoft Internet Explorer version 3.0 and greater

Java was developed by Sun Microsystems in 1995. The original version of the software was plagued by security and performance problems that made some developers wary of using it for commercial Web sites. The current version of Java (Version 1.2, with a 1.3 beta version available at the time of this writing) corrects both security and performance issues.

Java is an extremely powerful programming language that may be used to produce anything from a user input form to a three-dimensional graphic in real time.

Java actually consists of three primary components: **Java programming language**, **Java virtual machine**, and the **Java platform**. The Java programming language is an object-oriented code that is relatively simple compared to languages with similar capabilities such as C. The fundamental unit of a Java program is called a **class**. A class describes the attributes of a program, or a portion of a program. The **attributes** (called members) may consist of fields within a form, methods used to perform a calculation, or any other directive that the program is designed to do.

The Java virtual machine (VM) describes the portability features of a program written in Java. When a Web browser encounters Java, it interprets the information contained in the program into 16-bit pieces of data that use Unicode characters. (Unicode, described in Chapter 7, was developed to represent nearly all of the phonetic languages in the world, as well as many extinct languages.) Java relies on an interpreter that's installed in the client browser to translate the source code into 16-bit units. The 16-bit units are then used to interface with an operating system that supports Java.

The Java platform describes the functions that are available to Java programmers. The functions are organized as classes. Each class contains subsets known as **packages**. A package is a way of specifying the general use of a class. For example, under the java.awt class are graphical packages that allow a programmer to insert a button or other shape on a screen.

Java programs are designed to be written, then run on any machine that supports Java. This is an important concept because it means that Java doesn't rely on the operating system of the machine it runs on. The same Java program will run on a Windows 98, Apple Macintosh, or UNIX computer—as long as each of these machines has a Java interpreter installed. Other programs, such as Visual Basic and C++, must be customized for the operating system they will run on.

To create a Java program, you need the Java Software Development Kit (SDK), Standard Edition, version 1.2. The kit is available from Sun Microsystems. The SDK contains a Java compiler. A compiler is used to convert the source code of the program into machine language that the program is run on. Once the program has been compiled, it may then be executed on the Web site.

When a user visits a site running Java, the executed code will be downloaded to the Java-enabled browser. The Java interpreter in the browser will interpret the code by converting it into 16-bit Unicode chunks. The Unicode data will then access APIs running on the machine.

Java programming
language

Java virtual machine

Java platform

class

attributes

packages

C and C++

C has been around for nearly thirty years (it was originally developed by Dennis Ritchie in 1972) and was originally developed as a "high-order assembly language" for writing software to microprocessors. For each microprocessor coming onto the market, unique assembly language software had to be written. C was intended to introduce portability among microprocessor types so that one program could be written and run on different processors.

Assembly language

Background Info

Assembly language relies on mnemonics (alphanumeric characters) that represent the functions of the microprocessor. Mnemonics used with assembly language are a single step above binary machine code. The mnemonics used with each microprocessor are determined by the processor manufacturer, so each processor has a unique set of mnemonics. A program written for one type of processor in assembly language won't run on a different type of processor because the two use different mnemonics to represent the binary microprocessor code. Because the two assembly language programs can only run on one type of machine, they are said to be "not portable."

C has the capability to extend far above the machine level, however. The graphical interface used with Windows operating systems, for example, is created with C. As a programming language, C—originally—had the singular distinction of being the only language that could traverse from the bit-level manipulation of a microprocessor to developing complete operating systems. To this day, it's the choice language for developing many graphical and complex screens as well as for embedding functions into silicon-based components such as application-specific integrated components (ASIC) used for software-configuring many hardware devices.

function

The basis for C is a set of functions. A **function** is a named entity that causes something to happen when used in the program. For example, the atoi function is used to convert a string of digits into some value. If a program had a need to convert a decimal number into a percentage, the atoi function could be used as:

atoi(x)
y=100*atoi(amount)

This causes any value to be entered in the (amount) parameter field to be multiplied by 100, thus converting the decimal number to a percentage value.

keyword

In addition to a set of standardized functions, C also uses a set of keywords. A **keyword** is used in the program to initiate some common action. For example, the keyword *break* will cause the program to immediately exit that portion of the program where it occurs. The keyword is used in conjunction with an operator such as one that causes a portion of the program to repeat over and over until some event occurs. When the event occurs, break will cause the program to exit that point and go to another part of the program.

C must be compiled before it can be executed. A compiler is used to convert the human-readable source code into binary machine language that the computer on which the program is run can understand.

C++ represents an improvement to C in that C++ contains far more functions than those used with C. Any C++ software package (such as Microsoft Visual C++) also supports C. The inverse, however, isn't true. A program written with C++ function extensions won't run as a C program once it's compiled.

For Internet applications, C++ is typically used to build many of the graphic details that are frequently found on Web sites. When a user at a client browser accesses the site, the server executes the C++ program, and it's converted to HTML and downloaded to the client Web browser.

Visual Basic

Visual Basic is a server-side language that's primarily used to collect database information. However, it doesn't have to be because Visual Basic shares many aspects of the original BASIC language.

Visual Basic

Visual Basic, however, is object-oriented. This means that it consists of chunks of code (objects) that represent some **event** such as a link to another site, a form that a user inputs data into, or an arithmetic operation. BASIC programs, on the other hand, are sequentially executed (like HTML) from top-to-bottom.

event

Because Visual Basic is object-oriented, a program can be executed at any point in the program. The part of the program that will be executed next typically depends on some user action such as pressing a submit button on a form, or not pressing the submit button. A Visual Basic programmer has the flexibility to create a program that responds to many potential actions of users on a Web site.

Visual Basic relies on the use of classes and defining the characteristics of the class for a particular application. This is similar to C and C++. A typical Visual Basic package has a number of classes bundled in the software that a programmer can use in a program.

In addition to a set of classes, Visual Basic comes with form modules, global modules, and a general module. The form module is used to create user input forms by defining them on a screen, then allowing Visual Basic to replace the screen with the appropriate code. A global module contains procedures that are applied to the entire program. The general module contains text-oriented code that doesn't apply to graphics.

Microsoft Visual Basic is a commonly used package that is used to create input forms for large and complex Access databases. While the same forms could be created in Access, the time and effort needed to do so often doesn't make it worthwhile. Microsoft Visual Basic allows Access programs to be imported directly into the Visual Basic environment. In addition, forms and other links can be created quickly with tools specifically designed for Access (or other relational database software).

Perl

Perl (Practical Extraction and Report Language)

Perl (Practical Extraction and Report Language) was developed by Larry Wall in 1987. The language has been through several revisions and is currently at version 5.

Perl is used primarily as a server-side scripting language, particularly for writing CGIs that cause some event on the server to execute. It certainly doesn't have to be specialized for writing scripts, because Perl was fundamentally designed to process text on powerful computers such as Web servers.

Programmers like Perl as a scripting language because it's more efficient for basic tasks (such as a CGI script) than any other high-level language. This means that a script can be written in less time and with fewer lines of code than in comparable languages such as C or C++.

Perl is mostly portable across different machine types. A script can be written once and it will probably run on most machines. The only requirement is that Perl must be installed on the machine where it will be run, and that the directory where it will be stored uses a specific syntax, as in:

- For UNIX systems: /user/bin/perl is most common

- For Windows systems: c:\Perl\Bin\Perl.exe is most common

Perl is difficult for beginning programmers because a single expression (a line of code) may have two, three, or more meanings when read. Each expression that appears in a Perl program is evaluated, and the result of the evaluation determines the impact that the expression will have on the program. This can be confusing since three Perl programmers may write three different programs, all of which will do exactly the same task.

For experienced Perl programmers, the open-ended use of Perl syntax is what makes the language fun and challenging. Other languages are far more structured. It's said that before you can evaluate a Perl program written by someone else, you need a Perl reference manual to interpret the code. This is due to the fact that subtle syntax changes in the code will have far different effects on what the program does.

When Larry Wall developed Perl, he applied his training and experience as a linguist to the language. The rationale for doing so was that when we speak, we alter the meaning of a sentence by changing syntax, such as emphasizing one word in a sentence, or not emphasizing the word. A similar approach has been taken with Perl; hence, the apparent difficulty in interpreting Perl programs.

VRML

VRML

VRML, Virtual Modeling Reality Language, is a server-side language. VRML is an ISO standardized programming language used to create three-dimensional objects for Web sites. The ISO standard is officially called VRML97. VRML was adopted with only minor changes from the original (and still in widespread use) VRML version 2.

VRML has languished in popularity because it requires specialized tools and may require a considerable amount of memory. The idea of three-dimensional authoring software is to create exotic graphics and animation, and just about any graphic can drain memory and bandwidth resources. But in recent years, it's seen a revival of sorts due to more efficient ways of delivering audio, video, and graphical files to browsers from servers.

In order to see a VRML file, a VRML-enabled browser is needed. The most common VRML viewer is available from Cosmo Software for Windows 9x and Windows NT/2000 browsers. A VRML file is known as a "world." A world is loaded into the viewer, or browser plug-in, in the same manner as you'd open any other file in a browser.

The world file will be recognizable from the .wrl extension. Many VRML files are created using an ASCII text editor such as Notepad. But like HTML editors, there are also VRML authoring tools available in a GUI format.

The syntax used with VRML resembles Java and to a lesser extent C++. It resembles Java in that it is used for producing three-dimensional graphics, but has the added benefit in that users can interact with the image.

JavaScript

JavaScript (or Jscript as the Windows look-alike is called) is a client-side language that allows you to embed certain functions—similar to the functions associated with Java—into an HTML document, and have the functions executed on a client browser that supports JavaScript. At this time, the following support JavaScript:

- Netscape Navigator, version 2.0 and later

- All Sun Microsystems browsers

- Microsoft Internet Explorer, version 3.0 and later

To use JavaScript, you add a script tag to an HTML file, as in:

```
<html>
<script language=JavaScript>
<!--
...
```

The three dots above represent where the actual JavaScript begins. A script can occur anywhere in an HTML file, but typically, scripts are declared early, such as in the beginning or in the end portion of the file.

Like Java, JavaScript comes with functions, objects, and properties. The functions are similar to those used with Java but lack the flexibility of many Java functions. An object consists of several functions that, when grouped together, do something. For example, an object may display a graphic while simultaneously playing an audio file associated with the object. **Properties** are the attributes, or values, used with an object.

An example of an object associated with the properties of the object is:

Document.bgcolor = "orange"

This means that the object document has the property background color equal to the color orange.

JavaScript is interpreted by the client browser. It does so by reading the script following the <script> tag and storing the functions for later use. The browser may or may not execute the function as it's encountered. HTML is read in a similar manner. HTML tags are interpreted (and executed) as they are encountered in the HTML file; that is, from top-to-bottom of the page. JavaScript, however, will execute the script only when told to do so by the script.

For example, a script may tell the viewer to complete a form, then press the submit button. When the submit button is pressed, the script will check the form to make sure it's complete, then send the data off to a Web server. JavaScript won't execute the submit action until it has verified that the data in the form is complete.

JavaScript competes directly with Visual Basic Script, described in the next section. To create JavaScript, all that is needed is a text editor (such as Notepad) or an HTML editor that supports scripting (such as FrontPage). As you'll see shortly, Visual Basic Script demands a bit more from the developer.

VBScript

VBScript, or **Visual Basic Script**, is a client-side scripting language that allows you to create dynamic HTML files on a client computer. Access to a server and extensive software aren't required.

To run a VBScript, the client Web browser must be VBScript-enabled. Currently, Microsoft Internet Explorer, version 3 and later, will recognize HTML documents that contain a reference to VBScript.

The advantage of VBScript, to the Web developer, is that you can develop a complete Web page and test it on a client computer—where it will be run—before placing the page on a Web server. When a user visits the Web site, the VBScript will be downloaded in HTML to the client browser. A browser that supports VBScript will interpret the scripting language and initiate the content of the script.

In other words, you create a VBScript, place it on a Web server, and it executes on the client Web browser. Of course, the client-side Web browser must support VBScript.

The client browser that supports VBScript will come with a VBScript engine. This means that the client will interpret the language used in the downloaded HTML, compile the script, then run the Web page on the browser. As with all scripting languages, VBScript is intended to delegate some of the Web server work to the client computer; consequently, be prepared to tax the resources of client computers when a VBScript is run.

A VBScript is placed in the HTML file that resides on a Web server. A typical example begins as:

```
<html>
<script language="vbscript">
<!--
...
```

After the three dots above comes the VBScript code. On the client side, the browser will interpret the code and execute whatever action is indicated in the script.

VBScript competes directly with JavaScript. Essentially, the two languages serve the same purpose: They both off-load some of the work done on a Web server to the client browser.

Jscript

Jscript is the Microsoft version of JavaScript. Jscript is an interpreted language that must be run on a server or client computer that has a Jscript interpreter installed. Microsoft Internet Explorer and Internet Information Server have a Jscript interpreter installed.

Jscript

Although Jscript is object-oriented, it's limited. You can't use Jscript to write stand-alone application software, for example. However, you can use it to track the amount of time that has elapsed, and to notify a server that a specific amount of time has elapsed. Banner ads that run on Web sites change after a certain period and Jscript can be used to tell the server that it's time to run another ad.

Jscript is particularly well suited for Internet Web site applications because the script can be written in an HTML document. When a server encounters the script, it evaluates the code in the script in the Jscript interpreter. The outcome of the script isn't required to be executed sequentially because Jscript is object-oriented. This level of flexibility is convenient when a Web site visitor is faced with several options. The options can all be addressed in a single script that will be run based upon what action the visitor takes.

XML

XML, or **eXtensible Markup Language**, is an alternative to HTML that's being developed by the **World Wide Web consortium (W3C)**. XML will extend the terseness inherent with HTML so that a document can be made to appear exactly as the author intends it to appear, rather than appearing as the static set of HTML tags allows it to appear.

eXtensible Markup Language (XML)

World Wide Web consortium (W3C)

In other words, you can create your own XML tags to be used in a document and the Web browser that displays the document will interpret them as you intend. Note how different this is from HTML. With HTML, you apply a rigid set of tags (head, p, bold, etc.) to points in a document where you think they'll get your point across. XML also uses tags, but the tags are your own creation.

Original tags are defined in a model called the **Document Type Definition**, or **DTD**. The DTD is created along with an XML document that defines the original tags. For example, a typical DTD may look like:

```
<!DOCTPYE letter [
<!ELEMENT letter (return, address, date, para)>
<!ELEMENT return (#PCDATA)
<!ELEMENT address (#PCDATA)
<!ELEMENT date (#PCDATA)
<!ELEMENT para (#PCDATA)
]>
```

This DTD is used to specify the tags used in a document called a letter. The letter will consist of a return address (return), the address of the recipient (address), the date that the letter is sent (date), and a paragraph (para). Each of these tags has an attribute that's shown in parentheses as #PCDATA. This is an XML attribute that means that text will be used.

Once the tags have been defined, the document can be prepared using the defined tags. The finished product may appear as:

```
<letter>
<return>Bill Barney
111 2nd Ave.
Sometown, AL</return>

<address>Bob Basil
222 3rd Ave.
Another town, OH </address>

<date>January 12, 2000</date>

<para>Bob, I'm thinking of packing it in and moving to Alaska and living off the land for the
rest of my life. What do you think?</para>
</letter>
```

Notice that XML provides the author with entire creative control over the document content by defining the tags to be used in the document. The DTD is actually based on a small set of keywords that are used to define the elements used in the document.

In order to display XML, a browser must have an XML interpreter installed. There is some support for it at the time of this writing but it's not extensive since the W3C has yet to resolve a finished standard for XML. However, once they do so (it's difficult to know when that will happen since standards bodies are notoriously slow), expect Web browsers to fully support XML.

MULTIMEDIA SOFTWARE

To fully experience the multimedia capabilities of the Web, users must have the proper plug-in installed on their machine. A **plug-in** consists of software that is compatible with the Web browser installed on the user computer. Examples of plug-ins include Apple's Quick Time, Macromedia Shockwave, Real Audio, Media Player, and Adobe Acrobat.

The plug-in is used to display software that's typically—or, at least, initially—proprietary. Netscape Navigator and Microsoft Internet Explorer ship with many plug-ins, and many more can be downloaded from the Internet.

The vendor of the plug-in creates software that can only be displayed by the plug-in. The vendor may license the software used to create a multimedia file, and the viewer must install the appropriate plug-in in order to view the multimedia file. For example, Apple offers Quick Time for free. Quick Time allows you to view full-motion video clips stored on the Internet. However, Apple also sells developer software that's used to create video clips that can be viewed on a computer.

There are many plug-ins available as well as many varieties of multimedia developer software. This section previews some of the more common varieties.

QTVR

QuickTime Virtual Reality (QTVR) is produced by Apple. It consists of software that allows you to develop, then display, three-dimensional objects or scenes. Once an object is captured by the software, it can be manipulated or changed.

The QuickTime plug-in is available from Apple's Web site. It's a free download and must be installed on a Web browser that will be displaying files with the MOV extension. Both Netscape and Explorer include the QuickTime viewer pre-installed.

QuickTime Virtual Reality authoring software (called QuickTime Pro) is also available from Apple's Web site for a reasonable fee. The authoring software allows you to convert digital images into MOV file formats, then create a series of frames that will be used in the full-motion video.

QTVR supports audio and video streaming. Streaming means that the Web browser will begin displaying the file as soon as it begins to arrive. A plug-in that doesn't support **streaming** will download the entire file before it starts to display the file. A plug-in that supports streaming is less frustrating for the user because video files are larger and may take quite some time to download.

QuickTime Virtual Reality (QTVR)

streaming

Flash

Flash is a vector-based authoring software that allows you to create full-motion videos for source material that is, typically, in a common file format, such as a series of JPG files. Flash is distributed by Macromedia and is frequently used in conjunction with other Macromedia products for developing Web sites such as Dreamweaver.

Flash may be used with many multimedia file formats. For example, to create a video suitable for playing on the Internet, you can use a series of JPG stills, then frame them into a unit consisting of twelve frames a second using QuickTime Pro. Flash will then convert the QuickTime MOV files into video.

Flash

Flash supports audio and video streaming. Recall that streaming refers to the delivery of data packets that are opened as they arrive. Since the entire file doesn't have to be downloaded before it's opened, Flash is popular on Web servers because it allows for low-bandwidth connection for audio or video files that are typically large files.

Shockwave

Shockwave

Shockwave is a plug-in used to view games, tutorials, and complex presentations. Shockwave supports files that originated in Macromedia Director authoring software, as well as others, but Director is the most common.

Shockwave finds its greatest application with animated three-dimensional graphics. You create Shockwave files by using a series of vectors from which a reader plots the final three-dimensional image. Most games that you play on the Internet are best viewed using Shockwave.

RealPlayer

RealPlayer

RealPlayer, from RealPlayer Networks, is similar to QuickTime. It's a plug-in that's used to display video and audio files. RealPlayer, however, uses a proprietary protocol to interpret the received files, while QuickTime uses an open standard protocol.

Windows Media Player

Windows Media Player

Windows Media Player is a stock item on Windows 9x and NT/2000 operating systems. Windows Media Player allows you view most of the common video, audio, and graphical formats that you're likely to encounter on the Internet.

RELATIONAL AND NON-RELATIONAL DATABASES

relational database

non-relational database

A **relational database** consists of items in columns and rows that can be extensively cross-referenced to data contained in one or more databases. A **non-relational database** consists of a single set of row and column data that can't be cross-referenced to other databases.

Microsoft Access is a relational database because queries can be written that span more that one database.

In most cases, databases found on the Internet will be relational databases. All search Web sites, for example, consist of relational databases because the information contained on the site is located in many discrete databases.

Depending on the database used, you may be required to save the data in the database in a specific file format. For example, if you use Access, the file extension will be .mdb. One of the problems with creating a database is to determine the type of source file to use so that the data can be copied into more than one type of database. The usual method for creating source data is to create it using an ASCII text editor such as Notepad. Nearly all database software will allow ASCII (also called "flat files") to be imported.

There are many database languages in use. One of the challenges that Web developers face is determining how to integrate databases for use on the Web as well as within networks in which different operating systems and database types are used. In 1992, the Open DataBase Connectivity (ODBC) standard was first released. The purpose of ODBC was to provide an interface in order to access different database types. For example, today there are ODBC interfaces that allow access to Visual Basic, SQL, Access, Paradox, or Excel databases.

OBDC allows developers an acceptable way of adding a database to an existing Web site.

INTERNET WEB SITE SEARCHES

The volume of information available on the Internet is almost overwhelming. If not for specialized tools that allow us to search for and locate specific documents, we would spend most of our time following links that may or may not lead to the desired documents.

Search tools used on the Internet are called **search engines**. A search engine is a specialized database that contains Web site addresses, key words or phrases, or all words used in a document that's posted on the Internet. Common Internet search sites include Yahoo!, Northern Light, Alta Vista, and Ask.com.

search engines

A large Web site may also include a search tool so that you can quickly locate information on the site. Most commercial Web sites that offer a large number of products and services include a search mechanism so that you can quickly find the product you're looking for.

Most Web sites include a META tag in the HTML. A META tag can be used to provide information about a site to search engines. A search engine canvasses the Internet on a routine basis looking for new sites. When a new site is found, the search engine will key on information that's included in the META tag. Typically, this includes a site name, a brief description of the site that's about twenty-five words or less, as well as key words and phrases that can be used to link searches to the site.

When a user enters a word or phrase into the search window of a search site, the site looks for the information that was included in the META tags.

The following sections contain general information about the types of search mechanisms popular on the Internet, as well as common techniques used to structure a search query.

Static Index

static index

A **static index** consists of a list of headings that include links to detailed information related to each heading. A large or complex Web site may employ a static index as an option to quickly locate a specific area of the site.

A static index includes links to various areas of the site. The information is displayed in a manner that's similar to a directory structure with sub-directories listed under each directory heading.

site map

A **site map** is a variation of a static index. A site map also uses headings as key descriptors to various areas of the site, but the headings are typically arranged in a logical manner that's similar to a graphical road map.

A static index may also be included on the homepage of a Web site. The various areas of the site are frequently listed as headings or titles in a table or toolbar. The location of the index headings may appear near the top, bottom, left, or right of the page. When headings are placed in a frame, it's customary to also include a static listing of the index near the top or bottom of the page. This is done for those browsers that don't support frames, or for users who have turned graphics off for the site.

Keyword Index

keyword index

A **keyword index** examines the relevance of a word or phrase before listing it in the search database. Words or phrases that are used frequently are most likely to be included in the search database, while those words that are mentioned once or twice may not be listed at all. The advantage of a keyword index is that irrelevant words and phrases tend to be ignored. When a search is conducted, the results of the search are returned quicker.

Table 2-12 summarizes characteristics of a keyword index.

Table 2-12 Keyword Search Index

ADVANTAGES	DISADVANTAGES
Index only includes frequently occurring words or phrases.	May not return a result for obscure information.
Size of database may be customized to site content.	Requires complex database and programming skills.
Time to generate search result is short.	

Full Text Index

A **full text index** is a list of all terms and URLs that are found on a Web site. When a visitor wants to locate specific information on the site, a keyword or phrase is entered in a search field, and the search engine will compare the entry to similar words or phrases that the site contains.

A full text index often includes words or phrases that will never be queried by a visitor to a site, but the words are still maintained in the search database. Even though the words are never queried, the index includes them, which tends to slow the results of the search.

Most newer site search engines utilize a keyword search rather than the resource-intensive full text index.

Table 2-13 lists the advantages and disadvantages of a full text search.

ADVANTAGES	DISADVANTAGES
Includes most words and phrases found on the site.	Requires a large database size.
Likely to return obscure information.	Time to search complete index may be long.

Table 2-13 Full Text Search

Search Query Operators

Search query operators are the rules used with a search engine to define a query. Each search tool used on the Internet or on a specific Web site may differ in conventions used, but there are some common operators used with most search engines.

Most search engines used on the Internet rely on the use of Boolean or plus/minus operators to return search results. By including Boolean operators with a search query, the results are more likely to match the query and the number of results are more likely to be manageable. Let's take a look at the most common operators.

Boolean operators utilize the logical operators AND, OR, NOT, and NEAR between words and phrases in a query. When using Boolean operators, be sure to capitalize each operator as follows:

- **AND**: All terms in the query must be located in the documents being searched. An example of the AND operator is:

> spoon AND fork

When entered in this manner, only those documents that have both the words spoon and fork will be returned. If a document has only the word spoon, but not the word fork, it will not be listed in the query result.

- **OR**: If one or both terms in the query are found in a document, a return will be generated. An example of the OR operator is:

spoon OR fork

When entered in a query, all documents that contain either spoon, fork, or both words will generate a result.

- **NOT**: All terms that immediately follow the NOT operator are excluded in the result. The most common use of the NOT operator is to eliminate common associations that aren't relevant for the search. An example of the NOT operator is:

aircraft NOT helicopters

Notice that the NOT operator is used in this example to exclude helicopters from a search for aircraft. Without excluding helicopters, a search of the Internet would be sure to include information about the many types of helicopters.

- **NEAR**: If both terms of the query are typically associated in the same context, but not necessarily together, the NEAR operator may be used to locate documents containing the two words. Most search engines that support NEAR will examine a document to see if the queried words occur within twenty or twenty-five words of one another. If so, the documents will be listed in the search results. An example of the NEAR operator is:

bear NEAR cub

When entered in the query, any document that contains the words bear and cub in association will generate a result.

Table 2-14 summarizes the use of Boolean operators.

Table 2-14 Boolean Search Operators

BOOLEAN OPERATOR	DESCRIPTION
AND	Use to match an exact result for a phrase.
OR	Use when any term in a phrase is to be matched.
NOT	Use to exclude a commonly associated word.
NEAR	Use to locate documents in which words are frequently associated.

Plus and minus operators are a simplified way to use Boolean operators. Broadly speaking, the plus operator (+) corresponds to the Boolean AND operator, while the minus operator (-) corresponds to the Boolean NOT operator.

+: To use the + operator, preface each word in the query with + if you are looking for documents that exactly match the word. If a phrase is to be matched, preface each word in the phrase with + (with no spaces). An example of the plus operator is:

+cat+dog

When a search engine is queried in this manner, all documents that contain the words cat and dog are returned. However, the words may or may not appear in the document together. Like the AND operator, the plus operator will search all documents that contain the words anywhere in the document.

-: To use the minus operator, place a – symbol before each word that's to be excluded from the results. An example of the minus operator is:

+cat-dog

When entered in this manner, the results will include all documents that contain the word cat, but not documents that contain the word dog. Notice the effect of the minus operator is to narrow a search by excluding unwanted information.

Table 2-15 summarizes the use of the plus and minus operators.

PLUS/ MINUS OPERATOR	DESCRIPTION
Plus Operator (+)	Use when an exact match of a word is required.
Minus Operator (-)	Use when a word is to be excluded from a search result.

Table 2-15 Plus and Minus Operators

Double quotes are the most common operator to use when searching for a phrase. The result that's returned may be an exact match or a close match (which resembles the Boolean NEAR operator) to the query.

An example of the use of double quotes is:

"internet search engine"

When entered as a query, the results will include documents that contain either the exact phrase *internet search engine,* or closely related phrases.

Double quotes are frequently combined with Boolean operators to refine a search. For example, to include results for related phrases, link the phrases with the AND operator, as in:

"internet search engine" AND "internet databases"

This query will search documents that contain both phrases in a single document.

Stemming (also called **truncation**) is a technique that allows you to enter a partial word or phrase in the search query. Normally, an asterisk or some other wild card symbol is used to indicate any variations of the main word used in the search (for newer search engines, stemming is done automatically, without the need for entering the asterisk wild card symbol).

Double quotes

Stemming

truncation

An example of stemming is:

com*

When entered in this manner, the partial word *com* is likely to return matches for *communication, company, commerce, commercial,* or *complex.*

When setting up a search tool on a Web site, you should make sure that the operators you use and the type of search index are appropriate for the site. Table 2-16 lists several popular search sites along with the type of search index used and types of operators supported. Visit each site and try entering a few searches to get a feel for how each of them works.

Table 2-16 Common Internet Search Sites

SITE NAME	SEARCH TYPE	BOOLEAN	PLUS AND MINUS	DOUBLE QUOTES	STEMMING
Alta Vista	Keyword	Yes	Yes	Yes	Yes (*)
Excite	Keyword	Yes	Yes	Yes	No
HotBot	Keyword	Yes	Yes	Yes	Yes
Northern Light	Keyword	No	Yes	Yes	No
Yahoo!	Keyword/Directory subject search	Yes	Yes	Yes	Yes (*)

Yahoo! uses a slightly different approach to searches. You have the option of searching by subject and gradually narrowing the subject, until you arrive at the subject where the information is likely to be found. At that time, you can revert to a keyword search.

MULTIMEDIA FILE FORMATS

Multimedia file formats refer to the various file types that may be found on the Internet. This section previews the most common formats and briefly describes each type.

There are several important terms associated with file formats that you should be aware of. Literature that you read, or questions on the i-Net+ test, may make references to:

Streaming

- **Streaming**: Streaming may be used when referring to an audio or video file. It means that the file will be opened and displayed as it arrives. In a typical application, a live audio broadcast will stream audio to a Web browser. The audio will be packaged at the source as an audio file and sent in packets to browsers. The packets will be opened and the audio interpreted as they arrive, rather than waiting until the source broadcast is completed. Streaming video is structured and packaged in a similar manner. It's sent to browsers in packets and each is opened as it arrives. To the viewer, it appears as if a single stream of video is being sent to the browser.

- **Color Depth**: Color depth refers to the number of colors that can be displayed by a graphical file. Color depth is derived by assigning a specific number of bits to represent a color. For example, the most common color depth (also called bit depth) used on the Internet is 8-bits. With eight bits to represent each color, $2^8 = 256$ colors that can be displayed. Color depth is important because it affects the resolution of a displayed graphic. For example, if a graphic is created using a color depth of 24 ($2^{24} = 16.7$ million colors), a browser that only supports depths of 8-bits will garble the image.

- **Bitmap Image**: A bitmap image, also called a raster image, is composed of pixels (pixels are the dots painted on a monitor that, taken together, form an image) arranged so that a graphic emerges based upon the color of the pixels. Each pixel must be activated so that the correct image is displayed. Examples of bitmap images are bmp, jpeg, tiff, and gif files. A bitmap image is resolution dependent. This means that if the resolution of the browser is less than that of a downloaded bitmap image, the quality of the graphic will be degraded.

- **Vector Image**: A vector image is described using mathematical algorithms. The algorithm describes the location where an image is to be placed on a screen. Because each image is described with a separate algorithm, a complex graphic can be separated into hundreds of individual graphics. Software such as Illustrator and AutoCAD use vector images to represent graphics. A great deal of flexibility is available to a graphics designer since any of the parts of a graphic can be changed without affecting the rest of the image. Vector images are resolution independent. This means that a vector image can be displayed on browsers with different resolutions without affecting the quality of the image.

GIF

GIF, or Graphical Interchange Format, is a format widely used for displaying graphical files on the World Wide Web. The file extension used with GIF files is .gif. There are two versions of GIF: GIF87a and GIF89a. GIF89a is an improved version of GIF87a. The improvements that it offers include:

- Multiple images within a single file. With GIF89a you can create animations and save the animation as a single file.

- **Interlacing**: Interlacing means that an image will be "painted" across a screen in a series of passes. The advantage of an interlaced graphic over a non-interlaced graphic is that graphics downloaded on a slow connection will be visible to the point that a viewer may decide to click off the image. Without interlacing, the viewer will have to wait until the complete image downloads before deciding whether to move on to another site.

A disadvantage of the GIF format is that is uses a compression technique that is proprietary to Unisys. The compression technique is called LZW compression. If you develop software that includes GIF graphics, you must sign a licensing agreement with Unisys. If the software you develop will be used for commercial applications (that is, you'll make a profit from the software), you must pay Unisys a royalty. However, it's permissible to make and view GIF files without paying a fee to Unisys.

JPEG

JPEG, an acronym for Joint Photographic Experts Group, is another widely used graphical file format. The file extension used with JPEG files is .jpg. Unlike GIF, there are no proprietary issues surrounding JPEG.

JPEG offers several advantages over GIF as a graphics format choice:

- It supports 24-bit color depths. With 24 bits, a total of 16.7 million colors can be displayed. Most GIF files, by comparison, are displayed as 8-bit depths for a total of 256 colors.

- JPEG supports variable compression rates. This means that you can determine the level by compression depending on the desired file size and the quality of the restored image.

progressive JPEG

You may see references to **progressive JPEG**. A progressive JPEG allows an image to be gradually decompressed as it's painted on a screen. The displayed image will gradually sharpen as it's decompressed. This allows you to determine whether you want to wait for the entire image to appear or click on to another site. Progressive JPEG is the equivalent to interlaced GIF.

Because of the wide array of colors available with JPEG, it's best suited for graphics that contain many colors or shades, such as naturalistic images. A GIF file, on the other hand, is best suited to simpler graphics such as line art or posters, because it is capable of displaying fewer colors and shades.

PNG

PNG, which stands for Portable Network Graphics, was developed by the Internet community to specifically replace GIF techniques. The idea was that if developers use PNG file formats for graphics, the issue of licensing with Unisys GIF files would be avoided. The file extension for PNG files is .png.

PNG offers several other advantages over GIF:

transparency

- It supports **transparency**. Transparency refers to changing the color of a pixel on a screen so that it isn't visible.

- Interlacing with PNG occurs three to four times faster than with GIF.

- Files in PNG format can be 10% to 30% smaller than the same file that's compressed using GIF.

Both GIF and PNG use **lossless compression**. Lossless compression means that all of the information in the original graphic is displayed upon decompression. A JPEG utilizes **lossy compression**. Lossy compression means that some elements of the image may be lost upon decompression. Since a JPEG file is typically larger than GIF or PNG (because JPEG supports far more colors), a trade-off is usually made between color quality and file size. The more compression applied to a JPEG, the greater the loss of quality, but the smaller the file size.

lossless compression

lossy compression

PDF

PDF, short for Portable Document Format, is used to create a collage of graphics and text documents. A PDF file is created using Adobe's Acrobat software, and is viewed by downloading a free PDF file reader called Acrobat Reader. A PDF file uses the file extension .pdf.

PDF files may be found on the Internet but are more likely to be used on CDs containing user manuals, books, or some other type of electronic version of a document.

Using Adobe Acrobat, an electronic document can be designed so that it mimics a newspaper or magazine article. The text is placed on the document with matching graphics. For long documents such as a book or user help manuals, the PDF file may be placed on a network server and made available to all network users. Since the file resembles a printed document in appearance, it is much more efficient than distributing a paper version of a document.

RTF

RTF, or Rich Text Format, is a file format that permits you to exchange text documents between different word processors. For example, a document created using Microsoft Word can be saved as an RTF file by choosing the .rtf extension. Then, as an RTF file, a reader with Correl WordPerfect can open the file and read it.

The key to the effectiveness of RTF is that the operating system of the computer where an RTF document is to be read must support RTF. Currently, all Windows 9x, Millennium, and NT/ 2000 operating systems contain an RTF reader.

TIFF

TIFF, or Tag Image File Format, is used for exchanging graphic files between two different applications. The most common use is for images that are scanned for eventual placement on a Web site. The extension associated with TIFF is .tif.

TIFF, originally developed by the Aldus Corporation along with other companies, is a public domain technology. TIFF was originally developed to be independent of the platform that it's run on; consequently, it offers developers considerable flexibility as a format for graphical files.

A TIFF file is composed of groups of 4-byte segments. The segments are compressed using one of several compression techniques. Since each segment can be individually manipulated, any portion of a large graphical file can be edited to the 4-byte segment level.

In addition to its use as a popular scanner format, TIFF is widely used in medical imagery, fax machines, and 3-D applications.

TIFF requires a browser plug-in viewer before TIFF files can be displayed. Many graphical editing software packages, such as Photoshop, ship with a TIFF viewer. The viewer can be associated with the browser used to surf Web sites containing TIFF files. If the viewer isn't installed on the machine where the browser is located, it can be downloaded from the Internet.

PostScript

PostScript is a proprietary language used on PostScript printers. The language is a script that's used to interpret graphics files (which use an .eps extension) and text files (which use a .ps extension) that were created with PostScript.

Adobe currently owns PostScript. PostScript software, while able to print various file formats, is best suited for interpreting PostScript specific graphics and text.

BMP

BMP is short for BitMap. A BMP file is created by specifying the color of each pixel in an image. The file extension associated with BMP files is .bmp.

The most common application of BMP files is the Windows application Paintbrush. When a BMP file is saved, there is no native compression used to conserve the size of the file (other than "white spaces," which are the parts of the file where color wasn't applied). Due to the lack of effective compression and the mapping of pixels to colors, the sizes of BMP files are large. For most applications involving the Internet, the size of a BMP file makes it unacceptable.

In a general sense, large files of any type should not be used on a Web server. Because these same files will be downloaded to browsers, they will create a considerable load on the available bandwidth that's available to the server. As a general rule, for any bit-mapped image, the lower the dot-per-inch (DPI) of pixels in the image, the faster the image will download.

MOV

MOV stands for Movie. The MOV file format is proprietary to Apple and is used with the QuickTime plug-in. MOV is associated with the file extension .mov.

Apple created MOV in order to view video files on the Internet, as well as other multimedia situations. MOV requires a reader in order to interpret the file, a QuickTime reader that can be downloaded for free from Apple's Web site. All modern Web browsers come equipped with a QuickTime reader.

MPEG

MPEG, Moving Pictures Expert Group, develops standards for the compression of digital audio and video files. To display a MPEG file with a .mpg extension, you must use a viewer. Nearly all modern Web browsers include a MPEG viewer.

The MPEG group develops audio and video standards, and you'll see these referred to as MPEG-1 or MPEG-3. The most recent standard is MPEG-4.

AVI

AVI is an acronym for Audio Video Interleave. AVI is proprietary to Microsoft and is installed on the Windows 9x, Millennium, NT, and 2000 operating systems. The file extension associated with AVI files is .avi.

As the name implies, AVI uses interleaving to present audio and video files. The audio and video are separated into small packets and sent to a Web browser one after another so that a portion of the audio is heard, then a portion of the video is displayed. To the observer, the audio and video appear to occur simultaneously and without interruption since the packets are maintained as small units.

KEY POINTS REVIEW

- An API consists of a set of functions provided by an operating system or a hardware device that allows software to use it.

- CGI, which stands for Common Gateway Interface, is a program that runs on a server and is typically used to execute some other program.

- SQL, or Structured Query Language, is used to manipulate data in a database as well as to define the data that a user wants to see.

- The NSAPI (Netscape Server Application Programming Interface) was developed to provide a set of commonly used server functions to handle HTTP requests and responses.

- ISAPI (Internet Server Application Programming Interface) allows Web developers to extend the functionality of a server running Microsoft Internet Information Server.

- A DLL, or Dynamic Link Library, is used to access the functions of an operating system.

- Active Server Pages (ASP) is a proprietary server-side scripting language developed by Microsoft. ASP runs on the Windows operating systems, primarily Windows NT with Internet Information Server software installed on the server. ASP allows dynamic Web documents to be displayed on the client browser.

- HTML is an abbreviation for HyperText Markup Language. It provides a way to code a document so that it can be displayed on the World Wide Web area of the Internet.

- Java is a server-side programming language that was developed to avoid the use of CGI and to relieve some of the complexities of C and C++.

- C and C++ are compiled languages that rely on using a set of pre-defined functions in the source code.

- Visual Basic is a server-side language that's primarily used to collect database information.

- Perl is used primarily as a server-side scripting language.

- JavaScript is a client-side language that allows you to embed certain functions into HTML documents and have the functions executed on a client browser that supports JavaScript.

- VBScript, or Visual Basic Script, is a client-side scripting language that allows you to create dynamic HTML files on a client computer.

- Jscript, from Microsoft, is an interpreted language that must be run on a server or client computer that has a Jscript interpreter installed.

- XML, or eXtensible Markup Language, is an alternative to HTML that will extend the use of specific tags and allow developers to define their own tags.

- Multimedia software consists of authoring software used to create multimedia applications and plug-ins that allow the applications to be viewed.

- A relational database allows the information contained in many different databases to be merged.

- A large or complex Web site includes a search engine so that visitors can quickly find information.

- Multimedia files are used to represent graphics, text, video, or audio.

- Examples of graphical file formats include GIF, JPEG, BMP, and PNG.

- Examples of video file formats include MOV, AVI, and MPEG.

- Examples of audio file formats include MPEG and AVI.

The following questions test your knowledge of the material presented in this chapter:

1. What is the HTML tag that links to a Web site?

2. What is the meaning of the <head> tag?

3. What is the meaning of the <body> tag?

4. What HTML tag do you use to bold text?

5. Which Internet programming language allows you to create HTML tags?

6. What HTML tag is used for a numbered list?

7. What HTML tag is used for a definition list?

8. Study the HTML document shown below. Troubleshoot the tags to discover which tag is missing.

```
<html>
<head>
<title> This is an HTML document </title>
<body>
<p> Can you find the problem? </p>
<p> Let's hope so. </p>
</head>
</html>
```

9. What is the difference between a <br> tag and a <p> tag?

10. What happens when you set the height and width parameters for an HTML image?

11. What server-side utility is commonly used to execute a program so that information is sent to a client from the server?

12. Which server-side software entity allows a Web developer to summarize the core functions of a server to suit the needs of a Web site?

13. Which server-side language uses a "virtual machine"?

14. What is the color depth of a JPEG file?

15. Which type of search index includes a list of all terms and URLs that are found on a Web site?

1. In HTML, what is used to identify document parts, and tells the browser how to display them?

   a. Tag

   b. Object

   c. Attribute

   d. Map

2. What is the minimum number of characters in a color tag?

   a. Four

   b. Six

   c. Eight

   d. Ten

3. What does HTML stand for?

   a. HyperText Marking Language

   b. HyperText Markup Language

   c. HyperText Market Language

   d. HyperText Mark Language

4. What is the default background color of an HMTL document once it has been opened in a browser?

   a. Black

   b. White

   c. Gray

   d. Blue

5. What is the common server-side scripting language?

   a. Perl

   b. HTML

   c. Java

   d. C++

6. In the example cat+dog, what is the function of the plus?

   a. An exact match of a word is required.

   b. You want it to look better.

   c. The database is very large.

   d. The inquired database is too small.

7. When must you use a minus in an Internet search?

   a. When you want the search narrowed down.

   b. When a word is to be excluded from a search result.

   c. When you want to include a word.

   d. When more than one word is being searched.

8. What is the most common operator to use when searching for a phrase?

   a. Plus

   b. Minus

   c. And

   d. Double quotes

9. What is a common search engine that does not support Boolean?

   a. Yahoo!

   b. Northern Light

   c. Alta Vista

   d. HotBot

10. What Boolean operator is used to exclude a commonly associated word?

    a. AND

    b. OR

    c. NOT

    d. NEAR

11. Which of the following is commonly used to display video in a Web browser?

    a. QTVR

    b. Java

    c. Perl

    d. HTML

12. Which of the following uses a series of vector points to display three-dimensional objects?

    a. Visual Basic

    b. Shockwave

    c. QTVR

    d. JavaScript

13. Which of the following executes on a server?

    a. DLL

    b. Flash

    c. CGI

    d. XML

14. A video clip that begins to play as it downloads to the browser uses:

    a. Streaming

    b. Tables

    c. SQL

    d. CGI

15. What color depth is most widely used on the Internet?

    a. 8 bits

    b. 16 bits

    c. 24 bits

    d. 48 bits

CHAPTER 3

INTERNET PROTOCOLS

LEARNING OBJECTIVES

LEARNING
OBJECTIVES

Upon completion of this chapter and its related lab procedures, you should be able to perform the following tasks:

1. (4.4) Describe the nature, purpose, and operational essentials of TCP/IP. Content could include the following:

    *   What addresses are.

    *   Determining which ones are valid and which ones are not.

    *   Public versus private addresses.

2. (4.3) Describe Internet domain names and DNS. Content could include the following:

    *   DNS entry types.

    *   Hierarchical structure.

    *   Role of root domain server.

    *   Top-level or original domains.

3. (4.5) Describe the purpose of remote access protocols. Content could include the following:

    *   SLIP

    *   PPP

    *   PPTP

    *   Point-to-point/multipoint

4. (4.6) Describe how various protocols or services apply to the function of a mail system, Web system, and file transfer system. Content could include the following:

    *   TCP/IP
    *   SMTP
    *   POP3
    *   FTP
    *   Gopher

    *   Telnet
    *   NNTP
    *   LDAP
    *   LPR

5. (4.7) Decide when to use various diagnostic tools for identifying and resolving Internet problems. Content could include the following:

    *   Ping

    *   IPConfig

    *   WinIPCfg

    *   ARP

    *   TraceRT

Internet Protocols

INTRODUCTION

The Internet is a functional network because there are systematic rules that govern the services available on it. The rules are called protocols. A protocol specifies the attributes of a network function. For example, there are protocols specific to e-mail, file transfers, and remote access connections.

The most widely deployed protocol on the Internet is TCP/IP. TCP/IP is a universal protocol because it can be run on nearly any type of hardware and operating system. This chapter begins with an in-depth discussion of TCP and IP.

Remote access protocols are an important aspect of Internet connections because many stand-alone computers and mobile users connect to the Internet with a remote access protocol. PPP, SLIP, and PPTP are the three most widely used remote access protocols and each is described in the following sections.

A network provides applications to users via a process of setting up and maintaining a connection between the user's computer and a server. This chapter describes a wide variety of applications that a user may require.

The i-Net+ exam is specific about diagnostic tools that should be applied to wide area networks such as the Internet. Several tools will be discussed in the chapter.

TCP/IP PROTOCOL SUITE

TCP/IP is an acronym for **Transmission Control Protocol/ Internet Protocol**. TCP/IP consists of the TCP protocol, and the IP protocol. Together, the two protocols form the **TCP/IP Protocol Suite**.

TCP/IP is a universal protocol, one that's independent of the type of machine that it runs on. This means that TCP/IP will run on a Windows 9x computer, a Windows NT workstation, a Windows 2000 computer, a UNIX computer, or an Apple computer. TCP/IP is the primary protocol used on the Internet.

TCP/IP

Transmission Control Protocol/ Internet Protocol

TCP/IP Protocol Suite

While the protocol suite has the capabilities to respond to many networking environments, the basic purpose of each of the protocols can be summarized as follows:

- TCP is responsible for reliable process-to-process communication between two devices, such as servers, or servers and workstations. Because TCP operates at the Transport layer of the OSI Model, the headers of the protocol must contain sufficient information to initiate data transfers with some guarantee that transfers between the two nodes will be successful. Note that TCP doesn't "know how" data will get from a source node to the destination node. Instead, the protocol ensures that data can be exchanged between the nodes; and, if there are problems with the transfer (such as lost or garbled data packets), the data will be recovered.

- IP is responsible for routing data packets from the source node to the destination node. Keep in mind that when a data packet leaves a workstation to go to a server across the Internet, the packet will encounter many devices, such as routers, switches, or servers, before it arrives. IP must determine the best route that the packet will take to get to the destination node. IP uses a logical addressing scheme (called an **IP address**) to locate the destination node. IP addresses are fundamental to locating devices on an internetwork, and are described later in this chapter in the IP Address section.

IP address

TCP

TCP

sockets

well-known port

TCP uses **sockets** as a means of setting up the communication link between two nodes. A socket is a packet exchanged between the two nodes that contains the logical addresses of the nodes (their IP address), the process that's to be used between the nodes (such as e-mail, a file transfer, or HTTP for the World Wide Web), and the Transport layer protocol that the nodes will use (TCP).

A process is identified with a 16-bit number called a **well-known port**. When the port number is specified in the socket, the destination node will initiate that protocol to be used between the two nodes. For example, if a workstation sends a socket to a remote server that includes the well-known port number 80 in the header, the server will know that the exchange between the two nodes will be on the Internet using HTTP between the two nodes.

Table 3-1 lists several process and their well-known port numbers.

Table 3-1 TCP Well-Known Port Numbers

PROCESS	WELL-KNOWN PORT NUMBER
FTP	21, 20
Telnet	23
SMTP Mail	25
HTTP (WWW)	80
POP3 (e-mail)	110
TCP	8080

Once a process is identified using a well-known port and a protocol that will be used between the two devices is agreed upon, the two nodes can begin exchanging data. Remember that TCP is also responsible for a reliable transfer of data. TCP handles reliability in several ways.

First, TCP may decide to fragment data that a node delivers from the process. **Fragment** means that the data will be organized into blocks called packets. TCP has no size restriction; so, in theory, it will transport a packet of any size. But the underlying protocols are limited in the amount of data that can be placed in their respective packets. IP, for example, is limited to about 65,000 bytes and Ethernet is limited to about 1,500 bytes.

Since the process delivers data with no regard to packet sizes, TCP will determine how much of the data can be placed in a packet. Notice that if TCP didn't have the ability to fragment data streams from the process, the number of bytes in an IP packet would likely be exceeded. If the source node is located on an Ethernet network, the maximum size of the Ethernet frame would be certain to overflow. Data that's not properly placed in a packet will be lost. TCP uses fragments as one way of ensuring a reliable connection between the two nodes.

A second technique used by TCP for ensuring reliability is to send an acknowledgment to the sending node when a packet is successfully received. The acknowledgment includes an indicator that specifies the packet or fragment. When the sending node receives the acknowledgment, additional packets are sent. It's not uncommon in a TCP connection for an acknowledgment to be sent after every three or four packets. Typically, the acknowledgment is included in a packet that's sent from the receiving node to the sending node. Because TCP is a full duplex protocol (meaning that data is sent simultaneously in both directions), data transfers occur very quickly even with the use of acknowledgments.

Background Info

Connection-oriented and Connectionless Transport Protocols

A **connection-oriented protocol** uses acknowledgments between the sender and receiver. TCP is a connection-oriented protocol. A **connectionless protocol** doesn't send acknowledgments between the sending and receiving nodes. **UDP (User Datagram Protocol)** is a connectionless protocol.

A connection-oriented protocol runs a bit slower than a connectionless protocol because the data transfer must be occasionally interrupted for acknowledgments. A slower data transfer rate is the trade-off for ensuring that the transfer is reliable.

A connectionless protocol, also called a "best effort" protocol, isn't hampered with acknowledgments, so data can be sent as quickly as the protocol and physical infrastructure permit. For example, live, interactive gaming uses UDP between the connected nodes. Although a connectionless protocol runs faster than a connection-oriented protocol, there are no mechanisms built into it for ensuring a reliable connection. If a packet of data is garbled, it won't be sent again.

IP

The Internet Protocol (IP) is a Network layer protocol used to route a data packet from source node to destination node. The current version of IP is version 4 (also referred to as Type 4 IP). Version 4 IP contains 32 bits. The predominant feature of IP is the use of logical addresses called IP addresses.

IP doesn't guarantee that a packet will arrive at the destination node. In other words, it's a connectionless protocol. TCP is the reliable half of the connection. But IP is said to be a "best-effort" protocol. This means that the protocol possesses the ability to get the data packet to the node destination, but it can't guarantee that the data won't be garbled or even incomplete.

When a data packet is sent onto the Internet, it may travel through many routers before arriving at the destination node. There's a possibility that a packet could be passed indefinitely between routers and not arrive at the destination. TCP recognizes this possibility and handles it with acknowledgments to ensure a packet arrives. Because IP has the responsibility for routing a packet through a maze of routers, it includes a header field that limits the amount of time that a packet may remain within a network. The field is called **time-to-live**.

time-to-live

Time-to-live is a one-byte field that specifies the amount of time (in seconds) that a data packet may remain in a network. The default value is 20 seconds for IP. If a packet is passed between routers for more than 20 seconds, the packet is assumed to be undeliverable and will be discarded. (Note that TCP will detect the lost packet since the sending node won't receive an acknowledgment. The sending node will then resend the packet.)

Background Info

The time-to-live field in an IP header is an absolute value in seconds. Many routers, however, allow you to configure the parameter for IP packets that pass through them by specifying time-to-live as the number of hops that a packet may make before being discarded. A **hop** refers to the number of routers that a packet passes through. A typical value is 15 hops.

hop

If, for example, a packet has been sent through 15 routers before arriving at the destination, the packet will be discarded. You may have seen evidence of this when connecting to an Internet site but before it loads in your browser, you get a message saying that the remote site couldn't be accessed. However, if you immediately try again, you get connected. The packet was discarded before the route could be finalized to the destination, but upon reconnection, the remainder of the path was reconciled.

Time-to-live ensures that a packet won't circle endlessly around the Internet. But before the packet will even be sent onto the Internet, it must have a sense of where the packet is to be sent. IP uses logical addresses to identify nodes. Because an IP address is critical for routing data packets, the next section discusses IP addressing in detail.

IP Addresses

An IP address consists of 32 bits. All nodes connected to the Internet, and many intranets, have unique IP addresses. The address must be unique for all nodes, so that when a packet is sent, it will be sent to only one destination.

An IP header includes fields for the IP address of the sending node and for the destination node. Why include both addresses? TCP relies on IP for providing the source address so that acknowledgments can be sent back to the sending node.

An IP address consists of two parts, a **network address** and a **host address**. The network address identifies the network that a node is connected to. Network addresses are analogous to including a city and state on the address of postal mail. The host portion of an IP address identifies the specific machine connected to a network. Host addresses are analogous to the street name and house number used with postal mail.

Figure 3-1 shows the structure of a typical IP address. The address has a network portion and a host portion. The full 32 bits are divided into 8-bit octets separated by a decimal point. The only function of the decimal point is to divide the octets.

The native format of an IP address uses binary numbers to represent the numerical address. Because, for most of us, it's easier to work with decimal numbers, IP addresses are normally shown as decimal numbers. But notice in Figure 3-1 that the decimal address is based on a direct conversion from binary.

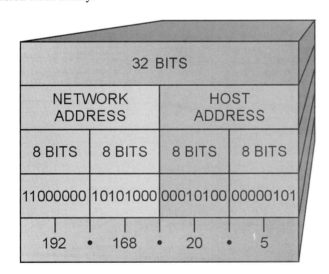

Figure 3-1 An IP Address

For the IP address 192.168.20.5, a host machine has been assigned the address 20.5. The host machine is connected to a network that has an address 192.168. The reason that IP addresses are divided into network and host addresses is so that a single network address can be assigned to a network that has many nodes connected to it. In Figure 3-1, the network 192.168 can have $2^{16} = 65,536$ host machines connected to it.

IP addresses are organized into classes. The specific class of an IP address refers to how many bits are assigned to the network portion of the address, and how many bits are assigned to the host portion of the address. The IP classes are organized as follows:

- **Class A**: The first octet is reserved for the network address, and the last three octets are reserved for the host address. All class A IP addresses begin with a decimal number from 1-126. For example, 10.154.26.6 is a class A IP address. The network portion of the address is 10 and the host portion of the address is .154.26.6.

- **Class B**: The first two octets are reserved for the network portion of the address, and the last two octets are reserved for the host portion of the address. All class B IP addresses begin with a decimal number from 128 through 191. For example, 172.16.54.7 is a class B IP address. The network portion of the address is 172.16, and the host portion of the address is .54.7.

- **Class C**: The first three octets of the address are reserved for the network portion of the address, and the last octet is reserved for the host portion of the address. All class C addresses begin with a decimal number from 192 through 223. For example, 192.168.65.4 is a class C IP address. The network portion of the address is 192.168.54, and the host portion of the address is .4.

Table 3-2 IP Classes

Table 3-2 summarizes IP classes.

CLASS	ADDRESSES BEGIN WITH	NETWORK OCTETS	HOST OCTETS
A	1-126	First	Last three
B	128-191	First two	Last two
C	192-223	First three	Last

Not all of the bit combinations in the 32-bit IP address are available for assignment to networks and hosts. There are some IP addresses that are used for private networks, testing, and link management functions between nodes on a network. (See the Invalid Addresses and Private IP Addresses sections in this chapter for more information.)

Subnets

A **subnet** means that a single IP address is used to represent more than one network. Workstations use a subnet mask to determine which network they are located on.

A class B network address may contain $2^{16} = 65,536$ individual host addresses. This represents a huge network, a network that's not likely to be found in a practical situation. In order to permit networks that are of a manageable size, IP addresses are routinely subnetted using a **subnet mask**.

A conventional subnet mask corresponds to the decimal number 255 placed in the network portion of an IP address. Each of the three classes of IP addresses has a subnet mask, as in:

- Class A Subnet: 255.0.0.0
- Class B Subnet: 255.255.0.0
- Class C Subnet: 255.255.255.0

A workstation uses the subnet mask to determine if a message is to remain in the same network, or if the message is to be sent to another network. The workstation will perform a logical AND operation between the source IP address and the source subnet mask, and the destination IP address and the source subnet mask.

Table 3-3 illustrates the truth table used for the logical AND operation. Notice that the only time the X-output is equal to a logical 1 is when both A and B inputs are logical 1s. For any other combination of the A and B inputs, the X-output will be a logical 0.

If the result of the AND comparison is the same, the workstation will send the message directly to the node on its network. But if the two aren't the same, the workstation will send the message to a router. The router will then determine where the destination network is located.

Notice that a subnet mask is required in order to connect to the Internet. The reason for this is that the workstation won't be able to determine whether a message is to remain on a local network, or if it is to be sent to another network.

Table 3-3 Logical AND Operation

A INPUT	B INPUT	X INPUT
0	0	0
0	1	0
1	0	0
1	1	1

Let's work through an example. Figure 3-2 shows a typical application of IP subnets. Network A contains two workstation nodes labeled A1 and A2. Network B contains a workstation node labeled B1. The two networks are connected with a router.

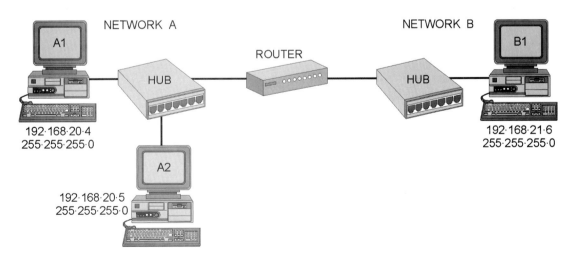

Figure 3-2 Subnet Mask Application

When A1 sends a message to A2, the steps for reconciling the route are as follows:

1. A1 converts its 32-bit IP address to binary.

    102.168.20.4 is 11000000.10101000.00010100.00000100

2. A1 performs a logical AND operation of its IP address and the subnet mask 255.255.255.0.

    11000000.10101000.00010100.00000100 = 192.168.20 .4

    <u>11111111.11111111.11111111.00000000 = 255.255.255.0</u>

    11000000.10101000.00010100.00000000 = 192.168.20 .0

3. A1 converts the destination IP address to binary.

    192.168.20.5 is 11000000.10101000.00010100.00000101

4. A1 performs a logical AND operation between the destination IP address and the source subnet mask 255.255.255.0.

    11000000.10101000.00010100.00000101 = 192.168.20 .6

    <u>11111111.11111111.11111111.00000000 = 255.255.255.0</u>

    11000000.10101000.00010100.00000000 = 192.168.20 .0

5. A1 compares the results of both AND operations. If the two are the same, the message is destined for a node on the local subnet. As you can see, the network portions of both ANDed results are the same; consequently, A1 will send the message directly to A2.

If the two aren't the same, A1 will send the message to the router, and the router will assume responsibility for locating the remote network. For example, assume A1 sends a message to B1. The steps are repeated for B1 as follows:

1. A1 converts its 32-bit IP address to binary.

    102.168.20.4 is 11000000.10101000.00010100.00000100

2. A1 performs a logical AND operation of its IP address and the subnet mask 255.255.255.0.

    11000000.10101000.00010100.00000100 = 192.168.20 .4

    <u>11111111.11111111.11111111.00000000 = 255.255.255.0</u>

    11000000.10101000.00010100.00000000 = 192.168.20 .0

3. A1 converts the destination IP address to binary.

    192.168.21.6 is 11000000.10101000.00010101.00000110

4. A1 performs a logical AND operation between the destination IP address and the source subnet mask 255.255.255.0.

$$11000000.10101000.00010101.00000110 = 192.168.21 .6$$

$$\underline{11111111.11111111.11111111.00000000 = 255.255.255.0}$$

$$11000000.10101000.00010100.00000000 = 192.168.21 .0$$

5. A1 compares the results of both AND operations. Because the masked network portions of the source and destination IP addresses aren't the same, A1 will deliver the message to the router. The router will then reconcile the network address to Network B.

The example of IP subnets shown in Figure 3-2 is conveniently masked at the end of the third octet with 255.255.255.0. This permitted 256 host addresses ($2^8 = 256$). But, what if you needed to divide the 256-node network into two smaller networks consisting of 128 nodes each? All that's required is to reposition the mask. Figure 3-3 shows an example of a subnet that extends into the fourth octet.

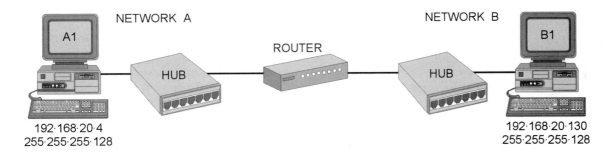

NETWORK A
NETWORK B
A1
B1
ROUTER
HUB
HUB
192·168·20·4
255·255·255·128
192·168·20·130
255·255·255·128

Figure 3-3 Extending the Subnet Mask

Notice in Figure 3-3 that the 192.168.20 subnet has been divided into two subnets with the subnet mask 255.255.255.128. The subnets will be numbered 192.168.20.1 through .126, and 192.168.20.129 through .254. When node A1 sends a message, the logic used to determine if the destination node is on the same subnet, or on another subnet, follows the same steps as described above. Assume that the message is to be sent to node B1.

1. A1 converts its 32-bit IP address to binary.

$$192.168.20.4 \text{ is } 11000000.10101000.00010100.00000100$$

2. A1 performs a logical AND operation of its IP address and the subnet mask 255.255.255.128.

$$11000000.10101000.00010100.00000100 = 192.168.20 .4$$

$$\underline{11111111.11111111.11111111.10000000 = 255.255.255.0}$$

$$11000000.10101000.00010100.00000000 = 192.168.20 .0$$

3.   A1 converts the destination IP address to binary.

192.168.20.130 is 11000000.10101000.00010100.10000010

4.   A1 performs a logical AND operation between the destination IP address and the source subnet mask, 255.255.255.128.

11000000.10101000.00010100.10000011 = 192.168.20 .130

<u>11111111.11111111.11111111.10000000 = 255.255.255.128</u>

11000000.10101000.00010100.10000000 = 192.168.20 .128

5.   A1 compares the results of both AND operations. Since the results differ, A1 will send the message to the router, and the router will determine the best route to the destination network.

Invalid IP Addresses

this host

this network

IP includes several special addresses that are invalid. All 0s in the host or network fields are interpreted to mean **this host**, or **this network**. When a host does not know the number of the network it's attached to, it may send a message with all 0s in the network field, meaning "this network." Other hosts will respond to the request with the network number, and the host records it for future transmissions.

For example, a workstation with an IP address of 192.168.20.24 sends a message with 0.0.0.24 in the source IP address field This means that the workstation has a host address of .24 but doesn't know its network address. Other workstations will send a response with 192.168.20.x in the network portion of their source IP address fields. The workstation with host address .24 will then learn it has a network address of 192.168.20.

The same workstation may not know its host address or its network address. In this situation, the workstation sends 0.0.0.0 as its source IP address. Other stations will send a return message that has 192.168.20.24 in the destination IP address field. The workstation will then know it is host .24 on network 192.168.20.

An IP address that contains the decimal number 255 is also invalid. The number 255 is reserved for network broadcasts. When a node has a message to send to all other nodes on the network, the decimal number 255.255.255.255 can be placed in the destination IP address field and all nodes will receive the message.

loopback address test

Any network address beginning with 127 is an invalid address. The network address 127 is reserved for testing. A common test is 127.0.0.1, or a **loopback address test**. This test IP address is entered at a workstation or server to determine if the network interface card (the NIC card) is operational. A packet sent to a local loopback address never arrives on the network wire.

To perform the local loopback test, you enter the local loopback IP address in conjunction with the ping command (for more information on ping and other TCP/IP diagnostic utilities, see the section titled Diagnostic Tools later in this chapter).

The following describes the steps for conducting a local loopback test:

1. Start the DOS shell on a Windows 9x workstation, NT server, or NT workstation, Windows 2000 workstation, or Windows ME workstation.

2. At the DOS shell command prompt, enter ping 127.0.0.1.

3. The screen will return a series of packets sent to the NIC card installed in the workstation or server. A successful loopback means that the card is communicating with the network software installed in the workstation or server. Figure 3-4 shows an example of a successful loopback test.

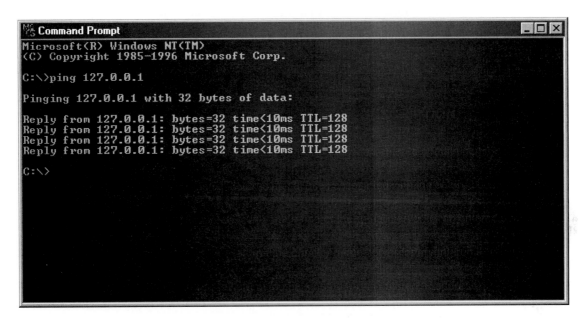

Figure 3-4 Successful Local Loopback Test

4. If the test is unsuccessful, it means that a network protocol hasn't been configured for the server or workstation, or it may mean that the NIC isn't working correctly.

Table 3-4 summarizes invalid IP addresses.

INVALID IP ADDRESS	DESCRIPTION
0.0.0.0	Reserved for unknown IP addresses.
255.255.255.255	Reserved for broadcast addresses.
127.x.x.x	Reserved for testing and troubleshooting.

Table 3-4 Summary of Invalid IP Addresses

Private IP Addresses

private IP addresses

proxy server

A range of IP addresses have been reserved for experiments, and for networks that aren't connected to the Internet. These IP addresses are called **private IP addresses**.

Private IP address schemes are commonly used for intranets in which the workstations don't connect directly to the Internet. Instead, the connection is made through a **proxy server**. A proxy server converts private IP addresses to conventional IP addresses. The conventional IP address—which is tracked by the proxy server—is the address that is communicated to the Internet on behalf of the network workstation. A network administrator will devise the addressing scheme for all workstations connected to the network side of the intranet. The proxy server will supply a valid IP address when a packet arrives from the workstation that's intended for the Internet.

You may need to conduct network experiments on occasion. For example, you may need to test a piece of hardware such as a bridge or a router before actually integrating it into a network. For testing and experimental purposes, you can use private IP addresses to configure servers and workstations or routers.

The IP addresses reserved for private networks are shown in Table 3-5.

Table 3-5 Summary of Experimental IP Addresses

IP ADDRESS CLASS	EXPERIMENTAL IP ADDRESS
Class A	10.x.x.x
Class B	172.16.x.x through 172.32.x.x
Class C	192.168.x.x

For example, you can configure workstations on a LAN with TCP/IP by using the class C network IP address 192.168.x.x. The third octet should be consistent for all workstations, and the last octet will be unique for each workstation. In other words, two workstations may have IP addresses of 192.168.20.24 and 192.168.20.25. Note that in this example, the subnet mask for the workstation will be configured for 255.255.255.0.

A private IP address can only be used on networks that aren't connected to the Internet because they can't be globally routed. If you attempt to use an experimental IP address with the Internet, the connection will fail because Internet routers won't return packets to an experimental IP address. For example, if your workstation uses the private IP address 10.100.10.15 with a subnet mask of 255.0.0.0, you won't be able to connect to the Internet because routers and servers will reject the address.

You may choose to use a private IP addressing scheme. A private IP address can be anything you want it to be, but there are a couple of basic rules:

- A private IP address must follow the four-octet format of a public (conventional) IP address.

- The value of each octet cannot exceed 255.

- If you subnet the network, no two subnets can have the same host number (this is also true for a network that uses the standard scheme for private IP addresses or conventional IP addresses).

A private IP address scheme is appropriate for a network that will never be connected directly to the Internet. If, at some time in the future, you believe that the network will be connected to the Internet, use public IP addresses and save yourself the trouble of a considerable IP address reconfiguration.

DNS STRUCTURE

DNS, or Domain Name Service, is used to translate Internet domain names to IP addresses. A domain name is the name of an Internet site, such as netscape.com. When an Internet domain name is entered into a Web browser, DNS will reconcile the name to a static IP address that has been assigned to the name.

A server on the Internet has no understanding of domain names; it only understands numbers, and particularly IP addresses. To reach a Web site on the Internet, all routers between your computer and the remote Web site server must be supplied with the IP address of the remote server. If you know the IP address of the remote server, you can enter it in the address field of a Web browser, and you'll connect to the Web site associated with the IP address that was entered.

Realizing that not many of us were keen on memorizing long lists of IP addresses, the designers of the Internet created DNS. DNS permits you to enter the domain name of the remote Web site server without knowing the assigned IP address of the server. The translation of the domain name to an IP address will be handled automatically with DNS servers.

Background Info

An Internet domain name is unique for all domain names used on the Internet. No two identical domain names are permitted. A domain name must be formally registered as described in Chapter 7, in the section DNS Structure.

Likewise, the IP address assigned to a domain name is unique for all IP addresses used on the Internet. No two Web sites will have the same IP address.

A registered domain name can't be accessed until an IP address has been assigned to it. However, a remote server or Web site that has been assigned an IP address can be reached by entering the IP address in the address window of a Web browser—even if the site doesn't have an assigned domain name.

Domain names were created as a convenience for users. Without them, navigating the Internet would be difficult, but not impossible. But without IP addresses (or a similar addressing scheme) navigating the Internet would be impossible.

DNS Zones and Country Codes

zone

DNS reconciles domain names to IP addresses by first examining the **zone** portion of the name. The zone of a domain name consists of three letters that broadly describe the type of Internet site. Examples of zones include .com, .org, and .edu. Table 3-6 lists common zone names.

Table 3-6 Internet Zone Designations

ZONE	DESCRIPTION
com	Commercial organization
edu	Educational institution
gov	State and federal government departments
int	International
mil	Military sites
net	Network-specific sites
org	Non-profit organizations

A zone is important to the DNS system because a domain name is interpreted from right to left. That is, when you enter a domain name such as internet.com, the DNS system will first look at the .com portion of the name during the IP address translation. Once the zone is identified, the remainder of the name will be reconciled.

In North America, domain names end with the zone. But outside of North America, a country code is included with the name. For example, an Internet site in the United Kingdom would be entered as internet.com.uk. The country code for the United States is us. You can include it with a domain name if you want, but DNS servers in North America will ignore it. When a site based in the United States is entered in a browser from outside the U.S., it's not necessary to add the .us suffix. For example, entering internet.com.us and internet.com will take you to the same Web site.

Table 3-7 shows a list of common country codes.

Table 3-7 Common Country Codes

ZONE	COUNTRY CODE	ZONE	COUNTRY CODE
au	Australia	it	Italy
at	Austria	jp	Japan
be	Belgium	nl	Netherlands
ca	Canada	no	Norway
dk	Denmark	ru	Russian Federation
fi	Finland	es	Spain
fr	France	se	Sweden
de	Germany	ch	Switzerland
in	India	tw	Taiwan
il	Israel	uk	United Kingdom

DNS Server Hierarchy

The DNS system follows a hierarchical structure when reconciling domain names to an IP address. The structure is pictured in Figure 3-5.

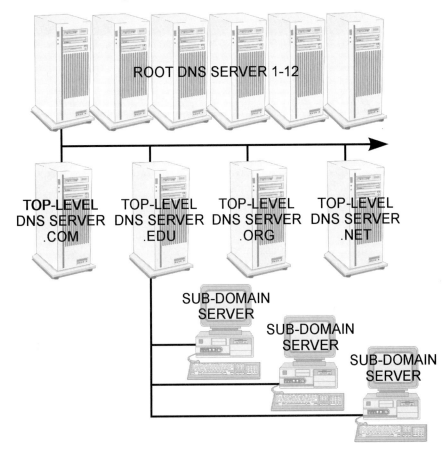

Figure 3-5 DNS Server Hierarchy

At the top of the hierarchy is a **root DNS server**. All DNS requests forwarded to the Internet are initially sent to a root server. A root server has authority for all zone designations. There are currently twelve root DNS servers in the United States.

Next in the hierarchy are **top-level domain servers**. A top-level domain server is specialized to a zone. For example, there are top-level DNS servers for .com. There are other top-level domain servers for .edu. There are still other top-level domain servers for .org. There are thousands of top-level domain servers. All root DNS servers know where all top-level domain servers are located.

When a domain name is sent to a root server, the root server examines the zone, then forwards the request to the appropriate top-level domain server. For example, if a root server receives the domain name internet.com, it will look only at the .com portion of the name, then forward the name to a .com top-level domain server.

root DNS server

top-level domain servers

Background Info

A root DNS server can translate domain names to IP addresses. Because the root servers in the United States can reconcile IP addresses to domain servers, they also function as top-level domain servers. But the root server is usually too busy to perform the translation.

sub-domain servers

Top-level domain servers are frequently subdivided. The subdivisions are called **sub-domain servers**. The purpose of a sub-domain server is to handle frequently accessed sites, or to refer a domain request to another country. For example, a sub-domain server may be specialized for .com.uk DNS requests. The sub-domain server will refer all .com.uk requests to a root server in the United Kingdom.

Let's look at an example of a DNS request as shown in Figure 3-6. The workstation user enters the Internet domain name internet.com into a Web browser. The domain name is first sent to a local DNS server. The local DNS server may be located at an ISP (for stand-alone users), or it may be located on the same network as the workstation. The local DNS server will attempt to reconcile internet.com to an IP address. If the local server contains a match for internet.com, the internet.com assigned IP address will be included with the HTTP request sent from the workstation Web browser, and the user will be connected to the internet.com Web site.

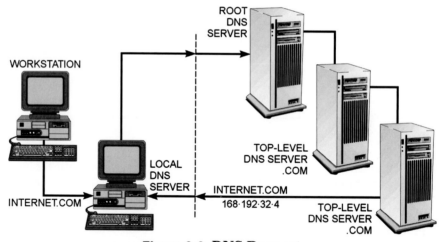

Figure 3-6 DNS Request

If the local DNS server can't find a match, the name is referred to one of the root DNS servers. The root DNS server will forward the request to a .com top-level domain server. The particular .com top-level server that's chosen will be selected based upon the least busy server that's in close proximity to the user. The top-level server may reconcile the internet.com name to an IP address, or it may hand off the request to a sub-domain server.

Once the domain name is matched to an IP address, the IP address is sent back to the local DNS server. The local DNS server will update the list of domain names and corresponding IP addresses in its database. The next time the user enters internet.com in the Web browser, the local DNS server will reconcile the name to the IP address without using the DNS hierarchy.

The IP address for internet.com is included in the HTTP protocol (or some other protocol specified in the Web browser such as FTP) and sent to a router that interfaces to the Internet. The IP address will be passed from router to router along the path to the actual site for internet.com.

If you know the IP of a site, you can enter it in the address window of a browser and you'll be taken to the site that has been assigned the static IP that you entered. For example, assume a site with a static IP address of 102.23.56.1 and a domain name of internet.com. The internet.com site can be reached either by entering the IP at the browser address window, or by entering the domain name.

But consider what happens if a DNS server fails, or if a browser hasn't been configured for the address of a DNS server. You could reach a Web site by entering an IP address. However, if you entered the domain name of the site, the name couldn't be reconciled to an IP address and you wouldn't reach the site. A quick check to determine if a DNS server is working is to try reaching an Internet site by using the IP address of the site, and by using the domain name of the site. If you're successful with the IP but not the domain name, it's likely that the DNS server is down.

DNS Entry Types

A DNS server contains records that may be used to provide information about the server to other DNS servers, or to network administrators. The records are called **resource records (RR)**. The resource that the RR contains is identified by *type*. A RR type contains specific information about the DNS server such as the domain name of the server, the IP address of the server, or the name of the e-mail server associated with a specific domain name.

resource records (RR)

To access the information in a RR, you must specify the record type. The most frequent way of entering record types is with the utility **nslookup**. The nslookup utility is entered from the command line screen of a Windows NT/2000 server or workstation, or from a UNIX server or workstation. Windows 9x operating systems do not support nslookup.

nslookup

Table 3-8 lists several DNS record types that are found in a DNS server RR.

Table 3-8   DNS Record Entry Types

RECORD TYPE	DESCRIPTION
a (a records)	Returns the IP address of an entered domain name.
cname (canonical name records)	Returns any aliases associated with the entered domain name.
mx (mail exchange records)	Returns the name of the e-mail server for an entered domain name.
ns (name server records)	Returns the primary name server for an entered IP address.
prt (pointer records)	Returns domain name for an entered IP address.
soa (source of authority records)	Returns site contact information for an entered domain name.

To use nslookup, go to the command line screen and enter nslookup record type. For example, to learn the IP address of a site called internet.com, enter nslookup a internet.com

There are several GUI nslookup tools that can be used in place of the command line version of nslookup. One such tool is called DNScape that will run on Windows NT/2000, and Windows 9x systems.

REMOTE ACCESS PROTOCOLS

remote access protocol

A **remote access protocol** is used to provide a connection from a stand-alone computer or a local network, to a remote server. For stand-alone computers and for workstations in a network, a remote access protocol is used to transfer data across serial communication links.

A remote access protocol can be described as point-to-point and multipoint. A point-to-point protocol exists between two devices. An example is the connection between a stand-alone computer and an ISP Web server. As far as the stand-alone computer is concerned, the remote server is connected to the stand-alone and no other devices. PPP, discussed in the following section, is a point-to-point protocol. A point-to-point protocol is characterized by a lack of addressing data in the protocol header. Addressing is easy because there are only two devices.

multipoint protocol

A **multipoint protocol** depends on addressing schemes in order to locate remote servers and workstations. TCP/IP is a multipoint protocol. IP contains a source address and a destination address. The destination address may be changed to reach any number of remote servers, or points, on the Internet. Multipoint protocols won't be described in the Remote Access Protocol section of this chapter. For more information on TCP/IP, refer to the beginning of this chapter.

Most ISPs or Web servers utilize a combination of PPP and multipoint. The Web server will include two or more modems that are used to establish and maintain two or more simultaneous connections to the single Web server.

In the following sections, the characteristics of three remote access protocols are discussed. The protocols are PPP, SLIP, and PPTP.

PPP

PPP (Point-to-Point Protocol)

PPP (Point-to-Point Protocol) is a communication protocol used to send data across serial communication links. PPP is almost universally used for the connection between stand-alone computers and an ISP.

Beyond the physical characteristics of the protocol, PPP specifies three components that comprise the protocol:

- The PPP Link Layer Protocol
- The PPP Link Control Protocol
- The PPP Network Control Protocol

The **Link Layer Protocol** describes the frame format and operation between two connected nodes. The length of the frame is set by default to 1,500 bytes. It includes a 1-byte start flag (01111110) that's used to denote the beginning of the frame. A 1-byte control field is used to specify the frame as unsequenced, which means that acknowledgments aren't sent between the nodes. An error detection field that consists of two to four bytes, is used to detect bit errors in the frame. A protocol field is used to indicate the Network layer protocol that's used (such as IP or IPX). A data field is included in the frame that contains user data and upper layer protocol information.

User data is placed in the data field of a PPP frame along with protocol headers from upper layer protocols such as TCP and IP. For example, when a stand-alone computer connects to an ISP, the computer is assigned an IP address for the duration of the Internet session. The assigned IP address is placed (encapsulated) in the data field.

The **Link Control Protocol** is responsible for setting up, configuring, maintaining, and terminating the connection. During establishment and configuration, the **maximum receive unit (MRU)** is specified. The MRU is the maximum length of the data field in the PPP frame. The quality of the link is tested to determine if it's sufficient for communication to occur between the two nodes. Negotiation for Network layer protocols is handled by the Link Control Protocol. Network protocols can be set up and taken down at any time during the communication, and may be run simultaneously. But, both ends of the link have to agree on what protocols will be used.

The **Network Control Protocol** is concerned with negotiating the dynamic allocation of IP addresses. Dynamic IP address allocation means that IP addresses are temporarily assigned by a server to a computer or workstation. Depending on the Network layer protocol specified in the protocol field of the PPP frame, this layer will respond differently.

PPP may, as an option, use **authorization protocols** when the link is first set up. An authorization protocol is a security measure that ensures that the user who requests access to the remote server is a valid user.

There are two types of authorization protocols commonly used with PPP:

- **Password Authentication Protocol (PAP):** Requires the user to enter a username and password. The remote server then compares the username and password to the list of usernames and passwords in its database. If it finds a match, the connection is opened.

- **Challenge Handshake Authentication Protocol (CHAP):** The server generates a random string of bits and sends them, along with its hostname, to the client. The client uses the hostname to look up a cipher key, encrypts the random string, and sends it back to the host. The host uses the same key to decrypt the random string. If it matches the original random string sent to the client, the connection is opened.

Link Layer Protocol

Link Control Protocol

maximum receive unit (MRU)

Network Control Protocol

authorization protocols

Password Authentication Protocol (PAP)

Challenge Handshake Authentication Protocol (CHAP)

PPP runs transparently across any Physical layer interface, such as EIA/TIA-232, V.35, EIA/TIA-422, or EIA/TIA-423. PPP doesn't specify data rates. The type of bandwidth technology dictates the actual data rate. For example, a connection over dial-up telephone lines won't exceed 53 Kbps. The protocol does require that the link be full duplex and use either asynchronous or synchronous operation.

Table 3-9 summarizes the characteristics of PPP.

Table 3-9 PPP Summary

PARAMETER	PPP CHARACTERISTIC
IP Address Assignment	Dynamic
Configuration Method	Automatic
Protocols Supported	TCP, IP, IPX, DECNet, AppleTalk
User Authentication	CHAP, PAP

SLIP

Serial Line Interface Protocol (SLIP)

SLIP, or **Serial Line Interface Protocol**, is used to connect two nodes in a point-to-point configuration. The most common application is the connection between a stand-alone computer and a remote server at an ISP.

SLIP is the forerunner to PPP. While the two remote access protocols share a similar purpose in connecting two nodes using serial communication, there are significant differences in the capabilities of the two.

SLIP can only transport TCP/IP. That is, if the workstations on a network are using the NetWare Network layer protocol IPX, they can't use SLIP to connect to an Internet ISP. Normally, this is more of an inconvenience than a problem because most remote access connections will use TCP/IP.

With SLIP, many configuration parameters are set up manually. The most important is the IP address. An IP address used in a SLIP connection is static. The address is assigned to the workstation that will be using SLIP to access the remote server. The disadvantage of a static IP address, compared to dynamic IP addresses, is that the IP address is assigned even if the workstation user isn't accessing the remote server. Because the IP address is permanently assigned, other workstations or computers can't use it.

Maximum Transmission Unit (MTU)

Other parameters may also need to be set up manually. For example, MRU (maximum receive unit) must be manually configured when SLIP is installed. MRU is the maximum length of the data field in a SLIP (and PPP) frame. Another parameter that must be manually configured for SLIP is **Maximum Transmission Unit (MTU)**, which is the maximum size of the frame.

Another drawback of SLIP is that it doesn't support logon authentication. Logon authentication refers to a mechanism whereby the user that logs on has the actual permission to log on to a remote host. PPP uses PAP or CHAP for authentication. SLIP doesn't support logon authentication. The logon is generated manually with a text script that traverses to the remote server unencrypted.

SLIP, like PPP, may be run across any Physical layer interface.

Table 3-10 summarizes the characteristics of SLIP.

PARAMETER	SLIP CHARACTERISTIC
IP Address Assignment	Static
Configuration Method	Manual with scripts
Protocols Supported	TCP/IP only
User Authentication	Manual login script

Table 3-10 SLIP Summary

PPTP

PPTP, or **Point-to-Point Tunneling Protocol**, is a protocol used to securely transport PPP packets over a TCP/IP network such as the Internet. This makes it an ideal choice for mobile users or telecommuters who need access to a remote server but lack a direct connection for dialing into the server. With PPTP, the user dials into their ISP using a local telephone number, then encapsulates the PPP packet in a TCP/IP frame addressed to the IP of the remote server.

Once the packet arrives at the server, the TCP/IP headers are stripped and the PPP packet, which may be carrying TCP/IP data or NetBEUI or IPX packets, is reformatted for the remote server. When responding back to the remote client, the server follows a similar approach. For example, if the remote server is a Windows NT machine, it may encapsulate NetBEUI packets in the PPTP packet and send them onto the Internet in a TCP/IP packet. At the receiving end, the TCP/IP headers are discarded, and the encapsulated NetBEUI frame is downloaded onto the client machine.

Notice that in order to transport various protocols such as NetBEUI or IPX, PPTP must have the capability of managing flow control between the communicating nodes.

PPTP offers two distinct advantages over PPP. It allows non-TCP/IP frames to be sent through the Internet. It requires that data be encrypted (with PPP, encryption is an option) using either PAP or CHAP. The end result is a very secure connection between client and remote server that doesn't require the use of expensive dedicated lines between client and server. In effect, a PPTP connection is a virtual private network because it uses the Internet as the communication medium.

When PPTP is used with a Win 9x workstation, **RAS (Remote Access Service)** must be installed on the workstation. RAS contains the encryption algorithms needed to transport

Point-to-Point Tunneling Protocol (PPTP)

data across the Internet. Windows NT and Windows 2000 operating systems install with RAS.

Table 3-11 summarizes the characteristics of PPTP.

Table 3-11 PPTP Summary

PARAMETER	PPTP CHARACTERISTIC
IP Address Assignment	Dynamic
Configuration Method	Automatic, with Remote Access Service software installed on the remote client computer
Protocols Supported	TCP, IP, IPX, DECNet, AppleTalk, NetBEUI
User Authentication	CHAP, PAP, encryption required

INTERNET APPLICATION PROTOCOLS

Internet application protocols

Internet application protocols are specific for services available at the Application layer of the OSI model. The applications include e-mail, file transfers, newsgroup access, Web file transfers, and remote printing applications.

The following sections describe how each of the protocols are used with the Internet.

TCP/IP

Transmission Control Protocol/Internet Protocol (TCP/IP)

TCP/IP is the **Transmission Control Protocol/Internet Protocol**. TCP/IP was described at length at the beginning of this chapter. TCP/IP is a required protocol for using the Internet.

TCP provides reliability for end users such as a client workstation and a remote server. IP provides logical addresses that are reconciled from domain names so that servers on the Internet can be located.

As mentioned previously, TCP/IP is the primary protocol used on the Internet. Even when a RAS protocol such as PPTP is used between workstation and server, TCP/IP is still used to transport the data. This is true for networks such as virtual private networks (VPNs, which use the Internet as a networking infrastructure between communication devices) that are implemented for proprietary networks that run IPX or NetBEUI.

HTTP

HTTP, or **HyperText Transfer Protocol**, is a client-server protocol used to send and receive files on the Internet. A client is any network workstation that sends a request to a Web server. A client may be a stand-alone computer connected to the Internet through an ISP, or it may be a workstation on a network that is connected to the Internet through an ISP. Nearly any file type can be sent using HTTP. Most Internet applications on the World Wide Web use HTTP.

HyperText Transfer Protocol (HTTP)

HTTP consists of a **request-response process**. This means that a client will initiate a request to a server for files contained at the server, and the server will respond to the request by sending the files. Let's look at an example.

request-response process

Before the client can send a request, it must be running the HTTP protocol. HTTP is packaged with all Web browsers and is the default protocol with browsers such as Microsoft Internet Explorer and Netscape Navigator. When HTTP is initiated from a workstation, the HTTP application is started at a remote server. HTTP applications are stipulated in the protocol by specifying the well-known port number 80.

From the client side, the user interaction with HTTP is straightforward. In the address windows of the browser, HTTP is entered along with the domain name of the server, and optionally, the path to the requested resource. A typical client-side request may appear in the Web browser address window as:

> http://internet.com/file.htm

When the user enters the request, the domain name is reconciled to an IP address and the site internet.com is found.

At the internet.com site, the HTTP server will respond to the request. Depending on the HTTP server software, the response may vary somewhat, but the following server response steps are accurate for most web servers:

1. **Authorization Translation**: The server will verify that the request is from an authorized source if necessary. For public Internet sites, a password and username aren't required, so this step is skipped. But for many intranet sites, a valid username and password are required before access is granted. If the site is password-protected, the server will check the username and password to determine if they are valid before processing the request.

Authorization Translation

2. **Name Translation**: The server translates the requested resource into a local file path. The resource is called a **Uniform Resource Identifier (URI)** and consists of the portion of a URL following the domain name. For example, when a user enters www.internet.com/file.htm, file.htm is the URI.

Name Translation

Uniform Resource Identifier (URI)

3. **Path check**: Once the URI is converted into a local path, the server will check that the requested resource is valid and that the requestor (the client-side user) is authorized to receive the file. This step is necessary because documents on an HTTP server are extensively linked. The URI file.htm may actually consist of many linked files, all of which will be returned to the client computer. Before sending the file, the server will ensure that the user is authorized for all of the files. The user may be authorized to receive some of the files, but not all of them, in which case the server will send only those files that the user is authorized to receive.

Path check

Object Type

Multi-Purpose Internet
Mail Extensions
(MIME)

Response

Log

4. **Object Type**: the server will next determine the type of file that's to be sent using **MIME**, which is **MultiPurpose Internet Mail Extensions**. MIME is a protocol used to standardize file extensions so that if a Web server has a file called file.htm, the client computer will know that the file will be displayed using HTML. Or, if a file is called file.jpg, the client Web browser will know to display the file as a graphic using the JPG standard.

5. **Response**: The server will send the requested file to the client computer.

6. **Log**: Once the file is sent, the server will record the transaction in a log file. Web server logs may be as simple as a brief entry that notes the time of the transaction, the outcome of the request, and the size of the request. Or they may be extensively logged to track usernames, record any errors that were generated, or note the amount of time that the server was occupied while responding to the request.

A Web server may not be able to respond to a client request. For example, the requestor may not be authorized to receive the resource, the server may not be able to translate the request to a local file path, or the path to the requested file may not be valid. If any steps of the response process fail, the server should still send a response back to the client indicating that the request couldn't be completed.

SMTP and POP3

Electronic mail
(e-mail)

Simple Mail Transfer
Protocol (SMTP)

Electronic mail (e-mail) is a staple of the Internet. E-mail is a quick and reliable method of sending messages. In addition to a basic text message, e-mail includes provisions for attaching nearly any file type to a message so that graphics, sound files, or video files can be easily sent to individualized recipients.

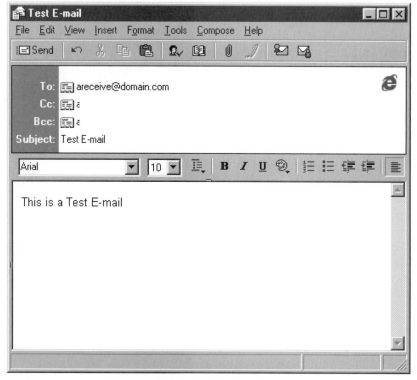

The protocol that defines e-mail is called the **Simple Mail Transfer Protocol**, or **SMTP**. Before you can send or receive e-mail, you must have access to a server running the SMTP protocol. The client workstation connected to the mail server must have access to the e-mail server that runs SMTP.

Figure 3-7 shows a typical e-mail screen with headers completed. This is typical of most e-mail software. You're required to insert the recipient's e-mail address, and (in some packages) include a subject. The message is entered in the body of the message and is in ASCII format.

Figure 3-7 Typical E-mail Screen

Notice the format of the sender and receiver names. The username comes before the @ symbol and usually represents the name of the individual or business holding the e-mail account. The domain names of the computer where the e-mail account is maintained are placed after the @ symbol. You may see that this system is very similar to DNS used with TCP/IP addressing. When an e-mail is sent, it's first uploaded into an e-mail server. (E-mail, as it's organized on most networks, follows a client-server arrangement with the sender acting as client and the receiver acting as server.) The local server will query DNS servers to resolve the receiver's address. Once this is done, the server contacts the remote server that holds the receiver's account and notifies it of a message. The two servers engage in a bit of handshaking that follows the following format:

1. Sender sends **TCP connection established**, and the receiver responds with a **receiver ready** message.

2. Sender sends a **HELLO** (Hello) command.

3. Receiver responds with an **acknowledgment** that includes its domain name.

4. Sender compares the received domain name to the name in the To: field of the message.

5. Sender sends a **MAIL** command that includes the reverse path back to the sending server. This is done so that any errors will be reported to the correct sending server.

6. The receiver responds with an **OK**.

7. There may be more than one recipient of a message, and the sender will now notify the receiver of all recipients one-by-one. The receiver will determine that all receivers are valid and send back an OK.

8. Sender sends a **DATA** command, which is used to tell the receiver that the body of the message will be sent next.

9. Receiver responds with a **start mail** input.

10. The sender sends the message line by line.

11. The receiver sends an OK for each line received.

12. Once all lines are sent, the sender sends a **QUIT** command to terminate the session.

13. The receiver responds with a **service closing** transmission channel command.

> TCP connection established
>
> receiver ready
>
> HELLO
>
> acknowledgment
>
> MAIL
>
> OK
>
> DATA
>
> start mail
>
> QUIT
>
> service closing

The receiver may have messages of its own to send and if it does, the roles of the two servers will swap and the forging (beginning with step 5) will be repeated.

If you had a constant connection to the Internet, SMTP would be all that's needed to send and receive e-mail. If you can't send e-mail, the first place to look is to see if you have a valid connection to the server that runs SMTP.

Most of us don't have a continuous connection, even when the connection is through a network; thus, there are times when we disconnect from the Internet. If, during one of those times, an e-mail is received, we wouldn't be able to receive it because our end of the SMTP handshaking process would be turned off.

However, we still want to be able to receive e-mail messages—usually at our leisure. The protocol used to handle e-mail reception is called **Post Office Protocol v.3**, or **POP3**. (There are earlier versions of POP but they aren't compatible with version 3, and shouldn't be used.) POP3 mimics the SMTP end of an e-mail dialogue and stores the received message until you ask to retrieve it. POP3 is a client-side protocol that must be installed on the workstation in order for e-mail to be downloaded to the client. That way, your e-mail is automatic and continues to receive when you're not around to handle it yourself, or when you're not connected to the Internet.

A client e-mail package such as Eudora, Lotus Notes cc:mail, or Microsoft Outlook Express contains a POP3 e-mail client that conforms to the SMTP protocol.

FTP

FTP, or **File Transfer Protocol**, is a means of downloading files to your computer, or uploading them from your computer to an FTP server. Like e-mail, FTP retains a distinct structure, probably because it too was introduced early in the formation of the Internet. The most common application for FTP is for downloading software or software enhancements. For example, many vendors have a download section at their Web site. If you've bought a product from them in the past, you can use the site to download the latest revision of the software that's used in the product. Patches, upgrades, or fixes to problems are routinely posted at a company's download area.

Most Web browsers support the FTP service, but the degree of support varies. At a minimum, you can assume your browser will include an FTP client that permits you to download files from an FTP site. However, your browser may not permit you to upload files.

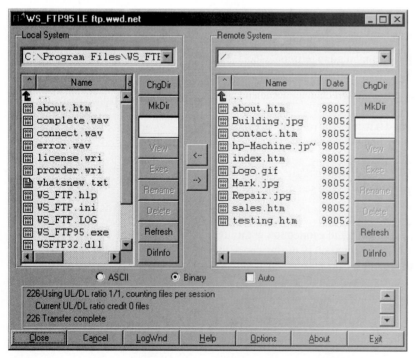

Figure 3-8 shows an FTP client (called WS_FTP95 or 98) that can be installed on a Windows 9x computer that provides full FTP functionality. To use the client, you connect to the Internet, then start the FTP client. You must know the name of the FTP server where you want to upload files, the exact directory where they will be uploaded to, and, in some cases, enter a username and password. The files are then sent to the FTP server name and placed into the specified directory at the FTP server.

Figure 3-8 FTP Client

Gopher

Gopher is an Internet database. Originally, gopher consisted of a series of menu headings that led to files of information, usually via sub-menu headings. Beginning at a top-level menu, you chose a topic and gradually descended through the menu, moving from one heading to the next. Search tools were available and the most widely used was called Archie. Much of the information contained at the gopher sites has now been converted to Web sites.

The most famous gopher is at the University of Minnesota, which is where the service was originally created. Figure 3-9 shows a screen shot of the root directory for the University of Minnesota gopher site. Note that to run the gopher service from a Web browser, you must specify gopher in the address window, as in:

gopher://gopher.tc.umn.edu

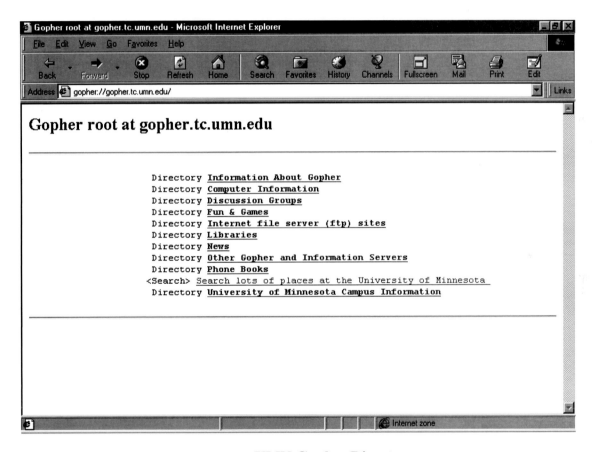

Figure 3-9 UMN Gopher Directory

Telnet

Telnet

terminal emulator

Telnet is a service that allows you to "telephone-net" into another computer so that you can utilize the resources of the computer. Telnet includes a command line interface similar to a DOS-based system. Most Web browsers do not include a client for telnet access. Most operating systems include a utility that allows you to launch telnet from a DOS shell (for Windows) by entering telnet at the command prompt. For other operating systems, a **terminal emulator** may be needed along with a telnet client. A terminal emulator is a software package that allows a terminal to mimic another terminal type.

Figure 3-10 shows a telnet screen launched from a Windows 98 workstation. With the telnet service running, you must now connect to a telnet host. The host can be specified by choosing Remote System from the Connect drop-down menu. Figure 3-11 shows the host name dialog box.

Figure 3-10 Telnet Screen

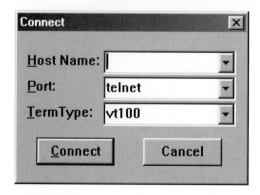

Figure 3-11 Telnet Host Dialog Box

Telnet allows a user at a remote computer to connect to a remote server. The computer doesn't have to be running the same operating system as the remote server. This is an ideal situation for a PC-to-mainframe connection because the PC will have a radically different operating system than the mainframe.

NNTP

NNTP is the acronym for the **Network News Transfer Protocol**. News is an Internet service that includes Usenet news. Usenet news is a huge bulletin board of discussion groups organized by topic. Articles related to the topics are posted on the Usenet discussion groups.

NNTP is the protocol that allows a client to read the Usenet articles from a server running the NNTP protocol. In addition to allowing articles to be posted and read, NNTP specifies how articles in the discussion groups are distributed around the Internet. Consider a typical Usenet discussion group called news.announce.newusers, which is an actual news group and should be the place to start for those new to Usenet. If an article is posted to this news group, NNTP contains provisions for distributing the article to all news servers in the world.

Figure 3-12 shows a sample news groups listing from the news client for Microsoft Outlook.

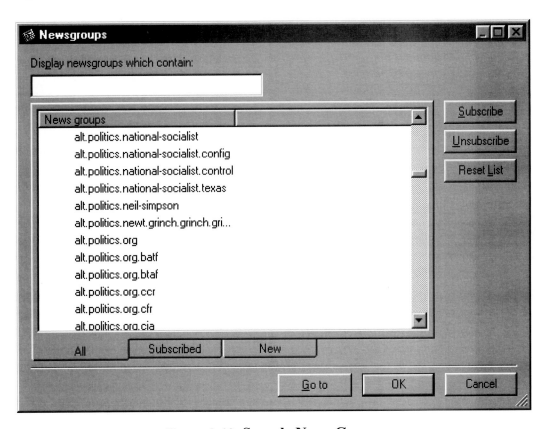

Figure 3-12 Sample News Groups

LDAP

LDAP stands for **Lightweight Directory Access Protocol**. LDAP is a client-server protocol that allows users to access remote database servers. LDAP uses TCP/IP as the Transport layer protocol, which allows any client running TCP/IP to access a LDAP server.

A user at a client computer sends a database request to an LDAP server. The LDAP server will then access the database and respond to the request. The LDAP listens at well-known port number 389 for requests (and at port number 636 for encrypted requests). When the request arrives, the LDAP server will direct it to a **Directory Information Tree**, or **DIT**.

A DIT is composed of data classes that are assigned to **object classes**. An object class may be a user, a department in an organization, or a geographical area. Each class has a number called the object identifier that is assigned by the American National Standards Institute (ANSI). Within the object identifier, a developer may create sub-object identifiers for a particular operating system. Windows 2000, for example, uses LDAP. Microsoft has been assigned the object identifier 1.2.840.113556 and may use any of the numbers from that point down with the Active Directory service included with 2000.

The advantage of LDAP is that client resources aren't taxed in order to use the protocol. Prior to LDAP, the client computer did most of the work in requesting database access, then accessing the database directly.

LPR

LPR is a **Line Printer protocol** first described in the Berkeley release of the UNIX operating system. An LPR print spooler contains the software to manage the remote print job and is installed on a print server with a printer attached to the server. The significance of LPR for internetworking is that a client computer user can use LPR to print to a remote printer over a TCP/IP connection.

LPR is described in **RFC** (**Request For Comments**) 1179. The RFC describes four basic processes handled by the protocol:

- **LPR**: Assigns a print job to a print queue.

- **LPQ**: Displays the print queue.

- **LPRM**: Removes the queue from the printer.

- **LPC**: Used to control the queue.

Users connect to the print server running LPR source software. The print server requires that each user have a name and assigns the print request a number that may range from 0 through 999.

LPR spoolers are available for operating systems besides UNIX, such as Windows 9x and Windows NT/2000. An updated version of LPR is **LPRng** (for next generation). LPRng includes enhancements not found in the original LPR RFC. These include support for redirecting print requests to multiple printers, enhanced security, and automatic job holding while print requests are being printed.

Table 3-12 lists each of the protocols described in this section and describes how they relate to the Internet.

SERVICE OR PROTOCOL	DESCRIPTION
TCP/IP	Transmission Control Protocol/ Internet Protocol, used for all Internet connections.
HTTP	HyperText Transfer Protocol, used between clients and servers to send and receive files on the Internet.
SMTP	Simple Mail Transfer Protocol, used to send and receive e-mail to an e-mail server.
POP3	Post Office Protocol, version 3, used to receive e-mail being held in an e-mail server.
FTP	File Transfer Protocol, used to send and receive files over a TCP/IP connection.
Gopher	Used to access Internet-based databases.
Telnet	Used to connect to a remote computer and use the resources of the computer, usually by emulating a terminal connected to the remote computer.
NNTP	Network News Transport Protocol, used between client computers and a news server for reading and posting Usenet articles.
LDAP	Lightweight Directory Access Protocol, used to access remote database servers without requiring excessive client resources.
LPR	Line Printer protocol, used to print to a remote printer over a TCP/IP connection.

Table 3-12 Protocols and Services Used on the Internet

DIAGNOSTIC TOOLS

Diagnostic tools presented in this section are limited to TCP/IP utilities. The i-Net+ exam specifies five tools that are appropriate for wide area connections. The tools are ping, IPConfig, WinIPCfg, ARP, and TraceRT.

Ping

Ping

Ping is a tool used to check connectivity between network devices, such as between workstations or between workstations and servers. When ping is run, a small packet is sent to a specified destination server or workstation. If the server or workstation receives the packet, it sends the packet back.

If the destination node doesn't receive the packet, a message is displayed saying that the transaction has timed-out.

Typically, five packets (called echo packets) are sent to a destination node. If the connection is good, a response should be received on at least three out of the five.

Ping is initiated from the DOS shell. At the C: prompt or equivalent, enter ping and the IP address of a workstation or server. Figure 3-13 shows an example of a successful ping to a server.

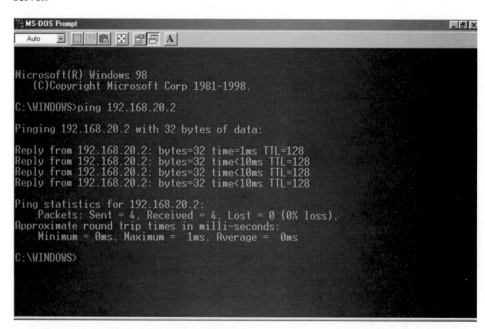

Figure 3-13 Successful Ping

Time To Live (TTL)

The notation "**TTL**" stands for **Time To Live** and is a field in the IP header. It's an instruction to any devices receiving the packet to discard the packet if the time specified in the field is exceeded. You can see the result of an unsuccessful ping by using an unknown IP address such as 123.456.789.123. Because this is an invalid IP address, an echo packet won't be returned and you'll see a message saying that the connection has timed-out.

Ping can be a helpful tool when a workstation is unable to connect to a server. The server may be local or remote. A successful ping to the server tells you that the connection between workstation and server is working. If the ping is successful, but a connection can't be made from workstation to server, then the source of the problem is likely to lie with permissions and rights to the server, rather than with a physical problem between the two devices.

IPConfig and WinIPCfg

IPConfig, short for **IP Configuration**, is a diagnostic tool used to learn addressing information about the network or computers on a network. When initiated, IPConfig will reveal IP addresses, MAC addresses, and subnet mask addresses, as well as NetBIOS information for Windows computers.

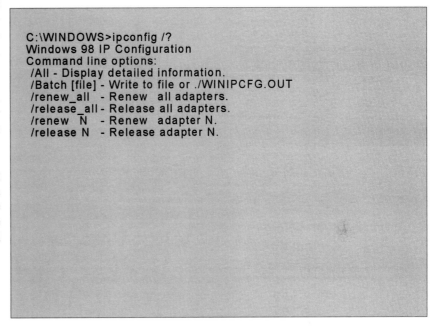

IPConfig is entered from the DOS shell. At the command prompt, enter ipconfig /?. The commands available with ipconfig will be displayed. The commands are shown in Figure 3-14.

To see the IP address, subnet mask, and default gateway address for the computer that ipconfig is entered at, type ipconfig at the prompt. Figure 3-15 shows a typical display.

If you want to see the complete addressing information for a node, enter ipconfig /all. In addition to the IP addressing information, the physical MAC address of the node will be displayed, along with the subnet mask and addressing information related to the server.

```
C:\WINDOWS>ipconfig /?
Windows 98 IP Configuration
Command line options:
/All - Display detailed information.
/Batch [file] - Write to file or ./WINIPCFG.OUT
/renew_all   - Renew  all adapters.
/release_all - Release all adapters.
/renew   N   - Renew   adapter N.
/release N   - Release adapter N.
```

Figure 3-14 IPConfig Help Screen

```
C:\WINDOWS>ipconfig

Windows 98 IP Configuration

0 Ethernet adapter :

     IP Address . . . . . . . . . . : 0.0.0.0
     Subnet Mask. . . . . . . . . . : 0.0.0.0
     Default Gateway . . . . . . :

1 Ethernet adapter :

     IP Address . . . . . . . . . . : 0.0.0.0
     Subnet Mask. . . . . . . . . . : 0.0.0.0
     Default Gateway . . . . . . :

2 Ethernet adapter :

     IP Address . . . . . . . . . . : 192.168.20.2
     Subnet Mask. . . . . . . . . . : 255.255.255.0
     Default Gateway . . . . . . :
```

Figure 3-15 IPConfig Display

WinIPCfg is the addressing diagnostic tool used with the Windows 95 operating system. The command is entered from the DOS shell of a Windows 95 workstation by entering winipcfg. (Note that WinIPCfg can be used with other Windows operating systems such as Windows 98 and ME, but ipconfig can't be used with the Windows 95 operating system.)

The addressing information that's returned is similar to the abbreviated information returned for ipconfig. An example of WinIPCfg is shown in Figure 3-16.

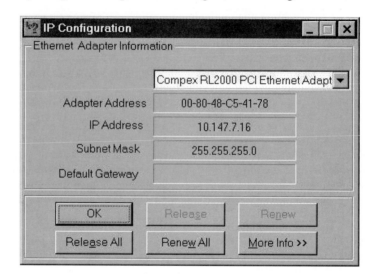

Figure 3-16 WinIPCfg on a Windows 95 Workstation

ARP

```
C:\WINDOWS>arp

ARP -a [inet_addr] [-N if_addr]

-a          Displays current ARP entries by interrogating the current
            protocol data.  If inet_addr is specified, the IP and Physical
            addresses for only the specified computer are displayed.  If
            more than one network interface uses ARP, entries for each ARP
            table are displayed.
-g          Same as -a.
inet_addr   Specifies an internet address.
-N if_addr  Displays the ARP entries for the network interface specified
            by if_addr.
-d          Deletes the host specified by inet_addr.
-s          Adds the host and associates the Internet address inet_addr
            with the Physical address eth_addr.  The Physical address is
            given as 6 hexadecimal bytes separated by hyphens. The entry
            is permanent.
eth_addr    Specifies a physical address.
if_addr     If present, this specifies the Internet address of the
            interface whose address translation table should be modified.
            If not present, the first applicable interface will be used.
Example:
> arp -s 157.55.85.212  00-aa-00-62-c6-09  .... Adds a static entry.
> arp -a                                   .... Displays the arp table.
```

Figure 3-17 ARP Commands

Address Resolution Protocol (ARP) is a convention used to map IP addresses to physical, MAC addresses. The resolution maps may be contained in servers, and are always collected in tables maintained by routers. Routers use ARP to reconcile a logical IP address to the MAC address of a physical machine.

As a diagnostic tool, ARP is used to reveal the IP address, MAC address, and Internet domain name. To see the commands available with ARP, enter arp at the DOS command prompt. The commands are duplicated in Figure 3-17.

To display information about a current connection to a remote server, enter arp -a at the command prompt.

You should see the following:

- *INTERFACE:* This is the IP of the machine running the ARP utility.

- *INTERNET ADDRESS:* This is the address of a server that the machine is connected to.

- *PHYSICAL ADDRESS:* This is the Ethernet address of the local machine.

- *TYPE:* This is the type of connection from local machine to server, and may be Dynamic or Static.

In addition to querying the ARP cache, entries may be added to it with the -s command, or deleted from it with the -d command.

TraceRT

TraceRT (also called **traceroute**) is a diagnostic tool used to show the path to a remote server or workstation. Typically, the tracert command is used in conjunction with the IP address of the remote node. TraceRT will list the number of hops to the destination along with the IP addresses of each router along the way.

TraceRT is initiated from the DOS shell. Figure 3-18 shows the commands that are available with TraceRT. To see these commands on your screen, enter tracert at the DOS prompt.

TraceRT (traceroute)

```
Microsoft(R) Windows 98
 (C)Copyright Microsoft Corp 1981-1998.

C:\WINDOWS>tracert

Usage: tracert [-d] [-h maximum_hops] [-j host-list] [-w timeout] target_name

Options:
  -d                    Do not resolve addresses to hostnames.
  -h maximum_hops       Maximum number of hops to search for target.
  -j host-list          Loose source route along host-list.
  -w timeout            Wait timeout milliseconds for each reply.
```

Figure 3-18 TraceRT Commands

Figure 3-19 shows an example of TraceRT. The information that's returned to the screen shows the IP address of each router to the destination along with the time (in milliseconds) that it takes a packet to travel to each router.

Figure 3-19 TraceRT to Remote Server

TraceRT can be used to specify the number of hops to the destination in order to determine the most efficient route. It's also a good tool to use to determine if a problem originates at the remote address, or is within the route to the destination.

For example, assume you ping a remote server but don't receive a response. The problem may be with the remote server, or it could be with any of the routers between the source node and the server. The problem can be pinpointed by connecting to the last router between the source and destination. From the last router, you can attempt to connect to the server. If the connection fails, the problem likely is with the last router.

If, however, the connection is successful, it means that the problem is with a previous router. Simply work your way back, until you can no longer connect to the remote server. The last router that you connected to—and that couldn't connect to the server—is the source of the problem.

Netstat

Netstat is a diagnostic tool used to display network statistical information along with protocol and port information. In a typical case, netstat will show the number of packets sent and received.

The netstat utility is started from the command prompt screen. To see a listing of all options available, enter netstat ?

A list of the options available will be listed on the screen

Table 3-13 summarizes the uses of diagnostic tools described in this chapter.

DIAGNOSTIC TOOL	PURPOSE
Ping	Used to check the connection between nodes.
IPConfig	Used to display IP address, MAC address, and subnet mask address, as well as NetBIOS information for Windows computers.
WinIPCfg	Used with Win 95 workstations to display IP address and MAC address.
ARP	Used to display IP address, MAC address, and domain name of remote server.
TraceRT	Used to display IP addresses of routers between source and destination nodes.
Netstat	Used to display statistical and port information for a TCP/IP connection.

Table 3-13 Summary of Diagnostic Tools

KEY POINTS REVIEW

This chapter has presented an exploration of TCP/IP and other protocols used on the Internet.

- TCP/IP is a universal protocol, one that's independent of the type of machine that it runs on.

- TCP is responsible for reliable process-to-process communication between two devices.

- IP is responsible for routing data packets from the source node to the destination node.

- An IP address consists of 32 bits. An IP address consists of two parts, a network address and a host address. The network address identifies the network that a node is connected to. The host portion of an IP address identifies the specific machine connected to a network.

- A conventional subnet mask corresponds to the decimal number 255 placed in the network portion of an IP address. A workstation uses the subnet mask to determine if a message that's sent is to remain on the same network, or if the message is to be sent to another network.

- An IP address is invalid if it contains the decimal numbers 255 or 0. If the network portion begins with the decimal number 127, the address is invalid because 127 IP addresses are used for testing and troubleshooting.

- The following IP addresses have been reserved for experimental purposes: 10.x.x.x, 172.16.x.x through 172.32.x.x, and 192.168.x.x.

- DNS extensions generally correspond to the type of Internet site. Examples of DNS types are .com, .edu, and .org.

- A DNS entry refers to the type of resource record found on DNS servers.

- The DNS system consists of a hierarchy of DNS servers that begin with a root server. Root servers delegate authority for translating domain names to IP addresses to top-level servers.

- A root server knows the location of all top-level servers and will forward requests for domain name translations to top-level servers.

- A top-level server is specialized to DNS types such as .com or .net.

- The purpose of the remote access protocol SLIP is to provide a serial connection running only TCP/IP.

- The purpose of the remote access protocol PPP is to provide a serial connection that runs more than one Network layer protocol such as TCP/IP or IPX.

- The purpose of the remote access protocol PPTP is to provide a secure connection over the Internet from a client computer to a remote server.

- The purpose of the point-to-point access method is to provide a connection between two devices such as a client computer and a remote server.

- The purpose of the multipoint access method is to provide a connection from a remote server to more than one client computer.

- The various functions of the Internet—Web access, file transfers, e-mail, etc.—are provided by specific protocols.

- Ping is a diagnostic tool used to check the connection between two devices.

- IPConfig is a diagnostic tool used to display workstation and server IP addresses.

- WinIPCfg is a Windows 95-specific utility used to display workstation and server IP addresses.

- ARP is a diagnostic tool used to reveal IP addresses, MAC addresses, and Internet domain names.

- TraceRT is a diagnostic tool used to show router hops and router IP addresses from source node to destination node.

- Netstat is a utility that displays statistical data along with TCP/IP connection information.

REVIEW QUESTIONS

The following questions test your knowledge of the material presented in this chapter:

1. Which protocol ensures that the connection between nodes is reliable?

2. Why is IP a "best effort" protocol?

3. What are the parts of an IP address?

4. What is the difference between a valid and an invalid IP address?

5. What is the purpose of DNS?

6. Describe the DNS hierarchy.

7. What is the purpose of PPTP?

8. Which protocol specifically addresses file transfers over a TCP/IP connection?

9. Which protocol is used to transfer HTML files from a Web server to a client computer?

10. To show the IP addresses of all routers between a client workstation and remote server, which diagnostic tool should be used?

MULTIPLE CHOICE QUESTIONS

1. Which of the following IP addresses is a valid address?
   a. 208.34.52.16
   b. 255.255.255.0
   c. 0.0.0.0
   d. 127.0.0.1

2. Which of the following IP addresses is reserved for experimental purposes?
   a. 127.0.0.0
   b. 124.56.82.4
   c. 192.168.0.0
   d. 255.255.0.0

3. The domain name computer.org is sent to DNS for translation. Which of the following statements is accurate?

   a. The client computer will translate the domain name to the IP address.

   b. A .net root server will translate the domain name to the IP address.

   c. The first router will translate the domain name to the IP address.

   d. A .net top-level domain name server will translate the domain name to the IP address.

4. Which of the following is most likely to support multipoint protocols?

   a. A stand-alone computer.

   b. A network workstation.

   c. A Web server.

   d. A file server.

5. Which of the following supports automated user authentication scripts for remote access connections?

a. SLIP

b. PPP

c. IP

d. TCP

6. In order to access Usenet news groups, which of the following must be set up on a client computer?

a. NNTP

b. Telnet

c. HTTP

d. LPR

7. Which of the following protocols is used to print to a remote printer over a TPC/IP connection?

a. LDAP

b. Telnet

c. POP3

d. LPR

8. Which of the following protocols is used to access a database server?

a. SMTP

b. LDAP

c. HTTP

d. NNTP

9. Which of the following diagnostic tools will display the domain name of a remote Web server?

a. IPConfig

b. TraceRT

c. WinIPCfg

d. ARP

10. Which of the following diagnostic tools is the best choice to use for displaying the IP address of a workstation?

a. IPConfig

b. TraceRT

c. Ping

d. ARP

CHAPTER 4

INTERNET CLIENTS

Upon completion of this chapter and its related lab procedures, you should be able to perform the following tasks:

1. (2.1) Describe the infrastructure needed to support an Internet client. Content could include the following:

   - TCP/IP stack
   - Operating system
   - Network connection
   - Web browser
   - E-mail
   - Hardware platform

2. (2.3) Explain the issues to consider when configuring the desktop. Content could include the following:

   - TCP/IP configuration
   - Host file configuration
   - DHCP versus static IP
   - Configuring browser

3. (2.2) Describe the use of Web browsers and various clients within a given context of use. Examples of context could include the following:

   - When you would use each.
   - The basic commands you would use.

4. (2.4) Describe MIME types. Content could include the following:

   - Whether a client can understand various e-mail types.
   - The need to define MIME file types for special download procedures, such as unusual documents or graphic formats.

5. (2.6) Explain the value patches and updates to client software and associated problems. Content could include the following:

   - Desktop security
   - Virus protection
   - Encryption levels
   - Web browsers
   - E-mail clients

6. (2.7) Describe the advantages and disadvantages of using a cookie and how to set cookies. Content could include the following:

   - Setting a cookie without the knowledge of the user
   - Automatically accepting cookies versus query
   - Remembering everything the user has done
   - Security and privacy implications

7. (2.5) Identify problems related to legacy clients. Content could include the following:

   - Checking the revision date, manufacturer/vendor
   - Troubleshooting and performance issues
   - Compatibility issues

Internet Clients

INTRODUCTION

A computer that's connected to the Internet may be referred to as a workstation or a client. Both terms, in the context of an Internet connection, mean the same thing—a computer that has the necessary hardware and software to access and utilize the services available on the Internet.

A **workstation** is the term generally given to a computer that's in a local area network. When a computer is directly connected to the Internet, it's normally called a **client**, or **stand-alone** computer. In this chapter, the terms workstation or stand-alone computer will be used synonymously with client. That is, a client is any computer that contains the hardware and software needed to access servers on the Internet.

The **infrastructure** of a client refers to the specific hardware and software used to initiate the Internet connection and to utilize the services on the Internet. As you'll see shortly, there are minimum requirements that must be met for software and hardware.

Because the Internet is composed of various areas such as the World Wide Web, e-mail, and gopher, there are various software packages needed to use any or all of the different areas.

There are also hardware requirements that a client computer must have in order to access the Internet. The minimum hardware needed depends on how the client is accessing the Internet. For example, the hardware installed in a workstation in a local network differs from the hardware installed in a stand-alone computer.

In this chapter, you examine common software and hardware elements used on the client side of an Internet connection.

workstation

client

stand-alone

infrastructure

CLIENT INFRASTRUCTURE

The infrastructure required to support Internet access on the client side varies with the type of Internet access. A stand-alone computer requires different hardware than a workstation in a network.

Common to all Internet connections, however, is a TCP/IP protocol stack. TCP/IP must be installed in any computer that will use the Internet, so this is where we'll begin.

TCP/IP Stack

TCP/IP stack

The **TCP/IP stack** refers to the software protocol needed to establish and maintain an Internet connection. At a minimum, this includes the TCP protocol and the IP protocol.

Frequently, the TCP/IP stack that's installed on a client or server includes other components, or protocols, related to TCP/IP. Table 4-1 lists common TCP/IP protocols and services that may be included in the TCP/IP stack.

Table 4-1 Components of a TCP/IP Stack

PROTOCOL OR SERVICE	DESCRIPTION
FTP	File Transfer Protocol used to upload and download files.
E-mail	Used to send and receive electronic messages.
HTTP	HyperText Transport Protocol used in Web browsers to send HTML and other file types.
Gopher	Gopher is a database area on the Internet.
Socket	A socket is used to initiate a TCP connection at a well-known port.
Utilities	TCP/IP utilities such as ping and TraceRT are used to troubleshoot an Internet connection.
PPP, PPTP, or SLIP	These are serial protocols used to access an ISP over a dial-up telephone connection.
Telnet	Telnet allows a user to login to a remote computer as if the user were directly connected to the remote machine.

A TCP/IP stack may be included in the operating system of the client or server, or it may be installed as an add-on to the machine operating system. For example, Windows 9x computers have TCP/IP installed along with a remote access protocol (PPP or SLIP), e-mail capabilities, and several TCP/IP utilities such as ping and IPConfig. Windows NT as well as Windows 2000 computers include an enhanced TCP/IP stack that includes the ability to dynamically assign IP addresses from a server using **DHCP (Dynamic Host Configuration Protocol)**. A UNIX machine may or may not have a complete TCP/IP stack. While UNIX machines are frequently used in a network, UNIX may also be used in a stand-alone environment so that a TCP/IP stack must be added to the stand-alone machine before it can be used to access the network.

DHCP (Dynamic Host Configuration Protocol)

In order to connect to any device on the Internet, both devices must have a valid (public) IP address. But recall from Chapter 3 that on a local area network, a subnet address is also needed. The reason is that the NIC in a workstation needs to determine if a message from the workstation is destined to remain on the local network, or if it's destined for a remote network. If the client workstation will be connected to a remote server on the Internet, or even to another PC across a WAN, both devices must have an IP address and a subnet address. The communication will be routed through a router. The router may be located on the same network as the workstations, or it may be located at an ISP.

Regardless, communications from a workstation to the Internet won't occur without a router.

Operating Systems

The operating system of a computer must be able to support TCP/IP before the client computer can access the Internet. Most commercial operating systems currently on the market include some type of TCP/IP stack that includes some or all of the protocols and services listed in Table 4-1.

The following lists operating systems that include a TCP/IP stack:

- Windows 9x
- Windows NT 3.5 and higher
- Windows 2000
- Apple Macintosh
- UNIX
- Linux

Some older operating systems don't directly support TCP/IP. For example, Windows 3.11 for workgroups doesn't support an Internet connection. However, there are protocols available that allow TCP/IP to be installed and run on a Windows 3.x machine such as Trumpet Winsock. See the section titled Legacy Client Troubleshooting later in this chapter for information related to older operating systems.

Network Connection

In addition to an operating system that supports a TCP/IP tack, the client or server must have the physical hardware needed to access the Internet. There are two common methods used for connecting: a network connection and a stand-alone connection.

A typical network connection is shown in Figure 4-1. Four workstations are connected to a hub along with a server running a network operating system such as Windows NT, UNIX, or NetWare. Each of the workstations and the server will have a network interface card (NIC) installed that allows them to exchange files through the hub. Each of the workstations has been configured to connect to the Internet through a "proxy" IP address. A **proxy** is an IP address assigned to the router or server that all workstations refer to when connecting to the Internet. When the router receives the proxy IP address, it dials out through the modem to an Internet service provider.

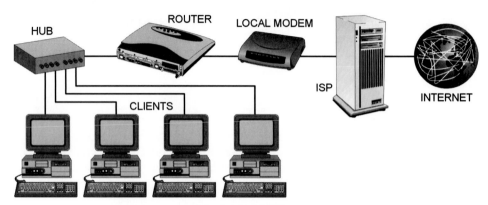

Figure 4-1 Typical Network Connection

The advantage of using the router is that all workstations are able to access the Internet simultaneously and with a single IP address. The proxy IP address protects the workstations from outside intruders because the actual addresses used by the workstations (their IP address or MAC address) are never advertised on the Internet.

A second method of connecting to the Internet is by using a stand-alone client computer. Figure 4-2 shows this scenario. A single computer with TCP/IP installed uses a remote access protocol such as PPP to connect to an ISP through an analog modem. This is a common Internet connection for home-based users.

As you can see, a stand-alone connection to the Internet is much simpler than a network connection. However, the disadvantage to the stand-alone connection is that there's a potential for intruder access to the stand-alone computer and a lack of multiple user access to the Internet.

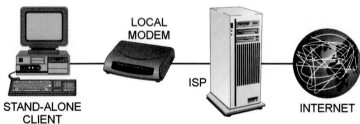

Figure 4-2 Typical Stand-Alone Connection

Web Browser

An Internet client must have a **Web browser** in order to make full use of the services available on the Internet. The World Wide Web, which is rich in graphics and multimedia content, requires that a client have a Web browser installed.

Two browsers currently dominate the market: Microsoft Internet Explorer and Netscape Navigator/Communicator. Both are available for free. Explorer is included with Windows 9x, Windows NT, and Windows 2000 operating systems. Figure 4-3 shows an example of Microsoft Internet Explorer. Navigator can be downloaded from the Netscape Web site, located at www.netscape.com. Figure 4-4 shows an example of Navigator.

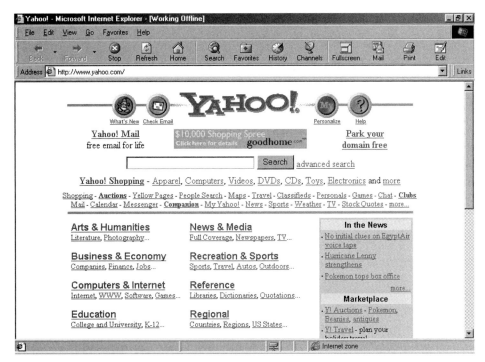

Figure 4-3 Explorer Web Browser

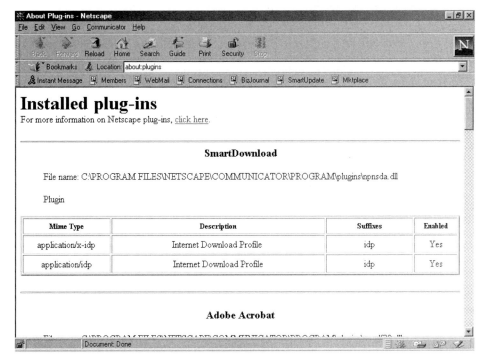

Figure 4-4 Navigator Web Browser

A Web browser includes the HTTP protocol that allows you to see and use HTML, as well as other file types. Most browsers also include full or partial implementations for using other Internet services such as FTP, gopher, and e-mail. The tools and services that are available vary with each browser and, in particular, vary with the version of Web browser that's installed.

Typical tools that are available with a Web browser include:

- *Refresh:* Refresh is a tool used to update files in the browser cache. It's used to ensure that the content displayed in the browser is the most current.

- *Home:* Home is a configuration setting that will automatically connect the browser to a default Web site.

- *Search:* Search is an input window in which a browser will search the Internet for a specified URL.

- *History:* History lists the sites that have been visited. The time covered by the listing may be configured from a session to many days.

- *Favorites:* Favorites contains a list of Web sites that have been specifically bookmarked.

The most current version of a Web browser varies with time. A new version is released when additional tools are to be added to the browser or as fixes to a past problem are developed. Be sure to check for browser version compatibility issues for any of the following:

- Failure to launch Java scripts on the client.

- Graphics files that won't display on the browser.

- Newer HTML tags are ignored.

- New digital certificates aren't being recognized. (See Chapter 6 for information about digital certificates.)

- New versions of video or audio files fail to operate on the browser.

E-mail

e-mail

An Internet client is likely to have an **e-mail** client installed. An e-mail client contains the Simple Mail Transfer Protocol (SMTP) used to send e-mail, along with the Post Office Protocol version 3 (POP3) that's used to receive e-mail from an e-mail server.

E-mail clients typically come with various options that allow you to attach files to an e-mail message, send carbon copies of the e-mail to more than one recipient, reply directly to the author of an e-mail that you received, and to organize your e-mail in address books. Figure 4-5 shows the Microsoft e-mail client, Outlook Express, that ships with Windows 9x operating systems.

File Edit View Insert Format Tools Compose Help

Send ↶ ✂ 🗎 🖺 🔍 📇 📎 ∕ ✉ 🗃

To: 📇 user@email.net
Cc: 📇 < click here to enter carbon copy recipients >
Bcc: 📇 < click here to enter blind carbon copy recipients >
Subject: Test

Arial ▼ 10 ▼ 🖹 **B** *I* U ✎, ⋮≣ ≣ ⌐≣ ≣⌐ ▤ ≣ ≣ — 🌐 🖼

This is a test email.

Figure 4-5 Outlook Express E-mail

Hardware

The hardware needed to access the Internet includes several types of devices. The most common is a **personal computer (PC)**. A personal computer must have an operating system that will support a TCP/IP stack. Nearly all operating systems in use today can support TCP/IP. Windows, UNIX, and Macintosh computers all support TCP/IP.

In a stand-alone environment, a PC must also have an analog modem to access the Internet over a dial-up connection. A dial-up connection means that the PC and modem will dial into an ISP using the telephone network. The analog modem used in the connection may be a card that slips into an expansion slot of the computer, or it may be an external modem that plugs into an available serial port of the computer.

A stand-alone computer may also use a cable modem to access the Internet over coaxial or fiber optic lines to a cable television operator. A cable modem may be installed internally in the computer or as an external modem (the most common). Figure 4-6 illustrates a typical connection using a cable modem.

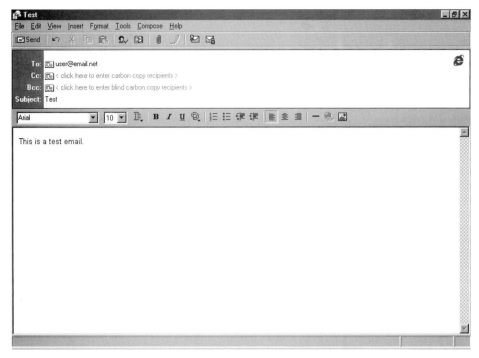

NETWORK ENTERPRISE HUB

SUBSCRIBER

BROADBAND MODEM

NIC

COAX CABLE

LOCAL CABLE OPERATOR (DOWNLOADS 27M-38MBPS TCP/IP)

CABLE MODEM

UTP CABLE

Figure 4-6 Cable Modem Connection

Cable modems use TCP/IP to transport data to and from the client computer. The cable modem has a coaxial connection that connects the modem to the CATV infrastructure. It also has a RJ45 connection that connects the modem to a NIC card (10/100BaseT) that's installed in the computer.

WebTV, which allows users to access the Internet through a television set or personal computer, frequently uses the CATV system. When a television set is used to display Internet sites, you must have a wideband amplifier that connects to the television and coaxial cable leading to the CATV operator. When used with a personal computer, you must have software installed in the computer that allows video images to be displayed. Typically, the images are sent as AVI files. While WebTV is a reality for PCs, the fidelity of the image doesn't equal that of television sets.

Increasingly, business travelers use handheld devices that allow them to access the Internet, particularly for e-mail. A handheld device may contain a modem for connection to a telephone, or it may use cellular phone technology to send and retrieve e-mail. The handheld device comes with a small liquid crystal display that permits the user to read e-mail and a keypad for composing e-mail.

Internet phone is used for **voice conferencing** over the Internet. A computer that will use Internet phone must be equipped with a sound card and microphone. Typically, Internet phone is used for voice conferencing on intranets. Users at workstations are essentially using the intranet as a voice extension of the intranet wiring infrastructure. Windows 98 and Windows 2000 client computers support Internet phone. In addition to the sound card and microphone, the client computers must be in a network (have a NIC card installed) and have TCP/IP installed.

DESKTOP CONFIGURATION

When a client computer is to be configured for Internet access, there are numerous choices that must be made. The first is to decide if the computer user will access the Internet through a network connection or as a stand-alone computer. Once the decision is made, you then must decide how the workstation will use the network resources to connect to the Internet.

TCP/IP Configuration

Before any TCP/IP services can be utilized, TCP/IP must be installed on the workstation. Typically, TCP/IP is not the default network protocol installed on a computer, except with UNIX machines. The following steps are used to install TCP/IP on a Windows 9x workstation:

1. Click the Start button and choose Settings.

2. From Settings, choose Control Panel.

WebTV

voice conferencing

3. In Control Panel, double-click the Network icon. The Network dialog box, shown in Figure 4-7, will open.

4. Choose the Configuration tab and press the Add button. The Select Network Component Type box, shown in Figure 4-8, will open. Select Protocol and press the Add button again.

5. The Select Network Protocol box, shown in Figure 4-9, will open. Choose Microsoft (or the network operating system manufacturer that's used with the network) under the Manufacturers column.

6. Under the Network Protocols column, choose TCP/IP.

7. Press the OK button.

You will return to the Network dialog box (Figure 4-7). For Windows computers, you must also enable file and print sharing. Press the File and Print Sharing button. The File and Print Sharing box will open as shown in Figure 4-10. Click both fields shown and press the OK button.

This completes the basic installation of the TCP/IP stack on a Windows computer. Now, you must configure TCP/IP for the specific environment that the workstation will be in.

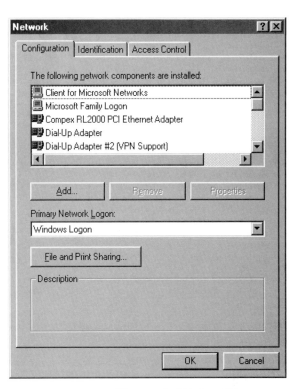

Figure 4-7 Network Dialog Box

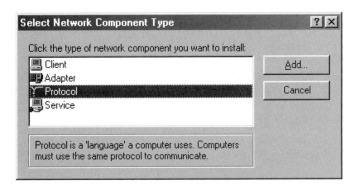

Figure 4-8 Select Network Component Type

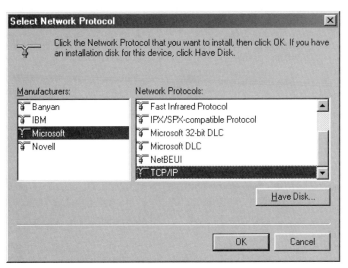

Figure 4-9 Select Network Protocol

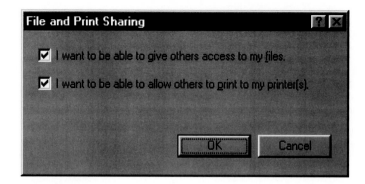

Figure 4-10 File and Print Sharing

NetBIOS Protocol

NetBIOS (Network Basic Input Output System) is a programming interface that allows computers on a network to send and receive files. Operating at the Session layer of the OSI Model, NetBIOS establishes, maintains, and terminates a connection between two computers.

Computers that have a Windows operating system installed use NetBIOS names. A NetBIOS name is given to each computer. All names must be unique and none of the names can exceed 15 characters.

When a computer is first started, it broadcasts its NetBIOS name to all other computers connected to it. The computers that receive the broadcast store the NetBIOS name of the computer. Because all NetBIOS names are unique for each computer on the network, requests to a particular computer will be ignored by all computers except for the one matching the NetBIOS name in the request.

NetBIOS is a **non-routable protocol**. This means that a request that relies only on NetBIOS names can't be sent to a network other than the local network. In other words, if two computers are connected via a router, they won't be able to communicate using only NetBIOS.

When a workstation connected in a network accesses the Internet, TCP/IP will be installed on the workstation. NetBIOS, operating at the Session layer, retains control over the connection, but relies on lower-layer protocols to route data traffic between the workstation and server on the Internet. There are several ways to configure a workstation for using TCP/IP, and the next sections describe each method.

Windows Internet Naming Service

Windows Internet Naming Service (WINS) is a protocol used to reconcile NetBIOS names to IP addresses. Once TCP/IP is installed on the workstation, the workstation will have an IP address assigned to it (see the DHCP and Static IP section for more information on assigning IP addresses).

When WINS is configured on the workstation, it will contact a local WINS server at power-up to notify the server of its NetBIOS name and IP address. The WINS server will add the name and IP address to its database of computer NetBIOS names and matching IP addresses. Then, if a workstation sends a file request to another computer on the network by specifying the name of the computer, the WINS server will translate the name to the IP address of the other workstation. Because IP is a routable protocol, the request may be sent to a computer (workstation or server) on another network though a router.

To configure a workstation for WINS, follow these steps:

1. From the workstation desktop, press the Start button and choose Settings.

2. Choose Control Panel from the Settings menu.

3. Under Control Panel, double-click the Network icon. The Network folder will open. Choose the Configuration tab.

4. Choose TCP/IP for the installed network adapter card and press the Properties button.

5. The TCP/IP Properties dialog box will open. Choose the WINS Configuration tab and the Configuration window, shown in Figure 4-11, will open.

6. Click the field labeled Enable WINS Resolution.

7. In the field labeled WINS Server Search Order, enter the IP address of the WINS server. If the network uses more than one WINS server, click the Add button and enter the IP address of the other WINS server.

8. Click the OK button.

Note that in order to use WINS, the network must have a server configured for WINS. The Scope ID field shown in Figure 4-11 is normally entered at the server and is used to group NetBIOS names so that all members of a group will be able to "hear" broadcasts sent by other members of the group.

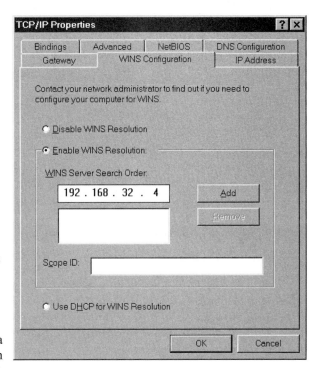

Figure 4-11 WINS Configuration Tab

When a name is entered at a workstation, WINS may not be able to translate it into an IP address. If the name/ IP address combination isn't cached in the WINS server database, the server will return a message saying that the computer couldn't be found. However, if the workstation also has DNS enabled, the server will refer the request to a DNS server for translating before returning the error message.

Domain Name Service

The Domain Name Service (DNS) is used to translate Internet domain names to IP addresses. Before DNS can be used on a workstation, it must be enabled. The network that the workstation is connected to must also have a DNS server.

To configure a client to use DNS, follow these steps:

1. Press Start and choose Settings, then Control Panel.

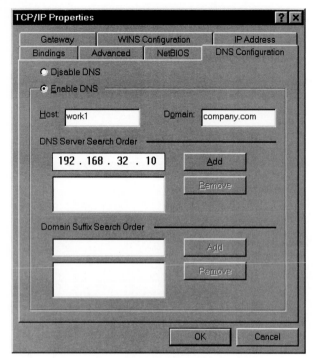

Figure 4-12 DNS Configuration Tab

2. Double-click the Network icon in the Control Panel. From the Network dialog box, select TCP/IP for the installed network adapter card and press the Properties button.

3. The TCP/IP Properties dialog box will open. Choose the DNS Configuration tab and the DNS Configuration window, shown in Figure 4-12, will open.

4. Click the field labeled Enable DNS.

5. Enter the Host name of the computer. This may be the same name as the NetBIOS name, or a name unique for Internet access.

6. Enter the Domain name that the client computer is connected to. Typically, this is the Internet domain name used by all computers in a network such as company.com.

7. In the DNS Server Search Order field, enter the IP address of the DNS server. This is usually a local server that caches a list of recently accessed Internet site domain names and their corresponding IP addresses.

8. If the network has more than one DNS server, enter the IP address of the secondary server and click the Add button.

9. Optionally, you can enter the domain names that you want DNS to search first in the DNS Suffix Search Order field.

DNS is always used to reconcile Internet domain names to IP addresses for a stand-alone Internet connection. Unless you have a static IP address assigned to the stand-alone machine, all settings will be assigned by the remote server located at the ISP.

To configure DNS on a stand-alone computer for Internet access, follow these steps:

1. Press Start and choose Programs, Accessories, Communications, then Dial-up Networking. From the Dial-up Networking window shown in Figure 4-13, select the specific connection icon, then right click and press the Properties button.

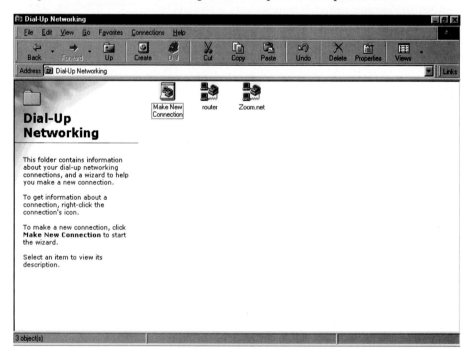

Figure 4-13 Dial-up Networking

2. The parameters dialog box for the selected connection will open. Press the Server Types tab.

3. The parameters for the connection will be displayed as shown in Figure 4-14. Press the TCP/IP Settings button.

4. The TCP/IP Settings dialog box, shown in Figure 4-15, will open. Typically, all settings are assigned by a server located at the ISP.

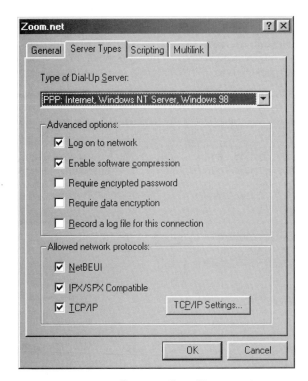

Figure 4-14 Connection Parameters

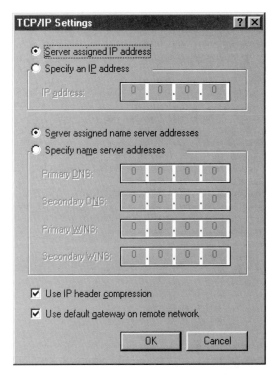

Figure 4-15 Dial-up TCP/IP Settings

Default Gateway

A **default gateway** is a router used to connect different networks. Figure 4-16 shows a typical application of a default gateway. As you can see in the figure, the IP address of the router is 192.168.20.1. When any of the workstations in the LAN attaches to the Internet, they'll do so through the router.

The IP address must be specified at each of the workstations. The IP address assigned to the router is a permanent (static) address.

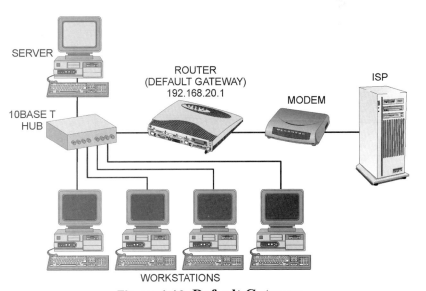

Figure 4-16 Default Gateway

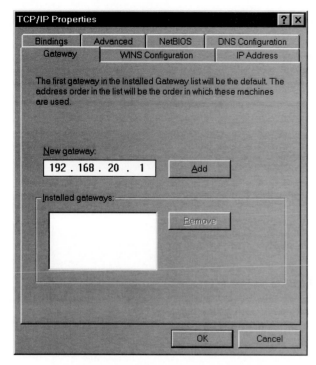

Figure 4-17 Gateway Tab

To configure a workstation with a default gateway, follow these steps:

1. Press Start, choose Settings, then Control Panel.

2. Double-click the Network icon in the Control Panel.

3. From the Network dialog box, choose TCP/IP for the installed network adapter card and press the Properties button.

4. Select the Gateway tab in the TCP/IP Properties dialog box, and the Gateway configuration window, as shown in Figure 4-17, will open.

5. Enter the IP address of the gateway (router) in the New gateway field, and press the Add button.

6. The list of gateways that the workstation may connect to will be listed under Installed gateways. If there is more that one router used to connect, enter the IP address of each router and press the Add button.

7. Click OK to return to the Network folder, then press OK again.

If the workstations don't connect to the Internet, or to other networks, a default gateway isn't needed.

Host File

host file

The **host file** contains mappings of IP addresses to computer names. If a network isn't using WINS to translate IP addresses to computer names, the host file can be manually configured to translate all computer names on a network to unique IP addresses.

The key word to host file configuration is "manually". For each computer name or IP address on a network, all workstations on the network must be updated manually. WINS will also perform computer name-to-IP address translations but does so automatically by broadcasting the information to all workstations.

The host file will be located in the Windows directory on a workstation. The file is a simple text file that contains the IP address and corresponding computer name. The IP address is listed first, followed by a space, then the computer name is listed. For example, the format may appear as:

192.168.20.5.1	internet.com	# Web site
192.168.20.5.3	roger.internet.com	# server
192.168.20.5.2	bill.internet.com	# client

The # sign is used for "comments". A comment is a note included in the file that provides some additional information for anyone reading the file. In the case of the examples shown above, the comments describe what is located at the designated IP addresses and domain names. The # signifies to the operating systems that the information to follow should be ignored.

For Windows 9x computers, the host file will be called "**hosts**". If the Windows 9x computer is in a Windows NT network, you'll also see a file called "**lmhosts**". Lmhosts is also used to map IP addresses to computer names but provides additional options, such as allowing you to specify the NT domain that the computer is in.

If a workstation is part of an NT network, name resolution will first be attempted using WINS (assuming WINS has been enabled), but if the translation fails, and there are no other means of reconciling names to IP addresses, the lmhosts file will be used. Hosts and lmhosts have been largely relegated to a backup method for reconciling IP addresses and NetBIOS names.

DHCP and Static IP Addresses

DHCP, or Dynamic Host Configuration Protocol, is used to temporarily assign IP addresses to workstations and Internet clients. Each time the computer is powered up, it will be issued a different IP address. When the computer is powered down, or disconnects from the network or Internet, the IP address is eligible for assignment to another client. A group of IP addresses will be maintained at a server specifically for temporary assignments to workstations.

The alternative to using DHCP is to use static IP addresses. A static IP address is permanently assigned to a workstation or client. Each time the computer is powered up, it will have the same IP address.

The advantage of using DHCP versus static IP addresses is that IP addresses can be more efficiently managed. Consider an ISP with thousands of home-based customers. Most of the customers will connect to the ISP for brief periods each day to check e-mail or for cruising Web sites. Once the user is finished, they disconnect. The ISP can estimate the average number of users that will use their facilities and ensure there's a sufficient supply of IP addresses. For example, if on average, 500 users connect to the Internet, the ISP can specify 500 IP addresses for temporary assignment. If the ISP has 3,000 customers, this represents a considerable savings of IP addresses.

When a stand-alone computer is configured for connection to an ISP, the IP address will be temporarily assigned using DHCP. This was described in the TCP/IP Configuration section earlier in this chapter.

When a workstation in a network is connected to an ISP, the IP address is likely to be assigned from a local server. A group of IP addresses will be specified in the local server for assignment using DHCP. But, before the workstation will accept an IP address using DHCP, it must be configured to do so. The following lists the steps required for configuring DHCP at the workstation:

1. Press the Start button, choose Settings, then Control Panel.

2. In the Control Panel, double-click the Network icon. For the installed network adapter card, choose TCP/IP and press the Properties button.

3. In the TCP/IP Properties dialog box that opens, click the IP Address tab. The IP Address window is shown in Figure 4-18.

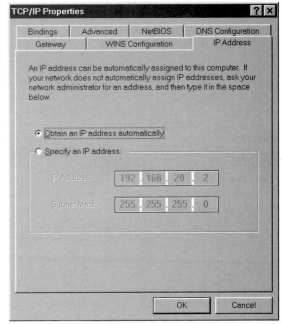

Figure 4-18 IP Address Tab

4. Click the field Obtain an IP address automatically.

5. Press the OK button.

Once the computer is restarted, it will query the server for an IP address. The server will issue an IP address using DHCP. The computer will retain the address for the duration of its session.

Background Info

DHCP at the server includes several configuration options such as specifying the length of time that the workstation may retain the IP address. The time that a workstation may keep the IP address varies from a few hours to several days. An ISP is likely to assign an IP address in the hours range.

A workstation may be assigned a static IP address instead of a temporary address. The advantage of a static IP address is that the address won't expire. To assign a static IP address to a workstation, follow these steps:

1. Press the Start button, choose Settings, then Control Panel.

2. In the Control Panel, double-click the Network icon. For the installed network adapter card, choose TCP/IP and press the Properties button.

3. In the TCP/IP Properties dialog box that opens, click the IP Address tab. Click the field Specify an IP address.

4. Enter the static address in the IP Address field. The IP Address screen is shown in Figure 4-18.

5. Enter the subnet mask in the Subnet Mask field.

6. Press the OK button.

A Windows workstation won't check the validity of the subnet mask you enter when configuring for a static IP address. This means that you can enter the subnet mask for a class A IP address, even if the address is actually a class C address. You won't get an error message from the workstation. For details and precautions on using subnet masks, refer to the TCP/IP Configuration section of this chapter.

Browser Configuration

A Web browser is used to access and display HTML documents and graphical files, particularly on the World Wide Web portion of the Internet.

Web browsers are installed in computers with default settings that require no user configuration interaction for direct Internet connections. A direct Internet connection is one in which a stand-alone computer connects to an ISP through a modem.

If, however, the browser is installed in a workstation located on a local area network, you may need to adjust a couple of settings. This section describes how to configure Microsoft Internet Explorer and Netscape Navigator Web browsers for a proxy server connection and how to configure the browser cache.

Proxy Configuration

Local area network users connect to the Internet through a **Web server**. The Web server may also be referred to as a **proxy server**. A proxy server is a barrier that prevents outsiders from entering a local area network. All addressing information sent to the Internet will use the IP address of the proxy server. Because the IP address of the workstation that's connecting to the Internet isn't used, an outside intruder has no way of accessing the workstation. A proxy server is also called a **firewall**.

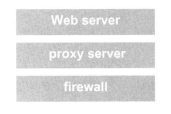

The proxy server is used to administer Internet access for workstation users. The actual physical connection to the Internet is usually via a router or ISDN adapter. Note that the server administers Internet access while a router (or ISDN adapter) provides the physical path to the Internet.

Workstation access is configured from the Web browser of the workstation. You have the option of manually configuring the workstation for addressing information of the proxy server, or you can create a single configuration file on the server and use this file to automatically configure each workstation browser.

To configure a workstation using a Microsoft Internet Explorer browser for a proxy server, follow these steps:

1. Start Microsoft Internet Explorer. From the toolbar menu, choose View, then Internet Options.

2. Select the Connection tab and your dialog box will appear similar to Figure 4-19. Enter the name of the proxy server in the Address field. An IP address may be entered in the Address field instead of the server name.

3. Enter the port number of the server in the Port field. The port number is usually a well-known port number.

4. Click the Apply button, then the OK button.

The proxy server will now supply the workstation with the addresses and port numbers for Internet services that are available to the workstations. The services include HTTP for transferring HTML documents, FTP for file transfers, Gopher for Internet gopher databases, or telnet.

The proxy can be customized by clicking the Advanced button on the Connection tab of the Internet Options dialog box. The customized Proxy Settings dialog box is shown in Figure 4-20. For each service, you can enter a specific server address along with the port number of the service.

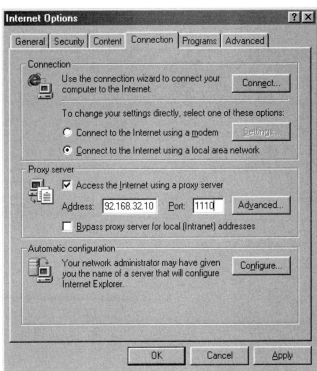

Figure 4-19 Explorer Proxy Configuration

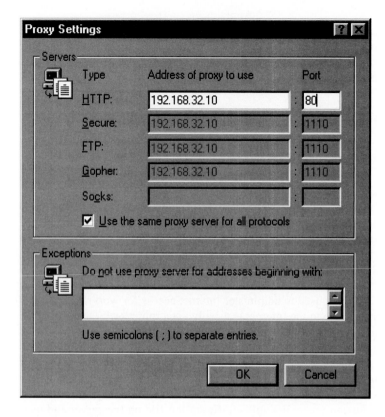

Figure 4-20 Advanced Proxy Configuration

Background Info

The port number referred to in the discussion concerning proxy servers are "well-known" port numbers such as 80 for HTTP. Assigned port numbers should be consistent with the standardized well-known port numbers. However, on an intranet that doesn't connect to the Internet, any port number will work. For Windows NT, you may receive an error message if you configure the proxy server using non-standard port numbers.

If the proxy server will be offering specialized services to users on the proxy server, use port numbers above 1024.

An alternative to customizing the address and port number for each proxy service is to create a configuration file on a server. From this single configuration file, all workstations can be configured quickly and easily. To automate the workstation configuration, follow these steps:

1. Create the proxy configuration file on the proxy server. Note that in a Windows NT network, the server must have **Internet Information Server (IIS)** running, as well as proxy server software (available from Microsoft or a third party).

Internet Information Server (IIS)

2. At the workstation, start Microsoft Internet Explorer, choose View, then Internet Options.

3. Click the Connection tab in the Internet Options dialog box.

4. Press the Configure button in the Automatic Configuration field. The Automatic Configuration dialog box, shown in Figure 4-21, will open.

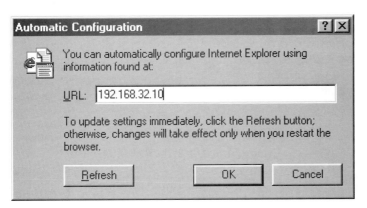

Figure 4-21 Automatic Proxy Configuration

5. Enter the address of the server where the proxy configuration file is located and press OK. Notice that a Refresh button is included with this dialog box. If changes are made to the configuration file at the server, the change can easily be communicated to the workstations by pressing the Refresh button.

6. Press the OK button. In Internet Options, press the Apply button, then the OK button.

7. The proxy configuration file will now be copied to the workstation.

Most commercial Web browsers provide for proxy configuration in a manner that's similar to the steps described above. For example, follow these steps to configure the workstation proxy settings for Netscape Navigator:

1. Start Netscape Navigator. From the toolbar menu, choose Options, then Network Preferences. Click the Proxies tab in the Preferences dialog box.

2. Click the Manual Proxy Configuration radio button, then press the View button. Figure 4-22 shows the Manual Proxy Configuration dialog box for Navigator.

3. Enter the name or IP address of the proxy server for each service along with the port number of the service.

4. Click the Apply button, then the OK button.

Navigator also permits you to use an automatic proxy configuration for workstations by entering the address where the proxy configuration file is located. Enter the address in the Automatic Proxy Configuration field of the Preferences dialog box.

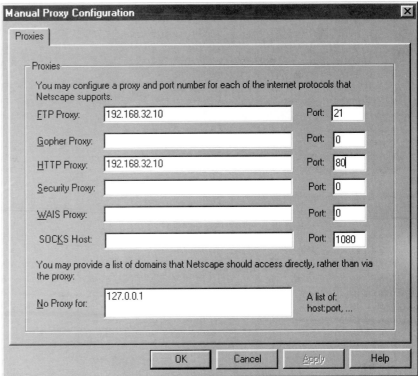

Figure 4-22 Navigator Proxy Configuration

Client-side Cache

A **cache** refers to a section of memory in a computer that has been specified for a particular use. Web browsers routinely cache information related to Web sites that you've visited. For example, the browser cache may store the URLs of sites you've visited, graphics, sound files, links, or video files.

The reason that the information is cached is that the contents on a Web site will load faster from your hard drive than from the remote server. Typically, the browser compares the information in your cache to the information at the Web site. If there's no difference in the version of a file, it's loaded from the cache. But if the file has been changed since the last visit to the site, the newer version is loaded in your browser and the older version is replaced in the cache.

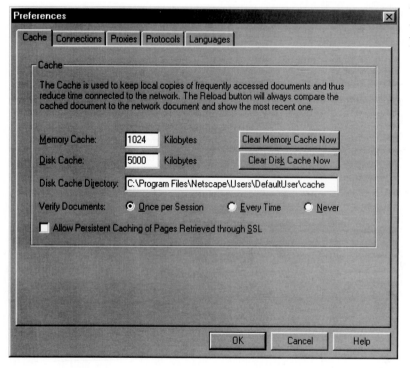

Figure 4-23 Navigator Cache Configuration

The size of the cache is configurable from a workstation. To configure the cache using Netscape Navigator, follow these steps:

1. Start Navigator. From Options, choose Network Preferences. Click the Cache tab in the Preferences dialog box. The Cache screen, shown in Figure 4-23, will open.

2. Enter the size of the amount of memory devoted to Internet files in the Memory Cache field. The default size is 600K bytes.

3. Enter the amount of disk memory to be used for storing Internet sites in the Disk Cache field. The default size is 5000K bytes.

4. Accept the default location of where the cache will be located in the Disk Cache Directory field, or enter a different location.

5. For the field labeled Verify Documents, choose whether Navigator will check Web site page revisions once each session, each time you visit a site, or never. The default is to check Once per Session.

6. Click the OK button.

A large cache may slow the performance of a workstation. If it seems to take a long time to exit from a browser, a likely culprit is the size of the cache. As an alternative, clear the contents of the cache in Preferences by pressing the Clear Memory Cache Now and Clear Disk Cache Now buttons.

In a similar manner, if you set the cache size to be too small, each visit to a Web size may result in the site files not being available in the cache. Consequently, the files will have to be downloaded from the remote Web server, which may cause the site to load very slowly in the browser. The remedy for this is to increase the cache size. So, what is best, increase or decrease the cache size? Start with the default settings for the Web browser. If you find that sites are loading too slowly, increase the cache size. If the time required to exit the browser begins to seem excessive, decrease the cache size.

Cache configuration for Microsoft Internet Explorer is similar to the steps described for Netscape Navigator. To configure the cache using Internet Explorer, follow these steps:

1. Start Internet Explorer. Choose View from the menu, then Internet Options.

2. Select the General tab in the Internet Options dialog box as shown in Figure 4-24.

3. Temporary Internet files contain the pages you've visited on the Internet. To configure the cache, press the Settings button. The Settings dialog box, shown in Figure 4-25, will open. As with Navigator, you can specify how often Internet Explorer will check for newer versions of a file. The size of the cache is specified with the slider bar. The minimum cache size is 16M bytes and the maximum size is the size of the hard drive.

4. Select the preferences and press the Apply button, then the OK button.

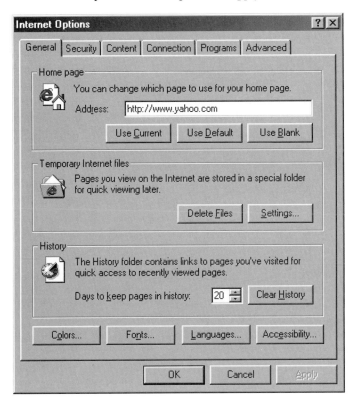

Figure 4-24 Explorer General Tab

Figure 4-25 Temporary Internet Files Settings

If the size of the cache is configured too large, the computer will slow when exiting Internet Explorer. To remedy the loss in performance, reduce the size of the cache. You can also empty the contents of the cache from the General tab of the Internet Options dialog box. Press the Delete Files button under Temporary Internet files to empty the cache. Press Clear History under History to empty the cache holding links of all sites visited.

INTERNET CLIENTS

In addition to viewing files on the World Wide Web, there are other services available on the Internet such as FTP, telnet, gopher, and e-mail. In this section, several **Internet clients** will be examined. An Internet client, when used in the context of accessing the Internet, refers to the software needed to use a particular service. To access an FTP site, for example, you must have FTP client software installed on your computer.

Most commercial Web browsers include client software in the TCP/IP stack. The client that's included with the browser is usually limited to providing the minimal level of service that most users require. For example, some later versions of Microsoft Internet Explorer allow you to upload and download files to an FTP site, but not all file types are supported. The same is true of Netscape Navigator.

In order to have the full range of services available with an Internet client, you must install the full client on a computer. Some desktop operating systems include Internet clients. For example, Windows 9x and 2000 operating systems both come with an FTP client that offers more flexibility than is found with Internet Explorer. However, the FTP client uses a command line interface from the DOS shell rather than a graphical user interface.

In this section, several clients will be examined.

FTP Client

An **FTP client** is used to upload files to an FTP server and to download files from an FTP server. One of the most common uses of FTP is to download software from an Internet server. Most software companies have download areas on their Web site. When you go to the download area, you're connected to an FTP server. When you click on a program to download it to your computer, the FTP client on your Web browser handles the transaction using the File Transfer Protocol.

Figure 4-26 shows a typical FTP site. This site is reached from a Web browser that supports FTP. An FTP server usually permits downloads of the information maintained at the site. To upload information, you need a password. An intranet may have an FTP server at which users can upload as well as download files, but uploads to a public FTP server are rarely permitted.

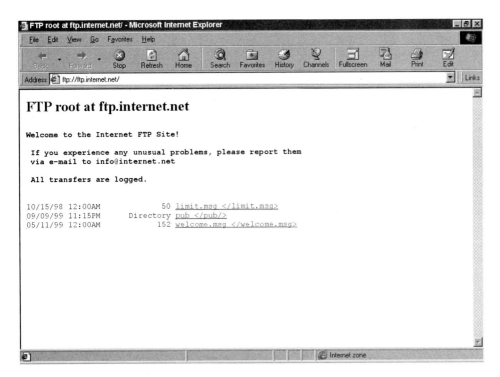

Figure 4-26 FTP Site

Windows 9x and 2000 operating systems also include an FTP client that's launched from a DOS shell. While a bit more difficult to navigate, the command line version of the FTP client allows a user more flexibility. Table 4-2 lists common commands used with FTP.

Table 4-2 Common FTP Commands

FTP COMMAND	DESCRIPTION
get	Receive (download) a file from the remote server.
mget	Receive multiple files from the remote server.
bye	Terminate the FTP session and exit.
cd	Change the remote working directory.
ls	List contents of the remote directory.
mkdir	Make a directory on the remote machine.
mput	Send multiple files to the remote server.
put	Send one file to the remote server.
connect	Establishes the connection from client to FTP server.

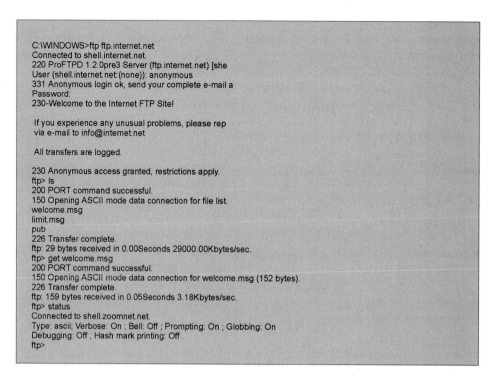

```
C:\WINDOWS>ftp ftp.internet.net
Connected to shell.internet.net.
220 ProFTPD 1.2.0pre3 Server (ftp.internet.net) [she
User (shell.internet.net:(none)): anonymous
331 Anonymous login ok, send your complete e-mail a
Password:
230-Welcome to the Internet FTP Site!

If you experience any unusual problems, please rep
via e-mail to info@internet.net

All transfers are logged.

230 Anonymous access granted, restrictions apply.
ftp> ls
200 PORT command successful.
150 Opening ASCII mode data connection for file list.
welcome.msg
limit.msg
pub
226 Transfer complete.
ftp: 29 bytes received in 0.00Seconds 29000.00Kbytes/sec.
ftp> get welcome.msg
200 PORT command successful.
150 Opening ASCII mode data connection for welcome.msg (152 bytes).
226 Transfer complete.
ftp: 159 bytes received in 0.05Seconds 3.18Kbytes/sec.
ftp> status
Connected to shell.zoomnet.net.
Type: ascii; Verbose: On ; Bell: Off ; Prompting: On ; Globbing: On
Debugging: Off ; Hash mark printing: Off .
ftp>
```

Figure 4-27 FTP Site

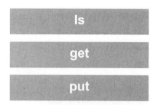

Figure 4-27 shows a screen capture of the command-line interface FTP client. (Note that the screen capture shown in Figure 4-27 is the same FTP site as shown in Figure 4-26.) As you can see from Figure 4-27, the **ls** command is used to list the directory contents. A file—welcome.msg—has been downloaded from the FTP site using the **get** command. If a file is to be sent to the server, the **put** command, followed by the file name, would be used.

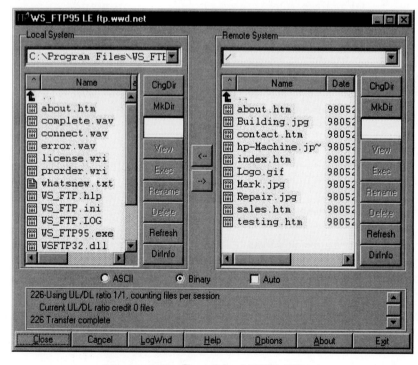

There are also many FTP clients available that provide a graphical interface for transferring and receiving files. These clients are commercial software packages that support many file types such as HTML and most graphic formats. Note that in order to use FTP, the TCP/IP protocol stack must be installed on the client machine.

Figure 4-28 shows an example of WS_FTP_95, a graphical interface FTP client for Windows 95 computers.

Figure 4-28 Graphical FTP Client

Telnet

Telnet is a tool that allows you to login to a remote computer and use the computer as if you were directly connected to it. Telnet is available as a utility that's launched from a command prompt on most desktop operating systems. Some Web browsers support telnet for specific applications such as Netscape Navigator which provides for remote connections to IBM machines using telnet.

Figure 4-29 shows a telnet screen. To launch telnet, start the DOS shell. At the command prompt, enter telnet. The telnet client as shown in the figure will open.

To connect to a remote machine, press Connect on the menu bar, and select Remote System. A dialog box will open. Enter the address of the telnet machine in the Host Name field of the dialog box.

Telnet

Figure 4-29 Telnet Screen

E-mail

E-mail is used to send and receive electronic messages across the Internet or an intranet. E-mail is conducted on the Internet using well-known port numbers to launch the e-mail process on an e-mail server. Most Web browsers support e-mail directly from the browser to a remote mail server. To initiate e-mail from the browser, enter mail and the address of the e-mail server in the address field of the browser.

E-mail

This will connect you to the remote mail server. Note that using the mail process requires no e-mail client software on the client computer; all e-mail software resides on the remote mail server. The advantage of using the remote server for all e-mail is that a local client computer is relieved of storing and maintaining e-mail that was sent or received. The disadvantage is that a user has no control over storing or organizing messages. Files on the remote mail server will be periodically purged as the mail server space fills, thereby deleting messages that a user may have wanted to keep.

From a user's perspective, an e-mail client installed on their computer provides more flexibility than storing all messages on the remote server. Although the user's account will still be purged at the mail server periodically, the user will have copies of all messages on the workstation to keep, delete, and organize as needed.

An e-mail client is installed on the local computer or workstation. There are many e-mail clients available. Most commercial Web browsers either include an e-mail client, or will launch e-mail residing on the computer.

Typical features included in e-mail packages include:

- *Address Book:* An address book is used to store e-mail addresses. Normally, a recipient's name is entered with their e-mail address. When sending an e-mail, you select the name of the recipient, and the e-mail address is automatically placed in the e-mail header.

- *Archive:* An archive tool is used to compress a large database of e-mail addresses. In a time when many business users get hundreds of e-mails each day, an archive tool allows the large amount of disk space that they consume to be reduced.

- *Import/Export:* An import and export tool is typically used to update large e-mail address databases into the client. In a business setting, there may be thousands of employees with e-mail addresses. If you change e-mail clients—to another package or to update the version of an existing package—the import tool allows you to retain the list of all e-mail addresses without entering each one again. In a similar fashion, the export tool allows you to save received e-mails to a disk in order to reduce space dedicated on the machine memory.

- *Encryption:* E-mails may be encrypted when sent, or when stored on a machine. E-mails are relatively easy to intercept and advanced network management tools allow network administrators to browse nearly anyone's e-mail. Encryption is useful when an e-mail contains sensitive data that shouldn't be read by others.

Each e-mail client on a computer must be configured for the address of the e-mail server that handles all e-mail. To configure e-mail using Microsoft Outlook Express, for example, follow these steps:

1. Start Outlook Express. From the menu bar, choose Tools, then Accounts.

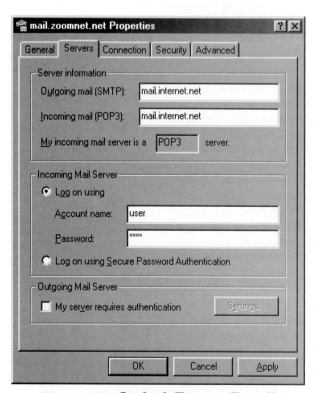

Figure 4-30 Outlook Express E-mail Configuration

2. Click the Mail tab. Press the Add button and the Mail Properties dialog box will open. Click the tab labeled Servers and a window similar to the one shown in Figure 4-30 will open.

3. Enter the name of the SMTP (Simple Mail Transfer Protocol) server, as well as the name of the POP3 (Post Office Protocol, version 3) server. Frequently, the same server handles both activities.

4. In the Incoming Mail Server area, enter the user Account name and Password.

5. Click the General tab and enter the name of the mail account. For network users, the mail account will be the same for all users. Complete the fields under User Information.

6. Click the Connection tab. Select the appropriate radio button for a stand-alone computer using a modem to connect to an ISP or for user on a network.

7. Click the Apply button, then the OK button.

Most e-mail clients provide users with various options for organizing e-mail. The options may include folders to store messages sent and received, an option for sending carbon copies of e-mail, an option for replying to a received e-mail, or an Address Book to maintain mail recipients.

MIME Types

MIME, or **Multipurpose Internet Mail Extensions**, is an Internet standard describing how messages are to be formatted in order for the messages to be exchanged between different e-mail systems. MIME allows nearly any file type to be sent with an e-mail message.

The MIME standard was first approved in 1992. Prior to the approval, e-mail was quite limited because only messages with ACSII characters could be sent. The size of the e-mail was limited to about 1,000 bytes. Once the MIME standard was approved, e-mail messages could:

- Contain more than one object in a single message such as links to Web sites, a graphic file, and a text file connected to the e-mail as attachments.

- Be sent without limits on line length or size of the e-mail.

- Allow characters other than ASCII to be sent, such as non-English languages.

- Allow various font styles to be used in the message along with formatting options such as bold and italics.

- Be sent as binary or application specific lines.

- Allow attachments featuring audio, graphics, or video.

There are hundreds of approved MIME types. To ensure that there exists an orderly process for defining a MIME type, each file to be listed as "MIME-compliant" must be submitted to the **Internet Assigned Number Authority (IANA)**. The IANA will then check to see if the file conforms to the MIME specification. For a listing of approved MIME types, go to LANTech Sweden at *www.ltsw.se/knbase/internet/mime.htp*.

A MIME-compliant email will contain the following in the first three headers of the message:

1. *MIME Version:* The MIME version is included so that any clients that receive the message will know whether the contents can be displayed for the installed version of MIME extensions on the client.

2. *Content Type:* The Content Type header specifies the format of the message that is in the e-mail. A typical entry in this field is "multipart/mixed," which means that the message contains attachments or consists of one or more replies, and contains mixed formats.

3. *Content Transfer Encoding:* This field in the header is a numerical number that describes the encoding mechanism used for the message. The receiving e-mail client needs to know this so that the message can be decoded correctly.

Many UNIX computers use uuencode (Unix-to-Unix Encoding) for sending non-ASCII e-mail. **Uuencode** converts binary files (usually graphical files) into ASCII text so that they can be sent either in an e-mail or as an attachment to an e-mail. When the message is received, a **uudecoder** converts the ASCII text file back to a binary image.

Less common than uuencode is **base64**, a file format used to convert binary data to ASCII formatted text files. Base64 is more common on older e-mail clients. The characters supported by base64 include:

ABCDEFGHIJKLMNOPQRSTUVWXYZabcdefghijklmnopqrstuvwxyz0123456789/+

The binary data is input a byte at a time into a register. The bit count in the register will correspond to the ASCII value according to the characters specified above. At the receiving end, the ACSII characters are converted back into binary.

For Macintosh e-mail users, **BinHex** is a utility that converts files into ASCII text files. An 8-bit binary stream is placed in one-byte registers and the bit pattern in the register will correspond to the bit pattern of a 7-bit ASCII character.

Many commercial e-mail packages use HTML to encode messages. An HTML encoded e-mail is sent to the recipient and can be viewed in any Web browser. HTML is a MIME-compliant file type, so attachments containing word processing files or multimedia files can be attached to it.

If you view the details of an e-mail you'll see the following MIME information listed:

- MIME-Version
- Content-Type

These two entries describe the version of MIME that the e-mail client is using, such as Version 1.0, and the type of content contained in the e-mail. For example, if the e-mail contains an attachment, the content will be "multipart/mixed" to indicate that there are more than one type of document formats in the e-mail and that the formats are "mixed"; that is, the e-mail may contain an ASCII text file and a Microsoft Word file.

MIME types are also associated with most Web browsers. A Web server will notify the receiving Web browser of the type of files (MIME-compliant) that will be sent. The browser will display those files that are MIME-compliant. A browser may be updated to include MIME types that it doesn't currently display. The update can usually be found at the browser vendor's Web site.

Universal Clients

A **universal client** contains a Web browser, FTP client, e-mail client, and occasionally a telnet client. It may contain many other options such as a programming interface for creating JavaScripts or for launching a Java file.

Microsoft Internet Explorer and Netscape Navigator are universal clients. They contain most of the tools needed to utilize the services available on the Internet.

There are specialized universal clients that cater to specific operating systems, such as universal clients for Macintosh computers and UNIX machines.

CLIENT PATCHES AND UPGRADES

Software running on an Internet client computer will need to be updated eventually. The update may be necessary because of a problem with the original release of the product or to add increased functionality to the product.

Software updates intended to fix a problem are called **patches**. For example, the vendor may discover, after the release of a Web browser, that it won't display a specific file type. A patch will be released that corrects the problem. Updates that increase the functionality of the product are called **upgrades**. For example, older Web browsers can be updated so they can run Java programs.

Patches and updates may be needed for client computers in order to address the following areas that are specific to Internet access:

- **Security**: All newer Web browsers include some type of security measures that are intended to prevent intruders from accessing a client machine and for protecting the user from accessing Web sites where downloadable files can't be verified as to their authenticity. For example, if a Web server begins to send files for displaying in a browser, the files should be MIME-compliant. But if the client browser can't determine that the files are actually compliant, the user should receive a warning message.

- **Virus Protection**: Many Web browsers include some type of minimal check for viruses that a file may contain. The problem is that new viruses are created each day and the precautions used by the browser may be out of date. A commercial anti-virus software package is the best solution to detecting viruses.

- **Encryption Levels**: Browsers are configurable for encrypting data that's sent on the Web or that's included in e-mails. The default setting for most browsers is to turn encryption off. The exception is when e-commerce sites are accessed and an order is placed with a credit card. The transaction will be encrypted at the site. When you enter credit card data on your computer, there's a risk that the information you send is not encrypted, unless your browser is instructed by the remote server to encrypt the numbers. The specific level of encryption varies for each browser, with the trend moving toward sophisticated techniques such as **public-key encryption**.

- **Web Browser**: Web browsers can be updated extensively so they'll run newer applications. Check the revision level of the browser to determine the current revision, and then check the vendor Web site to see what new versions are available. For most software, you can find the version level by locating an About file. Typically, the About file can be found under the Help drop-down menu.

- **e-mail Clients**: Because new MIME type files are frequently added to the list of approved file types, you should check for updates to e-mail packages.

The installation of software updates and patches should be proceduralized so they can be installed without adversely affecting the client machine, or other machines on a network. For example, a software patch may be released that addresses a weakness in the original software. The patch may be beneficial to some users, but not all, and may, in fact, cause some performance losses when installed. For those who need it, the loss in performance is compensated by the benefits of the patch. But for those who don't need it, the patch simply causes problems.

patches

upgrades

Security

Virus Protection

Encryption Levels

public-key encryption

Web Browser

e-mail Clients

The same is true for newer versions of a software package released from the vendor. A procedure should be in place that requires the software to be installed and tested before upgrading all clients and servers. The bugs that the upgrade addresses may not be appropriate or needed and, consequently, will only disrupt an otherwise functioning system.

test documentation

Visit the download area of a vendor Web site. You're likely to find patches and upgrades for both hardware and software. The upgrade will have a file that describes the bug or describes the benefits of the upgrade. The file is called **test documentation** because it typically contains the following information:

- Description of the bug or known weakness.

- The problem the patch or upgrade is designed to remedy.

- A listing of any known conflict that may arise when the patch is installed.

- Download and installation directions that are archived with the download.

Revision control of the product will normally follow a dotted decimal revision system. For example, a software package at the time you buy it may be at revision level 1.2. The next scheduled release of the package may be advertised as 1.3. In the meantime, bug fixes, patches, and interim upgrades may be at revision 1.2.1 or 1.2.1A, etc.

Before installing an upgrade or patch, read the vendor literature related to it. There are good reasons. It may not address your application, it may cause conflicts with other applications running on the client or network, or the cost of installing the upgrade may not be worth the benefit.

On the other hand, the upgrade documentation will also tell you pertinent information about the installation, such as configuration changes you must manually make before installing it.

COOKIES

cookie

A **cookie** is a piece of information generated by a Web server that is stored on the user's computer. A cookie contains information concerning the user's preferences when visiting a Web site. For example, most sites contain links to other pages at the site. A user may access any, or all, of the pages during a visit. A cookie can be created that determines how many users visit any portion of the site, rather than using a Web counter that counts each visit to each page of the site.

Cookies are also used to customize a Web site according to the user's preferences. Many search sites, for example, allow users to create categories related to their interests so searches will be restricted to those areas. The user's preferences for a "personalized search engine" are stored as cookies on the user's computer.

The use of cookies is controversial because they frequently occur without the user's knowledge. The average layperson who surfs the Internet doesn't understand cookies, doesn't know how to limit their use, and doesn't know how to delete them from their computer. The sections to follow describe configuration settings for Netscape and Microsoft Web browsers, as well as describe privacy implications of using cookies.

Cookies and Privacy

The setting of a cookie is a two-step process. First, a Web browser creates a cookie containing the user's preferences and then transmits the cookie to the user's browser. The browser will then store the cookie as a text file on the user's computer.

The second step occurs when the user revisits the Web site. The cookie that is stored on the client computer is transmitted to the Web server where it was initially created. The Web server uses the information in the cookie to return text and images based on the user's preferences.

A cookie is created using CGI scripts that are typically written in Perl. Recall that a CGI script executes on a server. During the request-response process of an HTTP connection, the script will be referred to in the HTML that's downloaded from the server to appear on the client browser screen. The Web server will fetch the script from the server and send it back to the client computer. When a user re-visits the Web site, the cookie that's stored on the client invokes another script to run on the server. This script contains instructions for the server to record pages on the site the user has visited, to note links that weren't clicked on, and so on.

Cookies not only save time for users, they also extend the capabilities of the Web server and client computer relationship. A single Web site can be customized to the individual preferences of thousands of users. This was the original intent of cookies and, in many cases, this is exactly what happens with them.

The use of cookies becomes controversial when the steps described above occur without the user's knowledge. It essentially becomes a breach of privacy. The issue is compounded when the server that the cookie was meant for shares the cookie with other Web browsers. Or, worse, when the user information contained in a cookie is sold—all without the user's knowledge.

Early browser versions simply admitted cookies. A file was created in the browser directory for storing them and the user had little control over the cookies. Newer versions of all commercial Web browsers allow you to specify how the browser will handle cookies—accept them, ask your permission before accepting them, and so on. The default for all Web browsers is to accept all cookies.

Background Info

Privacy protection from electronic snoops in the United States is in the infant stage compared to the European community. In Europe, data protection is provided by the European Union Directive on the Protection of Personal Data. The directive contains very specific measures that must be taken before electronic data may be solicited or shared—such as consent from the individual. The United States has no similar law protecting Web surfers against privacy invasion from information gleaned with cookies.

An interesting note is that if a corporate Web server in the United States also connects to Web servers owned by the same corporation in Europe, a company may find itself in a legal battle concerning inappropriate use of cookies.

Cookies may also represent a security breach for technically competent hacks. Whenever a browser is active (that is, when it has been started), the cookies are available to anyone who can access your computer.

Figure 4-31 shows a typical cookie taken from Microsoft Internet Explorer. The information in the cookie doesn't readily lend itself to interpretation. In fact, only the server that originally created the cookie may be able to decipher it. There are two parts of the cookie shown in Figure 4-31 that are common to all cookies—the domain name of the server that created the cookie and the IP address of the server.

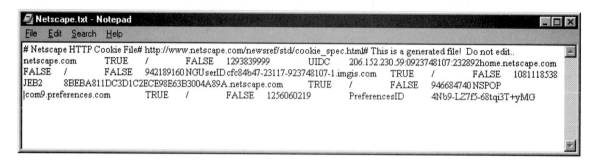

**Figure 4-31
Example of
a Cookie**

Setting Cookies

Most Web browsers contain a dialog box that allows you to specify how the browser is to treat cookies. For Internet Explorer, follow these steps for configuring (setting) client cookies:

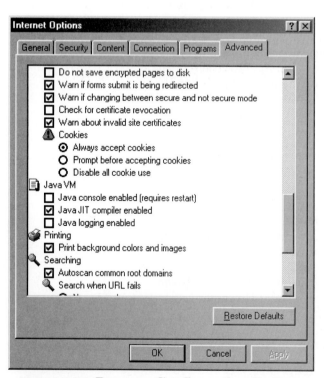

Figure 4-32 Browser Configuration Options

1. Start Internet Explorer.

2. Choose View from the drop-down menu and select Internet Options.

   The Internet Options dialog box will open.

3. Click the Advanced tab. The configurable options for Internet Explorer will be listed as shown in Figure 4-32.

4. Scroll down the Security heading to the Cookies sub-listing. You have three options:

   - Always accept cookies: When this option is selected, cookies will be created and accessed automatically.

   - Prompt before accepting cookies: When this option is selected, you'll receive a warning message each time a cookie is sent to your computer. You must accept or reject the cookie.

   - Disable all cookie use: When this option is selected, no cookies will be stored on your computer.

You may choose to accept all cookies and then edit the cookie file that's created to hold cookies. When using Internet Explorer, you can usually find the cookie folder at c:\windows\cookies. When you enter the cookie subdirectory, you'll see a listing of all cookies stored on the computer. Double-clicking a cookie will open a text file. At a minimum, you should be able to see the IP address of the server that the cookie points to, along with the domain name address of the server.

When you edit the cookie folder, delete those cookies from Web servers that are inappropriate or that are unknown.

Notice that because each cookie contains a domain name and IP address, it is a clear record of sites visited by a user. Cookie files aren't deleted when you delete an Internet cache such as Temporary Internet files.

To configure a Netscape Navigator browser for cookies, follow these steps:

1. Start Navigator.

2. Choose Preferences from the Edit menu. When the Preferences dialog box has opened, click Advanced from the Category menu listing on the left side of the dialog box.

3. The Advanced Preferences, shown in Figure 4-33, will display. You have four options:

   • Accept all cookies: When this option is selected, cookies will be automatically created and stored on the computer.

   • Accept only cookies that get sent back to the originating server: When this option is chosen, the browser will only store cookies that are returned to the server that created the cookie. The purpose of this option is to avoid the practice of copying cookies and replicating them to other servers.

   • Disable cookies: When this option is selected, no cookies will be accepted by the browser.

   • Warn me before accepting a cookie: This option may be used with either of the first two options described above.

The cookies used with Navigator can usually be found on a Windows computer at C:\Program Files\ Netscape\Navigator\Cookies. As with Internet Explorer, the cookie includes cryptic information that is difficult or impossible to decipher. But you will see the domain name of the server that created the cookie, along with the IP address of the server. Edit the cookie file by deleting those cookies that are inappropriate or from unknown servers.

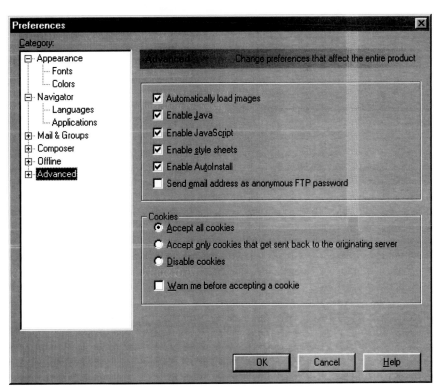

Figure 4-33 Advanced Preferences

LEGACY CLIENT TROUBLESHOOTING

You may encounter computers that access the Internet or an intranet that have older operating systems installed on them. Examples of older operating systems include DOS, Window 3.1, and Windows For Workgroups 3.11.

Because older Windows products didn't ship with a TCP/IP stack, it had to be installed alongside the operating system. While there were, and are, many personal computer TCP/IP stacks available, the most widely installed has been Trumpet Winsock (written by Peter Tappin and sold as shareware). DOS and Windows 3.x computers require a TCP/IP stack.

Typically, Trumpet Winsock is downloaded using FTP to the user's computer. Because the file is compressed, a decompression utility (such as WinZip) is needed to open the file. The particular version of the stack is normally included in the download file name. For example, twsk20b.zip means that the file is Trumpet Winsock, version 2.0b. The latest version for a particular operating system should be installed on the client computer.

Once the stack is installed, the version of the software can be determined by locating an About file. With each successive release of a TCP/IP stack, the user is offered additional features such as client utilities (telnet, for example) that may not have been included in the previous version.

The TCP/IP stack must be specific to the operating system. For example, there are stacks available for DOS, Windows, and Macintosh computers. Normally, the vendor or FTP site where the files can be downloaded organize the file names according to the operating system. Make sure that the stack that you're downloading is for the operating system that it will be installed on, and that you're downloading the most current version of the software.

The most troublesome aspect of setting up an Internet connection in the pre-Windows 95 days was related to SLIP and problems in the DOS client autoexec.bat file. SLIP requires that the IP address of the client be assigned as a static address. When setting up a SLIP account, you also have to specify the domain name of the ISP server, enter the correct subnet mask, and enter the IP address of the default gateway.

In some cases, the script used by the modem to dial in to the ISP must be altered by editing the .ini file where the script is stored. Figure 4-34 shows a typical configuration dialog box used to set up a SLIP account to an ISP.

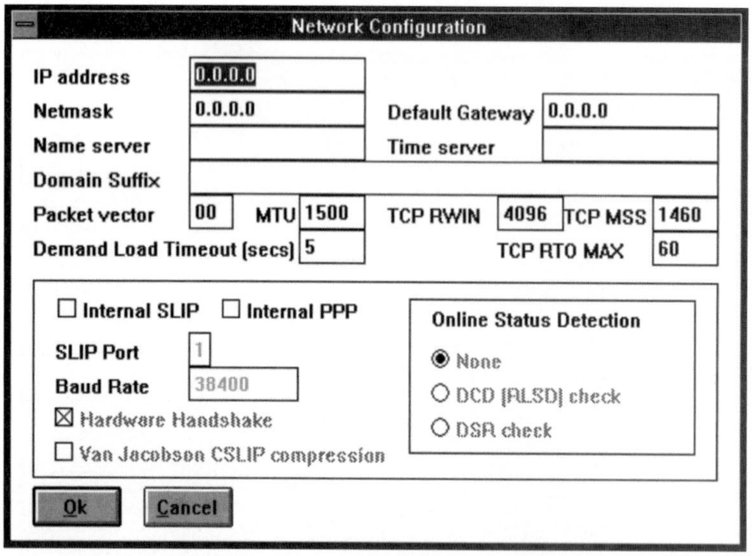

Figure 4-34 SLIP Configuration

If the path to the TCP/IP stack was left out of the autoexec.bat file in a DOS machine, the Internet connection won't initiate. To check for the proper path on a DOS computer, follow these steps:

1. At the DOS prompt, type **c:** and press enter.

2. At the **c:** prompt, type **edit autoexec.bat**, and press enter.

3. The DOS editor will display the commands in the autoexec.bat file. Look for the Path statement. If the Internet path is there, you'll see a reference to a **c:\internet statement**. If the statement is there, close the editor and exit. If the statement isn't in the Path command line, move the cursor to the end of the line and enter **;** **c:\internet**. Under the File drop-down menu, choose Save. Close the editor and exit DOS.

4. Restart the computer to allow the changes to take effect.

If the computer has Internet clients installed, such as gopher or telnet, check the version levels of the clients to make sure the latest version is installed. Check the file names of the clients to make sure they are correct for the operating system that they're installed in.

Other potential troubleshooting hotspots include:

- Client computers may not connect to the Internet if the client is on a network and the correct IP address of the proxy server is listed in the TCP/IP configuration.

- If the proxy server is down, a network client will not have Internet access. But note that the same computer may be able to send and receive e-mail if a separate e-mail server is used. The inverse is also true; if the e-mail server is down but the proxy server is up, a client will be able to connect to the Internet but won't be able to send and receive e-mail.

- For clients connected to an ISP through an analog modem, the connection may drop out if the analog telephone line is noisy.

- If call-waiting is enabled on the analog phone line that a client is using, an Internet connection will drop out each time a call is received unless the browser is configured for call waiting.

KEY POINTS REVIEW

This chapter has presented an exploration of the Internet clients.

- The TCP/IP stack refers to all of the ingredients needed to establish and maintain a network connection running the TCP/IP protocol suite. At a minimum, this includes the TCP protocol and the IP protocol.

- The operating system of a computer must be able to support TCP/IP before the client computer can access the Internet.

- Client computers may connect to the Internet over a network connection via a network interface card (NIC) installed and connected to a server. The NIC allows the exchange of files through a hub. Each of the workstations will be configured to connect to the Internet through a "proxy" IP address for the server or router.

- Stand-alone computers may connect to the Internet via a modem and an installed serial line protocol such as PPP, SLIP, or PPTP.

- A Web browser includes the HTTP protocol, which allows users to see and use HTML files. Most browsers also include full or partial implementations for using other Internet services such as FTP, telnet, gopher, and e-mail.

- An Internet client is likely to have an e-mail client installed. An e-mail client contains the Simple Mail Transfer Protocol (SMTP) used to send e-mail, along with the Post Office Protocol, version 3 (POP3), that's used to receive e-mail from an e-mail server.

- A variety of hardware platforms are available to support Internet access. These include a computer with analog modem, a computer with a NIC connected to a cable modem, or software to support Internet telephone, WebTV, or e-mail.

- The extent of configuration required at the client desktop is determined by the type of Internet connection such as a stand-alone connection or a network connection. Parameters that may need to be configured include WINS, DNS, default gateway, subnet mask, host file, DHCP or static IP address, proxy server address, and cache maintenance.

- An Internet client refers to software needed to utilize services available on the Internet. Internet clients include FTP, telnet, e-mail, and universal clients.

- MIME refers to standardized file types that allow nearly any file type to be sent in an e-mail message. MIME is also used with Web browsers to identify the type of file that will be sent to a client from a Web server.

- Patches and upgrades may be installed on a client in order to fix a problem or to enhance the functionality of software.

- A cookie is a small software object sent from a Web server to a client that contains information about the preferences of the client user. How the client computer handles cookies is configurable from the client computer.

- Legacy troubleshooting refers to managing Internet access to a computer using an older operating system. Typical problems associated with legacy troubleshooting involve setting up a serial line protocol and troubleshooting listings in the autoexec.bat file on a DOS computer.

REVIEW QUESTIONS

The following questions test your knowledge of the material presented in this chapter:

1. At a minimum, what protocol must be installed on a client in order to access the Internet?

2. List the hardware components needed for a network connection to the Internet and a stand-alone connection to the Internet.

3. What is the purpose of WINS?

4. What parameter must be enabled on a client computer if IP addresses will be temporarily assigned?

5. Describe the difference between a default gateway and a proxy server.

6. Which type of Internet client is best for downloading files from an FTP server?

7. What does it mean if a file is "MIME-compliant"?

8. A UNIX client is sending a graphical file to a remote server. What code is used to send the file?

9. An anti-virus package installed on a computer hasn't been updated in several months. Describe why it's important to check the installed version of the package for updates that are available from the vendor.

10. What is an Internet cookie?

11. List the steps for configuring the cache for Microsoft Internet Explorer.

MULTIPLE CHOICE QUESTIONS

1. Which of the following is used to display HTML files transferred from a Web server to a client?

   a. Web browser

   b. TCP/IP

   c. FTP

   d. Cable modem

2. A stand-alone client computer has the following components installed for accessing the Internet: TCP/IP, FTP, e-mail, Windows 98 operating system, and PPP. What component is missing?

   a. WebTV

   b. NetBIOS

   c. Web browser

   d. Modem

3. During a session with an FTP server, which of the following commands will download a file named "documents"?

   a. put documents

   b. ls documents

   c. get documents

   d. cd documents

4. Which of the following statements best describes the Netscape Navigator Web browser?

   a. Universal client

   b. FTP client

   c. Telnet client

   d. e-mail client

5. Client computer names are to be translated to IP addresses. Which of the following must be enabled on the client?

   a. DHCP

   b. WINS

   c. DNS

   d. HTML

6. A user has asked you to install Trumpet Winsock on a Windows 2000 workstation. Which of the following best describes an accurate response to the user?

   a. Trumpet Winsock can only be used on Macintosh computers.

   b. A Windows 2000 computer already has a TCP/IP stack installed.

   c. The stack installed on the Windows 2000 computer is at an earlier version date than the Trumpet Winsock version.

   d. Trumpet Winsock is a patch that's only used to fix problems.

7. In order to protect the IP addresses of workstations from Internet intruders, which of the following should be configured for the workstations?

   a. DNS

   b. WINS

   c. Proxy address

   d. NetBIOS

8. Which of the following best describes the behavior of a cookie?

   a. A cookie is required to access a Web server.

   b. A cookie reveals the IP address of the client workstation.

   c. A cookie is created by the client workstation and stored on a remote server.

   d. A cookie contains information regarding the preferences of a user accessing a Web server.

9. Which of the following statements best describes how cookies remember sites visited by a user?

   a. A cookie stored on the client includes the IP address and domain name of sites visited by the user.

   b. Cookies are stored in a cache along with other files for quick reloading when a user revisits a Web site.

   c. A cookie file contains a listing of all routers encountered during each Internet session.

   d. A cookie initiates TCP/IP.

10. After installing the latest version of a Web browser, you receive notification from the vendor concerning a problem with the browser. What should you do now?

    a. Uninstall the browser.

    b. Check the vendor's Web site for a patch.

    c. Install anti-virus software.

    d. Reconfigure the browser so that the cache is smaller.

11. After an Internet session, you notice that it takes the Web browser an extended amount of time to close. Which of the following should be done?

    a. Increase the amount of RAM in the client.

    b. Increase the Internet cache size.

    c. Decrease the Internet cache size.

    d. Reduce the amount of time spent on the Internet.

CHAPTER

5

INTERNET SERVERS

**LEARNING
OBJECTIVES**

LEARNING OBJECTIVES

Upon completion of this chapter and its related lab procedures, you should be able to perform the following tasks:

1. (1.2) Identify the issues that affect Internet site functionality. Content could include the following:

    - Bandwidth
    - Internet connection points
    - Audience access
    - Connection types
    - Corrupt files

    - Internet Service Provider (ISP)
    - Files taking too long to load
    - Inability to open files
    - Resolution of graphics

2. (4.8) Describe hardware and software connection devices and their uses. Content could include the following:

    - Network Operating System
    - Internet-in-a-box

    - Cache-in-a-box
    - Firewall

3. (4.10) Describe the purpose of various servers—what they are, their functionality, and features. Content could include the following:

    - Proxy
    - Mail
    - Mirrored
    - Cache
    - List
    - Web

    - News
    - Certificate
    - Directory
    - E-commerce
    - Telnet
    - FTP

4. (3.8) Describe the process of pre-launch site/application functionality testing. Content could include the following:

    - Checking hot links
    - Testing different browsers
    - Testing to ensure it does not corrupt your e-commerce site
    - Access to the site
    - Testing with various speed connections

5. (4.2) Identify problems with Internet connectivity from source to destination for various server types. Content could include the following:

    - E-mail
    - Slow server
    - Web site

CHAPTER 5

Internet Servers

INTRODUCTION

For many Internet visitors, their experience is limited to the rich displays of text, graphics, and links that stream from Web servers. But, in fact, there are many other types of servers used on the Internet. The other servers are working behind the scenes or in specialized applications that are removed from many folks who simply use and enjoy the incredible variety and depth of knowledge found on the Internet.

This chapter takes a look at many of the servers that, together, comprise the Internet.

In addition to describing the server types, the most common network operating systems are briefly reviewed.

Ensuring that the Internet remains viable, functional, and secure is a never-ending task for those who work with the Internet each day. Common server testing practices will be described that reveal details of server performance, functionality, and reliability.

Finally, specific problem areas that could reduce the effectiveness of an Internet Web site will be reviewed, along with troubleshooting practices for servers.

SITE FUNCTIONALITY

A Web site is functional if it works the way it's supposed to work. Specifically, functionality refers to the performance, reliability, and security of a Web site:

- **Performance** means that the site displays graphics properly, links to other pages on the site work, order processing is operational for e-commerce sites, and that contact information that launches e-mail will allow visitors to actually send an e-mail.

- **Reliability** refers to how well the site works under conditions such as responding to various versions of Web browsers, server maintenance and outages at the ISP, or heavy load conditions that occur when many clients access the site.

- **Security** refers to internal security at the Web site and also to security of the site visitors, particularly when the site is used to sell products that are paid for with credit cards. Because security threats are greatest from employees and those closest to a network, a secure site administrator should carefully screen business partners, check the Internet access provider's security precautions, and install a firewall to thwart intruders.

Performance

Reliability

Security

The following sections summarize aspects of a site that may affect functionality.

Bandwidth

The available bandwidth on the Internet directly affects the performance of a Web site as viewed from the client user. Compared to the speed of local networks, the Internet is painfully slow. Consider that a 10 BaseT Ethernet LAN transfers data at 10 Mbps while a full T-1 connection has a bandwidth of only 1.544 Mbps.

Bandwidth and the amount of data that's transferred are directly proportional. If the bandwidth is increased, the amount of information transfer will increase as well. Because the bandwidth of the Internet is slow compared to the networks connected to it (as well as the microprocessors that power the machines connected to it), a Web site must be built with a critical eye to the available data transfer rate.

For example, assume the total size of a Web page is 10,000 bytes. The page will load much faster in a browser connected to the site over a 128 Kbps ISDN line than it will over a 56 Kbps dial-up line. If the site is intended for the general public, with the assumption that most visitors will connect using a modem and dial-up connection, the content of the site should be designed to load quickly. This means that graphics, Java, CGIs, and other programming options should be kept to a minimum. On the other hand, if the site is built with the intention of providing information or services to large businesses, then the assumption can be that users are connected using a faster technology such as T-carrier or ISDN.

Internet Connection Points

Internet connection points refer to the physical connections that a Web site has to the Internet. An ISP has a direct connection to the Internet infrastructure, either through the Internet backbone or to a NAP.

A corporate Internet site uses an ISP for the physical access it provides at the connection point. The servers on the corporate site may connect to the ISP via any of the bandwidth technologies described in Chapter 1 such as Frame Relay, ISDN, or T-carrier. The number and the quality of the Internet connection points between the corporate site, the ISP, and the Internet all affect how the performance of the site will be perceived. The greater the connections, the slower a page will load.

The number of connection points and the quality of the connections will also affect the reliability of the connection. For example, if a corporate Web server is located in an area where the Internet connection infrastructure has intermittent problems, then visitors to the site will perceive that the site is unreliable.

Internet connection points

Audience Access

Technologically, a Web site may be reliable and well designed for fast downloads to clients, even though the site receives few visitors. A deliberate effort should be made to attract visitors to a Web site. There are numerous ways to attract visitors and Web designers are developing new methods on a daily basis. The following lists several techniques used by site designers:

- Use META tags in the HTML home page for the site. A **META tag** contains specific keywords and phrases that are used by all major search engines for listing and classifying a Web site. META tags are discussed in detail in Chapter 7.

- Use banner ads on search engines to advertise a site.

- Incorporate links to other sites and enter reciprocal agreements with other Web sites for including a site in their links.

- Offer visitors a service, information, demo product, or other incentive for visiting the site.

- Advertise the site in other media such as television, radio, or trade publications.

META tag

ISP

The ISP used to provide access to the Internet is crucial to the performance, security, and reliability of a Web site. Choose an ISP carefully to ensure it meets the requirements and goals of the site.

The range of services available with an ISP varies widely. Some provide only a basic dial-up connection to the Internet for home-based computer users and aren't equipped to offer business services.

Others offer a full range of services that may include:

- Web site design and development that includes all HTML and specialized programming such as Java scripts, database design, and customized DLL or CGIs. The ISP may be able to produce extensive graphics for still prints, video, or audio.

- Customer site installation and configuration, which includes a range of access technologies such as T1, Frame Relay, or ISDN. The ISP will frequently handle all aspects of purchasing equipment such as routers, install and configure the equipment, and test the suite for performance.

- Provide a secure server for conducting credit card transactions used with e-commerce sites.

- Analysis capabilities for determining the number of site visitors and the preferences of those who visit the site. In addition, the ISP may (should) be able to provide information as to how much exposure a site is given in search engines and suggest methods or changes that will improve search results.

Care must be taken when selecting an ISP. This requires doing some legwork on your own to determine the precise goal of a site, then matching an ISP to your goal. For example, if a site is intended to sell products via credit cards, the ISP should have a secure server installed and be able to describe each step required to set up the site. There is quite a bit that must be done before an e-commerce site can be activated and the process can be daunting without some knowledgeable help.

Web Page Files

Web page

A **Web page** consists of linked files that, when downloaded to the client browser, constitute the Web page. Web pages are also linked. A Web site frequently includes links to other sites. If any of the parts of the Web site don't work as intended, then the site is neither reliable nor a good performer. In addition, the security of the site may be compromised if visitors are permitted to upload files or send e-mail to a central site server. The uploads may contain viruses or be designed to return information about the site (via cookies, for example) that the site designer didn't intend to reveal.

corrupt file

Corrupt files placed on a Web site will quickly send a visitor off to another site. A **corrupt file** is a file that doesn't display because there's something wrong with it. For example, a photograph that has been scanned can be cropped when linked to a Web page. To the site visitor, only a portion of the graphic will be visible.

Exotic files require long load times. As a general rule, a complete Web page should load in a browser under 30 seconds. If a graphic includes audio and video, for example, users with dial-up connections may become frustrated waiting for the file to load.

The client will display graphics quicker if the cache size is increased because repeat visits will ensure that some, or all, of the site page is in the client cache. Additional RAM as well as a high-performance video card (a 64-bit video card versus an 8-bit video card) will also improve load times. Unfortunately, the Web site administrator can't control the configuration of most client machines. Instead, the site administrator must be knowledgeable about who the customers are that will visit the site, and estimate the capabilities of their browser and computer. For more information on load times, see the section Server Testing later in this chapter.

The resolution of a graphic is also a concern. If the resolution is set higher than the resolution of the client browser, the graphic won't appear to the user as it appears to the graphic designer. Some portions of the graphic may not be displayed at all. For more information about graphics resolution, refer to Multimedia File Formats in Chapter 2.

dummy graphic

Incompatible file extensions will cause a graphic to display in a browser as a **dummy graphic**. A dummy graphic is a generic icon that may be labeled "graphic". Because the graphic to be displayed isn't supported by the browser, the browser ignores the graphic—along with any height and width information—and replaces it with the dummy icon.

In order to be viewed, many file types require plug-ins. Video files, for example, require that the client have a plug-in such as QuickTime so the file can be seen. Because there's no realistic way that a Web site designer can determine the capabilities of all browsers that will visit a site, the site should be tested using all current versions of a browser as well as older versions.

SOFTWARE CONNECTION DEVICES

Software connection devices include software packages that may be required to access the Internet. Users on a corporate network with Internet access will undoubtedly be connected to a **network operating system (NOS)**. A fundamental understanding of the most widely used NOSs is important to understanding connection problems to the Internet.

network operating system (NOS)

For some companies, it makes sense to buy and install a software package that includes all the software needed to connect users to the Internet as well as to develop a Web site. Universal solutions are available that include all the tools needed for most applications.

A firewall is essential to preventing intruder access to a corporate network. A firewall may consist of a software-only implementation, or it may include a combination of hardware and software. Firewalls are briefly described in this section.

Network Operating System

A network operating system, or NOS, consists of software used to manage network security, user accounts, file and printing functions, and other features for computers connected in a network. Users who connect to the Internet from a local area network will likely do so through a NOS at the local level.

The ISP that provides access to local network users will also use a NOS for servers at the ISP. The NOS used at the local level may not be the same as the NOS used at the ISP. But, the two must be compatible at the Network layer in order to communicate. In order to be compatible for Network layer functions, the two NOSs will use TCP/IP between them. TCP/IP will be used as the common protocol that allows users to send and receive data packets.

Three network operating systems currently dominate the market. They are Windows NT, Novell NetWare, and UNIX. The following sections will provide an overview of each NOS.

Windows NT

Windows NT firmly established Microsoft in the networking business. The software is relatively easy to set up. Once set up, users can be added using pre-defined profiles for access to the network resources in which groups of users can be logically organized.

Windows NT

The Windows NT operating system actually extends to the workstations on a network with Windows NT Workstation. However, NT Workstation isn't required. The server and workstation versions of Windows NT are modular components added to the basic operating system making the package complete and enabling it to run across a common source code. All Windows 9x operating systems are supported by Windows NT Server (as well as Windows 2000).

domain

workgroup

Windows NT was designed for 32-bit applications; consequently, it won't support 16-bit device drivers found in older PCs. The software was designed for network servers that have several microprocessors. It supports hard drives larger than 2 Gigabytes.

Client computers on an NT network may be assigned to either a **domain** or a **workgroup**. A workgroup consists of computers that share access to files and applications. Each computer in the workgroup maintains a list of user accounts that contain passwords and access rights. The user account information must be configured for each workstation in the workgroup. Workgroup members use the same network protocol and share the same workgroup name.

A domain is a collection of client computers that are administered by a server. For example, an NT server can be installed on a network and client computers are assigned to the domain name given to the NT server. From the NT server, a network administrator can organize the complete network simply by referencing the domain name.

Administering workgroups is difficult when users frequently change workstations or move from one workgroup to another. The difficulty arises because all user account information resides in each computer. If a change is made in workgroup membership, the user account information on each computer in the workgroup must be changed as well. However, for a small network in which user changes aren't likely to occur frequently, workgroups may be a very good organizational tool.

Table 5-1 Network Protocols Supported by Windows NT

PROTOCOL	DESCRIPTION
NetBEUI	NetBIOS Extended User Interface is a proprietary, non-routable Microsoft protocol.
NWLink	Microsoft implementation of the NetWare IPX/SPX proprietary protocol, and routable protocol.
TCP/IP	Used for all internet connections and to access Web servers on the Internet.
Remote Access Server	Includes dial-up protocols such as SLIP, PPP, PPTP, and ISDN.
AppleTalk	Network protocol used with Macintosh computers.

Windows NT supports a wide variety of protocols. Table 5-1 lists several of the major protocols supported by Windows NT. For secure connections across the Internet to a remote server, NT also supports the PPTP protocol.

File Allocation Table (FAT)

NTFS (NT File System)

Windows NT supports two file structures, FAT and NTFS. **FAT** is short for **File Allocation Table** and is the file system used with DOS, Windows 3.x, Windows 9x, and OS/2. Because a huge base of installed operating systems use FAT, it may be tempting to use on an NT server. However, FAT lacks the security features found in the other option, NTFS.

NTFS (NT File System) is the recommended choice for Windows NT. NTFS is recommended over FAT because NTFS is the more secure of the two and utilizes the disk space far more efficiently than FAT.

Novell NetWare

NetWare is the proprietary network operating system of Novell. With a long history of developing NOS software, NetWare is currently the dominant NOS on the market. The current version of NetWare (5.0) is the most robust implementation of NetWare to date due to the use of public-key encryption techniques for securing file transfers.

NetWare

All Microsoft client operating systems such as Windows 3.x and Windows 9x, as well as Microsoft's newest iteration, Windows 2000, support NetWare. In order to run NetWare on a client computer, the NetWare Client software must be installed on the workstation.

The basis of the Novell directory services is called the Novell Directory Service, or NDS. NDS is based on the ITU standard X.500.

The directory structure starts with a **root.** A root is the primary object from which the directory structure is constructed. A company name or the name of a department within a company follows the root. The root typically branches out to **Organizations**. An organization consists of logical groupings of users that require similar levels of access to the network resources. Examples of organizations include Sales, Accounting, or Administration. The organization may also follow a geographic rationale such as by region, state, or group of cities.

root

Organizations

Branching off from the Organization level are **Organizational Units**. An organizational unit can refer to individuals within a department or cities within a state. Figure 5-1 shows an example of the NDS directory structure from the NetWare online documentation.

Organizational Units

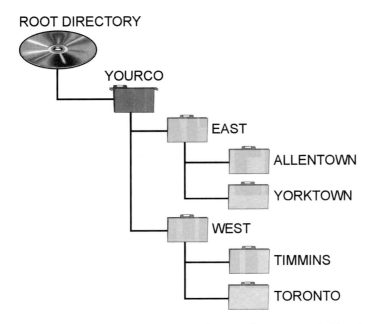

Figure 5-1 NetWare NDS Structure

Organizational branching with NDS can continue as long as needed by the network administrator. However, NetWare ships with a default structure that Novell recommends for networks containing fewer than 1,000 objects. The default structure allows administrators to quickly design the network for efficient user access to the network resources.

Table 5-2 lists network protocols supported by NetWare. See the section Networking Protocols, later in this chapter, for more information.

Table 5-2 NetWare Network Protocols

PROTOCOL	DESCRIPTION
IPX/SPX	Internet Package Exchange/Sequenced Packet Exchange, the proprietary routable protocol from Novell.
TCP/IP	Used for all internet connections and to access Web servers on the Internet.
AppleTalk	Used to permit Macintosh client computers to share files on a NetWare server.
NetWare Link	The remote access protocols supported by NetWare. They include PPP, ATM, X.25, and Frame Relay.

volumes

partitions

The Novell file system includes **volumes** and **partitions**. A partition is used to separate operating systems. For instance, a hard drive may be separated into two partitions with one containing NetWare and the other containing DOS. Up to four partitions may be placed on a single disk.

A volume is used to subdivide partitions into smaller units. With four allowable partitions on each disk, eight volumes may be used on a disk. Whereas a partition is limited to a single disk, a volume may span multiple disks. A volume is organized into logical groupings such as user directories for various departments such as sales, production, etc. A volume may also be created to contain application software available across the network.

Partitions and volumes are managed by two types of file services: Novell Storage Services (NSS), which is available only on version 5.0, and NetWare File System (NFS), which is the file service used on earlier versions of NetWare, but is also available on version 5.0.

With either service, directories and files are stored in volumes as just described. You specify which objects can access other objects along with the level of access: read only, read/write, or print. With NSS, space on all server hard drives is more efficiently utilized than with NFS. NSS collects all free space, as well as any space not used by a volume, and pools it. From this pool, additional volumes may be created.

UNIX

UNIX began as an experiment, commissioned by the U.S. government, to ensure that data communications lines would remain available if the United States were attacked. In the early days of computers, all data resided on centralized mainframes. If the mainframe were destroyed during an attack, the information it contained would be destroyed. UNIX sought to find a way to spread the data around to several computers so that if any one were destroyed, the data could be recovered from another computer.

UNIX is a non-proprietary network operating system that includes many provisions for remote connections such as e-mail. UNIX computers communicate using the TCP/IP protocol. TCP/IP is the only protocol supported by most versions of UNIX. Between UNIX and TCP/IP, users are supplied with a portable data structure that is machine independent. TCP/IP allows any machine type to communicate with any other machine type, and UNIX allows the machine users to efficiently exchange information such as files and e-mail.

UNIX is a 64-bit operating system. It supports graphic-intensive applications. It's capable of **multitasking**, which means that more than one operation can be addressed at the same time by the operating system. To access a UNIX server, the client computer will also have UNIX installed. However, there are several "front-end" programs that mask the use of a UNIX server to client workstations such as Windows operating systems.

The file and directory structure used with UNIX resembles a tree cluster. Figure 5-2 shows a typical example of a UNIX directory. At the top of the hierarchy is the **root**, indicated by the forward slash. Directories that branch from the root are called **subdirectories**. Subdirectories may branch into other subdirectories. In the figure, the subdirectories /sales, /account, and /admin are subdirectories of /home, which is a subdirectory of /. When written on a command line, the /doc directory appears as:

/home/admin/doc

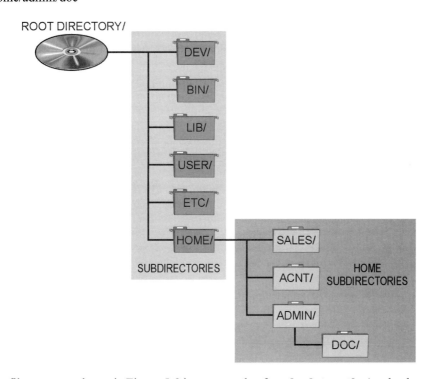

Figure 5-2 UNIX Directory Structure

The file structure shown in Figure 5-2 is an example of an **absolute path**. An absolute path includes all upper-level directories, including the root. Another way to specify files is to use a relative path. A **relative path** is specified at the time of login and will start at a specified file name. By specifying a relative path, the user logs on directly to their personal directory. For example, a relative path may appear as:

/admin/doc

If a relative login isn't specified, the user must enter the appropriate UNIX commands to get to the desired file or directory.

user

groups

all other users

Files on a UNIX system are organized into **user**, **groups**, and **all other users**. This convention is helpful in applying security to files and directories. Admin, in the figure, may want to give permission to other group users so they'll be able to read the contents of the doc file. The level of access is selectable to include read-only, read-write, and execute (for programs that can be executed).

UNIX is a very powerful operating system that's widely used on Internet Web servers. It runs on both types of popular microprocessor-based systems (CICS used on Intel machines and RISC used on Sun Microelectronics machines). An experienced administrator can fully equip a server with UNIX and TCP/IP for free using downloads from the Internet. Because, natively, UNIX employs a command line interface, it doesn't require the extensive use of server resources that NetWare and Windows NT require; that is, many older computers are being effectively used as UNIX servers.

Universal Internet Solutions

Internet-in-a-box

A universal Internet solution means that all tools needed to set up and maintain an Internet server are sold in a single package. The package is sometimes referred to as **Internet-in-a-box**. The package typically contains extensive troubleshooting and testing software, a full TCP/IP suite of protocols, Web development software such as a Java package and compiler software, and a network operating system such as a UNIX flavor, and may also include all hardware.

The vendor that sells the solution may also contract to set up, install, and maintain the server. The scope of many ISPs, for example, has become so extensive that it's not uncommon to contract out some or much of the software development and customer installations.

cache-in-a-box

Closely related to universal Internet solutions is **cache-in-a-box**. This is also a single package that frequently includes the software needed to setup a cache server, proxy server, and firewall. All three components are included in a single server. The package may also include the necessary hardware, installation, configuration, and continuing maintenance.

Universal solutions make sense for a company that doesn't have extensive technical expertise. A company such as Cisco or Nortel has in-house experts that can design, develop, and maintain a Web presence. But a company that doesn't have technology, and particularly network applications, as its core business, may be at a technical disadvantage. The convenience of purchasing a complete Internet solution is very attractive to companies such as these.

Firewall

A firewall is used to prevent corporate network users from accessing the Internet and to prevent outside intruders from accessing a corporate network. A firewall is a security system consisting of hardware and software. Figure 5-3 shows an illustration of a firewall used between a corporate network and the Internet.

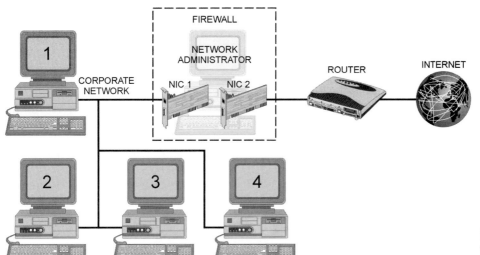

Figure 5-3 Internet Firewall

The firewall is usually a computer that has at least two network interface cards (NIC) installed. In the figure, NIC 1 connects back to the corporate network. NIC 2 connects to the router and the Internet. Before any of the network users can access the Internet, they must first go through the firewall. The firewall contains firewall software configured by a network administrator. The software is configured either to allow the user workstation to access the Internet or to deny the workstation access to all or parts of the Internet. For example, many companies configure the firewall so that users are denied access to sites that don't have a legitimate business purpose.

On the other side of the firewall, NIC 2 connects to the router and the Internet. If an intruder attempts to enter the corporate network from the Internet, the firewall software will deny access. The software is set up so that it will only permit access from approved domain names, IP addresses, or host names. If a packet arrives in which the source address isn't recognized by the firewall, it will be rejected.

Note that if the firewall is down—that is, if either of the NICs or the computer isn't working—no users will be able to access the Internet.

In many cases, a firewall does double-duty as a proxy server. A proxy server is used to replace the IP address of a client workstation with a proxy IP address. The idea behind using proxies is that the client workstation IP address will never be advertised on the Internet; consequently, an intruder won't be able to use a valid IP address that a firewall may admit to the corporate network. Proxy servers are discussed in more detail later in the following section.

SERVER TYPES

When you connect to a domain name on the Internet, you actually connect to a server that sends back the content of the domain name Web site. For many that cruise the Web, their interaction with the Internet is limited to receiving downloads of HTML files and related graphics. But for those who work with the systems that power the Internet, there are many servers operating behind the scenes. This section contains descriptions of the most common server types likely to be encountered while working with Internet applications.

Proxy Server

A **proxy server** is used to keep secret the IP address of a workstation on a network when the workstation accesses the Internet. A proxy IP address is assigned to the workstation and the proxy IP address is used in the IP packet header, rather than the actual IP address of the workstation.

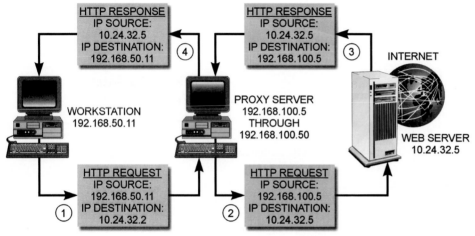

Figure 5-4 Proxy Server

Figure 5-4 shows how a proxy is used by a workstation.

The operation of the server is as follows:

1. The works100tation (one of many in a local area network) sends an HTTP request for a remote server. The source IP address used in the HTTP request specifies the IP address of the workstation.

2. The proxy server intercepts the request before it's sent to the Internet and replaces the IP address of the workstation with a proxy IP address. A proxy IP address assigned by the proxy server is taken from a pool of proxy IP addresses that have been reserved. Note that the source IP address in the HTTP request is no longer the IP address of the workstation, but is a proxy IP address assigned by the proxy server.

3. The destination Web server accepts the request and responds with the content of the Web site. The HTTP response is sent back to the proxy IP address.

4. When the proxy server receives the HTTP response, it reconciles the proxy IP address in the HTTP response to the IP address of the original workstation. Note that the destination IP address in the HTTP response is changed from the proxy IP address to the IP address of the workstation.

The advantage of using a proxy IP address is that the actual IP addresses of network workstations are never advertised on the Internet. Because the workstation IP addresses aren't advertised, it is impossible to physically locate the workstations by reconciling the IP addresses to workstation MAC addresses.

Proxy servers represent a potential hole through which intruders may enter a network. Chapter 6 details security precautions and types of threats that proxy servers, as well as Web servers, are exposed to. Since a proxy server receives all HTTP responses from Web servers, it may also be a source for viruses. The best protection against Web server viruses is to install anti-virus software on all proxy servers along with all client workstations.

A proxy server is used to substitute workstation IP addresses. They can, and sometimes are, used to filter IP address of remote servers. But filtering IP addresses to prevent unwanted visitors from accessing a network is best handled by a firewall.

In many business networks, user workstations are assigned a private IP address such as 10.100.24.15. The use of private IP addresses for network users offers considerable savings for a company. But a workstation with a private IP address won't get far on the Internet since Internet routers will reject (discard) private IP addresses. The proxy server replaces a private IP with a public IP address that will be recognized by Internet routers. However, the proxy has the problem of determining if a packet is destined for the Internet, or if it stays on the local network. The solution is actually resolved at the workstation where the packet originated but, in this case, the IP replacement at the proxy must confirm the workstation reconciliation, then substitute an actual IP address for the private IP. This process is called **Network Address Translation Service (NATS)**.

NATS involves replacing the private IP address with a public IP address, as well as creating a table containing the mappings of private and public IP addresses for each Internet connection. The map table is maintained at the proxy and updated for each new connection and for each discontinued connection.

Mail Server

A **mail server** is used to specifically send and receive e-mail, as well as to store e-mail records. All ISPs use an e-mail server that's separate from servers used to access Web servers, FTP servers, or any other type of server. The reason for doing so is twofold: E-mail comes with its own set of protocols, and the volume of e-mail that an ISP handles necessitates dedicating a server to handle the volume.

The protocol used with e-mail is called Simple Mail Transfer Protocol, or SMTP. SMTP must be installed on any client computer that will be sending or receiving e-mail. Figure 5-5 illustrates the basic operation of e-mail.

Each client has SMTP installed and is likely to be using a commercial software package such as Microsoft Outlook, Eudora, or Netscape Mail. When a user composes an e-mail, the message is first sent to the mail server. The mail server contains a list of authorized user accounts. The user may have to enter a password before the mail server will process the mail request.

The mail server will log all transactions. This means that all e-mail sent by all users will be saved on the server in an account set up for the user. In a similar manner, all received e-mail is copied to the user's account on the server.

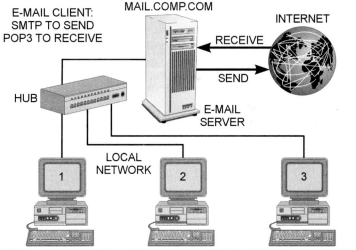

Figure 5-5 E-mail Server

Once the request to send a message is authenticated by the server, the message is sent to an e-mail address identified in the "To:" field of the e-mail message.

E-mail uses usernames to identify senders and recipients. The name of the e-mail server that sends a message is indicated by the domain name used. For example, a message from *user_1@comp.com* means that the username is "user_1". The @ symbol means that the packet is an e-mail using SMTP. The "comp.com" portion of the address means that the message originated from a domain called comp.com.

The name of the receiving e-mail server is implied by the e-mail address of the recipient. For example, assume an e-mail is sent to bob@happy.com. Bob is located at the domain name happy.com. When the sending e-mail server transmits the message, DNS servers translate the IP address of happy.com. When the e-mail message arrives at the happy.com IP address, it's transferred to the local e-mail server because the domain name is prefaced with "bob@", specifying an e-mail rather than another type of packet such as an HTTP response.

When an e-mail message is received, the e-mail server intercepts the message. Note that the formal domain name of the e-mail server in Figure 5-5 is mail.comp.com. The "mail" portion of the domain name is inserted in place of the username when a message is sent. DNS servers will then, first, reconcile the domain name (comp.com) of the e-mail server; then, reconcile the "mail.comp.com" name to an IP address. Note that e-mail server domain names are reconciled rather than the individual e-mail address of all recipients. Actual e-mail addresses are reconciled at the e-mail server.

In Figure 5-5, if the workstation's users are connected to the e-mail server and the server is connected to the Internet without interruption, then SMTP would be the only e-mail protocol required to send and receive e-mail. But, in practice, the workstation users won't be connected to the e-mail server all of the time. If a message arrives during the time that the workstation is shutdown or not connected to the e-mail server, the user needs a system for downloading received messages at some later time. The protocol used to receive e-mail is called Post Office Protocol, version 3, or POP3. (Note that there are earlier versions of the POP protocol. Earlier versions are incompatible with POP3.)

With the use of POP3, users can logon to the e-mail server and download messages received since the last logon. POP3 allows the received messages to be stored at the e-mail server until they are read from an authorized user.

In the majority of situations involving stand-alone connections to the Internet, the client computer will have both SMTP and POP3 installed. In most network connections to the Internet, both SMTP and POP3 will also be installed.

A word of caution concerning e-mail servers: Install anti-virus software on the servers. Typically, workstations will have (or should have) anti-virus software installed. But the server that either houses e-mail messages, or downloads them to client workstations, is often forgotten. This is a costly mistake. Be sure to protect the complete network from viruses. E-mail received from the Internet is the most common source of viruses.

Mirror Server

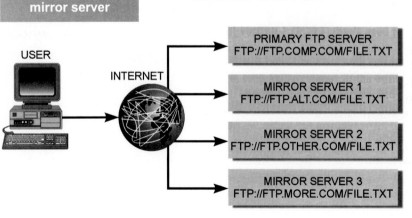

A **mirror server** contains exact copies of the contents of a primary server. Mirror servers frequently are used in conjunction with FTP servers. Figure 5-6 shows a primary FTP server and several mirror servers, or "FTP mirror sites".

Figure 5-6 Mirror Server

Users that connect to an FTP site may see a message that says downloads are also available from a list of mirror sites. If the primary site is busy, the user can select one of the mirror sites to download the same file. In some cases, a user will automatically be sent to a mirror site if the primary server is busy or not currently available.

Notice in the figure that when the user connects to the *ftp.comp.com* site to download the document *file.txt*, a list of mirror sites is displayed. The user then has the option of connecting to any of the listed sites to download the *file.txt* document.

Any type of server can be mirrored. Web servers identified by domain names are frequently mirrored so that if one of the servers is down, the site is still accessible to visitors at the mirror. Requests to the primary site are simply redirected to one of the mirror sites without the user having any knowledge of the change.

Note that a mirror server is also a **replication server**. A mirror server contains data that has been copied from another server. Replicating server data is also a common method of backing up the stored data on servers. The server may or may not be connected to the Internet. If you encounter the phrase replication server in conjunction with Internet-based servers (FTP, WEB, etc.), it's likely to be a reference to a mirror server.

replication server

List Server

A **list server** is used to generate messages to subscribers of a list, as well as allow subscribers to post messages that will be distributed to all other subscribers. The type of "lists" used with list servers runs the gamut of topics from the latest company news to very specialized messages related to medical topics or technical breakthroughs.

list server

A list server responds to subscribers. To subscribe to a list, an e-mail is sent to a subscription e-mail address. Messages may be posted to the list by sending a message to the post e-mail address. Generally, you must be a subscriber to receive list messages as well as to post messages to a list.

List servers use e-mail to send and post messages and the process is frequently referred to as "e-mail lists". There are several types of e-mail lists as described below:

- **Mail-merge Lists**: A mail-merge list compiles information contained in a database and uses e-mail to send the information to targeted recipients. Figure 5-7(a) illustrates the concept behind mail-merge lists. In the figure, a company with demographic information about its customers will enter the information in a database. When a new product is to be promoted, the database is searched for customers that would have an interest in the promotion and an e-mail containing the promotional material is sent to those targeted customers.

Mail-merge Lists

- **One-way Distribution Lists**: A one-way distribution list is used to send information such as newsletters to subscribers. Figure 5-7(b) shows a one-way list. The list resembles a print subscription to a magazine because the subscriber only receives the information, and doesn't interact with the list. Many companies use list servers for one-way list distributions to customers to announce new products.

One-way Distribution Lists

- **Discussion Lists**: A discussion list is interactive. Figure 5-7(c) shows an example of a discussion list. A list server that contains a domain name for sending messages sends an e-mail containing the latest posts to all subscribers. In the figures, subscriber 3 posts a message to the list server. The domain name for the post will be different than the send domain name. The post list server (usually, the send and post servers are the same server, although each uses a different IP address/domain name) forwards the new message to the send server. During the next scheduled send, the new message will be sent to all subscribers.

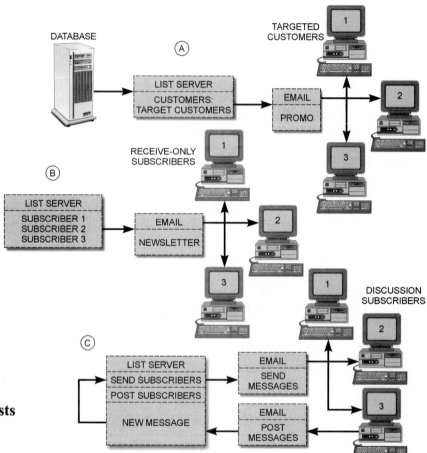

Figure 5-7
(a) Mail-merge Lists
(b) One-way Distribution Lists
(c) Discussion Lists

There are numerous software packages used with list servers—commercial network operating systems will bundle some type of list server in the package.

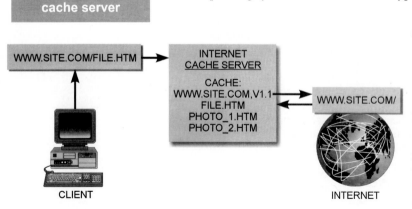

Figure 5-8 Cache Server

Cache Server

A **cache server** is used to store files. A cache server that's related to Internet applications will store Web site information for sites that users have recently visited. The intention of a cache server is to reduce the time required for a Web page to load in a client browser. Figure 5-8 illustrates how a cache server works.

In the figure, a client sends an HTTP request to *www.site.com* for a document called file.htm. The cache server intercepts the request. The cache server will first check its list of stored site names. If the requested site is in the cache, the server will then query the requested site and check the version of the requested page against the version of the page stored in the cache.

If the version at the remote server is the same as the version stored in the server cache, the cached version will be sent to the client. If the version of the requested file at the remote server is newer than the version stored in the cache, the cache server will download the newer version and replace the existing version with it. The newer version will then be forwarded to the client that originally made the request.

The effect of having a cache client is to speed the transfer of Web files to the client. Information travels across the Internet very slowly compared to data rates on local area networks. For example, a network with a T1 connection to the Internet will transfer data for each user at data rates in the 64 Kbps range. A packet of data on a 10 BaseT Ethernet LAN, on the other hand, will be sent in the 10 Mbps range.

A second advantage of a server cache, as far as network users is concerned, is that the cache in a client browser can be made smaller because the server can be used for storing the same information that a browser cache will store. This reduces the client resources that must be dedicated to Internet applications.

Web Server

A **Web server** uses the HTTP protocol to send HTML and other file types to clients. A Web server concentrates on the World Wide Web portion of the Internet, although not exclusively. Some Web servers also handle FTP requests or e-mail transactions.

Web server

A Web server is a powerful server because it must handle thousands of requests each hour. Notice that the server must handle the requests as if each of the thousands of clients were engaged in a one-to-one, dedicated session with the Web server. Because the server is accessed through a single point (the domain name), and returns information to many destinations simultaneously, it uses a point-to-point/multi-point protocol. This is accomplished by using multiple modems or routers at the server.

News Server

A **news server** uses the Network News Transport Protocol (NNTP) to store messages and to allow messages to be sent for others to read. The messages are organized by news groups in a general category called USENET News. The list of news groups that can be found in USENET cover thousands of topics listed alphabetically.

news server

In order to access a news group, the client computer must have a **newsreader** installed along with the NNTP protocol. A newsreader allows the user to read the messages posted in a news group, while the NNTP protocol allows the user to access a news server. Most e-mail packages as well as browsers include the reader and protocol. When the news client is configured, the domain name of the news server is specified at the client computer. An example of a news server name is *news.comp.com*.

newsreader

There are thousands of news servers on the Internet. When you connect to one news server, however, you see the same information that's contained in all news servers. In other words, there's no advantage in configuring a client to connect to more than one news server. News servers routinely exchange information by constantly transmitting updates to their neighbors. Because the process of updating news servers is dynamic, the updates ripple throughout the Internet very quickly.

Certificate Server

certificate server

A **certificate server** allows encrypted messages to be exchanged between a client and the certificate server. All modern Web browsers such as Netscape Navigator and Microsoft Internet Explorer support secure connections to a certificate server. Certificate servers are used at e-commerce sites where credit cards are used to purchase items, or they may be used to access sensitive information such as statistical data related to a Web site.

secure server

A **secure server** is identified with an URL beginning with https://. The "s" stands for the protocol used in the transaction, Secure Socket Layer, or SSL. SSL is described in more detail in Chapter 6, Internet Security.

A certificate server will have a certificate that authenticates the Web site to browsers that access it. The client browser will use the server certificate to do the following:

- Authenticate the identity of the Web server. This means that the browser will use the information contained in the certificate to determine if the Web site it's visiting is authentic or an imposter.

- Encrypt information sent to a validated certificate server.

- Decrypt information sent from a certificate server.

Certification Authority (CA)

Before the client browser can participate in a session with a certificate server, both the server and client must have a secure digital certificate issued by a **Certification Authority (CA)**. The purpose of the CA is to validate the identity of the certificate holder in such a way that the information contained in the certificate can't be modified. An example of a CA is VeriSign.

A certificate is a text file located on a client and certificate server. The following lists the information contained in the certificate:

- The name of the certificate holder. The name may be the name of an individual, URL of a Web site, or an e-mail address.

- The CA that issued the certificate.

- A serial number that is unique for each certificate issued. The serial number is similar to the number assigned to a credit card.

- A public encryption key. Public key encryption uses two keys, a private key that is kept secret by the parties that will exchange encrypted data, and a public key that's widely distributed. The public key can't be used without the private key to decrypt an encrypted message. If a message is encrypted with a public key, it can only be decrypted with the private key.

- Expiration date of the certificate that includes the date the certificate was valid and a date it will no longer be valid.

- Signature of the CA. The signature isn't a written signature, but is a digital (hexadecimal) number that will reveal to the server or browser if any part of the certificate has been tampered with.

All e-commerce sites as well as many sites containing data that's not intended to be shared with the public over the Internet use certificate servers to authenticate users, browsers, and Web servers.

When the protocol designated for a secure server uses "https", you may be prompted for a username and password. This can be implemented in a couple of ways. First, you go to the secure site by entering the domain of the site. Once there, you'll be prompted for a username and password. After successfully entering the correct logon information, you'll be given site access.

Another way is to enter the username and password at the same time that you enter the domain name of the site. This technique requires less time and fewer steps to enter the secure site. The syntax for entering the logon information at the same time as the domain name is as follows:

https://username@password/domain name

For example, assume that you have a Web site called spend-money.com. If you wanted to check statistics related to traffic on the site, you could do so by entering https://username@password/spend-money.com.

Since the statistics are for your eyes only, they are housed on a secure server. Only those with the correct username and password will have access to the information.

Directory Server

A **directory server** uses the **LDAP (Lightweight Directory Access Protocol)** protocol to access and search information that's distributed in a directory. Information in a directory server is likely to be any type of information that can be placed in a table, or that's organized in rows and columns. Examples of information placed on a directory server include telephone numbers of employees, user login accounts, e-mail and messaging, or addresses of people or businesses.

Almost all directory servers currently on the Internet are organized around the LDAP protocol. LDAP is based on the ITU X.500 protocol for directory services. **X.500** is an open systems protocol that covers all layers of the OSI Model. LDAP is a scaled-down version of X.500 because it only covers the Network and Transport layers of the OSI model.

Figure 5-9 illustrates a typical application on a directory server. A user at the client accesses the directory server via a standard URL domain name. Once the site has downloaded to the client, the user may enter search words or phrases to locate information in the directory. Frequently, many directory servers provide access to public directories that contain product information, catalog listings, or the locations of sales offices. This is shown in the figure as Public Directories.

directory server

LDAP (Lightweight Directory Access Protocol)

X.500

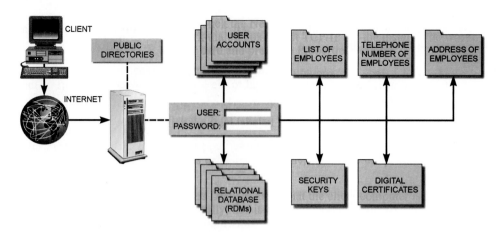

Figure 5-9 Directory Server

The same directory server may also have a private directory in which the user must enter a valid username and password before being admitted. The directory server maintains list of authorized users. Note that in the figure, a directory server may also include enhanced security for e-commerce applications. The boxes labeled Security Keys and Digital Certificates are used to validate purchases made from the site or encrypt data sent between the site and the client.

Typically, the distributed data found on a directory server is searchable. The figure shows several files related to employees that list their names, telephone numbers, and addresses. A search can be entered for any of the file attributes such as the addresses of an employee.

Background Info

relational databases management systems (RDMS)

Figure 5-9 may look similar to a conventional database. Most databases on the Internet are **relational databases management systems (RDMS)**. An RDMS requires a higher level of technical skills than does a directory database. If a directory structure can be used, then it should be used because the information content is likely to be returned quicker (for a properly set up directory service) than for a relational database service.

Many commercial directory servers (such as Netscape Directory) include provisions for integrating a directory server into a relational database that uses SQL. The directory service handles the user logins and maintains records of usernames and security certificates. The RDMS handles queries for complex object relationships such as preferences of users based on cookies returned from a client.

There are many directory server packages available. Netscape, Microsoft, and Novell offer commercial packages as add-ons to Internet server software packages. The one common element of directory servers is that they provide a single entry point to information that is likely to be distributed across many databases. This is particularly relevant to the Internet since a complex Web site is accessed through a single URL. From that URL, the visitor is able to browse many databases.

E-commerce Server

An **e-commerce server** is used to conduct secure financial transactions over the Internet. User purchases at the site occur with data encryption techniques similar to those described for certification servers. In most cases, an e-commerce site will use a standard Web server that incorporates a certificate server for purchases. All e-commerce sites use some type of merchant system such as MercanTec to handle credit card transactions.

One of the most widely employed tools used with e-commerce sites is **shopping carts**. A shopping cart allows a customer to place an item in a virtual cart while shopping the site. Once the customer has finished shopping, he may then view the contents of the shopping cart and add or delete any items.

When the customer is ready to pay for the purchases, the e-commerce software will total the prices of all items in the cart, add applicable taxes as well as shipping charges, and prompt the customer for credit card information. The customer enters the credit card information at the client browser. The e-commerce server will then validate the credit card by checking the expiration date of the card, the card number, and determine if the customer has sufficient credit on the card to pay for the purchases.

If, at any time, the e-commerce software can't validate the card information, a message will be generated to the customer.

If the card information is validated, the e-commerce software will transfer the amount of the purchase from the card issuer bank, then deposit the amount in an account specified by the owner of the e-commerce site. The money is typically deposited in a business checking account.

Notice that all of the steps described above occur with little-to-no human interaction at the e-commerce site.

E-commerce sites, also called **virtual storefronts**, are changing the way many of us make purchases. The process of setting up an e-commerce site, however, requires considerable technical expertise, time, and money.

Telnet Server

A **telnet server** is used to allow remote users to connect to a server that will display information as if the user were directly connected to the server. To utilize a telnet server, a telnet client must be installed on the client computer. Most client operating systems include some type of telnet client.

The vast majority of telnet sessions consist of entering information using the command-line interface, rather than a graphical interface.

e-commerce server

shopping carts

virtual storefronts

telnet server

FTP Server

An **FTP server** is used to transfer files across the Internet, extranet, or intranet. To access an FTP server, the client computer must have an FTP client installed. Modern Web browsers include a minimal FTP client that opens in the browser, which allows files to be sent and received using the FTP protocol.

Many companies utilize an FTP server for software downloads. The software may be free software, beta versions of software, patches and upgrades to existing software, as well as demonstration versions of software. By segregating software downloads from the company's Web server, traffic is reduced during downloads.

FTP is a viable alternative to using e-mail for transferring files. An FTP server is specifically designed to transfer files, whereas e-mail is specifically designed to handle messages. Large files included as attachments to e-mail take considerably longer to send and download to an e-mail server than do large files sent to an FTP server.

Table 5-3 Server Summary

Table 5-3 provides a summary of the servers described in this section.

SERVER TYPE	DESCRIPTION
Proxy	Replaces client IP with IP assigned by a proxy server.
Mail	Used to send, receive, and store e-mail messages; maintains list of authorized user accounts. SMTP is used to send e-mail and POP3 is used to receive e-mail from mail server to client.
Mirror	Used to replicate server contents. Many Web and FTP servers are mirrored. Additional servers reduce the bandwidth demands placed on a single server.
List	Used to maintain a list of message subscribers. List servers may auto-generate messages to subscribers as well as allow for auto-posting messages.
Cache	Used to save Web, FTP, or other files. A cache server compares the current version of a Web file to a stored version and replaces the stored version if not current. Documents may be sent directly to a client (at network speeds) from cache if the version hasn't changed.
Web	Used to store HTML and other file types. A Web server is identified with the HTTP protocol and usually is assigned a unique domain name.
News	Used to access USENET news groups. NNTP protocol must be installed on the client to read or post USENET articles.
Certificate	Used to provide a secured connection between client and server. Communications are encrypted and both client and server must possess a valid certificate.
Directory	Used to access or search distributed data. The LDAP protocol is associated with directory servers. It allows a user to access multiple directories.
E-commerce	Used for secure financial transactions over the Internet. An e-commerce site employs encryption techniques to secure credit card purchases. Many e-commerce sites utilize a shopping cart.

Table 5-3 Server Summary (Cont.)

SERVER TYPE	DESCRIPTION
Telnet	Used for remote logins to a remote server. A telnet server requires that the user's computer have a telnet client installed.
FTP	Used to upload and download files. An FTP session requires that the client have an FTP client installed. Most Web browsers provide an FTP client.

Messaging Server

A messaging server is used to allow network users to send e-mails or to auto-deliver simple notices (that are also referred to as **instant messages**). A message server may be maintained on an intranet, or it could be a server that serves a global audience.

instant messages

An example of a message server is Microsoft Back Office. A message server is particularly agile since it uses TCP/IP packets to transport encoded messages. A MIME e-mail, for example, can be sent to a message server over an Internet connection. At the receiving end, the TCP/IP headers are stripped away and the MIME encoded message is deciphered and delivered to the recipient.

A messaging server relies on the former CCITT X.400 protocol from which e-mail systems were developed. The server may be called a **network gateway server** since it has the ability to deliver messages from any type of machine—as long as the machine is running the TCP/IP stack.

network gateway server

SERVER TESTING

A server used on the Internet should be tested. The test should occur before the site goes "live", and periodically after the site has been in operation. Benchmarks are crucial to understanding test data concerning an Internet server. A **benchmark** is set a of attributes—values, times, speed, errors—from which the performance of the server can be measured.

benchmark

There are numerous sources for benchmark data. The first place to look is with the ISP hosting the Web site. The ISP will normally track much of the data used in testing (but for billing purposes rather than for testing purposes). In some cases, you may be able to access a protected test site maintained by the ISP that's specifically used for testing sites hosted by the ISP.

Another way to collect initial test data is to create the benchmark in the pre-launch phase of the site. The **pre-launch phase** occurs when the server is tested from a remote client, before the site goes live. The site is reached via an IP address only because the ISP has yet to associate the site domain name to the assigned IP address (therefore the site can't be reached through the DNS servers on the Internet and is, in effect, off line). Any data derived from pre-launch tests can be used as initial benchmark data.

Another alternative is to use the services of companies that test Web sites for a fee. The value of using outside testing is that the data is less likely to be biased and can be compared to similar sites that the company has tested.

Once the site is running, it's important to test the site performance. Tests should be scheduled and logs maintained for comparing the data so that trends can be pinpointed before they become a problem. The following sections describe various tests and include test data examples.

Hot Links

Hot link testing refers to checking links at a Web site to determine if they work. Each time a change is made to a site, the links should be checked to ensure they are still valid.

The Internet changes daily. A site that was available to users yesterday may be gone today. If a Web site that includes links to other sites is not changed frequently, then a plan should be developed for periodically checking links.

Table 5-4 shows a typical format for testing links. Notice that all links are referenced to lines in the HTML file for the site. The test includes links to other sites, links to graphic files, as well as links to other servers.

Table 5-4 Format for Checking Links

HTML LINE	LINK TYPE	LINK	STATUS
22	Image	Logo.gif	OK
55	HREF	Order.htm	OK
123	Image	Photo.jpg	OK
175	HREF	www.connect.com	Not valid

Links should be checked from a browser while connected to the site. That is, don't check links off line from the Internet.

Browsers

A Web site should be checked to see if most browsers on the market can interpret the content of the site. This means that older versions of a browser need to be loaded into a client computer and used to connect to the site. If an older version of a browser won't display certain attributes of the site, then a notice should be placed on the Web site that indicates what action should be taken.

Background Info

Check with the browser vendor to determine if an older browser version is automatically replaced when a newer version is installed. All versions of Netscape browsers install side-by-side so that you have access to any version that's installed on a machine. Microsoft browsers, on the other hand, will replace older versions of Internet Explorer, unless the machine is specifically told not to do so.

For example, a Web site may have video or audio files that a browser won't support. If the site requires plug-ins for the video or audio files, a link should be included for downloading the appropriate plug-ins.

Table 5-5 is a sample of a browser test used to check a site for several versions of Netscape Navigator and Internet Explorer.

HTML LINE	ATTRIBUTE	EXPLORER VERSION			NETSCAPE VERSION		
		3	4	5	2	3	4
23	ALINK	N	Y	Y	Y	Y	Y

Table 5-5 Format to Test Browsers

Web browsers that don't support an HTML tag simply ignore the tag. If a site is using the latest technology to display content, a quick test like the one shown in Table 5-5 can be used to indicate the visitors that may not be able to fully utilize the site because their browser won't support the technology.

E-commerce

An **e-commerce** site is generally tested in conjunction with the merchant software used to set up the site. This typically involves using a dummy credit card number that's entered while connected to the site.

e-commerce

The merchant software will then check the number and process an "order" as if an actual customer placed the order. The complete process will be examined as follows:

1. Encryption of the account number received from the browser.

2. Comparison of certificates between banks and credit card issuers.

3. Withdrawal of funds against a credit card.

4. Deposit of funds to the merchant account.

5. Transaction notification sent to merchant describing the transaction (completed, denied, etc.). Or, the transaction may be logged to be sent to the merchant at a later time, for example, within twenty-four hours.

Most merchant software, such as MercanTec, require that an e-commerce site be tested before going "live"; that is, before accepting actual orders.

Load Testing

Load testing

Load testing refers to the length of time required to open all files of a site in a Web browser. Typically, a load test is conducted at several modem speeds and, ideally, by using several bandwidth methods (T-carrier, dial-up, cable modem, etc.).

The reason that a site should be load tested under different conditions is so that it can be designed for most users. This is particularly important when the site incorporates technologies other than HTML to create the site. For example, if a site makes extensive use of Java applets, connects to an SAP server, or interfaces to a database, the load times will be slower.

Table 5-6 Load Test

Table 5-6 is an example of a load test used to download an image file at various speeds.

SPEED	TIME	FILE TYPE	FILE SIZE	FILE
14.4 Kbps	29.2 s	Image	1100 bytes	photo.gif
28.8 Kbps	15.35 s	Image	1100 bytes	photo.gif
33.8 Kbps	11.71 s	Image	1100 bytes	photo.gif
56 Kbps	8.32 s	Image	1100 bytes	photo.gif
128 Kbps (ISDN)	4.65 s	Image	1100 bytes	photo.gif
1.44 Mbps (T1)	2.45 s	Image	1100 bytes	photo.gif

In addition to measuring the load time of images, the load time of the entire page should be measured. As a general rule, a Web page should load in less than 30 seconds. If not, take a second look at the HTML specifying tables or image sizes. If the width and height of an image, for example, aren't specified in the HTML, the browser is forced to determine the best size of the file. This will cause the page to take longer to load. The same is true for cell attributes in a table. By specifying height and width sizes of the table and cells within the table, the table will load faster.

If the files that constitute a Web page are scattered among different servers, the page will take longer to load in a browser. When a client connects to a Web site, a port is opened for downloading files to the client. If more than one server is involved in downloading site content, then time-to-load at the browser increases because a port must be opened at each server involved in the download.

Decide if the number of graphics used at the site can be reduced. The fewer the graphics, the faster the site will load in a browser.

Site Access

Site access

Site access refers to options that screen some visitors, while allowing others full access. For example, if a portion of a site is password protected, check the password mechanism to determine if it works. Typically, passwords are randomly generated. Generate a test password as if you are an authorized visitor, and then use it to ensure the password allows you access.

In a similar manner, if a Web site contains a database (for conducting site searches or for locating product information, for example), then use the tool used to access the database to make sure it performs as intended.

Speed

The **speed** of a server refers to the time required for a client to connect to a Web server. Several attributes may be included in measuring server speed. Table 5-7 lists typical server speed tests and includes actual speeds as well as average speeds for comparison purposes.

speed

Table 5-7 Speed Tests

TEST	ACTUAL	AVERAGE
Ping Time	125 mS	400 mS
DNS Translation Time	.5 S	.8S
Connect Time	2.6 S	1.75 S
Download Time	4 S	5 S
Timeout	10 S	30 S

ping test

The **ping test** is conducted from the network driver installed on the server. The HTTP protocol utilized to access the site is not involved in a ping test, so this test provides a good indicator of speeds between the server and a client. If the ping times tend to be on the high side (longer than the average) it may mean congestion on the network where the server is located.

DNS translation times measure how long it takes to reconcile a domain name to the IP address assigned to the name. When a site is first set up, DNS translation times should be conducted because they will be longer than for a site that has been active for several weeks. The initial time provides a worst-case benchmark to measure against.

The **connect time** describes how long it takes for a client to connect to a Web server. Long connect times may be due to various factors including the network connection (the physical infrastructure used from client to server), the type of connection (dial-up, T-carrier, ISDN), and the configuration of the server. If the ping test is normal, but the connect time is long, the problem is likely to be with the server. For example, a Web server is configured for some maximum number of users that can connect to it. If the actual number of users exceeds the maximum number specified, then connect times will lengthen. If the connection times become too long—more than a minute or so—the user will receive a timeout message and won't be able to connect to the server.

The **download time** is the time required to download the complete Web page in the user's browser. A site that consists primarily of text files will load much faster than a site that includes extensive multimedia files such as audio and video. The trick is to strike a balance between a page that is visually appealing and that won't frustrate visitors due to long download times.

A **timeout** refers to the amount of time required to request services from a Web server. Sites that include search engines or searchable databases may timeout on users under heavy demands. The TCP protocol plays a role in determining how soon a connection will timeout, but you should check a Web site frequently to make sure visitors are able to access information in a reasonable amount of time.

SERVER TROUBLESHOOTING

Internet servers are, essentially, computers. This section lists several troubleshooting hotspots that can be applied to nearly any server. E-mail and the content of Web sites receive specific attention in this section because they have peculiarities not shared by most Internet servers.

When troubleshooting Web servers, it's helpful to know some of the more common HTTP codes that are generated for various conditions. HTTP error codes are returned automatically during the server response phase of a HTTP TCP connection. Table 5-8 lists several common HTTP codes.

Table 5-8 Common
HTTP Codes

HTTP CODE	CODE DESCRIPTION
200	Transmission to the server has been successful.
302	The HTTP request has been redirected to another URL.
304	The file that has been requested is in the client's cache and will be retrieved from there.
401	Access has been denied. This is normally for password protected sites.
403	Access denied because the request has been for explicit site files such as administrator files.
404	Request not found. The server may be indicating that the site doesn't exist, or that the request is from an unauthorized source.
500	The HTTP request can't be completed due to problems with the server, such as it may be down for maintenance.

E-mail

An e-mail server is typically set up as a different server than a Web server. This is because it uses a unique set of protocols by comparison with the protocols that users who simply access the Internet use. (Note that all transactions on the Internet use TCP/IP, even e-mail. But because e-mail requires SMTP, it's technically and historically treated separately from other Internet applications.) An e-mail server, if integrated into another server such as a Web server, may create bottlenecks due to the volume of e-mail sent and received.

An e-mail server must be assigned a domain name so that when a client is sent an e-mail, the DNS system will be able to resolve the domain name to the actual IP address assigned to the mail server.

Because a mail server usually has a unique IP address, it's possible that users may be able to access the Internet but not be able to send or receive e-mail. The most common cause of not being able to send or receive e-mail is that the mail server is simply down (for maintenance, due to a crash or some other problem). Other problems that will disable the mail server include using a protocol other than SMTP or using a domain name that hasn't been properly configured.

In order for a client to send e-mail, the SMTP protocol must be installed on each client. If the client is to have the option of downloading e-mail that's been placed on the mail server, the POP3 mail protocol should be installed on both the server and client.

Another area that can cause problems with e-mail is an improperly configured MIME file type. Examples of MIME types include base64 and Quoted Printable used with Microsoft operating systems. Most e-mail software allows you to configure the MIME type used for attaching documents to an e-mail message. The MIME type used on the client should be compatible with the MIME type used at the mail server.

The following list summarizes typical e-mail server problems:

- The e-mail server doesn't have a proper mail name.

- The mail server isn't configured properly.

- The protocol running on the e-mail server isn't SMTP.

- The client computer doesn't have SMTP.

- The client computer doesn't have POP3 installed.

- Incorrect MIME types.

Slow Server

Taxing the resources of the server can cause a slow server. For example, if the server isn't configured for the number of visitors accessing the site, there will be long waits and time outs for users waiting to open a connection at the site. The lack of simultaneous connections that accommodate the volume of visitors is configurable with the server software.

Most Web servers continuously monitor the number of connections that are being opened. When the number is around 70% of the maximum available, the server will generate an alarm message. The server administrator will then have a bit of time (hopefully) to reconfigure the connections, or take some other action, before users are forced to wait for access. Other alternatives to reconfiguring the server is to create replication, or mirror, servers that users will be redirected to if a primary server is busy. Many large, busy Web sites organize servers into rings. The ring of servers all have the same content and are used to balance the load volume of visitors.

The hardware used with the server may be causing the server to run slow. For example, the microprocessor used with the server may be slow, which will cause the server to run slow. Even if the microprocessor is the latest and fastest version on the market, it can't overcome mechanical latencies of hard drives. A hard drive can cause the server to slow since the read mechanism used with hard drives is mechanical. A typical read to a fast hard drive may take about .01 seconds, far slower than the microprocessor is operating.

Insufficient RAM is another hardware bottleneck that will slow both a server and a client machine. As far as a server is concerned, more RAM is better.

If a cache server is used on the client side of an Internet connection, the cache can be a source of slow connections. If access times tend to slow during peak periods of Internet usage—early in the morning and at lunchtime—then the cache size should be increased.

The following list summarizes common sources of a slow server:

- The server isn't configured properly for the volume of site visitors.

- The server RAM is insufficient.

- The server microprocessor is overloaded.

- The server cache is too small.

- The server hard drive mechanics are creating long queues.

Web Site

A Web site can be a source of problems due to the content used on the site. The most common problem occurs when HTML tags are used improperly or misspelled. The best fix for this problem is to have the HTML file edited by someone knowledgeable, or to hire an outside testing service that will check the syntax and spelling used with the file.

Unless a Web site is very large and complex, try to keep all files for the same site on a single server. If the page files are located on multiple servers, the client browser must open connections with each server in order to load the page, and this requires time to do so.

An attempt should be made to use pre-installed client scripts when possible. For example, if a Java script applet can be pre-installed on the client, this saves considerable time. If the script isn't pre-installed, the Web server must execute the file and download the content to the browser, which may be very time intensive if the server is busy and the executable is complex. Along the same line, CGIs—which must be executed—will cause a Web site to load slowly if they are used extensively at the site.

Graphic files should be checked to ensure they aren't corrupted. Be sensitive to the size of the file, the type of file extension used, and the resolution of the graphic. The best policy to implement when using a file type that's questionable as to whether a browser will display it, is to test known browsers first.

Some HTML editors insert graphic files into a page and make assumptions about the size attributes of the graphic. If the height and width of the file are specified, the print portion of the document will be placed on the Web page during download in the proper position. Then, as the graphic downloads, it will fill the space specified in the HTML. If the height and width aren't specified, the browser will assume a position for the text, but may have to change the position once the text arrives and graphics are downloaded. The time needed to format the page at the browser may be so long that a site visitor will click-off to another Web site.

Links must be routinely checked, especially links to other Web sites. If the links on a Web site aren't functioning, the entire site is questionable from the perspective of a visitor.

Web sites intended for the general public should be written to the level of the general public. The use of acronyms, for example, can be very confusing to novices. Consider this phrase:

HTTP, along with TCP, transports IP packets containing HTML and JPG files via end-user PPP accounts.

The sentence is technically correct, but if you don't know what all of the abbreviations mean, it makes no sense.

In a similar manner, avoid using colloquialisms that are common to the United States and particular to the English language. Here's an example:

It's raining cats and dogs.

It's probably not. More likely, it's raining hard.

The following list summarizes typical Web site problems:

- HTML syntax errors and misspellings.

- Page files from multiple servers.

- Lack of client-side scripts to handle executable files.

- Excessive use of executable files such as CGIs.

- Images that don't include height and width attributes.

- Corrupt files.

- Large files.

- Resolution conflict between the client browser and server page.

- Broken links.

- Unknown file extensions.

- Excessive and confusing acronyms and colloquialisms.

KEY POINTS REVIEW

- Bandwidth and the amount of data that's transferred are directly proportional. If the bandwidth is increased, then the amount of information transfer will increase as well.

- The number of connection points and the quality of the connections will affect the reliability of a connection to an Internet site.

- A deliberate effort should be made to attract visitors to a Web site using tools such as META tags, banner ads, and alternative media for advertising.

- The goals of a Web site should be matched to the services available from an ISP. The ISP can directly affect security, site performance, and site reliability.

- The files that compose the pages of a Web site should be tested and checked for HTML errors, corrupt files, mismatched file extensions, the resolution of graphics, and the relative size of graphic files.

- A network operating system, or NOS, consists of software used to manage network security, user accounts, file and printing functions, and other features for computers connected in a network. The most common NOSs are Windows NT, Novell NetWare, and UNIX.

- A universal Internet solution includes all tools and software needed to set up and equip an Internet Web site.

- A firewall is used to prevent corporate network users from accessing portions of the Internet and to prevent outside intruders from accessing a corporate network.

- A proxy server is used to replace a client IP address with an IP address assigned by a proxy server.

- An e-mail server is used to send, receive, and store e-mail messages; and to maintain a list of authorized user accounts. SMTP is used to send e-mail; POP3 is used to receive e-mail from mail server to client.

- A mirror server is used to replicate server contents.

- A list server is used to maintain a list of message subscribers and to automatically send the messages to subscribers.

- A cache server is used to save Web, FTP, or other files. A cache server compares the current version of a Web file to the stored version and replaces the stored version if not current.

- A Web server is used to store HTML and other file types.

- A news server is used to access USENET news groups via the NNTP protocol.

- A certificate server is used to provide a secured connection between client and server by using encryption and security certificates.

- A directory server is used to access or search distributed data via the LDAP protocol.

- An e-commerce server is used for secure financial transactions over the Internet. An e-commerce site employs encryption techniques to secure credit card purchases.

- A telnet server is used to allow a client to login and use the services of a remote server.

- An FTP server is used to upload and download files via the FTP protocol.

- Each time a change is made to a site, the links should be checked to ensure they are still valid.

- A Web site should be checked to see if most browsers on the market, including older versions of the browser, can interpret the content of the site.

- An e-commerce site is generally tested in conjunction with the merchant software used to set up the site. This typically involves using a dummy credit card number that's entered while connected to the site.

- Load testing refers to the length of time required to open all files of a site in a Web browser.

- Site access refers to options that screen some visitors, while allowing others full access. For example, a portion of a site may be password protected to screen some of the visitors.

- The speed of a server refers to the time required to connect to a Web server.

- Typical problems associated with an e-mail server include SMTP not installed, the server not available, and incorrect MIME type configuration.

- Typical problems associated with a slow server include too many visitors for the configured number of connections to the server, and inadequate resources such as a slow microprocessor and insufficient RAM.

- Typical problems associated with Web site problems include incorrect HTML syntax and misspellings, incompatible file extensions, lack of height and width attributes for graphics, corrupt files, and broken links.

REVIEW QUESTIONS

The following questions test your knowledge of the material presented in this chapter:

1. Describe how the bandwidth to a Web site affects page downloads.

2. How will a graphic file be displayed if the resolution of the graphic is set higher at the Web site than a client browser can display it?

3. In order to allow users access to the Internet, Windows NT, Novell NetWare, and UNIX must all support the _____ protocol.

4. What is a universal Internet solution?

5. Describe the difference between a firewall and a proxy server.

6. When an e-mail is sent to joe@comp.com, what is the domain name of the receiving e-mail server?

7. Describe the effect a cache server will have on client workstation load times in the browser.

8. What is the purpose of a certificate server?

9. If an e-mail server is down, what type of server is an alternative for sending e-mail attachments?

10. During pre-launch of a Web site, all links were tested and found to be working correctly. Why should links continue to be tested after the site is active?

11. You receive a complaint from a user that the user's browser ignores a new HTML tag used in your Web site. What is the likely problem?

12. What does it mean when a Web site is "load tested"?

13. After receiving complaints from users that they can't access the e-mail server, you check it and discover that 1) the protocol installed on the server is SNMP, 2) that the server MIME-type is the same as configured for users, and 3) that all clients are configured to access a POP3 server. What's wrong with the e-mail server?

14. Web server access slows considerably from 11:00 AM until 1:00 PM. Before and after these hours, server access is normal. What would make the server slow during the two-hour period?

15. What is the advantage to specifying the height and width of a graphic used in an HTML file?

MULTIPLE CHOICE QUESTIONS

1. A new Web site is expected to draw a very high number of visitors from around the world. Which of the following is the most important consideration for a high number of visitors?

   a. Browsers type

   b. Number of page links

   c. Bandwidth

   d. Banner ads

2. Which of the following is used to describe a Web site listing in search engines?

   a. META tags

   b. ref tags

   c. Certificate

   d. Proxy

3. What is used to prevent intruders from accessing a network from the Internet?

   a. Firewall

   b. Cache

   c. Base64

   d. Cookie

4. Which of the following client-side protocols will be configured for downloading e-mail from an e-mail server?

   a. HTTP

   b. FTP

   c. LDAP

   d. POP3

5. What network protocol must be installed in order to run UNIX?

   a. NetBEUI

   b. TCP/IP

   c. IPX/SPX

   d. AppleTalk

6. A Web server is configured for a maximum of 100 Internet connections. If the number of visitors to the site exceeds 100, what will happen?

   a. Load times will increase.

   b. The server cache will overload.

   c. The number of timeouts will increase.

   d. Links will be broken.

7. What type of server requires the use of the NNTP protocol on the server and client?

   a. List Server

   b. News Server

   c. Telnet Server

   d. E-commerce Server?

8. What type of server stores Web site files so that page loads to clients will be faster?

    a. Proxy Server

    b. Cache Server

    c. Mirror Server

    d. FTP Server

9. What type of server uses the SSL protocol?

    a. Certificate Server

    b. Directory Server

    c. Mail Server

    d. Cache Server

10. What type of server provides a single point of access to distributed information?

    a. Web Server

    b. Proxy Server

    c. Directory Server

    d. Mail Server

11. What type of server requires the use of merchant software?

    a. Telnet Server

    b. List Server

    c. News Server

    d. E-commerce Server

12. What type of server allows remote login to clients using a command-line interface?

    a. Mirror Server

    b. Web Server

    c. E-commerce Server

    d. Telnet Server

13. What type of server is used to replicate Web sites?

    a. Proxy Server

    b. Mirror Server

    c. FTP Server

    d. Mail Server

14. What type of server uses the SMTP protocol on clients and server?

    a. Mail Server

    b. News Server

    c. Directory Server

    d. Certificate Server

15. What type of server is used to automatically send messages to a group of subscribers?

    a. Mail Server

    b. Web Server

    c. List Server

    d. Directory Server

CHAPTER 6

INTERNET SECURITY

**LEARNING
OBJECTIVES**

LEARNING OBJECTIVES

Upon completion of this chapter and its related lab procedures, you should be able to perform the following tasks:

1. (5.4) Describe access security features for an Internet server. Examples could include the following:

    - Username and password

    - File level

    - Certificate

    - File-level access: read, write, no access

2. (5.1) Describe the following Internet security concepts: access control, encryption, auditing, and authentication, and provide appropriate types of technologies currently available for each. Examples could include the following:

    - Access control—access control list, firewall, packet filters, proxy

    - Authentication—certificates, digital signatures, non-repudiation

    - Encryption—public and private keys, socket layers (SSL), S/MIME, digital signatures

    - Auditing—intrusion detection utilities, log files, auditing logs

3. (5.3) Describe various types of suspicious activities. Examples could include the following:

    - Multiple login failures

    - Denial of service attacks

    - Mail flooding/spam

    - Ping floods

    - SYN floods

4. (5.5) Describe the purpose of anti-virus software and when to use it. Content could include the following:

    - Browser/client

    - Server

5. (5.2) Describe VPN and what it does. Content could include the following:

    - VPN is encrypted communications

    - Connecting two different company sites via an Internet VPN

    - Connecting a remote user to a site

Internet Security

INTRODUCTION

Security is a complex and challenging aspect of the Internet. The ultimate security goal of any network is to protect data from thieves, snoops, and intruders. A thief may use the information gleaned from a server for any number of reasons such as selling the information or using it to gain a competitive advantage. A snoop is someone who simply wants to know what's in a server that they don't have access to. By far, employees of a company are the greatest threat in the snooping category. Intruders typically have a malicious intent to disrupt or crash a server or network.

Network security comes with a price. While data can be reasonably protected, the protection comes with a loss of performance. The more extensive the security measures, the greater the performance loss. For example, time is required to encrypt a file before sending it across the Internet. Decryption on the other end of the connection also requires time.

This chapter is a comprehensive overview of network security. But security techniques used on the Internet change frequently. They have to because TCP/IP, the protocol of the Internet, was never intended to be a particularly secure protocol. There are many opportunities for intruders or hackers to find security holes in TCP/IP. As the holes are discovered, new countermeasures must be developed to preserve the integrity of Internet servers and the information in the servers.

INTERNET SERVER ACCESS SECURITY

There are numerous methods used to control access to Internet-based servers. In the case of e-commerce servers, access is stringent. But in the case of a public Web server, the level of access is restricted to certain linked files in a directory. In order to view files outside of the public directory, a password is required.

In this section, several types of server access will be defined.

Username and Password

A username and password is a means of authenticating and controlling access to servers. When a username and password is entered to access a server, the password is compared to a database of usernames and matching passwords. If the username and password that were entered match in the database, it's assumed that you are who you say you are, and you're admitted.

Background Info

Authentication

Authorization

Authentication is not the same as authorization. **Authentication** is the process of verifying identities. **Authorization** is the process of being given access to resources. Being admitted to a restricted area of a server may mean little unless you have been authorized to access some or all of the resources on the server. Access control lists or user profiles are created that stipulate the resources a user is authorized to use.

Username and password security means that you must enter the correct username and password before you can access a server, or a restricted part of a server. The information is typically entered in a form that's generated when you access the URL of a protected server.

Most extranets control access via usernames and passwords. Because the server is connected to the public Internet, any host on the Internet could connect to the server, but access will be denied to those without the correct password.

In many cases, no username or password is required to access a Web server. The server contents have been placed on the Internet with the hope that it will attract many visitors. However, there may be portions of the server that are not intended for the Internet public. For example, files that contain number counters so that the number of visitors can be tracked may not be accessible. Files that collect information about users so that a cookie can be sent back to the user's browsers won't be accessible.

Access to a secure FTP site may be via a graphical interface in which you enter a username and password in a manner that's similar to a network logon screen. Without the interface, however, you have the option of logging on at the time that the FTP site URL is entered. The syntax for logging on in this way is:

username:password@ftp.xxx.xxx

For example, assume a username of *bbrown* with a password of *getin*. To logon to an FTP site called *ftp.download.com*, the entry would be bbrown:getin@ftp.download.com

In cases where portions of a server are accessible via a username and password, some type of file level security has been applied to those sections of the server.

File Level Access

File level security is intended to restrict the level of access to the server content. The most common levels of file security are Read, Write, and Full.

- **Read-only access** means that you may view the file or directory contents, but you can't modify the content. A file with read-only access may be identified with the letter R.

- **Write access** means that you can view and modify the content of a file or directory on a server. A file with write access will be identified with the letters RW.

- **Full access** means that you can view, modify, and initiate executable software. A file with full access may be identified with the letters RWE.

Certificate

Certificate-level access refers to digital certificates that are used to authenticate users or Web sites. The most common application is for authenticating Web sites, particularly e-commerce sites.

A digital certificate eliminates the need for username and password authentication. In a typical situation, a client Web browser that accesses a secured server will request the digital certificate of the server. The server will encrypt its certificate and send it to the browser. The browser will decrypt the certificate and check the certificate for validity and to see if the certificate has been modified. If the certificate is valid and if it hasn't been modified, the browser will assume the secured server is authentic.

Certificates are used as part of the Secure Socket Layer protocol and are described in greater detail later in this chapter.

INTERNET SECURITY CONCEPTS

In order for a network to be reasonably secure, the security policy for the network must address the following areas:

- **Access control**: Access control refers to measures taken that admit, limit, restrict, or deny access to the resources of a network.

- **Authentication**: Authentication refers to a process of guaranteeing the identity of a user or server.

- **Encryption**: Encryption refers to hiding the content of data packets so that the information in the packets will remain confidential and unchanged.

- **Auditing**: Auditing refers to techniques used for monitoring network access and authentication.

The broad issues discussed in this section apply equally to the Internet, intranets, extranets, and **virtual private networks (VPN)**. A VPN consists of two devices that use the Internet infrastructure to exchange secured packets, and is described in the Virtual Private Network section later in this chapter.

The level of security that is applied to each of the network types may differ according to the type of network and the type of information that's exchanged. Use Table 6-1 as a general guide to determining the appropriate level of security.

**Table 6-1 Network
Security Guidelines**

NETWORK TYPE	ACCESS CONTROL	AUTHENTICATION	ENCRYPTION	AUDITING
Internet	Always	Minimal	Occasional (e-commerce)	Always
Intranet	None	Minimal	Rarely	Always
Extranet	Always	Always	Occasional	Always
VPN	Always	Always	Always	Always

Note that there are exceptions. For example, an intranet has little need to institute controls that limit or identify outside intruders, unless the intranet has a computer port that connects to any portion of the public Internet or telecommunications infrastructure.

Authentication for access to the Internet or an intranet is typically limited to a username and password. But the intent of the password is not so much to authenticate the user as it is to serve as a method for accessing authorized resources.

Note that auditing should be implemented on all types of networks.

The following sections provide detailed information for the core components of a security policy.

Access Control

Access control refers to security precautions that protect network users from Internet intruders. The most common components used to control access to a network are a firewall and proxy server. In small networks, the firewall and proxy may be housed in the same machine, but in larger networks, the two devices are physically separated.

A firewall is used to protect the users of a network from intruders outside the network. Typically, the intruder is at a remote host connected to the Internet. Figure 6-1 illustrates the components needed to protect a network from the Internet. The security system is composed of:

- A Firewall
- Proxy Server
- Detection Logs

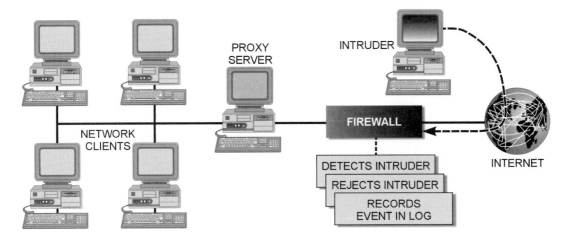

Figure 6-1 Intruder Protection System

The firewall may be configured in many ways, but the most common method is to use it to filter packets that arrive at the network from the Internet. The firewall may also be used to filter packets sent from the network to the Internet.

The proxy server (also called an **application gateway**) is used to screen certain Internet-related services from the connected network. For example, the proxy may be configured to prevent an outside host from telnetting to a workstation on the Internet. Telnet can raise some security issues since a knowledgeable intruder can use it to capture keystrokes from a workstation. If the proxy is configured to prevent any telnet connections initiated from outside the network, then the use of telnet for compromising network security is eliminated.

A proxy server, as described in Chapter 5, is also used to protect the IP addresses of network workstations. When a workstation connects to the Internet, the proxy server will replace the IP address assigned to the workstation with a proxy IP address.

Detection logs, when properly set up, will alert an administrator that a potential breach is occurring. The main weakness of many security systems is a lack of logging suspicious activities. If the activity isn't logged, a security break may be detected only after the intruder has breached the network.

The degree to which a firewall or proxy is effective at preventing unauthorized access to a network is determined by the type of firewall or proxy used and the method used to detect or thwart an intruder. The following section provides details of firewall types, methods used to prevent intruders, and the benefits of using both a firewall and a proxy server to secure a network.

Packet Filters

packet filtering gateway

A firewall may be set up to filter traffic that is in-bound from the Internet to a network workstation, as well as to filter traffic that's bound from a network workstation to the Internet. This type of filter is called a **packet filtering gateway**. The filter is specific to fields in a TCP/IP packet and may include any of the following:

- Protocol such as IP, UDP, FTP, Telnet

- Source IP Address from the host where the packet originated

- Destination IP Address for the host where the packet is to be sent

- Source Port Number such as 20 or 21 for FTP

- Destination Port Number such as 20 or 21 for FTP

In most cases, packet filtering is accomplished with a router. The specific vendor of the packet filter router will determine which of the filters listed above will be included in the router.

packet filter

The **packet filter** set up on a firewall is sometimes configured in an across-the-board manner to filter certain fields. For example, telnet may be eliminated for all network users. If, however, there are specialized users who routinely participate in telnet sessions, the telnet restriction may be lifted through the use of access control lists.

A packet filter set on an IP address is used to screen known sources of trouble. Many organizations use destination IP address packet filters to block employees from accessing Web sites that aren't appropriate to their business. At the same time, a block may be placed on all source IP addresses. Only source IP addresses that are known or trusted will be exempted from the filter. For example, a virtual private network (VPN) that uses the Internet for connecting networks may block IP addresses except for those that have been assigned by a DHCP server. Similarly, an extranet may block IP addresses except those that originate from a trusted business partner or authorized employee.

Block port filtering

In a similar manner, all TCP/IP port numbers may be filtered except those that are reserved for well-known ports (which range from 0 to 1023). This has the advantage of blocking an intruder using a port number that's disguised to appear legitimate when it's only intended to capture information about the connected client on the network. **Block port filtering** can cause problems when a company or ISP uses an unreserved well-known port number (numbers above 1023) for a specialized application. In a situation such as this, the port number must be exempted using access lists.

Access control lists

Access control lists may be employed in a firewall for directing exemptions to packet filters. For example, a file called telnet_access could be placed on the firewall. Listed in the file would be usernames that are permitted to establish a telnet connection to a remote site. The firewall will compare any packet with telnet in the header to the list of approved usernames, and if there's a match, open the connection to the remote telnet site. If there's not a match, the connection will be rejected.

FTP access is controlled in a similar way. In a large network, there may be a specific FTP server that accommodates all file uploads and downloads. But because FTP, like e-mail, is a source for viruses, a packet filter may be set so that uploads to the FTP server from the Internet are rejected. The filter is set so the **put command** entered during the FTP session is rejected. However, Internet users connected to the FTP server may download files using the **get command** because it won't be filtered.

put command

get command

Table 6-2 shows an example of packet filtering that is focused on TCP port numbers.

LINE NO.	SOURCE IP ADDRESS	DESTINATION IP ADDRESS	SOURCE PORT	DESTINATION PORT	ACTION
1	*	192.168.20.10	*	80	Accept
2	*	192.168.50.15	*	25	Accept
3	*	192.168.20.20	*	21	Accept
4	*	192.168.20.20	*	20	Accept
5	172.16.20.1	192.168.50.10	80	80	Reject

Table 6-2 Packet Filtering

Line 1 of the packet filter is set so that all IP addresses (indicated with the *) will be admitted to a server located at 192.168.20.10. The server will accept any source port number but the server will only be listening at port number 80, which is the TCP well-known port number for HTTP (the World Wide Web). The server will accept all Web connections.

Line 2 of the packet filter is set so that all traffic destined for port number 25 will be sent to 192.168.50.15. Well-known port number 25 is for SMTP, the e-mail protocol used on the Internet. The e-mail server is located at IP address 192.168.50.15 and all incoming mail will be sent to this server.

Line number 3 is also set so that all source IP addresses will be sent to a server located at 192.168.20.20 on well-known port number 20, which is the port number for FTP. The server will accept all FTP requests.

Line 4 is identical to the action described for Line 3 except the FTP server will be listening at port number 20 instead of port 21. Port numbers 20 and 21 are standardized for FTP use.

Line 5 of the packet filter is used to reject requests from the source IP address 172.16.20.1 on port 80. Notice that the incoming request is specified for the HTTP—Web—server. This line of the filter is used to block connections to the Web site located at 172.16.20.1.

Proxy

The most common use of a proxy server, or application gateway, is to prevent network workstation IP addresses from being advertised on the Internet. If a potential intruder captures a valid IP address, the intruder can use the address for several types of attacks that can cripple a network. (See the Intruder Detection section later in this chapter for more information about service attacks.)

In addition to preventing network IP addresses from being advertised to the Internet community, a proxy is useful in reverse situations. That is, it may be physically positioned so that the proxy is the only access point to a network. Because all in-bound traffic must first pass through the proxy, the proxy can be used to filter packets as described above.

A proxy server may be configured so that network users only have access to specified portions of the Internet. For example, the proxy could be set up so that no users are able to use FTP or telnet. In addition, specific sites may be placed off-limits to users.

There are several other advantages to using a proxy:

- It serves as a single device for gathering logging information from packets entering or exiting a network. Because only the proxy server (or servers, because an e-mail server is essentially a proxy server for e-mail users) is involved in logging Internet traffic, other network machines, such as network servers, will not have to dedicate resources for capturing and maintaining the logs. The logs may capture source and destination IP addresses, domain name information, and so on.

- It can reduce packet filtering schemes. Keep in mind that router packet filters can become complex if there are many users on a network and if there are many customized packet filters. With a proxy server, a router can be installed that passes all traffic to and from the Internet without regard to filtering because the proxy will handle all packet filters. This improves the performance of the router.

- It can be used to authenticate in-bound Internet traffic. For example, if an FTP file loaded with a virus is directed to the network, the proxy will first determine if an authorized FTP session has been opened with a network workstation or server. An authorized FTP session means that the user connected to the FTP server is authorized to do so, and the proxy will not interfere with the user's access. If the connection isn't authorized, the FTP connection will be rejected by the proxy.

Typically, a proxy server is located at the interface to the Internet and may be used as a stand-alone security precaution, or in conjunction with a firewall. To provide the highest level of security, a proxy server should be used with a firewall as described in the next section, Firewall Types.

Firewall Types

There are numerous ways to physically connect a firewall at the interface of the Internet and a network. There are also numerous software solutions that combine functions of a proxy server and firewall. In this section, four configurations will be described: Packet Filter, Dual-Homed, Choke-Gate, and Screened Subnet.

A **packet filter firewall** is pictured in Figure 6-2. The firewall is typically a router that supports packet filtering.

packet filter firewall

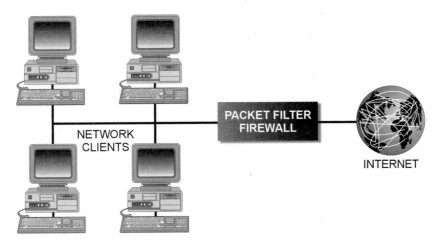

Figure 6-2 Packet Filter Firewall

A packet filtering firewall is most common in smaller networks in which the information stored on the network is not security-sensitive. The firewall is normally installed at the point where the network interfaces to the Internet. All network users accessing the Internet must pass through the firewall before being connected to the Internet. Filters that may be configured on the firewall include any combination of filters previously described.

For traffic in-bound from the Internet, the firewall may be configured to prevent any Internet application such as FTP uploads or e-mail. In addition, the firewall may reject all packets that are broadcast to all workstations connected to the Internet. This prevents the network workstations from being a target or unwitting accomplice in attacks against the network.

A **dual-homed firewall** is shown in Figure 6-3. A dual-homed firewall consists of a router and a proxy server that are contained in the same machine. The router is used as a single access point to and from the Internet. The proxy server is used to set all packet filters. Because a proxy server is essentially a computer, it can be software configured more efficiently than a router for setting filters. In addition, the proxy can be set up to capture traffic information for logging purposes.

dual-homed firewall

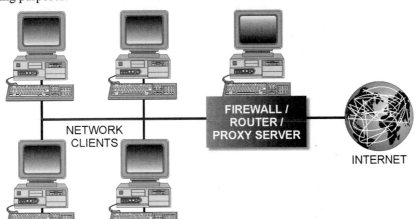

Figure 6-3 Dual-Homed Firewall

Note that in a dual-homed firewall, the router is used to specifically route data packets to and from the Internet, while the proxy is used to manipulate and control the data packets. The proxy is typically configured for filtering on usernames or user groups, and will replace the source IP address of all out-bound traffic with a proxy IP address.

The advantage of a dual-homed firewall is that a single machine is used to route packets and to set filters. Because both functions are being handled by the same device, dual-homed firewalls run somewhat slower that other types.

choke-gate firewall

A **choke-gate firewall**, shown in Figure 6-4, improves on the performance of a dual-homed firewall. A choke-gate firewall consists of a dedicated router and a dedicated firewall. The router is connected at the interface of the Internet. The proxy is connected to the internal side of the network. The router is responsible for handling packet flow to and from the network with no regard to filtering. Because the router is configured only for routing, it performs better than a firewall that combines the functions of a router and proxy server.

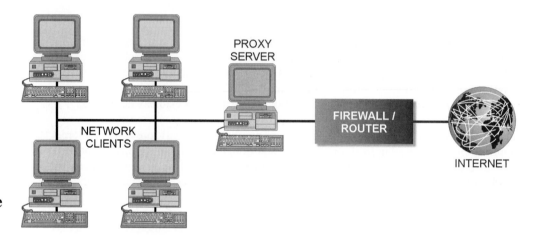

Figure 6-4 Choke-Gate Firewall

The proxy server performs all packet filtering. In addition, the proxy will replace workstation IP addresses with a proxy IP address and may also authenticate users via a password for connecting to the Internet. The proxy will typically log Internet-related activities such as the number of times that a user connects to the Internet, the length of the connection, and the sites that a user visited.

A choke-gate firewall adds another level of security for network users. Because the firewall consists of two devices that must be cleared, an intruder must pass through both devices before being admitted to a network.

screened-subnet firewall

A **screened-subnet firewall** is pictured in Figure 6-5. A screened-subnet firewall consists of a single router and multiple proxy servers. The proxy servers are normally dedicated to specific Internet applications such as e-mail, Web, or FTP. All traffic destined for the network will enter through the router. In some cases, the router may be configured to deny all traffic having certain characteristics, such as a packet with the FTP put command. This will prevent all file uploads to the network FTP clients or servers.

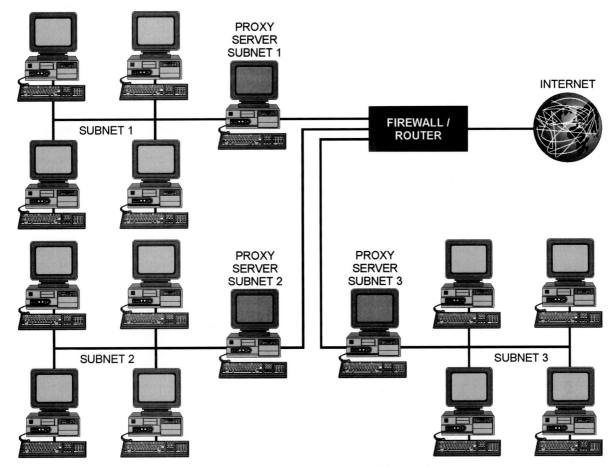

Figure 6-5 Screened-Subnet Firewall

The proxy servers are specified for functions such as e-mail or the Web. For example, one of the proxy servers may be configured with packet filtering so that it only accepts the SMTP protocol; hence, the proxy server is actually a dedicated e-mail server. Another server may be configured with packet filtering so that it only accepts the HTTP protocol; hence, it's a Web server.

A screened subnet is appropriate for larger networks where there are many users. Because numerous proxy servers are used in the firewall, a screened subnet offers the highest level of security. The major disadvantages of a screened-subnet firewall are the additional expense of the proxy servers and the level of complexity required to configure packet filtering on the dedicated servers.

Authentication and Encryption

The use of authentication and encryption must be defined for a network connected to the Internet. Users may need to be assured that the Web site they are connected to is actually the Web site they *think they are connected to*. Encryption may be a requirement if the information sent to or received from a server must remain confidential.

This section details common authentication and encryption schemes.

Authentication

Authentication is the process of identifying two parties engaged in communication across an open network such as the Internet. One of the earliest authentication systems is called Kerberos and was developed at the Massachusetts Institute of Technology. Kerberos authenticates the parties by embedding a key (that's assigned to each of the parties) in the messages that are exchanged. When a message is sent, the key in the message is compared to the key assigned to the sender. If the two match, then the receiving party will know that the message was sent by a trusted party.

Figure 6-6 shows the simplicity of Kerberos. The sender sends a request to exchange data with a receiver by including a message key in the request. The receiver compares the sender's message key with its key. Because the two keys are identical, the receiver returns a message indicating that the sender has been authenticated. Message packets will now be exchanged between the two parties.

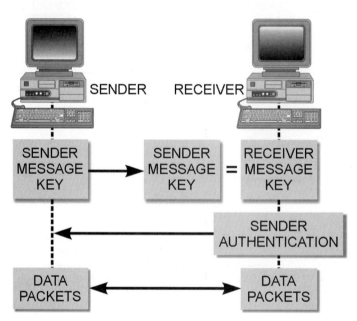

Figure 6-6 Kerberos Authentication

Other authentication systems require the usernames and passwords. A form that requires a user to enter a username and password is an authentication system. If you know the correct username and password, it's assumed that you are who you say you are. Password systems have weaknesses. The most apparent weakness is that passwords are compromised by writing them down, or by allowing others to see them when they're entered.

For secure communications over the Internet, the most common authentication system is contained in the Secure Socket Layer (SSL) protocol. SSL is described later in this chapter.

Encryption

Cryptography is the process of writing secret messages so that the message intelligence is hidden. In the past, secret communications have been the domain of governments, the military, and intelligence organizations. Today, these agencies still have a considerable need for cryptography, but the applications have broadened in the last decade or so with the explosion of commercial Web sites.

The basic concept of data cryptography is illustrated in Figure 6-7. The data is encrypted at the transmitter. Encryption is the process of transforming data into a secret code. **Decryption** is the process of transforming the secret code back to the original data, and is done at the receiver. The blocks labeled E and D in the figure represent encryption and decryption, respectively.

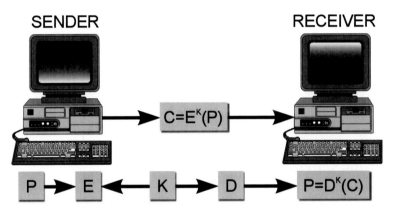

SENDER   RECEIVER

$$C = E^K(P)$$

$$P \rightarrow E \leftarrow K \rightarrow D \rightarrow P = D^K(C)$$

Figure 6-7 Data Encryption and Decryption

The data to be encrypted is called **plaintext** and is represented as P in the figure. Once the plaintext has been encrypted, it's referred to as **ciphertext**. Ciphertext is represented with a C in Figure 6-7.

All encryption techniques require the use of a **key**, shown in the figure as K. The key specifies the parameters of the secret code. For example, you may encrypt a message by changing all letters of the message to the next adjacent letter so that the word DATA becomes EBUB. The letter D is followed by E, A by B, T by U, and A by B.

The key used in this example may be written as:

$$K = X + 1$$

where for each plaintext letter (X), the cipher text results by using the next letter in the alphabet.

Encryption keys describe how the plaintext will be operated on to become ciphertext. The process of imposing the key on the plaintext is done with an encryption **algorithm**. The encryption and decryption blocks of Figure 6-7 represent an algorithm that will transform plaintext, through a series of permutations, to ciphertext. The algorithm is implemented in accordance with the encryption or decryption key. In our example of encrypting the word DATA, the algorithm is the necessary hardware and software needed to implement $K = X + 1$.

The encrypted data out of the transmitter of Figure 6-7 is $C = E^K(P)$. This means ciphertext (C) is produced by applying an encryption key (K) and algorithm (E) to the plaintext (P). Decryption takes place at the receiver according to $P = D^K(C)$. This means the plaintext (P) will be recovered by applying the decrypting key (K) and algorithm (D) to the ciphertext (C).

The strength of an encryption system is determined by the length and complexity of the key. For example, e-commerce Web sites use a 128-bit key to encrypt credit card transfers. For comparison, the minimum implementation of the **Data Encryption Standard (DES)** uses a 64-bit key.

Data Encryption Standard (DES)

Encryption systems are carefully protected in the United States. Most modern Web browsers support data encryption for use with 128-bit keys. Under current United States laws, no encryption system that uses a key length greater than 40 bits may be exported. If a computer, for example, that has a 128-bit encryption system is to be used outside the United State, the browser used in the computer must be replaced with an International browser that limits data encryption keys to 40 bits or less.

non-repudiation

The security process between two users on a network may use **non-repudiation**. Non-repudiation refers to proof of submission or delivery of information between two devices such as a Web server and a client. For example, non-repudiation can be used to guarantee that the data that was requested from a site (such as a Web server), was actually sent. The Web server, in turn, may also employ non-repudiation. The Web server may require that the client receiving the message cannot deny that it was received.

Encryption Schemes

substitution

transposition

product

Encryption systems can be divided into three classes: **substitution**, **transposition**, and **product** ciphers. Each of these is shown in Figure 6-8. The substitution class of Figure 6-8(a) is identical to our earlier example of encryption. A substitution cipher substitutes letters of the plaintext with other letters.

Plaintext: **DATA**
Ciphertext: **EBUB** (a)
Key: $K = X + 1$

Plaintext: **DATA**
Ciphertext: **ATAD** (b)
Key: $K = \overline{X}$

Plaintext: **DATA**
Ciphertext: **BUBE** (c)
Key: $K = \overline{X + 1}$

Figure 6-8 Encryption Schemes

Transposition classes of ciphers rearrange the sequence of the plaintext. In the example shown in Figure 6-8(b), the sequence of the letters in the word DATA have been reversed. Other transposition methods may involve route transposition of blocks of data, reversing the order of most- and least-significant bits in data streams, or by arranging messages in columns and transposing the columns.

The product cipher class of Figure 6-8(c) is a combination of substitution and transposition classes. The letters of the word DATA have been substituted by the next adjacent letter and then the order of the letters is transposed by reversing them.

The weakness of substitution encryption is that the code may be broken by analyzing patterns based on character frequency. For example, the letters E and T are commonly used letters. In our example of enciphering the word DATA, a frequency analysis would quickly reveal that the letter U corresponds to a frequently used letter. After a few trial-and-error attempts, our simple key would be broken.

Transposition is effective as long as any patterns in the plaintext don't exceed the length of the key. For example, mathematical equations that are long or complex, yet are duplicated many times over in a message, will reveal a pattern to a **cryptanalyst**. If the equations themselves can be derived by examining the redundancy in the ciphertext, the key itself will be revealed. Currently, 128-bit keys can be considered to be fully secure.

cryptanalyst

By combining substitution and transposition in a product cipher, the revealing nature of **character-frequency analysis** and the statistical properties of the ciphertext can be obscured.

character-frequency analysis

Private-Key Encryption

In a **private-key encryption** scheme, the same key is used to encrypt and decrypt an encoded message. Private-key encryption is also called **symmetric encryption**.

private-key encryption

symmetric encryption

Figure 6-9 shows an example of private-key encryption.

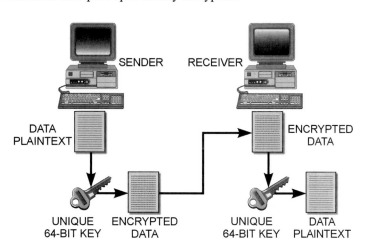

Figure 6-9 Private-Key Encryption

In the figure, a plaintext file is encrypted by the sender using a unique, 64-bit key. Typically, the key is generated by the encryption hardware and software. The encrypted file is then sent to the receiver. The receiver uses the same unique key to decrypt the file.

Note that the sender and receiver share the same key. Possession of the key authenticates each user. The idea is that if you possess the key, then you must be the one authorized to use the key. Symmetric cryptography is a very fast encryption method. However, the important disadvantage of private-key encryption is that the receiver has no way of knowing if the sender is actually authorized to possess the key.

The method of authentication used in private key encryption is weak. Frequently, users must either supply a username and password before using the scheme, or a third-party authentication scheme is used, such as Kerberos.

The most common private-key encryption scheme is the **Data Encryption Standard (DES)**. The **National Bureau of Standards (NBS)** adopted the Data Encryption Standard (DES) as a mandatory procedure in 1977. It's based on an IBM cryptographic scheme known as **LUCIFER**. The IBM technique successfully encrypted 64-bit blocks of plaintext under the control of a 56-bit key. The Bureau of Standards required government organizations to implement the DES and encouraged commercial vendors to do the same. The DES is the first algorithm offering strength of security over a wide range of applications.

The DES model is a product cipher that encrypts blocks of data. The substitution and superposition of bits is accomplished using a series of randomly generated keys during the encryption process. The electronic circuitry used to encrypt according to the DES model is composed of a series of digital registers. At specific points in the register path, the data is fed back to an earlier point in the register path. This process is called cyclic redundancy and is used to ensure that the data bits are operated upon during the encryption process many times over. Once data begins shifting through the registers, it does so according to the initial condition of the registers—that is, the data output is directly influenced by the logic 1's and 0's held in the registers at the time the data is fed through. The initial condition of the registers is determined by the algorithm, or key, used with the encryption scheme. The registers are initially set to the key, and data to be encrypted is then cycled through the generator. Decryption is the inverse of encryption.

Background Info

Cyclic redundancy is also used in the error checking fields of all layer 2 and 3 protocols. The error field is called a **Cyclic Redundancy Check**, or **CRC**. Protocols such as TCP, UDP, IP, Ethernet, and Token Ring all have a CRC (also called **check-sum**) field used to detect bit errors. The mechanics of an error checking process are very similar to the process used with data encryption.

Symmetric encryption will work only on 1's and 0's through substitution and transposition of the sequence of the 1's and 0's. It has the added advantage of cyclic redundancy, which produces ciphertext that's based on many permutations of the plaintext. Cryptoanalysts find it extremely difficult to find patterns in the ciphertext because each generated character is based upon the state of the registers for many cycles before the character. Another key advantage of symmetric encryption is that duplication of keys is unlikely. An 8-bit generator produces 256 keys, a 16-bit generator produces 65,536 keys, while a 24-bit generator can provide almost seventeen million unique keys.

The minimum key length used in the DES standard is 56 bits + 8 parity bits = 64 total bits. Depending on the sensitivity of data to be encrypted, the key length may be 192 bits long, or more. As a general rule, the more sensitive the data to be encrypted, the longer the encryption key.

Public-Key Encryption

One of the problems of receiving a secret message is deciding if the message originated with an authorized user, or was transmitted by someone who had gained access to the key. The assumption of the receiving user is that the message must be valid or it wouldn't have been sent. The flaw in that kind of logic is that the success of encryption lies in keeping the keys secret, while the object of unauthorized users is to uncover the keys without the knowledge of authorized users. A public-key cipher is intended to authenticate the message sender, as well as perform message encryption and decryption. Public-key encryption is also referred to as **asymmetric encryption**.

asymmetric encryption

Public-key encryption is shown in Figure 6-10. The sender wants to send an encrypted message to a receiver. First, the sender requests the receiver's public key. The sender uses the public key to encrypt a plaintext file, then sends the encrypted message to the receiver. The receiver uses its private key to decrypt the file. Note that the encrypted file can be decrypted only with the private key. Because the receiver possesses the only private key, no one else can decrypt the message. Although the private key is related to the public key, it can't be derived from the public key alone.

In a practical public-key system, all nodes on the network store the public keys of all other nodes. However, each node has its own, unique, private key. The advantage of public-key ciphers is twofold: the security of private keys is simple because they are protected at a single location, not at hundreds or thousands of sites. Secondly, erroneous secret messages are avoided, because message authentication depends on possessing a private key.

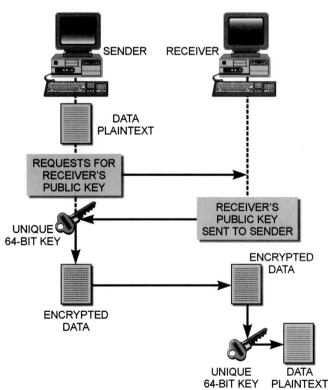

Figure 6-10 Public-Key Encryption

The challenge in using public-key ciphers is to generate two different keys—one public and one private—in which the encryption/decryption algorithms are related, but where neither key may be derived from the other. The most common public-key cipher is the **Rivest-Shamir-Adleman (RSA)** cipher. Keys are generated by factoring large numbers into **prime numbers**. A prime number is evenly divisible only by itself and 1. The primes are then manipulated mathematically, resulting in message decryption being the inverse of encryption.

The RSA cipher is one of the few ciphers having an inverse encryption/decryption property, based on prime numbers, which doesn't permit the revelation of either the private or public key with the use of the other.

The success of public-key ciphers lies in the computational difficulty of determining the original number from which the primes are derived. These ciphers assume that our limited mathematical knowledge (or lack of computer power) will remain their greatest security.

Normally, private-key encryption is limited to encryption/decryption. Although authentication can be incorporated into the exchange, it's usually handled by digital certificates.

A digital certificate is used to authenticate Internet users or Web sites. A digital certificate ensures that communication over the Internet is confidential and reliable. All e-commerce sites on the Internet use digital certificates in public-key encryption.

Figure 6-11 illustrates the use of a digital certificate.

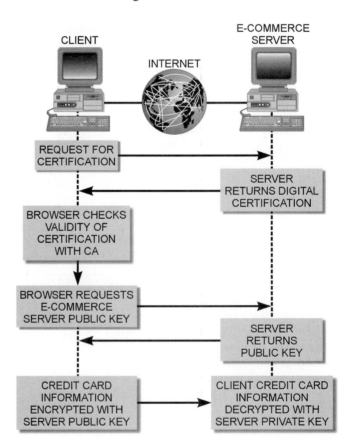

Figure 6-11 Digital Certificate Exchange

When a user wants to purchase an item on an e-commerce site using a credit card, the user's Web browser will authenticate the e-commerce server by checking its digital certificate. If the certificate is valid, the browser will request the e-commerce server's public key. The e-commerce server will send its public key to the purchaser's Web browser. The browser will encrypt the credit card information with the public key. When the e-commerce server receives the encrypted information, it uses its private key to decrypt the information. Because the e-commerce server possesses the only private key for the session, no other computer can decrypt the file.

For each session that the e-commerce server enters into with a Web browser, a new private key is created. Note that with public key encryption, there will be a unique set of public and private keys generated for each secure exchange between a server and client. Each of the private keys must be able to decrypt the file that's been encrypted using the public key, but none of the private keys can be derived from the public key.

The primary disadvantage to public-key encryption is that it's slow compared to private-key encryption. The key length of public-key ciphers used for credit card purchases on the Internet is 128 bits, whereas the private-key DES model allows for variable key lengths. Nearly all e-commerce sites on the Internet use public- key encryption that is designed into a protocol called Secure Socket Layer.

Secure Socket Layer Protocol

The Secure Socket Layer (SSL) protocol is used to authenticate users or e-commerce servers on the Internet, and to encrypt/decrypt messages (particularly credit card purchases) using public-key encryption. SSL encrypts data between the browser and the server.

The protocol consists of a digital certificate that the e-commerce site must possess before a Web browser will be able to authenticate the site. The digital certificate is issued by a Certificate Authority (CA). The role of the CA in the SSL session is to authenticate the holder of a certificate (such as an e-commerce server), and to provide a digital signature that will reveal if the certificate has been compromised.

CA certificates are pre-installed in all modern Web browsers. The browser uses the CA to authenticate a Web server.

Examples of CAs include:

- VeriSign
- Thawte
- Microsoft
- AT&T
- GTE
- InternetMCI

The digital certificate used in a public-key transaction is used to authenticate the Web site, typically an e-commerce site that accepts credit card orders. The reason that the site must be authenticated is that it's not too difficult to copy a complete Web site, then post the site using a domain name that's very similar to the "real" site. For example, it easy to mistake the site **micrsoft.com**, for **microsoft.com**. A purchaser may be lured to the first site, make a purchase, and never receive the purchased item.

The certificate will typically include the following information:

- The name of the holder of the certificate. If the certificate is to be used on a Web site, then the URL of the site will be listed.

- The name of the CA that issued the certificate.

- The date that the certificate became valid.

- The date that the certificate will expire.

- A digital signature.

The digital signature (a hexadecimal number) is used to indicate if the certificate has been modified in any way. If a certificate has been stolen for use on a bogus e-commerce site, then the thief must modify the certificate so that the bogus site can present the certificate to a Web browser. But when the certificate is modified, the signature will change. A change in the signature will create a change in keys used in the encryption process. Because the keys will change, the key held by the bogus site won't be able to decrypt information encrypted by the browser.

Background Info

hash secret

A digital signature may also be called a **hash secret**. A hash secret, or hash key, is generated by producing a number that's based on the content of the certificate. The key is encrypted with the remaining contents of the certificate during the initial setup of a SSL session and sent to a browser. The browser runs the hash function to produce the original digital signature. The message is then decrypted with the public key. If the digital signature that's decrypted matches the digital signature in the browser's database, then the browser knows that the server is authentic.

A connection to a certificate server that uses SSL will use a URL that begins with https://. For example, a site called *https://buy.now.com* is a secure site in which messages between the browser and server will be encrypted. The browser will indicate that the connection is secure by displaying a locked padlock, or key, near the bottom corner of the browser.

E-mail Encryption

Most commercial e-mail packages use the **S/MIME (Secure/MIME) protocol** for encrypting e-mail. S/MIME supports RSA (from RSA Data Security) encryption. RSA uses public-key encryption techniques.

Another e-mail encryption technique relies on the **Pretty Good Privacy (PGP)** encryption. PGP is a shareware tool. PGP uses a method that's similar to digital certificates. The digital certificates are used for authenticating the sender. In addition, PGP uses public-key encryption based on either RSA or Dixie-Hellman encryption algorithms (the two encryption techniques are not compatible). PGP is one of the most widely used encryption schemes used on the Internet. In addition to being available as a shareware download, a commercial version of the software can be obtained from Network Associates.

Microsoft Outlook, Microsoft Outlook Express, Netscape Messenger, and OpenSoft Express Mail all install S/MIME by default. However, there are PGP plug-ins available for all commercial e-mail packages.

The choice between PGP and S/MIME is one of preference because both methods use similar encryption techniques.

S/MIME (Secure/MIME) protocol

Pretty Good Privacy (PGP)

Auditing

Once a network is connected to an Internet Web server, all data on the network is at risk from intruders. **Intruders** refers to not only outside hackers, but employees within an organization. Employees offer the greatest security risk to a network because they have a greater inside knowledge of the network.

To get a handle on the security risks, a server that is connected in any way to the public Internet must audit the behavior of network users and log the results of the audit. Ideally, the server audits should encompass the following areas:

Intruders

- **Server configuration problems**: A Web server that's misconfigured or that contains bugs may permit remote users to access workstation or server files, execute server commands, or launch attacks that deny service to legitimate users.

- **Client-side Web browser problems**: A browser can unwittingly provide information about a user's work habits through the use of cookies. Some file types can crash a browser or contain viruses that may go undetected. Examples include **ActiveX controls** or any executable software such as CGI scripts, or Java scripts that have been intentionally written to crash a system.

- **Data interception**: Data can be intercepted at any point between a Web browser and a Web server. This includes any point on a local area network, between the local server (proxy, firewall, Web, or file server) and the ISP, between the ISP and regional access point to the Internet, and along the router path to a remote Web server.

Server configuration problems

Client-side Web browser problems

ActiveX controls

Data interception

The more complex the software that's installed on a Web server, the greater the security risk to users. A server that performs multiple duties such as file and print, proxy, Web access, or e-mail is at an even greater risk because the multiple functions leave the window open for more security holes. The best security practices dictate a separation of duties among servers when network users are granted Internet access. (Note that "Internet access" refers to the public Internet, extranet, intranet, or a virtual private network.)

All major network operating systems include software for auditing a network and for logging the audit results. Typically, the network administrator sets the audit parameters. The logs may be ongoing, or they may be temporary to capture statistical data. Generally, the following are tracked in audit logs:

- IP address or host/domain name of the remote servers.

- Requested URL. This includes links to other servers that may comprise a Web site.

- The user accessing a remote server. On a network connection, the user will be identified by a username. On a direct connection to an ISP, the user will be identified by an e-mail address.

- The size of file transmitted from the remote server to a local machine.

- Multiple failed logon attempts. Web servers will typically issue an alert for failed logons because this is the first sign that an intruder is attempting to access the network.

- Tracking of all IP broadcasts to a network from a remote host. A broadcast IP address contains 255 in the host portion of the IP address. A broadcast IP address may potentially mean that a network is being used to attack another network.

log files

An audit is composed of raw data, typically statistical information. The audit results are presented in **log files** so they can be reviewed for trends. A log file contains a summary of the raw data collected during an audit. A network administrator will review the log file and interpret the information according to insights gleaned from the logs.

There are commercial software packages available that are specifically designed to detect an intruder. For example, Axtant ITA is a company that provides a complete set of intruder detection utilities as well as auditing and logging software.

INTRUDER DETECTION

Intruder detection

Intruder detection refers to techniques designed to catch a remote user that's attempting to enter a network connected to the Internet. The intruder may intend to simply snoop around the network, infect the network with a virus, make configuration changes to servers, or to use the network as an intermediary in attacking another network.

This section is focused on network attacks. However, another type of intruder is one who never enters a network. An intercept intruder will intercept packets entering or leaving a network. The interceptor may copy the packets before forwarding them on, or the interceptor may capture the packets and never forward them.

A packet of data is, natively, in a binary number format. Many intrusion detection systems will interpret the binary data and present it either as hexadecimal numbers or in ASCII plaintext. Systems that identify the content of a data packet are called **host detection** schemes. Host detection is helpful in analyzing troubleshooting information contained in a TCP or IP packet, as well as for analyzing the packet for security threats.

Host detection

Multiple Login Failures

A multiple login failure occurs when an intruder attempts to login to a network but doesn't know the correct password. After a specified number of incorrect logins, the workstation will be locked out from the network. In order to unlock the workstation, intervention is required from the network administrator.

Multiple logins are a frequent method used by intruders for accessing a network. The task of the intruder is made easy when security policies are lax so that users aren't educated in choosing secure passwords. Many users choose the names of their children or spouse, special dates, or even their own name as a password. The intruder tries entering these common names at the login screen hoping to luck into the correct password.

The best method for defeating a multiple login intruder requires prevention and detection.

To prevent a successful multiple login security breach, users should be educated to choose secure passwords. Use the following as a general guide for secure passwords:

- Establish a minimum number of characters for passwords. The longer the password, the more difficult it will be for an intruder to guess it. At the same time, long passwords may result in users writing the password down so they don't forget it, which defeats the purpose of a password. Typically, most systems require that passwords be no less than eight characters.

- Require that passwords include a mix of letters, numbers, lower-case letters, upper-case letters, and symbols. An example of a secure password is: Rb3&kf5P.

- Require that passwords be changed on a monthly basis.

- Require that passwords can't be duplicated over a six-month period. For example, some users choose two passwords and alternate them each month. A predictable pattern such as this is fodder for intruders.

Detection can be accomplished using several methods. The most common is to specify some maximum number of incorrect logins. Network operating systems such as Windows NT and Novell NetWare allow administrators to specify the number of incorrect logins. An example of the security configuration screen for Windows NT is shown in Figure 6-12.

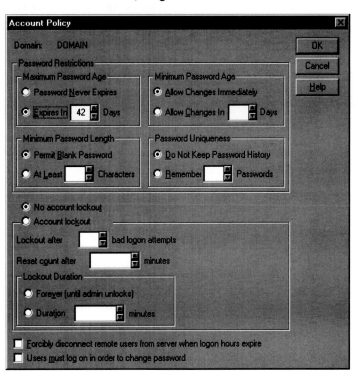

Figure 6-12 NT Security Configuration Screen

Notice that in the bottom half of the screen are fields for specifying account lockouts. If the first option is selected, an intruder won't be locked out from accessing the server resources. But if the field labeled Account lockout is selected, the administrator will then specify the number of attempts that can be made before the lockout occurs. Typically, a user is permitted four incorrect logins before the account is locked.

Once locked out, the account should be re-opened by the administrator. If the administrator must re-open the account, it forces an investigation to determine why the account was locked. The investigation may reveal the intruder. If the administrator doesn't have to re-open the account, the account will re-open when the computer is next re-booted.

Denial of Service Attack

A **denial of service attack** occurs when the resources of a computer—typically, a server—have been diverted so that users are unable to utilize the server resources. Because the computer is kept busy attempting to respond to the attack, users are unable to access the server resources.

For the most part, denial of service is intentional, an attempt to disrupt a network. Occasionally, however, a denial of service is accidental. For example, if a server runs low on memory, users may wait extended times before accessing the server, or may not be able to access the server at all.

In order to launch a denial of service attack, the hacker must be able to access a network from the outside. In other words, the hacker will use the Internet in order to gain access to a network. However, if a network isn't directly connected to the Internet, then a hacker can't access it. The only network type that is immune from denial of service attacks is an intranet. An intranet doesn't use public communications facilities such as the telephone network to exchange information; consequently, a hacker won't be able to access the intranet.

For this book, and for the i-Net+ exam, assume that all denial of service situations are intentional and designed to disrupt network communications.

There are several specific types of denial of service attacks including ping floods, SYN floods, IP spoofing, and ICMP echo (smurf) attacks. Each of these denial of service attacks is described in the following sections.

Ping Flood

Ping (an acronym for Packet Internet Groper) is used to test the connection between network devices, such as between a server and workstation. Ping, as described in Chapter 3, is a widely used diagnostic tool. A typical ping consists of sending a small (32-byte) packet to a device identified by an IP address. If the device receives the packet, an acknowledgment is returned to the sending computer.

Ping takes advantage of the connection-oriented nature of TCP. Because TCP is connection oriented, each received packet is noted at the receiver by sending an acknowledgment packet back to the receiver. Essentially, ping is a small and specialized TCP/IP packet.

Because it's a TCP/IP packet, the maximum size of the packet can be about 65,000 bytes. A **ping flood** occurs when the size of the ping packet is inflated to the maximum size, and the large packet is sent to a server. As the packet travels across the Internet to the server, it's fragmented into smaller sizes that when reassembled at the server, cause the server **buffers** (a buffer is a small amount of temporary storage) to overflow.

ping flood

buffers

The process of reassembling the packet fragments will fail because portions of the packet have been lost due to the buffer overflow. Legitimate requests received from clients will be denied by the server because the server's buffers are full. A ping flood typically crashes an unprotected server.

The remedy for ping floods is to install network operating systems that will detect the attack. Once the attack is detected, the server will immediately stop responding to the attack. All modern versions of Windows NT, Windows 9x, and Novell NetWare will recognize most forms of the ping attack.

SYN Flood

A **SYN flood** occurs when a half-open TCP connection is begun with a server, then never closed.

SYN flood

When a TCP connection is first initiated, the sending device (such as a computer or workstation used to access a Web server) sends a request for the server's service. The request will include an ID that identifies the sending device. The server will respond with an acknowledgment that includes the ID of the sending device. The acknowledgment is called a Synchronous Sequence Number packet.

The server will then wait for a Connection Acknowledgment from the sending device. When the sending device returns the acknowledgment to the server, the connection is opened between the two devices. At this time, data will be exchanged between the computer and server.

However, if the sending device includes a bogus ID in the initial request to the server, the server will return the acknowledgment packet to the bogus ID. Because the ID is bogus, the server will never receive a Connection Acknowledgment from the sender. Eventually, the half-open connection will time out and the server will close the connection.

If the server is deluged with half-open TCP connections, all of the server's resources are consumed waiting to close the connections. Legitimate users won't be able to establish a connection with the server.

The server will wait for the connection to close and when it doesn't, it will automatically close the connection. However, a typical SYN flood attack keeps requesting connections using bogus sender IDs. Because the server is so busy waiting for the half-open connections to time out, users trying to access the server may not gain access.

IP Spoof

Spoofing

Spoofing is a technique used to make a network message appear to originate from an authorized IP address, when it actually comes from a different IP address. Spoofing is commonly used with routers as a network management tool to reduce network traffic. For example, LAN software sends packets onto a network that are designed to return information about the network such as the status of workstations connected to the network. Because the bandwidth of LANs is much greater than the bandwidth of Internet connections, the use of network monitoring packets doesn't represent a problem.

But if the same packets are sent across an Internet connection to a remote network, the packets can increase traffic congestion, which will cause network response times to slow. A router will frequently identify a test packet and send it back to a local server with the IP address of the intended device inserted in the source IP address field of the packet header. To the server, it appears as if the returned packet actually originated from the remote device. But, in fact, the router has spoofed the server.

The advantage of spoofing is that network traffic is reduced. In addition to reducing traffic, costs are generally decreased because Web servers are charged for packet flows that exceed a predetermined number.

The same principle can be applied to a server by inserting an authorized IP address in the packet header and sending the packet to the server. For example, if the IP address of a router is inserted as the source IP address in the packet, then the test packet is likely to be forwarded on to the server. If the packet is sent over and over, then the server will be deluged with network monitoring packets and will either slow or be unable to respond to legitimate requests from users.

The remedy to IP spoofing is to place a firewall between the server and Internet router. Most firewalls will discard all specific test packets that originate from the Internet.

ICMP Echo Smurf

ICMP (Internet Control Message Protocol)

ICMP (Internet Control Message Protocol) is used to generate messages intended for the TCP/IP software. An ICMP message may involve an error between two devices such as "Error Message 404, host unreachable." ICMP is also used to determine the status of a network in a manner similar to the ping utility. Because ICMP communicates with only the TCP/IP software and not applications running on a machine, it doesn't set up ports between two devices. All that's needed to send an ICMP message is the IP address of the source and destination devices.

smurf

ping attack

Due to the simplicity of ICMP, it's used to initiate denial of service attacks against targeted Internet servers. The attack is called an ICMP echo attack, or **smurf**, after the name of the program used to set up the attack. Since smurf attacks use ICMP packets, an ICMP attack is also referred to as a **ping attack**.

A smurf attack is directed to Internet hosts and particularly to servers on the Internet. A smurf attack originates from a single host computer. An attacker at the computer sends an ICMP ping to a valid network address, and all recipients at the receiving network return the ping to a third IP address. The third IP address is the victim of the attack. Figure 6-13 illustrates the mechanics of a smurf attack.

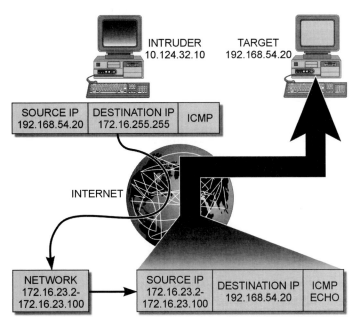

Figure 6-13 ICMP Echo (Smurf) Attack

The attacker modifies the ICMP packet so that the source IP address is the IP address of the target. The destination IP address of the packet contains the network address of the intermediary network in the network portion of the IP address field, and all 1's in the host portion of the address. This is a network-specific broadcast (called a **directed broadcast**), which will be received by all devices on the intermediary network that are connected at the time the packet arrives. When all computers on the intermediary network receive the ping packet, they return an **echo packet** to the host (the target) whose IP address is in the source field of the packet.

Because all workstations on the intermediary network return an echo packet, the target host is deluged with hundreds of echo packets. The result is a significant performance loss at the target server, or a complete loss of service to legitimate users.

The intermediary network is frequently called an amplifier network because the intermediary devices send many echoes in response to a single ICMP query.

A smurf attack can be devastating for periods lasting from a few minutes to several hours. The attacker often compounds the problem by making the packet larger than the usual 32 bytes. Typically, the packet size is filled to around 1500 bytes (the size of a filled Ethernet packet). When the target server receives hundreds of large ICMP echo packets, the server buffers overflow and none of the legitimate users are able to access the server.

The remedy for smurf attacks is to properly configure routers that connect users to the Internet. The routers should be configured so that the "directed broadcasts" configuration setting is turned off. Directed broadcast is a configuration parameter on nearly all routers, as well as switches with routing capabilities. By turning off directed broadcasts, a ping that originates outside the network that has a broadcast IP address will be rejected by the router.

directed broadcast

echo packet

Background Info

IP version 4.0 RFC1812 states that routers must default to turning on directed broadcasts so that the broadcasts will be forwarded by the router. However, many router vendors such as Cisco, Nortel, and Cabletron take the advice of RFC 2644, a Best Practice update to RFC 1812, to set directed broadcasts to off by default.

For any router connected to the Internet, the directed broadcast parameter should be turned off.

Another remedy to smurf attacks is to use a firewall that will trace the source IP address of any directed broadcast ping to determine if the packet can actually be traced to the source IP address inserted in the packet header. If the source IP address has been spoofed, the route won't be able to be traced to the source. The firewall will then reject the ping.

Mail Flood

Mail flooding

Mail flooding occurs when large e-mails are sent to an e-mail server. If the number of e-mails is large, and each e-mail contains a large file attachment, then the e-mail server will become preoccupied dealing with the large files and won't be able to respond to legitimate user requests.

spamming

Another method used to crash an e-mail server is called **spamming**. An e-mail spam is an e-mail sent to all e-mail addresses on a network. In the worst case, the number of addresses range into the thousands and a single server is taxed beyond its capabilities while forwarding the messages.

Background Info

In some cases, spamming is a legitimate technique to communicate with all users on a network. For example, a network administrator may use an e-mail spam to notify all users that the network will be unavailable on a specific day. These types of e-mail spams are short, sent infrequently, and sent during times when the network is lightly loaded such as before or after normal work hours.

Many commercial e-mail software packages permit e-mail users to utilize the same tool for sending messages. Rather than enter a list of designated recipients, a user may select a field such as "All" so that the message is sent to all users, regardless of whether the message is appropriate for all users.

This is an inappropriate use of spamming and should be discouraged.

Spamming is strongly discouraged on the Internet. All legitimate Web site administrators will solicit the permission of visitors before sending uninvited e-mail messages to the user. In addition, there are list servers (described in Chapter 5) specifically designed to communicate messages to users interested in a particular topic or product.

ANTI-VIRUS SOFTWARE

Anti-virus software is used to detect and/or clean a virus from a client computer, server, gateway, or router. Any device that interacts with the Internet should be protected against viruses. The anti-virus software should be updated frequently so that newly discovered viruses will be detected.

A virus can be detected by the "signature" it leaves. A **signature** refers to characteristics of the virus and the manner that the virus attacks a computer.

signature

It's particularly important that as soon as an anti-virus software package is installed, the software vendor be contacted for updates to the package. It's likely that between the time the software was shipped from the vendor and the time that it was installed, a new virus has been discovered. The quickest way to install the updates is to download them from the vendor's Web site. You should receive notice when the updates are available, or you can check their Web sites for the latest signatures.

There are two basic types of anti-virus software available:

- **Memory Resident Virus Scanners**: Detects a virus but can't correct the virus. Scans only selected files and will remain active on the desktop at all times that the computer is turned on.

Memory Resident Virus Scanners

- **On-demand Virus Scanners**: Will detect as well as correct a detected virus. Will scan all files on a disk, and must be manually activated.

On-demand Virus Scanners

Typically, a commercial anti-virus package will allow you to configure the software for either type or for a combination of the two types.

In order for an anti-virus software package to be most effective across a network, follow the guidelines listed here:

- Install the software on all machines that may be infected. This includes all types of servers, client workstations, routers, gateways.

- Require users to scan all e-mail attachments before opening them because e-mail is the most common carrier of viruses from the Internet.

- Before purchasing an anti-virus product, ensure that it has been certified by ICSA (International Computer Security Association).

- When installing a new application, deactivate the anti-virus scanner.

- When an anti-virus product is purchased, check the vendor's Web site for new updates because the vendor may have identified new viruses since the product was sold.

- Update virus signatures on a monthly basis (at a minimum), and more often for recent virus attacks.

- For users that have an FTP client, ensure that FTP files are scanned for viruses when opened, before being saved to a disk, and before being executed.

- Create documentation specifying how viruses are to be detected and how to install and update the software on all machines.

- Address the use of outside floppy disks from outside users.

- Require that the disks be scanned before they are run on a workstation.

VIRTUAL PRIVATE NETWORK

A Virtual Private Network, or VPN, is a secure and encrypted connection between two points across the Internet. The secure connection is realized by authenticating users at each end of the connection. The communication that's passed between the two end points is encrypted to prevent unauthorized reading of the data. The Internet is used as the network infrastructure for sending and receiving the private data messages.

There are two basic applications for VPNs:

Network-to-Network

- **Network-to-Network**: In a network-to-network VPN, two networks use the Internet to implement a secure wide area network that connects two or more LANs. A company with several branch offices can implement a VPN for each branch site that connects to a corporate data center. Or, a company may need to set up a temporary connection with a contractor while a product is in the development stage. The two companies could use the VPN as a temporary means of sharing information in a secure environment. Figure 6-14 shows an example of a network-to-network VPN.

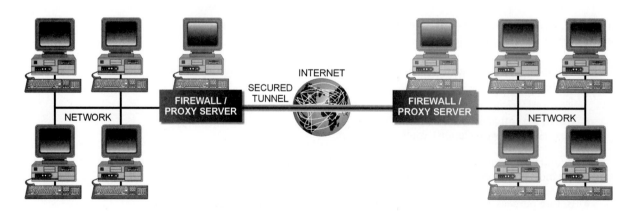

Figure 6-14 Network-to-Network VPN

A network-to-network VPN extends the security of a VPN to the connected networks. Using an appropriate access protocol such as PPTP, the data from either network is equipped with authentication headers and then encrypted. A proxy server will assign the packet a proxy IP address before sending the packet to the local ISP. The local ISP will route the packet to the Internet. At the receiving end, the proxy IP address is stripped from the packet and the data is decrypted, and then sent to the desired server.

- **Client-to-Network**: In a client-to-network VPN, a remote user establishes a secure connection to a server located at a corporate site. The remote user may be a mobile user such as a sales rep who connects temporarily to the corporate server to send and receive e-mail or download product literature. Employees who work at home as telecommuters can use a VPN to exchange sensitive files with a server. Typically, the remote user will connect to a local ISP, and the ISP will be used to route HTTP or e-mail requests to a remote server. Figure 6-15 shows an example of a client-to-network VPN.

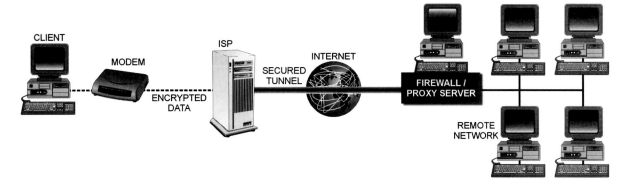

Figure 6-15 Client-to-Network VPN

When the client logs on to the ISP, a temporary IP address is issued using DHCP or the equivalent. The client machine uses a derivative of PPP for authentication, then encrypts the data message and sends it on to the ISP. The ISP will encapsulate the packet with source and destination IP addresses that have been specified for VPNs. Because the user packet is encapsulated in an IP packet that originates at the ISP, nearly any type of Network layer protocol can be sent across the Internet. (There are exceptions. See the next section, VPN Protocols.)

Note that dynamic IP addressing is always used in a VPN. The use of dynamic IP addresses is consistent with the intention of a virtual network. That is, a virtual network can be built, used for any length of time, then torn down. When it's not in use, the resources are returned to the Internet, ISP, or the local network. This represents only one of the efficiency advantages of a VPN.

The alternative to using a VPN is to select a bandwidth technology such as Frame Relay, ISDN, or T-carrier. In some larger networks, all of these bandwidth technologies are used in order to meet the needs of the many types of users who need to access a corporate network. Unfortunately, none of the technologies are directly compatible, and all require specialized equipment and trained personnel.

A VPN avoids the direct and indirect expenses of trying to support multiple bandwidth technologies because the cost of equipment and personnel is delegated to a third party such as an ISP. In the example where a company has many branch officers that require access to corporate servers, a VPN drastically reduces telecommunication costs because the client session to a remote server requires only a local telephone call (to the ISP) to initiate. Both Frame Relay and T-carrier technologies are billed based on the distance between connections, or the volume of data sent between end points.

A VPN avoids many of these costs. The disadvantage of a VPN is that data travels between the end points at Internet speeds that are typically slower than dedicated T-carrier, Frame Relay, or ISDN. In addition, there are no standardized solutions for implementing authentication and encryption over a VPN. There are, however, several competing security systems, and the following section describes each of them.

VPN Protocols

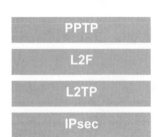

Currently, there are four protocols being used on VPNs:

- **PPTP**: Point-to-Point Tunneling Protocol
- **L2F**: Layer 2 Forwarding
- **L2TP**: Layer 2 Tunneling Protocol
- **IPsec**: IP Security

The PPTP protocol was described in Chapter 3. PPTP has been widely used since Microsoft included it on Windows NT 4.0, included a Windows 95 patch for PPTP, and included it as part of the Windows 98 operating system. Because PPTP, like PPP, relies on link information at Layer 2 of the OSI Model, it can be used to transport nearly any network protocol across the Internet. For example, a PPTP connection will transport IPX, NetBEUI, or AppleTalk packets to a remote server.

Compared to other VPN protocols described in this section, PPP has a huge disadvantage in that it can carry only one channel for each connection. This means that only a single user can connect to the Internet using PPP. Small networks often employ PPP for multiple users by installing Internet server software that allow more than one user access, but the time that each user connects is divided by all users. If more than one user is connected at the same time, download speeds drop significantly since the server manages connection on a round-robin basis.

PPTP encapsulates the data to be sent along with standard PPP headers. The PPTP protocol headers include fields for authenticating end-point connections (users, or a client machine and a server) and for encrypting the data.

The L2F protocol was developed by Cisco. It shares many of the strengths of PPTP but also addresses some PPTP weaknesses. L2F uses PPP to authenticate end-point connections. This means that a client-to-network connection will have PPP installed and use PPP to connect to a local ISP. The ISP will then employ L2F to create a tunnel to the remote server.

L2F is a layer 2 protocol so it can carry network protocols other than IP, such as IPX or NetBEUI. Unlike PPTP (and PPP) L2F may be used in about any type of network environment other than IP. Because Network layer protocols aren't recognized by L2F, it can be deployed on ATM networks or Frame Relay networks.

L2F can establish more than one connection in the tunnel established between the end points. This means that an ISP using L2F can select the best routes to send data packets so that they are likely to arrive at the server faster than if the connection used PPTP.

L2TP uses PPP to provide dial-up authentication access. It's currently being developed by the **Internet Engineering Task Force (IETF)** as a future replacement for PPTP and L2F. Like its predecessors, L2TP can carry packets from non-IP networks. The tunneling mechanism used with L2TP is based on the multiple-connection tunnel used with L2F. However, a tunnel protocol is being defined for technologies other than IP-based networks (such as the Internet) that includes X.25, Frame Relay, and ATM.

PPTP, L2F, or L2TP are essentially authentication protocols that are used to encapsulate data messages, and do not directly incorporate data encryption. Typically, the encryption scheme is a public-key cipher that's bundled with modern Web browsers. Note that SLIP does not provide authentication since it doesn't support encryption. However, the final version of L2TP is expected to incorporate the encryption methods that are stock with IPsec.

IP security (IP secretary) was developed in conjunction with the next version of IP, IP version 6. The security portion of IPv6 is compatible with the current version of IP, version 4. IP security, then, is being used to provide authentication and encryption for IPv4-based networks.

A data packet that's subjected to IPsec may be authenticated, encrypted, or both authenticated and encrypted. The two processes are separated at the Transport and Network layers so that only the Transport layer header (TCP or UDP) may be authenticated, encrypted, or both; or the Network layer data—which covers the entire packet—may be authenticated, encrypted, or both.

The first process is called the Transport mode and provides basic authentication and encryption. The second process is called Tunneling mode and provides the highest level of security. IPsec supports multiple tunnels over a single connection. In order to do so, IPsec must be supported by the PPP-MP protocol as described in Chapter 1.

IPsec is a layer 3 protocol. It can be used only with IP packets; consequently it won't carry IPX or NetBEUI packets. In a typical implementation, a workstation user will send data destined to a remote network and use the Internet as the VPN infrastructure. At the local router interface to the ISP connection, the packet is fitted with authentication and encryption headers, encrypted, then sent to the ISP over a PPP connection. The ISP encapsulates the packet with source and destination IP addresses, which are drawn from a pool of packets that have been specified for the VPN. The packet is then sent to the remote network where the packet headers are stripped and the data decrypted. Note that the ISP server must be set up in a PPP-MP configuration in order to track multiple connections back to the local network.

Because the source and destination IP addresses are drawn from a pool of addresses, the source of the packet is protected from intruders on the Internet.

IPsec provides for numerous encryption schemes. The list at this time is as follows:

- Private Key, DES, Triple DES
- Public Key, RAS
- Hash Key message digests
- Digital Certificates

But note that encryption doesn't alleviate the need for firewalls or proxy servers when IPsec or any of the other access methods are used. For network-to-network connections, an Internet tunnel will extend to both sides of a firewall—that is, to the network side of the connection. For client-to-network connections, the tunnel will extend from the ISP to the network side of the firewall of the remote network. Between the client and the ISP, authentication and encryption are intended to protect the user's data.

KEY POINTS REVIEW

This chapter has presented an exploration of Internet security.

- A username and password is a means of authenticating and controlling access to servers.

- Authentication is the process of verifying identities.

- Read-only access means that you may view the file or directory contents, but you can't modify the content.

- Write access means that you can view and modify the content of a file or directory on a server.

- Full access means that you can view, modify, and initiate executable software.

- Certificate level access is a means of verifying the validity of a Web site.

- Encryption refers to hiding the content of data packets so that the information in the packet will remain confidential and unchanged.

- Auditing refers to techniques used for monitoring network access and authentication.

- A firewall is used to protect the users of a network from intruders outside the network.

- The proxy server (also called an application gateway) is used to screen certain Internet-related services from the connected network, as well as to protect the IP address of a network computer.

- Detection logs will alert an administrator that a potential breach is occurring.

- A firewall may be set up to filter traffic that is in-bound from the Internet to a network workstation, as well as to filter traffic that's bound from a network workstation to the Internet.

- Encryption systems can be divided into three classes: substitution, transposition, and product ciphers.

- In a private-key encryption scheme, the same key is used to encrypt and decrypt an encoded message. Private-key encryption is also called symmetric encryption.

- In a public-key encryption system, one key is known to both parties in the exchange, while the other key is known to only one party. Either key may be used to encrypt or decrypt. Public-key encryption is also called asymmetric encryption.

- A digital certificate is used to authenticate Internet users or Web sites. A digital certificate ensures that communication over the Internet is confidential and reliable.

- The Secure Socket Layer (SSL) protocol is used to authenticate users or e-commerce servers on the Internet, and to encrypt/decrypt messages using public-key encryption.

- The role of the Certificate Authority in the SSL session is to authenticate the holder of a certificate and to provide a digital signature that will reveal if the certificate has been compromised.

- Most commercial e-mail packages use the S/MIME (Secure/MIME) protocol for encrypting e-mail.

- Intruder detection refers to techniques designed to catch a remote user that's attempting to enter a network connected to the Internet.

- A multiple login failure occurs when an intruder attempts to login to a network but doesn't know the correct password.

- A denial of service attack occurs when the resources of a computer have been diverted so that users are unable to utilize the server resources.

- A ping flood occurs when the size of the ping packet is inflated to the maximum size and the large packet is sent to a server, or a server is deluged with ping requests.

- A SYN flood occurs when a half-open TCP connection is begun with a server and then never closed.

- IP spoofing is a technique used to make a network message appear to originate from an authorized IP address, when it actually comes from a different IP address.

- ICMP echo (smurf) attacks consists of a test packet directed to all nodes on a network. The nodes respond to the test packet to a single IP address on a different network.

- Mail flooding occurs when large e-mails are sent to an e-mail server.

- Anti-virus software is used to detect and/or clean a virus from a client computer, server, gateway, or router.

- A Virtual Private Network, or VPN, is a secure and encrypted connection between two points across the Internet.

- There are four protocols being used on VPNs: PPTP (Point-to-Point Tunneling Protocol), L2F(Layer 2 Forwarding), L2TP (Layer 2 Tunneling Protocol), and Ipsec (IP Security).

REVIEW QUESTIONS

The following questions test your knowledge of the material presented in this chapter:

1. Describe the difference between authentication and authorization.

2. What type of access has been granted to a user that can view and modify the contents of a directory but can't execute software located in the directory?

3. What is the function of a firewall?

4. Why should a network administrator set up detection logs on a network connected to the Internet?

5. How many keys are used in a private-key encryption scheme?

6. What is another name for public-key encryption?

7. Summarize the encryption/decryption process in a public-key encryption system.

8. What is the purpose of a Certificate Authority?

9. If a user must take a computer outside of the United States, what must be done to the Web browser installed in the computer?

10. What is a digital signature?

11. What type of attack has been launched when a server is left with multiple half-open TCP connections?

12. How can a smurf attack be detected by the intermediary (amplifier) network?

13. List three network devices that should have anti-virus software installed.

14. Describe characteristics of a VPN.

15. List four protocols that may be used on a VPN.

MULTIPLE CHOICE QUESTIONS

1. In order to protect network users from Internet intruders, a _____ should be installed at the interface of the network and the Internet.

    a. Firewall

    b. Certificate Server

    c. Encryption Key

    d. SSL

2. From the following, choose the secured URL:

    a. http://company.buy.com

    b. ftp:// company.buy.com

    c. https://company.buy.com

    d. http:s//company.buy.com

3. What is a unique value that indicates if a digital certificate has been tampered with?

    a. Public Key

    b. Digital Signature

    c. Certificate Authority

    d. Proxy

4. Which encryption technique uses the same key for both ends of the connection?

   a. Symmetric

   b. Asymmetric

   c. Public Key

   d. RSA

5. Which type of network is most secure from denial of service attacks?

   a. VPN

   b. Internet

   c. Extranet

   d. Intranet

6. Which of the following is used to prevent network users from accessing a Web site with the IP address of 10.128.32.1?

   a. Non-repudiation

   b. DES

   c. ICMP

   d. Packet Filter

7. A network administrator determines that the network is receiving direct broadcast ICMP packets from an unknown source. What type of attack does this indicate?

   a. SYN Flood

   b. Smurf

   c. Mail Flood

   d. Spoof

8. Which of the following firewall types offers the most security?

   a. Packet Filter Only

   b. Dual-homed

   c. Screened-subnet

   d. Choke-gate

9. The process of identifying users or a Web site is called:

   a. Authentication

   b. Authorization

   c. Repudiation

   d. Encryption

10. What protocol will be used when L2TP is used between servers on a VPN?

   a. IPsec

   b. L2F

   c. SLIP

   d. PPP

11. Which of the following best describes access control?

    a. Measures taken that admit, limit, restrict, or deny access to the resources of a network.

    b. The process of guaranteeing the identity of a user or server.

    c. The process of hiding the content of data packets so that the information in the packet will remain confidential and unchanged.

    d. Techniques used for monitoring network access and authentication.

12. Which of the following occurs when a browser exchanges information with a certificate server?

    a. The browser and server encrypt and decrypt with the same key.

    b. A unique digital certificate is issued for each transaction.

    c. A unique set of public and private keys is created.

    d. IPsec is initiated between the server and browser.

13. After installing new anti-virus software, what should be done next?

    a. Run the software on all workstations and servers.

    b. Check the vendor's Web site for updates to the software.

    c. Scan all e-mail files for viruses.

    d. Check the software README files for changes.

14. Which of the following will not support more than one tunnel per connection?

    a. L2F

    b. PPTP

    c. PPP

    d. IPsec

15. Which of the following best describes a VPN?

    a. A SLIP connection between browser and ISP.

    b. Encrypted communication between two devices over the Internet.

    c. SSL running between a client and e-commerce server.

    d. The use of Kerberos at each end of a connection.

CHAPTER

7

BUSINESS ON THE INTERNET

**LEARNING
OBJECTIVES**

LEARNING OBJECTIVES

Upon completion of this chapter and its related lab procedures, you should be able to perform the following tasks:

1. (6.3) Define the following Web related terms within a given context:

    -   Push technology

    -   Pull technology

2. (6.1) Explain the issues involved in copyrighting, trademarking, and licensing. Content could include the following:

    -   How to license copyright materials

    -   Scope of your copyright

    -   How to copyright your material anywhere

    -   Consequences of not being aware of copyright issues, not following copyright restrictions

3. (6.2) Identify the issues to working in a global environment. Content could include the following:

    -   Working in a multi-vendor environment with different currencies

    -   International issues—shipping, supply chain

    -   Multi-lingual or multi-character issues

4. (4.9) Describe how to register a domain name.

5. (6.4) Describe the differences between the following from a business standpoint:

    -   Intranet

    -   Extranet

    -   Internet

6. (6.5) Define e-commerce terms and concepts. Content could include the following:

    -   EDI
    -   Online Cataloging
    -   Business to Business
    -   Relationship management
    -   Business to Consumer
    -   Customer self-service
    -   Internet commerce
    -   Internet marketing
    -   Merchant systems

CHAPTER 7

Business on the Internet

INTRODUCTION

This chapter is an overview of specialized business concepts related to Web sites. We begin with the fundamental thrust of the HTML that a site is composed of, which determines if the client or the server is the active component in driving dynamic updates to Web sites. The decision must be made early, during the development of a site.

The current copyright laws in the United States don't directly mention Internet Web sites. Web site owners are left to studying the law as it is and applying current laws to their Web site. Because a Web site is a business asset, it's important to be familiar with the current law so that your site content isn't infringed upon, and so that you don't inadvertently infringe upon another copyright.

If a business sells products to other countries besides the United States, the product must pass through the U.S. Customs Office during shipping. The Customs Office is interested in anything that leaves and will want to know what you're shipping. There is a specific filing system that you must adhere to when exporting and the system is described in this chapter.

For global Web sites, the issue of language becomes very important and complex when you consider that there are thousands of languages. In order to realize the maximum amount of exposure to their Web site, developers are using the Unicode Standard to bridge the language gap.

Last in this chapter is a discussion of how to register a domain name.

CONDUCTING BUSINESS ON THE INTERNET

Fundamentally, a Web site is composed of HTML or one of the many versions of HTML combined with one or more specific Web programming languages such as Java. One of the irritating aspects of HTML is that it was originally created to statically display information. The use of links to other pages or URLs was used to provide a dynamic feel to Web cruises.

E-commerce, and particularly advertising on the Internet, has left many Web site owners wishing for a more intimate relationship with their site visitors. That is, site owners and developers wanted to update their sites dynamically while visitors were viewing the site. In this way, advertisements could be displayed for a few seconds, then replaced with another advertisement. Or, the site could feature products on a continually changing basis so viewers will be tempted to stay at the site, explore, and hopefully purchase an item.

Dynamic HTML (See Chapter 2 for more information about HTML) uses two methods that allow a Web site developer to continuously update a Web site. The methods are called **client pull** and **server push**. Although both are used for the same purpose, they work in a complementary manner.

Pull Technology

The client pull method relies on opening and closing a TCP connection for each update to a Web page. Figure 7-1 illustrates a typical sequence. A browser has accessed the homepage of a Web site. The Web server homepage includes a graphic (image_1) that will change while the browser remains connected to the site. The graphic image will change but the surrounding text will not. A typical application for this example is to display product news on a rotating basis, or to include advertising that constantly changes.

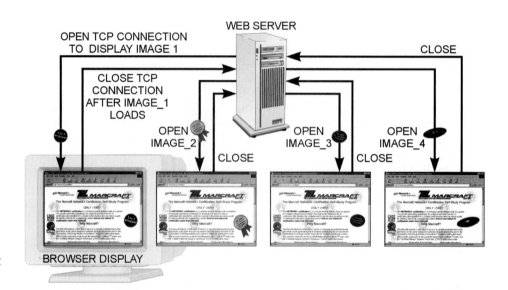

Figure 7-1 Client Pull Technology

Image_1 is loaded by first opening a TCP connection to the Web server. Once the graphic has loaded in the browser, the connection is terminated.

After a short time, the browser will open another TCP connection to the Web server and change the graphic to image_2. Once image_2 is loaded, the TCP connection will close.

After another short time, the browser will open another TCP connection and image_3 will load. Once image_3 has loaded in the browser, the TCP connection will close.

The last graphic will load by opening a fourth TCP connection so that image_4 will load in the browser and replace image_3. When image_4 has loaded, the TCP connection will close.

In the example shown in Figure 7-1, four TCP connections must be opened and closed so that the graphic can be changed. Each TCP connection requires a minimum of a second to open, and in many cases may require several seconds. Due to the time required to open multiple TCP connections, client pull reduces the efficiency of the Web transaction.

The server must be capable of providing multiple TCP connections as they are requested by the browser. The server may or may not be ready to download each time the browser sends a new request.

On the positive side, the browser is in control of the transaction because the HTML that's loaded in the browser dictates when the image is to change. The user sitting in front of the browser can interrupt the operation at any time by clicking to another site or by pressing the stop button.

Push Technology

The server push method relies on opening a single TCP connection between browser and Web server. The server will "push" updated information to the browser according to some predetermined time period, or whenever the server data changes.

Figure 7-2 shows an example of server push. When the browser sends an HTTP request to open a TCP connection, the server responds with the homepage from the site, which includes image_1. The TCP connection isn't closed after the image has loaded in the browser.

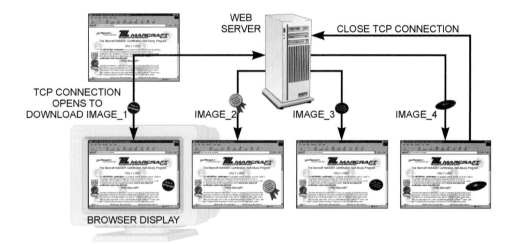

**Figure 7-2
Server Push
Technology**

After displaying image_1 for a short time, the server sends image_2 on the same TCP connection used to display image_1. Image_1 is now replaced with image_2.

After another pause, the server sends image_3 on the same TCP connection and image_2 is replaced.

Finally, image_4 is sent on the same TCP connection and image_3 is replaced.

Notice that the connection is never closed until the user clicks to another site or closes the browser window.

PointCast is a good example of how a Web server pushes information to browsers. There are others, including Microsoft, that use push technology to constantly update the information displayed in browsers. Most vendors have some technique for specifying, delivering, and defining how information will be displayed in browsers. **Channel Definition Format (CDF)** is a possible industry standard (proposed by Microsoft) that defines a framework for pushing technology across channels. Many vendors are supporting the standard, its implementation, and its eventual adoption as a standard. The benefit to users is that browsers can be CDF-compliant for all Web servers that use push technology.

The advantage of server push over client pull is that the efficiency of the TCP connection is increased because a single connection is used for the entire process. When client pull is used, the server must be capable of opening many TCP connections, as well as keeping track of all connections open to all browsers connected to the site.

The downside to server push is that the server must have sufficient TCP ports to handle all browser requests for as long as the browser is connected to the site. With client pull, the TCP ports can be alternated between all browsers, which means that, on average, fewer simultaneous (dedicated) TCP ports will be needed.

The updates from the server will be done quicker with server push because the time to open a unique port for each update is eliminated. The TCP port is never closed as it is with client pull.

The significance of client pull and server push for an ISP or company that's developing a Web site is that if you plan to make the site dynamic, you must decide which method is best for you.

Table 7-1 Client Pull and Server Push Summary

Table 7-1 summarizes the advantages and disadvantages of both methods.

CLIENT PULL	
Advantages	**Disadvantages**
The browser controls updates, relieving the server of doing so.	A TCP port is opened for each update, which may tax server resources.
The updates may be terminated by pressing the Stop button or clicking to another site.	The efficiency of the transaction decreases due to the time needed to open each TCP connection.
SERVER PUSH	
Advantages	**Disadvantages**
A single TCP connection is used throughout the connection, which improves efficiency.	The server must be capable of providing a single TCP connection for each browser, and tracking the connections.
The updates may be terminated by pressing the Stop button or clicking to another site.	

Intellectual Properties

Intellectual property is a reference to non-tangible assets of a business such as the content of a Web site, the name of a company, or a specific slogan used by a company.

In this section, copyrights, trademarks, and licensing are described.

Intellectual property

Copyrighting

A **copyright** is used to protect the author of an original work from infringement. Infringement, in this context, refers to the unauthorized use of copyrighted material.

copyright

Background Info

There are specific definitions that stipulate "who" is the author of an original work, as well as what constitutes "unauthorized use". For the latest information on copyrights, write the Copyright Office at:

Library of Congress
Register of Copyrights
101 Independence Avenue, S. E.
Washington, DC 20559-6000

Or visit the Copyright Web site at:

lcweb.loc.gov/copyright

Copyright laws extend to works created in the United States and to countries that have treaty agreements with the United States regarding protected works.

Although copyrights may be covered by various treaties, you shouldn't assume that any original work you produce is protected globally. There is no such thing as global protection from infringement. The copyright laws are primarily intended to protect works created in the United States.

Copyrighting may cover many original forms. For example, the following may be copyrighted:

- Literary works, including software

- Musical works, including any accompanying words

- Dramatic works, including any accompanying music

- Pantomimes and choreographic works

- Pictorial, graphic, and sculptural works, including software

- Motion pictures and other audiovisual works

- Sound recordings

- Architectural works

Examples of work that may not be copyrighted include:

- Titles, names, short phrases, and slogans

- Familiar symbols or designs

- Variations of typographic ornamentation, lettering, or coloring

- Listings of ingredients or contents

- Ideas, procedures, methods, systems, processes, concepts, principles, discoveries, or devices, as distinguished from a description, explanation, or illustration

- Works consisting entirely of information that is common property and containing no original authorship (for example: standard calendars, height and weight charts, tape measures and rulers, and lists or tables taken from public documents or other common sources)

At the time of this writing, the copyright law doesn't specifically mention Web sites. Most site owners still copyright the site as a precaution against unauthorized use of the site content. But note that even if the site has a copyright notice that's all-inclusive of the site, the copyright won't cover items as described above, and it won't extend to works that are in the public domain (works that have expired copyrights).

The general rule concerning the use of material on a Web site is that if the use will create economic losses for the owner of the copyright, you can't use it without paying the owner a fee (and then only with the permission of the owner). Before including text found on the Internet, a graphic, sound clip, or video clip on a site, attempt to establish ownership before using the file on the site. Request permission from the owner before including it in the site content. If you can't establish ownership, then don't use the file. Instead, create an original for your site.

The length that a copyright is in effect varies with the date that the work was produced. This portion of the U.S. copyright law is rather complex. Table 7-2, however, summarizes the length stipulations.

WORKS ORIGINALLY CREATED ON OR AFTER JANUARY 1, 1978	The author's life plus an additional 70 years after the author's death
FOR WORKS MADE FOR HIRE, AND FOR ANONYMOUS AND PSEUDONYMOUS WORKS (UNLESS THE AUTHOR'S IDENTITY IS REVEALED IN COPYRIGHT OFFICE RECORDS)	95 years from publication or 120 years from creation, whichever is shorter.
WORKS ORIGINALLY CREATED BEFORE JANUARY 1, 1978, BUT NOT PUBLISHED OR REGISTERED BY THAT DATE	The life-plus-70 or 95/120-year terms will apply to them as well.

Table 7-2 Lengths of Copyrights

For any original work produced after 1989, an official copyright notice or indication of copyright isn't required. That is, if you create a Web site that is original and don't place a copyright notice on the site, it is still protected by the copyright laws of the United States.

The problem with taking this approach is that others may innocently infringe upon the copyright without realizing that the work is, in fact, copyrighted. Rather than not placing a copyright notice on the work, you should always do so as explained in the next section.

For any work produced prior to 1989, a copyright notice is required.

You may or may not formally register an original work with the copyright office. Doing so will help to protect your work if it is infringed, or if others contest the authorship of the work. The section should help to clear some of the confusion surrounding how to copyright your work.

How to Copyright Original Work

Any work created after 1989 is copyrighted when it is in a fixed format. **Fixed** means that a copy of the work exists. A **copy** of the work means that the work "can be read or visually perceived, either directly or with the aid of a machine."

Fixed

copy

Examples of fixed copies of a work include:

- A copy of software source code

- Books

- Audio cassettes or CDs

- Lyrics and music for audio products, a script for video work

- The physical presence of the work, such as a graphic (JPEG or GIF files as well as original drawings and paintings)

- Sculpture (which also encompasses architecture)

- Web sites

- Movies, slides, photographs

A work may be prepared over a long period. The portion of the material that is completed and in a fixed format is copyrighted as of the date that the material is fixed. This is important for "works in progress" that may require months or years to complete.

Note that the work is copyrighted after 1989 without registering it, and without using the copyright symbol. However, it's prudent to use the symbol, and it may also be prudent to register the work.

Work produced between 1976 and 1989 is copyrighted at the time it's created. The work must include the familiar copyright symbol © with the work. See the next section of this chapter for the proper method of using the symbol. The work need not be formally registered with the U.S. Copyright Office in order to be copyrighted. The proper use of the symbol is all that's required, but see the note below on the advantages of registering a work.

Background Info

Work produced after 1989 doesn't need to have the copyright symbol displayed, and it doesn't have to be registered with the Copyright Office in order to be copyrighted. But there are several advantages to doing one of both.

Advantages to including the copyright symbol:

- The symbol advertises the work as proprietary.

- The symbol serves to notify others that the work is not to be distributed.

- The symbol will advert innocent infringements on copyrighted material.

- The symbol represents a level of professionalism on the part of the owner of the work.

Advantages to registering the work with the Copyright Office:

- Registration provides a public record for the copyright.

- Registration will permit you to register the work with the U.S. customs Service so that pirated copies of the work entering the United States will be detected.

- Registration provides validity of the copyright if ownership is challenged in court.

Publication

Work produced prior to 1976 is copyrighted by act of publication and the proper use of the copyright symbol, in addition to registering the work with the Copyright Office. **Publication** is generally interpreted to mean that the work was sold to the public. But there are many exceptions, however, and if you require assistance in securing a copyright for a work produced before 1976, consult an attorney or read the many circulars pertaining to the law before 1976.

An unpublished work could be copyrighted by registering the work with the U.S. Copyright Office. The copyright law of 1978 eliminated the "publication" criteria for securing a copyright; however, the work had to have the copyright symbol displayed. The 1978 law was important because it leveled the field for all works to be protected at the time they were created, regardless of whether they were actually published.

Table 7-3 summarizes the various requirements for copyrights.

DATE OF WORK	MANNER OF COPYRIGHT
After 1989	The work is copyrighted when it's "fixed." The use of the copyright symbol and registration is optional.
Between 1978 and 1989	The work must have the copyright symbol properly displayed. The work is protected at the time it was created.
Before 1978	The work must be published and have the copyright symbol properly displayed; or, unpublished works may be registered.

Table 7-3 Copyright Requirements

How to Display a Copyright

The U.S. Copyright Office is very specific on how to properly display the copyright symbol. Figure 7-3 illustrates an example.

A properly displayed symbol consists of three components:

1. **The copyright symbol**. The correct symbol is a "c" within a circle, as in ©. (Note that for phonograph products, a "p" within a circle may be required. See the Copyright Web site for more information.)

2. **The year that the work was fixed**. To avoid confusion, use all four digits in the year. That is, indicate the year as 2000, rather than as 00.

3. **The owner of the copyright**. The owner may be an individual, or it may be a company or organization.

Figure 7-3 Proper Use
of the Copyright
Symbol

©2000 VERY GOOD WEB SITE, INC.	
Required Display	**Description**
©	The copyright symbol, which consists of a "c" within a circle.
2000	The year that the work was fixed. For in-progress works, the year indicates the work at that point in the development.
Very Good Web Site, Inc.	The name of the owner of the work. The name may be that of an individual, or it may be the name of a company or similar organization.

Graphics used on the Internet may contain a copyright notice that isn't visible. The usual method of copyrighting a graphic file is to use a watermark that won't appear when the graphic loads. Before using a graphic found on the Internet, check the source code of the graphic and if a watermark is found, contact the owner before using the graphic. To locate the mark in an HTML file, look for the "watermark" tag.

How to Register a Copyright

You may choose to register an original work with the U. S. Copyright Office. Registration provides an important public record of the work. A work is frequently registered with the Copyright Office so as to deter challenges to the ownership of the work.

The copyright office lists three requirements that must be met when submitting original works for registration:

1. A properly completed application form.

2. A non-refundable filing fee of $30 (effective through June 30, 2002; after this date, the cost will likely change) for each application.

3. A non-returnable deposit of the work being registered. The deposit requirements vary in particular situations. Table 7-4 lists the requirements for several types of works.

To register the work, send the package to:

Library of Congress
Copyright Office
Register of Copyrights
101 Independence Avenue, S.E.
Washington, D.C. 20559-6000

TYPE OF WORK	DEPOSIT REQUIREMENT
If the work was first published in the United States on or after January 1, 1978	Two complete copies of the best edition.
If the work was first published in the United States before January 1, 1978	Two complete copies of the work as first published.
If the work was first published outside the United States	One complete copy of the work as first published.
Motion picture	One complete copy of the unpublished or published motion picture and a separate written description of its contents, such as a continuity, press book, or synopsis.
Literary, dramatic, or musical work published only in a phonorecord	One complete phonorecord.
Unpublished or published computer program	One visually perceptible copy in source code of the first 25 and last 25 pages of the program. For a program of fewer than 50 pages, the deposit is a copy of the entire program.
CD-ROM format	One complete copy of the material; that is, the CD-ROM, the operating software, and any manual(s) accompanying it. If registration is sought for the computer program on the CD-ROM, the deposit should also include a printout of the first 25 and last 25 pages of source code for the program.

Table 7-4 Types of Non-returnable Deposits

Before sending an original work to the copyright office, be sure to call the office first, or check the copyright Web site for specific requirements.

Trademarks

A **trademark** is a word, phrase, symbol, or combination of words, symbols, or phrases that are used to differentiate the products and services of one party from another. Examples of products and services protected by a trademark include Marcraft and Microsoft.

trademark

Trademarks are monitored by the U.S. Patent and Trademark Office. The Patent and Trademark Office is authorized to determine if a trademark can be registered. Once registered, a trademark may not be used by any other individual or organization in the United States. The Patent and Trademark Offices authority does not extend to other countries. To register a trademark in another country, you must submit a registration to that country.

Background Info

Trademark law is complicated and extensive. For detailed information about trademarks, contact:

U.S. Patent and Trademark Office
2900 Crystal Drive
Arlington, VA 22202-3513

Or visit the Patent and Trademark Office Web site at:

www.uspta.gov/

There are actually three different types of marks recognized by the United States Patent and Trademark Office:

Service Mark

Registered Trademark

- **Trademark**: Specifies the word, phrase, symbol, or combination of words, phrases, or symbol of a good or service.

- **Service Mark**: Identifies the source of goods and services.

- **Registered Trademark**: A trademark that has been formally registered and approved by the U.S. Patent and Trademark Office.

The difference between a trademark and service mark is one of context. A trademark is typically used on the packaging of a product, whereas a service mark is used to refer to the source of the trademark—such as a company name—and may be listed in the advertising of a product.

public domain

Trademarks are important to maintaining the identity of a company's brand and product image. Failure to register a trademark means that it will be classified as belonging in the **public domain**, which means that no one has legal recourse for using the trademark.

How to Display a Trademark Symbol

A trademark symbol may be displayed by anyone on any product. Registration of the trademark isn't required under U.S. law. However, as with copyrights, there are advantages to doing so:

- A trademark protects the image of a product.

- A trademark associates a product with a specific company.

- A trademark prevents infringement from others—either innocently or willfully.

You may use the trademark symbol ™ on any word, phrase, or symbol without approval from the U.S. Patent and Trade Office. Use of the symbol doesn't indicate ownership. However, if another party uses the symbol in conjunction with a product or service, and received approval from the Patent and Trademark Office, you must stop using it. Consequently, you should register a word, phrase, or symbol as soon as possible after you begin—or before—using it.

Once the Patent and Trademark Office has approved the word, phrase, or symbol, you can change the annotation from to. The use of an "R" within a circle means that the trademark is duly registered—and protected—by the U.S. Patent and Trademark Office.

When referring to products or service in advertising, you may use the symbol ℠ to refer to the source of a product.

Figure 7-4 shows the use of the three types of marks for a fictional e-commerce company. The first listing shows the name of the company, BigInternet.com. Because the ™ trademark is used, the name hasn't been registered with the Patent and Trademark Office but is used to warn others that the company intends to protect the name. The second listing is a slogan that the company wants to trademark. Because the slogan also uses the ™ symbol, it hasn't been registered either.

In listing three, the ® symbol is included because the company has now registered its name with the Patent and Trademark Office. The slogan in listing four has also been registered so the ® symbol is included with it. Note that the use of the symbol is likely to be found directly on the company's Web site because the site contains the product that the company offers.

In listings five and six, the ℠ symbol is used. If BigInternet.com runs a television advertisement, the ℠ symbol will be used because it indicates protected names of goods and services that the company offers, but doesn't actually show the product (you have to go to the Web site to see the product).

1. BigInternet.com™

2. We're a click away.™

3. BigInternet.com®

4. We're a click away.®

5. BigInternet.com℠

6. We're a click away. ℠

Figure 7-4 Proper Use of Trademarks

Note that the use of ™ does not constitute exclusive right to a word, phrase, or symbol. It's typically used during the registration and approval process with the Patent and Trademark Office. Once the registration is complete, the symbol will be changed to ®. If you are considering using a word, phrase, or symbol on a Web site that has the ™ or ℠ attached, think twice because by the time you use it—or sometime after you use it—the registration may be complete. At that time, you must include the symbol or note on the site that the word, phrase, or symbol is a registered trademark. Frequently, matters of this sort are described in a "Legal" section of a Web site.

How to Register a Trademark

A trademark is registered with the U.S. Patent and Trademark Office. There are three requirements you must fulfill when applying for registration:

- Complete the written application. The specific form number can be found at the Patent and Trademark Office Web site.

- Submit a drawing of the trademark symbol. The symbol may consist of a word, phrase, graphic, or any combination of words, phrases, and graphics.

- Pay the application fee. Fees vary for trademark-related services. The initial application fee for filing an application is $325 at the time of this writing. See the Patent and Trademark Office Web site for current fees.

Once you've submitted the application, the trademark office will conduct a search of existing trademarks to determine if yours is the same as any other trademarks. If it is, you'll receive a letter saying that your trademark can't be used. If it isn't, the proposed trademark will be listed in the Official Gazette, which is a weekly publication of the Patent and Trademark Office. If there is no opposition or challenge to the trademark, a registration certificate will be issued to the owner of the trademark.

The complete trademark process takes from about six months to a year.

Licensing

Licensing refers to requiring payment in exchange for using a copyrighted work. The owner of a work may sell access to the work by stipulating that a licensing fee be paid, or that royalties be paid for each copy of the work sold.

For example, writers may receive **royalties** from a publisher for each copy of a book that's sold. In other words, the writer has licensed the publisher to sell the work on behalf of the writer, and to share the proceeds of the sale with the writer.

Software is routinely licensed in a similar manner. The specific details of the license are contained in a contract between the owner of the software (an individual or, more often, a company), and the user of the software. The license agreement can be packaged in many ways but the following are the most common:

- A **flat-rate license** in which the user (an individual or a company) pays an agreed-upon price for unlimited use of the software.

- An **escalating rate license** in which a flat rate is structured based on the number of installations of the software, or on the number of users of the software. Typically, the owner of the software and a company will agree that a specified number of users may use the software for a flat rate, but if additional users are needed, an additional fee must be paid.

Licensing agreements are a means for users to have access to original software without infringing the copyright of the owner of the software. It's not unusual for a single software package to consist of many elements that are copyright protected. When the package is sold, the owners of each of the elements are paid a licensing (or royalty) fee by the publisher of the software.

When software is used and licensing agreements are ignored, the software is said to be **pirated**, which is another way of saying that it's been stolen. Information technology departments must develop a way to track the software used in an organization to ensure that all licensing agreements are being met, or run the risk of a lengthy and costly court engagement.

pirated

Global Internet Business

Doing business on the Internet means that consumers from anywhere in the world may buy your product. If you don't have a system for exchanging foreign currency, you're likely to lose business from foreign customers. Just as important as having a currency exchange system is the technology for communicating with your customers, no matter what language they speak.

Assuming you can exchange money and communicate with the foreign customer, you now have to ship the product outside of the United States, which involves working with the U.S. Customs Office.

The following sections provide an overview discussion of currency exchange, multi-language technology, and export filing.

Currency Issues Among Vendors

Much of the Internet has an English-based language, although this is changing quickly (see the Unicode section in this chapter). However, commerce on the Internet is often global and this means that a consumer from anywhere in the world may make an Internet purchase.

The consumer will make the purchase in their local currency so the owner of a Web site must be prepared for currency exchanges. Note that currency values change often—at times, on an hourly basis. Unless an e-commerce site has extensive resources for tracking currency changes and then making the appropriate deposits into banks, the details of foreign currency handling are contracted to banks or financial institutions that specialized in foreign currency transfers.

Figure 7-5 shows a typical process that occurs when a purchase is made from a country outside the country of an e-commerce site.

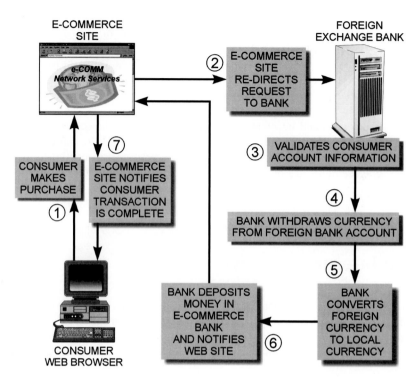

Figure 7-5 Typical Currency Exchange Process

1. The user/consumer makes a purchase from an e-commerce site located in another country.

2. The e-commerce site redirects the purchase request to a bank that has been contracted to handle foreign exchange transfers. Note that the bank—or similar institution—will typically provide software that will either automate the process or semi-automate it with minimal user intervention.

3. The foreign exchange bank will check to ensure the credit card used by the consumer is valid.

4. The bank will make a withdrawal from the consumer's account that's equal to the price of the purchased item, but in the currency of the consumer.

5. The bank will convert the foreign currency to the local currency of the e-commerce site. The value of the currency will be the exchange rate of the foreign currency to the local currency at the time of the purchase.

6. The foreign exchange bank will now deposit the money into an account specified by the e-commerce site.

7. Once the process has been completed—which may take from a few seconds to a day or two—the consumer is notified. The notification may be a message generated by the e-commerce site or it may consist of an e-mail sent to the consumer.

When a product is returned (or shipped) from the foreign location, a similar process is followed. The tricky part of a return is to know the currency exchange rate at the time a product was purchased versus the exchange rate at the time money is returned to the consumer. It's not likely that the two rates will be the same. A foreign exchange service, such as the type described in Figure 7-5, will be able to make the correct adjustment.

International Shipping

Commercial shipping from the United States to another country means that your product will pass through U.S. Customs. To do so, you must provide proper notification to customs concerning your shipment.

Customs uses a process called the **Automated Export System (AES)** that is used to detail the product that's being shipped. AES is a software solution that can be customized (Customs provides the source code on request) for electronic filing of export documentation. The level of detail required with the AES form depends on the product being shipped. The more sensitive the product that's being shipped, the more detail that is required. For example, if you export software that includes encryption, then expect to fill in more than the usual 20 fields in the form.

Automated Export System (AES)

You have several options for meeting export regulations. You can:

- Perform the filing yourself.

- Contract to an international shipper who is familiar with Customs regulations.

- Contract to an AES vendor for customized development.

When importing materials, expect the material to go through customs as well. As with exporting, if you're familiar with the import process, you should contract with an international shipper to act as your agent.

Unicode Concepts

Internet commerce has a potential for true global access. But if your customers are located in a country where English isn't the predominant language, you will effectively eliminate these customers from buying via your Web site.

The Unicode Standard represents a solution to language barriers by providing a single system for representing characters from the majority of languages from the past and present. The current version of Unicode provides for nearly 39,000 coded characters from the world's alphabets.

Unicode is based on the simplicity of standard ASCII by using a 16-bit encoding scheme (for a total of 65,000 characters) that's used to represent letters, numbers, punctuation, math symbols, technical symbols, and other symbols.

Table 7-5 lists a sample of Unicode.

Table 7-5 Unicode
Sample

UNICODE CODE (Hexadecimal)	CHARACTER
0020	Space
0021	Exclamation Mark
0022	Quotation Mark
0023	Number Sign
0024	Dollar Sign
0025	Percent Sign
0026	Ampersand
0027	Apostrophe
0028	Left Parenthesis
0029	Right Parenthesis
002A	Asterisk
002B	Plus Sign
002C	Comma
002D	Hyphen-Minus
002E	Full Stop, Period
0030	Digit Zero
0031	Digit One
0032	Digit Two
0033	Digit Three
0034	Digit Four
0035	Digit Five
0036	Digit Six
0037	Digit Seven
0038	Digit Eight
0039	Digit Nine

As you can see from the table, each character is represented by a 16-bit code, which is shown as a hexadecimal number in the table.

All Windows 9x operating systems, Windows NT/2000, and Apple Macintosh support Unicode. Because Unicode is widely deployed, the cost to implement it as a multi-language solution is minimal; frequently nothing more is needed other than to make sure the installed Unicode is the most current version (version 3).

Keep in mind that when you or a developer creates the content of a Web site, it will be viewed by users from any part of the globe. Make sure that the content will translate appropriately. As a general guide, avoid the following:

- Slang

- Colloquialisms

- Technical jargon not appropriate for the audience

- Slurs of any type

- Cultural bias (for a business Web site)

Domain Name Registration

A domain name is used to specify a site on the Internet by matching the name to an IP address. Domain names are unique and the corresponding IP address of the name is also unique. The use of a domain name is almost always associated with a World Wide Web address. In order to establish a presence on the Internet, you must have a domain name, or have access to a domain name.

A name can be registered without associating the name to an IP address. Registering the name is a way of reserving exclusive use of the name until the name is actually used for a functioning site.

The management of domain names is coordinated by the **Internet Corporation for Assigned Names and Numbers (ICANN)**. ICANN is a non-profit organization that accredits companies for registering domain names. A company that has been accredited by the ICANN is said to be an "accredited registrar," and is normally referred to as a **registrar**. Registrars are authorized to register domain names in the .com, .net, and .org domains.

Internet Corporation for Assigned Names and Numbers (ICANN)

registrar

For many years the source for domain name registration has been InterNIC. InterNIC is an informational organization formed by several companies in cooperation with the U.S. government. InterNIC has been synonymous with domain name registration and in particular with Network Solutions, a certified registrar. In recent years, InterNIC has been trying to establish itself as an information organization as opposed to a domain name registrar, while referring those seeking registration to a list of certified registrars.

In the United States, only accredited registrars may be used for registering a domain name. Table 7-6 lists those registrars that are ICANN accredited and operational at the time of this writing.

Table 7-6 ICANN
Accredited Registrars

REGISTRAR	LOCATION
A+ Net	US
AWRegistry	US
Alabanza	US
America Online	US
Columbia Analytical Services	US
CORE - Council of Internet Registrars	Switzerland
Domain Bank, Inc.	US
Domain Registration Services	US
domaininfo.com	Sweden
DomainPeople.com	US
eNom, Inc.	US
France Telecom Oléane	France
Internet Domain Registrars	US
interQ Incorporated	Japan
Melbourne IT	Australia
The NameIt Corporation	US
NameSecure.com	US
Network Solutions, Inc.	US
NORDNET	France
PSI-Japan, Inc.	Japan
register.com	US
Signature Domains, Inc.	US
TUCOWS.com, Inc.	Canada

A registered domain name may not be used by any other individual or organization. The registered name is submitted to a registry of registered domain names. Once a name is registered, it can be submitted to an ISP for hosting. The ISP will assign a static IP address to the domain name.

A registered domain name with a corresponding IP address can then be resolved to an actual Web site via the DNS servers.

Figure 7-6 shows the Network Solutions Web site. Network Solutions is an accredited registrar.

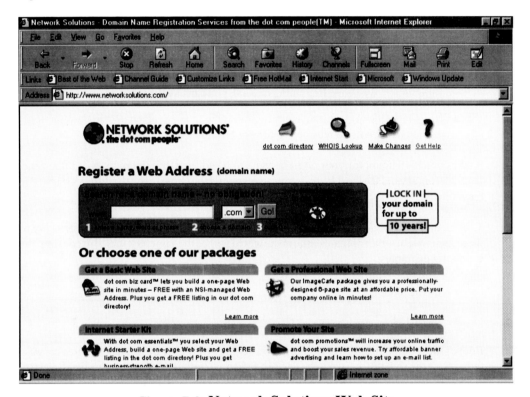

Figure 7-6 Network Solutions Web Site

To register a domain name, you follow these steps:

1. Enter the name of the domain name you want to register in the registry database. If the name is already in use, you'll receive a message telling you that the name isn't available.

2. Once you've received a message telling you that the domain name you've selected is available, you can register the name. You may select a .com, .net, or .org extension for the name (or choose all three). Generally, the accepted uses of the three extensions are:

    *   .com: Used for commercial, for-profit business.

    *   .net: Used for companies involved in the Internet infrastructure. Frequently, an ISP has a .net extension.

    *   .org: Used for non-profit organizations.

3. The next step in the registration process varies somewhat. At a minimum, you'll be asked to enter contact information that includes a name, address, and telephone number of an individual that can be contacted concerning any problems with the domain name. In addition:

- If you have an ISP that will be hosting the site, you will enter the IP address for the domain name (obtained from the ISP).

- The primary and secondary DNS servers used by the ISP. These will also be given to you by the hosting ISP and may be either domain names or IP addresses.

4. Pay the fee for registration. Fees vary widely among registrars (the fee at Network Solutions, for example, is $35 a year) and each is free to set their own pricing structures according to the services they offer. You may choose to contact an ISP and have them do the registration work for you. If so, check with the ISP for pricing information. In addition:

- You'll be asked to specify the length of the registration. You must pay a fee for a minimum of two years. Beginning in 2000, you can pay for a maximum of ten years.

- Once the registration period nears expiration, you must renew the registration or the domain name will be returned to the pool of unused domain names.

It takes about 48 hours for your domain name to be entered into the registry. At that time, DNS servers around the world will be able to reconcile the name to the IP address assigned to the name.

A .com, .net, and .org domain name is global. When you register a domain name in any of these domains, no other domain name in the world will be the same as yours. But consider the following examples:

- Internet.com

- Internet.uk

Both of these domain names may take a browser to two entirely different Web sites because they aren't the same domain name. The second name is appended with a top-level country code (for the United Kingdom). Many companies, when registering a domain name, also register the name in other countries using the country code of the country. The advantage to doing so is that brand names and service marks are reserved and can't be used by unscrupulous individuals who create Web sites that attempt to appear to be the same as a .com, .net, or .org Web site.

Fees tend to get expensive when registering top-level country code names (the fee may range from about $300 to $600 for each country code extension) because the registration process and requirements vary with the country where the name is registered. There are currently 191 recognized country codes. If you want to register a top-level country code for your domain name, check with your ISP (the process is complicated, so make sure the ISP has experience registering country code names), or contact an accredited registrar.

Country codes in 80 of the 191 countries that register top-level country codes are registered on a first-come, first-served basis.

Background Info

An ISP will generally redirect registered domain names to a single domain name address. For example, assume a company has registered the following domain names:

www.internet.com

www.internet.net

internet.com

internet.net

internet.houston.tx.us

internet.uk

internet.cc (Cocos-Keeling Islands)

internet.fr (France)

When any of these names are entered into a Web browser, the ISP can redirect them to a single site address such as internet.com.

E-COMMERCE CONCEPTS

Increasingly, the Internet is being used by companies for commerce. The Internet can offer huge savings over a traditional business with walls. Before discussing e-commerce concepts, it's important to describe how the different types of network arrangements fit into the e-commerce model.

The Internet is the primary network type used for e-commerce. The reason for this is that the Internet is accessible to the public, whereas other network types are not.

An extranet may be used for commerce between businesses, but not between a company and the general public.

An intranet is rarely used for e-commerce. An intranet is normally used exclusively for employees of a company and isn't readily accessible by the public.

Electronic Data Interchange

Electronic Data Interchange, or **EDI**, is a method used by companies for transferring business information over the Internet. The most common application of EDI is for invoices, purchase orders, or request for quotes from a buyer to a seller.

EDI is structured differently than human-readable information. EDI is structured specifically for computers to read and interpret. The appeal of EDI is that it is run on an open environment so that it doesn't matter what type of machines are connected to either end of the exchange; EDI is standardized so that it can be read by any machine that has an EDI interpreter.

There are two standards associated with EDI. The first is administered by the American National Standards Institute (ANSI) and is the **ANSI X12** Standard for EDI. The second is **EDIFACT**. Both standards serve the same purpose in defining the structure and sequence of an EDI interchange. EDIFACT, however, is supported by more organizations that ANSI X12. ANSI is moving toward integrating the specific conventions used with EDIFACT into the X12 standard, but is also maintaining the original X12 standard for companies that have invested significantly into the X12 standard.

Of the two standards, EDIFACT is the more efficient because data may be defined with fewer entries than with ANSI X12.

Source data from a company (such as the information input to an invoice) may be mapped to more than one data field. For example, pricing information contained in an invoice may be placed in the header of an EDI document, or it can be listed as a series of line items in the body of the invoice. To ensure that communicating companies agree to the methods used with EDI, they follow **EDI Implementation Guidelines**. The guidelines are developed by industry-specific groups to aid companies in following EDI standards.

The structure of an EDI document is hierarchical. Data is identified by the smallest amount of information that has meaning, to the full exchange of a completed EDI document. The following describes each element of an EDI document:

- **Data Element**: The smallest named item of the EDI document. An example of a data element is a date, weight, currency exchange rate, or a unit of measure.

- **Composite Data Element**: A code that represents several data elements. Only the later versions of the EDI standard support this. An example is a code to represent a street name with a street number.

- **Data Segments**: A data segment is a group of related data elements. For example, an address contains the data elements for a street name, street number, city, state, and zip code. Taken together, the data elements form a logically related data segment.

- **Transaction Set**: The smallest set of data that may be exchanged between two organizations. For example, a single invoice or purchase order is a transaction set.

- **Functional Group**: A functional group contains more than one transaction set. For example, an exchange may contain two purchase orders and three invoices. The two purchase orders represent one functional group, while the three invoices represent a second functional group.

- **EDI Interchange**: An EDI interchange contains the functional groups to be sent between companies. The interchange may have one transaction set or it may have many sets.

The EDI interchange is bound by a header and a trailer. The header includes:

- Name of sender

- Name of receiver

- Date and time of the interchange

- Security information

- A unique tracking number

The trailer contains:

- Number of functional groups in the interchange

- The same unique tracking number that's carried in the header

Figure 7–7 illustrates a sample EDI document structure for a simple invoice.

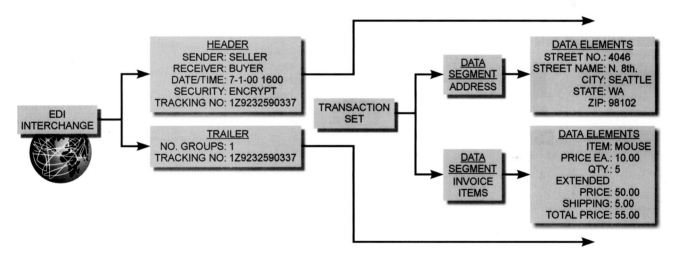

Figure 7-7 Sample EDI Document Structure

Notice that the document is structured so that data elements are defined. The data elements are organized to form data segments; one for the address and one for the invoice items. The data segments and data elements comprise a single transaction set. Although not specified in the figure, there is only one functional group, the invoice. Header and trailer are added to the transaction set to complete the EDI interchange.

While, in theory, EDI documents can be translated by any computer that have an EDI interpreter installed, the reality is that the connection between companies has proven to be difficult. Many companies forgo the potential problems by hiring a **Value Added Network Service (VANS)**. The VANS acts as a middle point for forwarding and receiving EDI documents. A company need only install the VANS EDI software, and the VANS will provide communication with all other organizations that a company does business with.

Business to Business

Business to business (B2B)

Business to business (often abbreviated **B2B**) refers to an e-commerce Internet site that exists to sell directly to other businesses. An example of a business to business site may be a supplier of bulk chemicals that sells the chemical to factories that fabricate products from the chemical.

Figure 7-8 shows an example of business to business e-commerce. In the figure, a company that sells gardening books has established an Internet-based relationship with a general publisher. The gardening book Web site purchases books from the general publisher over a B2B link using EDI.

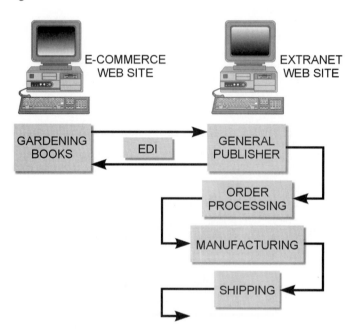

Figure 7-8 Business to Business Operation

The general publisher processes the orders from the gardening book site, then sends the orders to a factory where the books are produced. The finished books are then shipped from the factory.

Business to business commerce over the Internet can represent significant savings for the companies involved through telephone costs, time savings, and efficiencies in filling orders.

Business to Customer

business to customer

A **business to customer** site refers to an e-commerce site that markets directly to end users. An example of a business to customer site is illustrated in Figure 7-9.

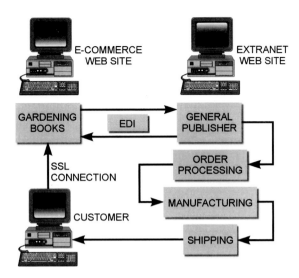

Figure 7-9 Business to Customer Operation

In the figure, a commercial site has been set up to sell gardening books. The customer will place an order for a book using a credit card over a SSL link between the user's computer and the commercial site server.

Once the gardening book site receives the order, the site will validate the credit card. Once the card is validated, the amount of the purchase, including any taxes and shipping charges, will be deducted from the card and deposited into a business bank account belonging to the gardening site.

The gardening book Web site may be little more than a virtual company. That is, a supply of books may not be stored in inventory at the site, and there may be few employees located at the site. In fact, the site may consist of little more than a storefront.

But to stay in business, the gardening book site must have a financial arrangement with a book supplier. The EDI link between the gardening site and the general publisher represents the financial link that ensures the general publisher will receive money for the books that are shipped. Frequently, an EDI interchange is structured so that money is deposited and withdrawn as a part of the exchange between companies.

In Figure 7-9, the general publisher ships an ordered book directly from its inventories to the customer, relieving the gardening book site from having to maintain an inventory.

Internet Commerce

Internet commerce refers to buying and selling over the Internet. The volume of money exchanged directly as a result of the Internet is increasing rapidly.

Internet commerce

Many companies find that the accessibility of the Internet allows them to dispense with many traditional walls and conventions. For example, Internet commerce often eliminates, or reduces, the need for the following:

- Extensive inventories
- Sales representatives

- Extensive bookkeeping

- Large buildings

- Traditional payment equipment such as cash registers

- Paper-based invoicing, order taking, and purchasing

- Personnel costs

Merchant Systems

A **merchant system** refers to software used on e-commerce sites that allows orders to be taken, filled, and administered electronically. **MercanTech** is an example of a merchant system. With MercanTech, a basic Internet storefront can be set up using a shopping cart to collect items to be purchased.

Once the items are purchased, the software will then present the buyer with screens for paying for the purchases with a credit card. The credit card information is encrypted with the same software. The buyer can purchase without worry because the site must be authorized for collecting from credit cards. The site will be issued a digital signature and the signature downloaded to the customer Web browser. The browser will then send the signature to a service such as VeriSign to ensure the site is authorized.

E-commerce uses SSL to ensure an encrypted connection between a Web browser and Web server. During the SSL session, all data is encrypted; consequently, an SSL session is secure. What SSL doesn't do, however, is authenticate the user at the browser end of the connection during a credit card purchase from an e-commerce site. The open industry standard used on the Internet that does authenticate buyers when making credit card purchases is called **Secure Electronic Transmission (SET)** protocol.

SET was developed by IBM, Microsoft, MasterCard, VISA and others as a method of using public-key encryption on the Internet for making purchases with credit cards. When a buyer uses a credit card to make a purchase from a Web site, the information (card number, buyer's name, bank issuer, etc.) is encrypted using a randomly generated key. The information is encrypted once again using a public key. The encrypted information is sent to the card issuer where it is decrypted using a private key (that was derived from the public key.) A symmetric key is then used to decrypt the original information.

SET is employed by all major credit card issuers and banks on the Internet and has proved to be more secure than paying with a credit card in a conventional "bricks and mortal" store. In addition to authenticating buyers, SET also ensures that the transaction will not be diverted during the purchase.

Online Cataloging

Online cataloging refers to placing a database of products on a Web site for sale to the public, or to other businesses. A customer may search the site for a specific product, then purchase the product with a credit card. In the case of a business customer, the purchase may be made through an EDI interchange.

There are many sites that offer online catalogs and Web sites are quickly replacing their paper-based predecessors. The single biggest advantage of offering an online catalog is that it saves printing and postage costs.

Online cataloging

Relationship Management

Relationship management refers to customs that a company engages in to keep customers satisfied. For example, it's one thing to sell a product on the Internet, but another thing to develop the site so that customers can receive help using the product, or for returning the product.

The following lists typical Web site areas devoted to maintaining relationships with customers:

Relationship management

- Help Desk access via e-mail

- Technical notes

- Download area that includes drivers, patches, or other software

- Feedback on the site, typical to the site administrator

- Return policies and a "how-to" area that describes the steps for returning a product

Customer Self-service

Customer self-service refers to Web sites that are automated to the point that the customer can locate a product to buy, make the purchase, and receive notification that the product has been sent—all without interacting with a human.

Customer self-service

Most e-commerce sites are structured to be self-service sites. The normal process is to provide the customer with an electronic shopping cart. The site software will keep track of the contents of the cart and total the purchases when the customer is ready to "check-out." At that time, the transaction will be sealed when the customer makes the purchase with a credit card.

Internet Marketing

Internet marketing refers to selling a product on the Internet. Advertisements are one method used to sell products. Banner ads placed on sites are a common method used to advertise a business. Figure 7-10 shows an example of a banner ad.

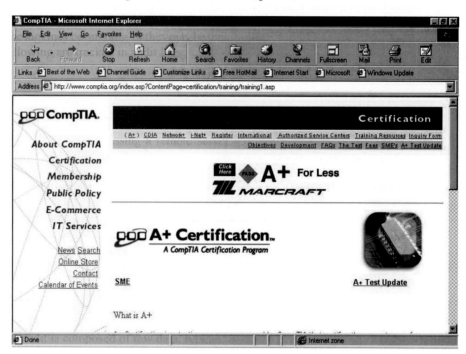

Figure 7-10 Example of a Banner Ad

Another method used to market a Web site is META tags. A META tag is placed in the HTML of the home page of a Web site. The META tags specify the site by name, and include a short description of the site content. Figure 7-11 shows an example of a META tag.

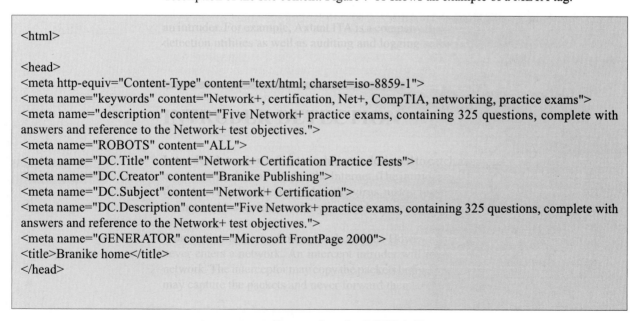

```
<html>

<head>
<meta http-equiv="Content-Type" content="text/html; charset=iso-8859-1">
<meta name="keywords" content="Network+, certification, Net+, CompTIA, networking, practice exams">
<meta name="description" content="Five Network+ practice exams, containing 325 questions, complete with answers and reference to the Network+ test objectives.">
<meta name="ROBOTS" content="ALL">
<meta name="DC.Title" content="Network+ Certification Practice Tests">
<meta name="DC.Creator" content="Branike Publishing">
<meta name="DC.Subject" content="Network+ Certification">
<meta name="DC.Description" content="Five Network+ practice exams, containing 325 questions, complete with answers and reference to the Network+ test objectives.">
<meta name="GENERATOR" content="Microsoft FrontPage 2000">
<title>Branike home</title>
</head>
```

Figure 7-11 Example of a META Tag

Nearly all search sites on the Internet use META tags to categorize Internet Web sites. Care must be taken when you add descriptive comments about a site because search sites will rank the site according to the words contained in the description.

KEY POINTS REVIEW

- Client pull technology relies on opening and closing a TCP connection for each update to a Web page.

- Server push technology relies on opening a single TCP connection between browser and Web server.

- A copyright is used to protect the author of an original work from infringement.

- The length that a copyright is in effect varies with the date that the work was produced.

- For any original work produced after 1989, an official copyright notice or indication of copyright isn't required.

- The use of the copyright symbol properly displayed is notice that the work is copyrighted and should always be used on original work to avoid infringement.

- A properly displayed symbol consists of the copyright symbol ©, the year that the work was fixed, and the owner of the copyright.

- A trademark is a word, phrase, symbol, or combination of words, symbols, or phrases that are used to differentiate the products and services of one party from another. A trademark may be displayed as ™, ®, or ℠.

- Licensing refers to requiring payment in exchange for using a copyrighted work.

- Because a global Web site will be doing business with consumers in many countries, the site must be able to make adjustments for varying currency values.

- The Customs Office requires advance notification of any product that is to be exported. The Customs Office requires that the shipper enter shipping information in the Automated Export System (AES).

- Multi-lingual issues are resolved with the Unicode Standard, which is a system that represents characters as 16-bit values.

- The management of domain names is coordinated by the Internet Corporation for Assigned Names and Numbers (ICANN).

- To apply for a domain name, you must contact a registrar that has been accredited by ICANN.

- EDI represents a structured method for exchanging business forms and documents between companies.

- Business to business refers to using the Internet as a channel for conducting commerce between two companies.

- Business to consumer refers to using the Internet as a channel for conducting commerce between a company and a buyer.

- META tags are placed in the HTML of a home page of a Web site and are used by Internet Search sites for cataloging and ranking sites.

REVIEW QUESTIONS

The following questions test your knowledge of the material presented in this chapter:

1. What type of technology is used between client and Web server in which a TCP connection is opened for site update?

2. What is needed to copyright an original work that was recently created?

3. What type of technology is used between client and Web site in which a single TCP connection is opened for all site updates?

4. Graphic files posted to a Web site were created last year. What is the length of the copyright for the graphic files?

5. List three advantages to registering an original with the copyright office.

6. List three advantages to using the copyright symbol with original works.

7. The Big Internet Company has a Web site that it wants to place a copyright notice on. Write the proper format for copyrighting the site.

8. Describe the difference between a copyright and a trademark.

9. A television advertisement displays the name of a company. In order to indicate that the company name is reserved, which symbol should be displayed next to the company name?

10. A company called BestBuy.com wants to protect the Web site name, but hasn't formally registered the name with the U.S. Patent and Trademark Office. How should the name be displayed?

11. You have created an original software package and want to sell the package to others but don't want to relinquish ownership of the package. How can you do it?

12. Why is currency exchange an important issue among global Web site owners?

13. What is the name of the software used by the U.S. Customs service?

14. What is the purpose of Unicode?

15. List the steps required to register a domain name.

MULTIPLE CHOICE QUESTIONS

1. From the following, select the proper copyright format.

   a. Copyright Company 2000

   b. ©2000 Company

   c. ™ 2000 Company

   d. © Company

2. Which of the following symbols is used to indicate that a trademark is registered with the U.S. Patent and Trademark Office?

   a. ®

   b. ™

   c. ©

   d. SM

3. From the following statements concerning domain names, select the statement that is true.

   a. Before a registered domain name can be used on the Internet, the name must have an IP address assigned to it.

   b. When a domain name is registered for a .com domain, it's automatically registered with .org and .net domains.

   c. When registering a domain name, it's not required that you divulge contact information for the name.

   d. Domain names must be re-registered every six months.

4. Which of the following should a global Web site be sure to use?

   a. License

   b. Cookies

   c. UDP

   d. Unicode

5. How many bits are assigned to each character in Unicode?

   a. 4

   b. 8

   c. 16

   d. 32

6. Which of the following statements is true regarding the use of the ™ symbol?

   a. The word or phrase that it's used with has been registered with the U.S. Patent and Trademark Office.

   b. The use of ™ does not constitute exclusive right to a word, phrase, or symbol.

   c. It's used to mean the same as the ® symbol.

   d. It may only be used by small businesses.

7. Which of the following best describes client pull technology?

   a. A single TCP connection is opened for all client-side updates.

   b. The client Web browser has the option to accept or reject Web site updates.

   c. Updates sent to the client Web browser takes less time than with server push.

   d. A TCP connection is opened for each update sent to the client Web browser.

8. A Web site that uses server push technology allows:

   a. The site to be viewed without specialized plug-ins.

   b. The client to determine when updates are to be received from the server.

   c. A single TCP connection to be used for updating each client Web browser.

   d. The client browser to control the content of the Web site.

9. From the following, which cannot be copyrighted?

   a. A JPEG file.

   b. A technical paper.

   c. A title.

   d. A Web site.

10. Which of the following allows you to copyright a document without registering the document?

   a. ©

   b. ®

   c. ™

   d. ℠

11. A Web site based in the United States has a domain name called company.com. To ensure the same site won't be confused in the United Kingdom with similarly named sites, how should the site be registered?

   a. company.org

   b. company.uk

   c. company.uk.com

   d. uk.company

12. When developing the content of a Web site, which of the following should be avoided?

   a. Graphics

   b. Hyperlinks

   c. Action verbs

   d. Colloquialisms

13. A company called Big Seller has registered the company name with the U.S. Patent and Trademark Office. How should the name be displayed?

   a. Big Company©

   b. Big Company®

   c. Big Company™

   d. Big Company℠

14. A Web site has been designed so that visitors will receive continuous updates on weather conditions in three different geographic regions at the same time. Which of the following is the most efficient technology to use for this application?

   a. Unicode

   b. Client pull technology

   c. Server push technology

   d. AES

15. How can you check a graphical file such as a JPG or GIF to determine if it is copyrighted?

   a. Check for a watermark that indicates the copyright.

   b. Computer generated files can't be copyrighted.

   c. Use the file, then wait for the owner to notify you.

   d. Check with the U.S. Copyright Office.

OSI Reference Model

The ISO (International Organization for Standardization) OSI (Open System Interconnection) Reference Model for Data Communications is a blueprint for large and small networks. The model is used by network designers as a baseline reference for evaluating the overall effectiveness of a network.

The OSI model consists of seven layers, as shown in Figure AA-1. Each layer describes key components of an ideal network. The layers are arranged in a hierarchical manner so that each layer is subordinate to the next higher layer. In an ideal networking environment, the model will exist with no dependence on the types of machines (computers, routers, hubs, etc.) connected to it. For this reason, the model describes an open system or architecture.

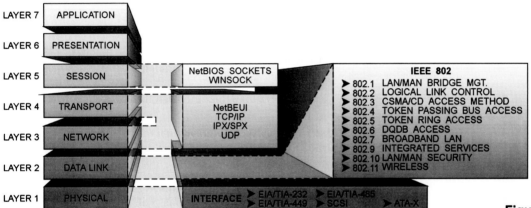

Figure AA-1 OSI Reference Model

The Physical layer resides at the bottom of the stack. The specific parameters of data bits, and the specifications of connectors and cabling media, are described at the Physical layer. The Physical layer is the only layer in which actual data bits and networking media can be found. All succeeding layers are logical layers and are implemented with software.

The next layer in the hierarchy is the Data Link layer. The Data Link layer is responsible for organizing the data bits that move at the Physical layer into organized units called frames. The Data Link layer is subdivided into the Media Access Control (MAC) sub-layer, and the Logical Link Control (LLC) sub-layer.

The MAC sub-layer is normally implemented with well-known protocols such as Ethernet, Token Ring, FDDI, and ATM. Since each of these protocols contains specifications of data rates and cabling types, the MAC sub-layer actually extends from the Data Link layer into the Physical layer. But they also describe the format of frames used such as the length of the frame and addressing schemes (the MAC address).

The LLC sub-layer is a software interface between the Data Link layer and the next layer, the Network layer. The LLC contains specific fields that detail the type of network (such as Windows NT, Windows 2000, or Novell Netware) in which a frame that was created in the MAC sub-layer will be sent along.

The Network layer is responsible for organizing MAC sub-layer frames into larger frames that are called packets, then ensuring that the packets are routed to the correct destination. This is an important layer for networking since a network may have hundreds or millions of nodes connected to it. The Network layer provides a standardized addressing scheme (the IP address) for forwarding a data packet across any size network and to the correct destination node.

The Transport layer is responsible for ensuring the reliability of a network. When a packet is sent to a remote node at the Network layer, there are few guarantees that the packet will actually arrive at the correct node. The Transport layer, as an option, will guarantee that the packet arrived at the correct address and the data that was sent is the same data received. The most common scheme used to do so is with acknowledgments. That is, the receiving node is required to send a packet back to the sending node indicating if the packet was received. If the sending node doesn't receive the acknowledgment, it will assume that the receiving node didn't receive the original transmission and re-send it. TCP (Transmission Control Protocol) is the most common Transport layer protocol.

The Session layer is responsible for setting up the initial communications dialogue between two communicating network nodes. A good example of a Session layer activity is a socket that is created using well-known ports. The socket specifies the protocol to use along with the processes (FTP, HTTP, etc.) that will be invoked during the data exchange between nodes.

The Transport layer is responsible for formatting data so that it can be shown appropriately on a screen or for a machine to read. For example, the format of data used in an EDI exchange is determined at the Presentation layer. Data encryption, as well as foreign language translations, occur at the Presentation layer.

The Application layer is used to launch a network application such as FTP, e-mail, or HTTP. Note that the Application has nothing to do with *application software* such as Microsoft Word or Excel. In the context of the OSI model, the Application layer is only concerned with specialized processes, or uses of a network.

A basic understanding of the OSI model is important to a conceptual understanding of networks since it's frequently used as a reference for classifying protocols. Common protocols and their associated layers in the reference model are shown in Figure AA-1. Networking vendors and manufacturers use the layers of the model in specifications and white papers describing their products.

i-Net+ Objective Map

i-NET+ EXAMINATION

The CompTIA organization has established the following objectives for the i-Net+ Certification exam.

1.0 i-Net Basics

This domain challenges the test taker to demonstrate basic knowledge of the Internet. This includes issues that can affect Internet site functionality, URLs and their appropriate use, caching, and search indexes.

> 1.1. Describe a URL, its functions and components, different types of URLs, and use of the appropriate type of URL to access a given type of server.

Content may include the following:

- Protocol - Chapter 1, Lab Procedure 1

- Address - Chapter 1, Lab Procedure 1

- Port - Chapter 1, Lab Procedure 19

> 1.2. Identify the issues that affect Internet site functionality (e.g., performance, security, and reliability).

Content may include the following:

- Bandwidth - Chapters 1 and 5, Lab Procedure 18

- Internet connection points - Chapter 5

- Audience access - Chapter 5, Lab Procedure 23

- Internet Service Provider (ISP) - Chapter 5

- Connection types - Chapter 5, Lab Procedure 15

- Corrupt files - Chapter 5

- Files taking too long to load - Chapter 5, Lab Procedure 9

- Inability to open files - Chapter 5, Lab Procedure 9

- Resolution of graphics - Chapter 5, Lab Procedure 9

1.3. Describe the concept of caching and its implications.

Content may include the following:

- Server caching - Chapter 5, Lab Procedure 18

- Client caching - Chapter 4, Lab Procedure 3

- Proxy caching - Lab Procedure 18

- Cleaning out client-side cache - Chapter 4, Lab Procedure 3

- Server may cache information as well - Chapter 5

- Web page update settings in browsers - Chapter 4

1.4. Describe different types of search indexes - static index/site map, keyword index, full text index.

Examples could include the following:

- Searching your site - Chapter 2

- Searching content - Chapter 2

- Indexing your site for a search - Chapter 2

2.0 i-Net Clients

This domain requires the test taker to demonstrate knowledge of Internet clients and the infrastructure needed for their support and performance. This includes the use of Web browsers, various clients, cookies, patches, upgrading, and desktop configuration issues.

2.1. Describe the infrastructure needed to support an Internet client.

Content could include the following:

- TCP/IP stack - Chapter 4

- Operating system - Chapter 4

- Network connection - Chapter 4, Lab Procedure 14

- Web browser - Chapter 4

- E-mail - Chapter 4, Lab Procedure 17

- Hardware platform (PC, handheld device, WebTV, Internet phone) - Chapter 4

2.2. Describe the use of Web browsers and various clients (e.g., FTP clients, Telnet clients, e-mail clients, all-in-one clients/universal clients) within a given context of use.

Examples of context could include the following:

- When you would use each - Chapter 4, Lab Procedure 15

- The basic commands you would use (e.g., put and get) with each client (e.g., FTP, Telnet) - Chapter 4, Lab Procedure 15

2.3. Explain the issues to consider when configuring the desktop.

Content could include the following:

- TCP/IP configuration (NetBIOS name server such as WINS, DNS, default gateway, subnet mask) - Chapter 4, Lab Procedure 14

- Host file configuration - Chapter 4, Lab Procedure 18

- DHCP versus static IP - Chapter 4, Lab Procedure 14

- Configuring browser (proxy configuration, client-side caching) - Chapter 4, Lab Procedure 3

2.4. Describe MIME types and their components.

Content could include the following:

- Whether a client can understand various e-mail types (MIME, HTML, uuencode) - Chapter 4, Lab Procedure 17

- The need to define MIME file types for special download procedures such as unusual documents or graphic formats - Chapter 4, Lab Procedure 17

2.5. Identify problems related to legacy clients (e.g., TCP/IP sockets and their implication on the operating system).

Content could include the following:

- Checking revision date, manufacturer/vendor - Chapter 4, Lab Procedure 16

- Troubleshooting and performance issues - Chapter 4, Lab Procedure 16

- Compatibility issues - Chapter 4

- Version of the Web browser - Chapter 4, Lab Procedure 16

2.6. Explain the function of patches and updates to client software and associated problems.

Content could include the following:

- Desktop security - Chapter 4

- Virus protection - Chapter 4, Lab Procedure 24

- Encryption levels - Chapter 4

- Web browsers - Chapter 4, Lab Procedure 16

- E-mail clients - Chapter 4, Lab Procedure 16

2.7. Describe the advantages and disadvantages of using a cookie and how to set cookies. - Chapter 4, Lab Procedure 3

Content could include the following:

- Setting a cookie without the knowledge of the user - Chapter 4

- Automatically accepting cookies versus query - Chapter 4

- Remembering everything the user has done - Chapter 4

- Security and privacy implications - Chapter 4, Lab Procedure 3

3.0 Development

This domain requires the test taker to demonstrate knowledge of Internet application development and terminology. This includes knowledge of programming languages, databases, HTML document structure, extensions or plug-ins, and various file formats.

3.1. Define programming-related terms as they relate to Internet applications development.

Content could include the following:

- API - Chapter 2

- CGI - Chapter 2, Lab Procedure 23

- SQL - Chapter 2, Lab Procedure 12

- SAPI - Chapter 2

- DLL - dynamic linking and static linking - Chapter 2

- Client and server-side scripting - Chapter 2

3.2. Describe the differences between popular client-side and server-side programming languages.

Examples could include the following:

- Java - Chapter 2

- JavaScript - Chapter 2

- Perl - Chapter 2

- C - Chapter 2

- C++ - Chapter 2, Lab Procedure 11

- Visual Basic - Chapter 2

- VBScript - Chapter 2

- Jscript - Chapter 2

- XML - Chapter 2

- VRML - Chapter 2

- ASP - Chapter 2

Content could include the following:

- When to use the languages - Chapter 2

- When they are executed - Chapter 2

3.3. Describe the differences between a relational database and a non-relational database. - Chapter 2, Lab Procedure 12

3.4. Identify when to integrate a database with a Web site and the technologies used to connect the two. - Chapter 2, Lab Procedure 12

3.5. Demonstrate the ability to create HTML pages.

Content could include the following:

- HTML document structure - Chapter 2, Lab Procedures 4, 7, and 8

- Coding simple tables, headings, forms - Chapter 2, Lab Procedures 5 and 6

- Compatibility between different browsers - Chapter 2, Lab Procedure 8

- Difference between text editors and GUI editors - Chapter 2, Lab Procedure 8

- Importance of creating cross-browser coding in your html - Chapter 2

3.6. Identify popular multimedia extensions or plug-ins.

Examples could include the following:

- QTVR (quick time) - Chapter 2, Lab Procedure 2

- Flash - Chapter 2

- Shockwave - Chapter 2

- RealPlayer - Chapter 2, Lab Procedure 2

- Windows Media Player - Chapter 2, Lab Procedures 8 and 16

3.7. Describe the uses and benefits of various multimedia file formats.

Examples could include the following:

- GIF - Chapters 2, 5, and 7, Lab Procedure 2 and 9

- GIF89a - Chapter 2

- JPEG - Chapters 2 and 7, Lab Procedure 2 and 9

- PNG - Chapter 2, Lab Procedure 2 and 9

- PDF - Chapter 2

- RTF - Chapter 2

- TIFF - Chapter 2

- PostScript - Chapter 2

- EPS - Chapter 2

- BMP - Lab Procedure 9, Lab Procedure 2

- MOV - Chapter 2, Lab Procedure 2

- MPEG - Chapter 2, Lab Procedure 2

- AVI - Chapters 2 and 4, Lab Procedure 2 and 10

- BinHex - Chapter 4

- Streaming media - Chapter 2

- Non-streaming media - Chapter 2

3.8. Describe the process of pre-launch site/application functionality testing.

Content could including the following:

- Checking hot links - Chapter 5, Lab Procedure 8 and 23

- Testing different browsers - Chapter 5

- Testing to ensure it does not corrupt your e-commerce site - Chapter 5

- Load testing - Chapter 5

- Access to the site - Chapter 5, Lab Procedure 23

- Testing with various speed connections - Chapter 5

4.0 Networking and Infrastructure

This domain requires the test taker to demonstrate knowledge of networking and Internet infrastructure and terminology, as well as the use of diagnosing tools for problem solving.

4.1. Describe the core components of the current Internet infrastructure and how they relate to each other.

Content may include the following:

- Network access points - Chapter 1

- Backbone - Chapter 1

4.2. Identify problems with Internet connectivity from source to destination for various types of servers.

Examples could include the following:

- E-mail - Chapter 5, Lab Procedure 18

- Slow server - Chapter 5

- Web site - Chapter 5, Lab Procedure 23

4.3. Describe Internet domain names and DNS.

Content could include the following:

- DNS entry types - Chapter 3, Lab Procedure 1 and 22

- Hierarchical structure - Chapter 3, Lab Procedure 1 and 22

- Role of root domain server - Chapter 3

- Top level or original domains - edu, com, mil, net, gov, org - Chapter 3, Lab Procedure 1

- Country level domains - .UK - Chapter 3

4.4. Describe the nature, purpose, and operational essentials of TCP/IP. - Lab Procedure 14

Content could include the following:

- What addresses are and their classifications (A, B, C, D) - Chapter 3, Lab Procedure 14

- Determining which ones are valid and which ones are not (subnet masks) - Chapter 3, Lab Procedure 14

- Public versus private IP addresses - Chapter 3, Lab Procedure 18

4.5. Describe the purpose of remote access protocols.

Content could include the following:

- SLIP - Chapter 3

- PPP - Chapter 3, Lab Procedure 25

- PPTP - Chapter 3, Lab Procedure 25

- Point-to-point/multipoint - Chapter 3

4.6. Describe how various protocols or services apply to the function of a mail system, Web system, and file transfer system.

Content could include the following:

- POP3 - Chapter 3, Lab Procedures 17 and 19

- SMTP - Chapter 3, Lab Procedures 17 and 19

- HTTP - Chapter 3, Lab Procedure 17

- FTP - Chapter 3, Lab Procedure 15

- NNTP (news servers) - Chapter 3

- TCP/IP - Chapter 3, Lab Procedure 14

- LDAP - Chapter 3

- LPR - Chapter 3

- Telnet - Chapter 3, Lab Procedure 15

- Gopher - Chapter 3

4.7. Describe when to use various diagnostic tools for identifying and resolving Internet problems.

Content could include the following:

- Ping - Chapter 3, Lab Procedure 13

- WinIPCfg - Chapter 3

- IPConfig - Chapter 3, Lab Procedure 13

- ARP - Chapter 3, Lab Procedure 13

- Trace Routing Utility (TraceRT) - Chapter 3, Lab Procedure 1

- Network Analyzer

- Netstat, Lab Procedure 1

4.8. Describe hardware and software connection devices and their uses.

Content could include the following:

- Network interface card - Chapter 1

- Various types of modems including analog, ISDN, DSL, and cable - Chapter 1

- Modem setup and commands - Chapter 1

- Adapter - Chapter 1

- Bridge - Chapter 1

- Internet-in-a-box - Chapter 5

- Cache-in-a-box - Chapter 5

- Hub - Chapter 1

- Router - Chapter 1

- Switch - Chapter 1

- Gateway - Chapter 1, Lab Procedure 18

- NOS - Chapter 5

- Firewall - Chapter 5, Lab Procedure 18

Content could include the following:

- T1/E1 - Chapter 1

- T3/E3 - Chapter 1

- Frame relay - Chapter 1

- X.25 - Chapter 1

- ATM - Chapter 1

- DSL - Chapter 1

Content could include the following:

- Proxy - Chapter 5, Lab Procedure 18

- Mail - Chapter 5, Lab Procedure 17

- Mirrored - Chapter 5

- Cache - Chapter 5, Lab Procedures 3 and 18

- List - Chapter 5

- Web (HTTP) - Chapter 5, Lab Procedures 17 and 23

- News - Chapter 5

- Certificate - Chapter 5

- Directory (LDAP) - Chapter 5

- E-commerce - Chapter 5

- Telnet - Chapter 5, Lab Procedure 15

- FTP - Chapter 5, Lab Procedure 15

5.0 i-Net Security

This domain requires the test taker to demonstrate knowledge of Internet security terminology, features, and requirements.

5.1. Define the following Internet security concepts: access control, encryption, auditing, and authentication; and provide appropriate types of technologies currently available for each.

Examples could include the following:

- Access control - access control list, firewall, packet filters, proxy - Chapter 6, Lab Procedure 18

- Authentication - certificates, digital signatures, non-repudiation - Chapter 6

- Encryption - public and private keys, secure socket layers (SSL), S/MIME, digital signatures, global versus country-specific encryption standards - Chapter 6, Lab Procedure 25

- Auditing - intrusion detection utilities, log files, auditing logs - Chapter 6, Lab Procedures 20 and 21

- SET (Secure Electronic Transactions)

5.2. Describe VPN and what it does. - Lab Procedure 25

Content could include the following:

- VPN is encrypted communications - Chapter 6, Lab Procedure 25

- Connecting two different company sites via an Internet VPN (extranet) - Chapter 6, Lab Procedure 25

- Connecting a remote user to a site - Chapter 6, Lab Procedure 25

5.3. Describe various types of suspicious activities.

Examples could include the following:

- Multiple login failures - Chapter 6, Lab Procedure 20

- Denial of service attacks - Chapter 6, Lab Procedure 20

- Mail flooding/spam - Chapter 6, Lab Procedure 19

- Ping floods - Chapter 6, Lab Procedure 20

- SYN floods - Chapter 6

Examples could include the following:

- Username and password - Chapter 6, Extended Lab Procedure 2 (see Instructor's Guide)

- File level - Chapter 6, Extended Lab Procedure 1 (see Instructor's Guide)

- Certificate - Chapter 6, Extended Lab Procedure 2 (see Instructor's Guide)

- File-level access: read, write, no access - Chapter 6, Extended Lab Procedure 1 (see Instructor's Guide)

5.5. Describe the purpose of anti-virus software and when to use it.

Content could include the following:

- Browser/client - Chapter 6, Lab Procedure 24

- Server - Chapter 6, Lab Procedure 24

5.6. Describe the differences between the following as they relate to security requirements:

- Intranet - Chapter 1

- Extranet - Chapter 1

- Internet - Chapter 1

6.0 Business Concepts

This domain requires the test taker to demonstrate knowledge of Internet business concepts. This includes knowledge of legal and regulatory issues, e-commerce concepts, e-commerce terminology, and audience development using Web-related mechanisms.

6.1. Explain the issues involved in copyrighting, trademarking, and licensing.

Content could include the following:

- How to license copyright materials - Chapter 7, Lab Procedure 26

- Scope of your copyright - Chapter 7, Lab Procedure 26

- How to copyright your material anywhere - Chapter 7, Lab Procedure 26

- Consequences of not being aware of copyright issues, not following copyright restrictions - Chapter 7, Lab Procedure 26

6.2. Identify the issues related to working in a global environment.

Content could include the following:

- Working in a multi-vendor environment with different currencies, etc. - Chapter 7

- International issues - shipping, supply chain - Chapter 7

- Multi-lingual or multi-character issues (Unicode) - Chapter 7, Lab Procedure 27

- Legal and regulatory issues - Chapter 7

6.3. Define the following Web-related mechanisms for audience development (i.e., attracting and retaining an audience):

- Push technology - Chapter 7

- Pull technology - Chapter 7

6.4. Describe the differences between the following from a business standpoint:

- Intranet - Chapter 7

- Extranet - Chapter 7

- Internet - Chapter 7

6.5. Define e-commerce terms and concepts .

Content could include the following:

- EDI - Chapter 7

- Business to business - Chapter 7

- Business to consumer - Chapter 7

- Internet commerce - Chapter 7

- Merchant systems - Chapter 7

- Online cataloging - Chapter 7

- Relationship management - Chapter 7

- Customer self-service - Chapter 7

- Internet marketing - Chapter 7

Glossary

A

Access Control: Refers to security precautions that protect network users from Internet intruders.

Active Server Pages: ASP is a proprietary server-side scripting language developed by Microsoft. ASP runs on Windows operating systems, primarily Windows NT with Internet Information Server software installed on the server. ASP allows dynamic Web documents to be displayed on the client browser.

Address Resolution Protocol: ARP is a tool used to map IP addresses to physical, MAC addresses.

Anti-virus Software: Anti-virus software is used to detect and/or clean a virus from a client computer, server, gateway or router. Any device that interacts with the Internet should be protected against a virus.

Application Programming Interface: An API consists of a set of functions provided by an operating system for a hardware device that allows software to use it.

Asynchronous Transfer Mode: Asynchronous Transfer Mode is a cell relay standard that uses 53-byte cells for transporting text, voice, video, music, or graphic messages.

Auditing: Auditing refers to techniques used for monitoring network access and authentication.

Authentication: The process of verifying identities.

Authorization: The process of being given access to resources.

Automated Export System: AES is used to detail the product that's being shipped. AES is a software solution that can be customized (Customs provides the source code on request) for electronic filing of export documentation.

B

Bandwidth: A specification used in networks that's stated in bits/second. The amount of data that's transferred is directly proportional to the bandwidth. If the bandwidth is increased, the amount of information transfer will increase as well.

Bridge: A bridge is used to reduce network traffic by filtering Data Link layer frames. A bridge examines MAC addresses to determine if the frame should be sent on to another portion or a network, or if it should remain in the portion of the network where it originated.

C

C: C was intended to introduce portability among microprocessor types so that one program could be written and run on different processors. C must be compiled before it can be executed.

C++: C++ represents an improvement to C in that C++ contains far more functions than those used with C. C++ must also be compiled before it can be executed.

Cable Modem: A cable modem uploads and downloads data using the existing cable television (CATV) wiring infrastructure.

Cache Server: A cache server is used to store files. A cache server that's related to Internet applications will store Web site information for sites that users have recently visited.

Cache: Refers to a section of memory in a computer that has been specified for a particular use. Web browsers routinely cache information related to Web sites that have been visited.

Certificate Authority: A CA is used in a SSL session to authenticate the holder of a certificate (such as an e-commerce server), and to provide a digital signature that will reveal if the certificate has been compromised.

Certificate-level Access: Refers to digital certificates that are used to authenticate users or Web sites. The most common application is for authenticating Web sites, particularly e-commerce sites.

Certificate Server: A certificate server allows encrypted messages to be exchanged between a client and the certificate server.

Ciphertext: Plaintext that has been encrypted.

Circuit Switching: A circuit switched network is one in which a path is set up and maintained between two devices for the duration of the transmission.

Class A IP Address: The first octet is reserved for the network address, and the last three octets are reserved for the host address. All class A IP addresses begin with a decimal number from 1-126.

Class A Private IP Address: The address 10.x.x.x.

Class A Subnet Mask: The network mask, 255.0.0.0, used with a Class A IP address.

Class B IP Address: The first two octets are reserved for the network portion of the address, and the last two octets are reserved for the host portion of the address. All class B IP addresses begin with a decimal number from 128 through 191.

Class B Private IP Address: The address 172.16.x.x through 172.32.x.x.

Class B Subnet Mask: The network mask, 255.255.0.0, used with a Class B IP address.

Class C IP Address: The first three octets of the address are reserved for the network portion of the address, and the last octet is reserved for the host portion of the address. All class C addresses begin with a decimal number from 192 through 223.

Class C Private IP Address: The address 192.168.x.x.

Class C Subnet Mask: The network mask, 255.255.255.0, used with a Class C IP address.

Client-side Languages: A client-side language runs on a client machine.

Common Gateway Interface: CGI is a program that runs on a server and is typically used to execute some other program.

Connectionless Protocol: Doesn't send acknowledgements between the sending and receiving nodes. UDP is a connectionless protocol.

Connection-oriented Protocol: Uses acknowledgements between the sender and receiver. TCP is a connection-oriented protocol.

Cookie: A text file generated by a Web server that is stored on the user's computer. A cookie contains information concerning the user's preferences when visiting a Web site. Cookies are also used to customize a Web site according to the user's preferences.

Copyright Symbol: The copyright symbol is a properly displayed symbol that consists of three components:

1. *The copyright symbol.* The correct symbol is a "c" within a circle, as in. (Note that for phonograph products, a "p" within a circle may be required.)

2. *The year that the work was fixed.* To avoid confusion, use all four digits in the year. That is, indicate the year as 2000, rather than as 00.

3. *The owner of the copyright.* The owner may be an individual, or it may be a company or organization.

Copyrighting: A copyright is used to protect the author of an original work from infringement. Infringement, in this context, refers to the unauthorized use of copyrighted material.

Cryptography: The process of writing secret messages so that the message intelligence is hidden.

D

Decryption: The process of transforming the secret code back to the original data.

Default Gateway: A router used to connect different networks.

Denial of Service Attack: A denial of service attack occurs when the resources of a computer—typically, a server—have been diverted so that users are unable to utilize the server resources. Since the computer is kept busy attempting to respond to the attack, users are unable to access the server resources.

Detection Logs: Alert an administrator that a potential network breach is occurring.

Digital Certificate: Used to authenticate Internet users or Web sites. A digital certificate ensures that communication over the Internet is confidential and reliable. All e-commerce sites on the Internet use digital certificates in public-key encryption.

Digital Subscriber Line: Digital Subscriber Line, or DSL, is a connection technology that uses standard twisted-pair telephone wires to send and receive data at high data rates.

Directory Server: A directory server uses the LDAP (Lightweight Directory Access Protocol) protocol to access and search information that's distributed in a directory.

Domain Name Service or System: DNS is used to translate Internet domain names to IP addresses.

Dynamic Host Configuration Protocol: DHCP is used to temporarily assign IP addresses to workstations and Internet clients.

Dynamic Link Library: A DLL is used to access the functions of an operating system. The functions of a DLL refer to communication with a serial port, accessing the Internet, or performing various functions on an operating system such as Microsoft Windows. On a Web server, a DLL is often used an interface to applications residing on the server.

E

E-commerce Server: An e-commerce server is used to conduct secure financial transactions over the Internet.

Electronic Data Interchange: EDI is the transfer of data between different companies using computers that are connected by a network, typically, the Internet.

E-mail Client: An e-mail client contains the Simple Mail Transfer Protocol (SMTP) used to send e-mail, along with the Post Office Protocol version 3 (POP3) that's used to receive e-mail from an e-mail server.

Encryption: Encryption refers to hiding the content of data packets so that the information in the packet will remain confidential and unchanged.

Extranet: An extranet is a private network that supports Internet applications and uses the public telecommunications system to share company information with users, customers and partners. Essentially, an extranet extends an intranet to the public Internet.

F

File Level Security: Intended to restrict the level of access to the server content. The most common levels of file security are Read, Write, and Full.

File Transfer Protocol: FTP is a means of downloading files to your computer, or uploading them from your computer to an FTP server.

Firewall: A firewall is used to prevent corporate network users from accessing portions of the Internet, and to prevent outside intruders from accessing a corporate network. A firewall may consist of hardware and software. *See proxy.*

Flash: Flash is an authoring software that allows you to create full-motion videos for source material that is, typically, in a common file format such as a series of JPG files.

Frame Relay: Frame Relay is a variable-bandwidth packet switched technology that utilizes Data Link layer concepts to send data. Its operation is similar to X.25.

FTP Client: Software that is used on a client computer to upload files to an FTP server, and to download files from an FTP server.

FTP Server: An FTP server is used to transfer files across the Internet, extranet or intranet. To access an FTP server, the client computer must have an FTP client installed.

Full Text Index: A full text index is a list of all terms and URLs that are found on a Web site.

G

Gateway: A gateway is a device used to convert from one incompatible protocol to another protocol.

Gopher: An Internet database.

H

Host File: Contains mappings of IP addresses to computer names.

Hot Links: Hot link testing refers to checking links at a Web site to determine if they work.

HTML Tags: A tag specifies the structure, or look, of a document. There are tags indicating the start of a paragraph, for example.

Hub: A hub is a device used to provide centralized access to the network. Hubs are used in a physical star topology.

HyperText Markup Language: HTML provides a way to code a document so that it be displayed on the World Wide Web area of the Internet.

HyperText Transfer Protocol: HTTP is a client-server protocol used to send and receive files on the Internet.

I

ICMP Echo (Smurf) Attack: A smurf attack is directed to Internet hosts and particularly to servers on the Internet. A smurf attack originates from a single host computer. An attacker at the computer sends an ICMP ping to a valid network address, and all recipients at the receiving network return the ping to a third IP address. The third IP address is the victim of the attack.

Internet Backbone: A backbone is a common channel that allows networks to be connected together. The Internet commercial backbone provides voice and data lines across the United States. Other parts of the world have similar backbones used to provide voice and data communications along with access to NAPs.

Internet Connection Point: Refers to the physical connections that a Web site has to the Internet. An ISP has a direct connection to the Internet infrastructure, either through the Internet backbone or to a Network Access Point.

Internet Protocol: IP is responsible for routing data packets from the source node to the destination node.

Internet Server Application Programming Interface: ISAPI is a proprietary software tool created by Microsoft and designed to run on servers with Microsoft Internet Information Server (IIS) installed.

Internet Service Provider: An ISP is used to provide access to the Internet.

Internet: The Internet is a network consisting of thousands of networks. It's a global, public network that uses an infrastructure consisting of network access points, a commercial backbone, and Internet service providers.

Intranet: An intranet is a private network that supports Internet applications and that doesn't use the public telecommunications system to connect users.

IP Address: An IP address contains 32 bits. It consists of two parts, a *network address* and a *host address*. The network address identifies the network that a node is connected to. The host portion of an IP address identifies the specific machine connected to a network. An IP address may be public or private.

IP Spoof: IP spoofing is a technique used to make a network message appear to originate from an authorized IP address, when it actually comes from a different IP address.

IPConfig: A diagnostic tool used to learn addressing information about the network or computers on a network.

ISDN Adapter: Used to connect to the digital ISDN telephone network.

J

JavaScript: JavaScript is a client-side language that allows you to embed certain functions into HTML documents, and have the functions executed on a client browser that supports JavaScript.

Java: Java is a server-side programming language. Java actually consists of three primary components: Java programming language, Java virtual machine, and the Java platform.

Jscript: Jscript is a client-side scripting language that allows you to create dynamic HTML files on a client computer.

K

Kerberos: An authentication scheme that authenticates the parties by embedding a key (that's assigned to each of the parties) in the messages that are exchanged.

Keyword Index: A keyword index examines the relevance of a word or phrase before listing it in a Web site search database.

L

Licensing: Licensing refers to requiring payment in exchange for using a copyrighted work.

Lightweight Directory Access Protocol: LDAP is a client-server protocol that allows users to access remote database servers. LDAP uses TCP/IP as the Transport layer protocol, which allows any client running TCP/IP to access a LDAP server.

Line Printer Protocol: LPR is used with internet-working so that a client computer user can print to a remote printer over a TCP/IP connection.

List Server: A list server is used to generate messages to subscribers of a list, as well as allow subscribers to post messages that will be distributed to all other subscribers.

Load Testing: Load testing refers to the length of time required to open all files of a site in a Web browser.

Loopback Address Test: The test IP address, 127.0.0.1, that's entered at a workstation or server to determine if the network interface card is operational.

M

Mail Flood: Mail flooding occurs when large e-mails are sent to an e-mail server.

Mail Server: A mail server is used to specifically send and receive e-mail, as well as to store e-mail records.

Mirror Server: A mirror server contains exact copies of the contents of a primary server.

Modem: A modem is used as an interface to the public telephone network.

Multimedia Software: Software used to view graphics, video, or audio files. Multimedia software is installed on client computers with plug-ins to Web browsers.

Multiple Login Failure: A security breach that occurs when an intruder attempts to login to a network but doesn't know the correct password.

Multipurpose Internet Mail Extensions: MIME is an Internet standard describing how messages are to be formatted in order for the messages to be exchanged between different e-mail systems. MIME allows nearly any file type to be sent with an e-mail message.

N

Netscape Server Application Programming Interface: NSAPI was developed to provide a set of commonly used server functions to handle HTTP requests and responses.

Network Access Points: A NAP provides high-speed interconnectivity to the Internet. Today, there are six major NAPs in the United States and all of them are commercially owned and operated.

Network News Transfer Protocol: NNTP is an Internet service that includes Usenet news.

News Server: A news server uses the Network News Transport Protocol (NNTP) to store messages, and to allow messages to be sent for others to read.

NIC: A network interface card (NIC), also called a network adapter, is a printed circuit card used to access the network resources. A NIC contains electronic circuitry that organizes data into unique frames so that the data can be sent, and received, on the network.

Non-relational Database: A non-relational database consists of a single set of row and column data that can't be cross-referenced to other databases.

P

Packet Switching: A packet switched network is one in which data may travel across many paths between two devices.

Patches: Software updates intended to fix a problem.

Perl: Perl is used primarily as a server-side scripting language, particularly for writing CGIs.

Ping Flood: A network attack that occurs when the size of a ping packet is inflated to the maximum size, and the large packet is sent to a server, causing the server buffers to overflow.

Ping: A tool used to check connectivity between network devices, such as between workstations, or between workstations and servers.

Plug-in: A plug-in consists of software that is compatible with the Web browser installed on the user computer. Examples of plug-ins include Apple's Quick Time, Macromedia Shockwave, Real Audio, Media Player, and Adobe Acrobat.

Point-to-Point Protocol: PPP is a communication protocol used to send data across serial communication links.

Point-to-Point Tunneling Protocol: PPTP is a protocol used to securely transport PPP packets over a TCP/IP network. PPTP is normally associated with a VPN.

Post Office Protocol: POP3 mimics the SMTP end of an e-mail dialogue and stores the received message until you ask to retrieve it. POP3 is a client-side protocol that must be installed on the workstation in order for e-mail to be downloaded to the client.

Private IP Address: A range of IP addresses that have been reserved for experiments, and for networks that aren't connected to the Internet.

Private-Key Encryption: The same key is used to encrypt and decrypt an encoded message. Private-key encryption is also called *symmetric encryption.*

Protocol: A protocol specifies the attributes of a network function.

Proxy Server: A barrier that prevents outsiders from entering a local area network. All addressing information sent to the Internet from the local network will use the IP address of the proxy server.

Public-Key Encryption: Two keys—one public and the other private—are used to encrypt as well as authenticate users. Public-key encryption is also referred to as *asymmetric encryption.*

Pull Technology: A method of downloading data from a server to a client. The client pull method relies on opening and closing a TCP connection for each update to a Web page.

Push Technology: A method of downloading data from a server to a client. The server push method relies on opening a single TCP connection between browser and Web server.

Q

QTVR: QuickTime Virtual Reality (QTVR) is produced by Apple. It consists of software that allows you to develop, then display, three-dimensional objects or scenes.

R

RealPlayer: RealPlayer is a plug-in that's used to display video and audio files.

Relational Database: A relational database consists of items in columns and rows that can be extensively cross-referenced to data contained in one or more databases.

Root DNS Server: All DNS requests forwarded to the Internet are initially sent to a root server. A root server has authority for all zone designations. There are currently twelve root DNS servers in the United States.

Router: A router is used to connect different networks and, occasionally, different network segments.

S

Search Query Operators: Search query operators are the rules used with a search engine to define a query. Examples include AND, OR, and NOT; as well as the operators + and -, and quotation marks.

Secure Socket Layer: The SSL protocol is used to authenticate users or e-commerce servers on the Internet, and to encrypt/decrypt messages using public-key encryption.

Secure/MIME: S/MIME is a protocol for encrypting e-mail. S/MIME is an RSA derivative that uses public-key encryption techniques.

Serial Line Interface Protocol: SLIP is used to connect two nodes in a point-to-point configuration and is a less secure serial protocol than PPP.

Server-side Language: Programming language that runs on a Web server.

Service Nark: A service mark is used to refer to the source of the trademark—such as a company name—and may be listed in the advertising of a product.

Shockwave: Shockwave is a plug-in used to view games, tutorials, and complex presentations.

Simple Mail Transfer Protocol: SMTP defines the use of e-mail on the Internet. To send e-mail, SMTP must be used.

Socket: A packet exchanged between the two nodes that contains the logical addresses of the nodes (their IP address), the process that's to be used between the nodes (such as e-mail, a file transfer, or HTTP for the World Wide Web), and the Transport layer protocol that the nodes will use (TCP).

SONET: SONET, or Synchronous Optical Network, is a carrier technology that uses optical signals.

Static Index: A static index consists of a list of Web site headings that include links to detailed information related to each heading.

Static IP Address: A static IP address is permanently assigned to a workstation or client.

Structured Query Language: SQL is used to manipulate data in a database as well as to define the data that a user wants to see.

Subnet Mask: The decimal number 255 that's used to identify the network portion of an IP address so that a single IP address can be used by more than one machine.

Switch: A switch allows each connected node to be dynamically connected to any other node port. The connections established between ports in a switch are handled with software. The connection is a virtual circuit that is built-up and torn-down each time a node connects to a different port.

SYN Flood: A SYN flood occurs when a half-open TCP connection is begun with a server, then never closed.

T

T-1 Carrier: Digital data is transmitted in a frame that has a data rate of 1.544 Mbps.

T-carrier: Digital technology transmission system in which data is transmitted at 64 Kbps (or 56 Kbps in older T-carrier systems) simultaneously in both directions.

TCP/IP: An acronym for Transmission Control Protocol/Internet Protocol. TCP/IP consists of the TCP protocol and the IP protocol. Together, the two protocols form the TCP/IP Protocol Suite.

Telnet Server: A telnet server is used to allow remote users to connect to a server that will display information as if the user were directly connected to the server. To utilize a telnet server, a telnet client must be installed on the client computer.

Telnet: A service that allows you to use the resources of a remote computer through a command line interface.

Top-level Domain Servers: A top-level domain server is specialized to a zone such as .com, .org, or .net.

TraceRT: A diagnostic tool used to show the path to a remote server or workstation.

Trademarks: A trademark is a word, phrase, symbol, or combination of words, symbols, or phrases that are used to differentiate the products and services of one party from those of another.

Transmission Control Protocol: TCP is responsible for reliable process-to-process communication between two devices, such as servers, or servers and workstations.

U

Unicode Standard: Represents a solution to language barriers by providing a single system for representing characters from the majority of languages from the past and present. The current version of Unicode provides for nearly 39,000 coded characters from the world's alphabets.

Uniform Resource Locator: A uniform resource locator (URL) is used to access services on the Internet.

Uuencode: Unix-to-Unix Encoding converts binary files into ASCII text so that they can be sent either in an e-mail, or as an attachment to an e-mail.

V

VBScript: VBScript, or Visual Basic Script, is a client-side scripting language that allows you to create dynamic HTML files on a client computer.

Virtual Circuit: A virtual circuit (also called a permanent virtual circuit) refers to a specified amount of bandwidth that's guaranteed for the duration of a transmission between two devices. Packet switched networks use virtual circuits.

Virtual Private Network: A Virtual Private Network, or VPN, is a secure and encrypted connection between two points across the Internet. The secure connection is realized by authenticating users at each end of the connection.

Virtual Private Network: A virtual private network, or VPN, uses the Internet infrastructure as the communication medium between different network sites.

Visual Basic: Visual Basic is a server-side language that's primarily used to collect database information.

W

Web Browser: Software used to view the World Wide Web, which is rich in graphics and multimedia content.

Web Page Files: A Web page consists of linked files that, when downloaded to the client browser, constitute the Web page.

Web Server: A Web server uses the HTTP protocol to send HTML and other file types to clients.

Well-Known Port: A 16-bit number that specifies a process to be initiated by a server.

Windows Internet Naming Service: WINS is a protocol used to reconcile NetBIOS names to IP addresses.

Windows Media Player: Windows Media Player, installed with Windows operating systems, allows you to view most of the common video, audio, and graphical formats that you're likely to encounter on the Internet.

WinIPCfg: The addressing diagnostic tool used with Windows 95 operating systems.

X

X.25 Packet Switching: X.25 packet switching is an older transport protocol used in WANs, and is modeled after the public telephone system. Data in an X.25 network travels at either 56 or 64 Kbps.

XML: XML, or eXtensible Markup Language, is an alternative to HTML that's being developed by the World Wide Web consortium (W3C).

Index

Point-of-presence, 6
Point-to-Point Tunneling Protocol, 10, 131
POP3 (Post Office Protocol, version 3), 136, 178
PPP (Point-to-Point Protocol), 128
PPTP, 10, 131, 198, 262
Pre-launch phase, 216
Pretty Good Privacy (PGP), 251
Primary Rate Interface (PRI), 25
Prime numbers, 248
Private IP addresses, 122
Private-key encryption, 245
Product, 244
Progressive JPEG, 100
Properties, 87
Protocol, 7, 111
Proxy, 156
Proxy server, 122, 169, 204, 235, 238
Public domain, 282
Public switched telephone network (PSTN), 21
Publication, 278
Public-key encryption, 181
Pulse Code Modulation (PCM), 30
Put, 176
Put command, 237

Q

QuickTime Virtual Reality (QTVR), 91
QUIT, 135

R

R Interface, 27
RAS (Remote Access Service), 131
Rate Adaptive DSL (RADSL), 29
Read-only access, 233
RealPlayer, 92
Receiver ready, 135
Reference Interface, 27
Registered Trademark, 282
Registrar, 289
Relational database, 92
Relational databases management systems (RDMS), 212
Relationship management, 299
Relative path, 201
Reliability, 193
Remote access protocol, 128
Repeaters, 14
Replication server, 207
Request-response process, 133
Resource records (RR), 127
Response, 134
RFC (Request For Comments), 140
RIP (Routing Information Protocol), 19
Rivest-Shamir-Adleman (RSA), 248
RJ11, 21
RJ45 connector , 12
Robbed bit, 35
Root, 199, 201

Root DNS server, 125
Router, 5, 16
Royalties, 284

S

S Interface, 27
S/MIME (Secure/MIME) protocol, 251
Screened-subnet firewall, 240
Search engines, 93
Search query operators, 95
Secure Electronic Transmission (SET), 298
Secure server, 210
Secure Socket Layer (SSL) , 242, 249
Security, 181, 193
Segment, 14
Serial data, 11
Serial Line Interface Protocol, 130
Server Application Functions (SAF), 62
Server configuration problems, 251
Server farm, 8
Server name, 49
Service closing, 135
Service Mark, 282
Set Asynchronous Balance Mode (SABM), 41
Set Asynchronous Response Mode (SARM), 41
Shockwave, 92
Shopping carts, 213
Signature, 259
Simple Mail Transfer Protocol (SMTP), 50, 134, 158, 205
Site access, 219
Site map, 94
SLIP, 130
SMTP (Simple Mail Transfer Protocol), 178
Smurf, 256
Sockets, 112
SONET (Synchronous Optical Network), 37
Source-route bridging, 14
Spamming, 258
Speed, 219
Spoofing, 256
SQL, 61
Stand-alone, 153
Start mail, 135
Static index, 94
Static router, 18
Stemming, 97
Store-and-forward, 20
Streaming, 91, 98
Structured Query Language, 61
Subdirectories, 201
Sub-domain servers, 126
Subnet, 116
Subnet mask, 116
Subscriber Interface, 24
Substitution, 244
Superframe, 32
Supervisory, 40

RC Jet-Cobra Race Car SE-1030

Leave the competition in the dust.....build this 1/18 scale, 2 wheel drive Baja racer from Marcraft. Select one of two forward speeds, punch the turbo power and go for it. The Jet-Cobra features a 5-function pistol grip controller that incorporates a turbo-boost circuit. Independent front and rear suspension provide excellent handling on sharp, high-speed corners. You'll find state-of-the-art IC technology coupled with fundamental transistor circuitry to demonstrate important electronics components such as: RF signal transmission and reception, digital information encoding and decoding, and motor control theory. A 72-page manual provides a thorough understanding of the electronics principles. As low as $36.95.

MARCRAFT *Electronics Kits*

PC Technician's Tool Kit IC-345

This professional technician's kit contains 29 of the most popular PC service tools to cover most PC service applications. Zipper case is constructed out of durable vinyl with room for an optional DMM and optional CD-ROM service disks. Includes: case (with zipper) has external slash pocket for extra storage (13½" L x 9¾" H x 2 3/8" W), slotted 3/16" screwdriver, IC Inserter, slotted 1/8" screwdriver, 3-prong parts Retriever, Phillips # 1 screwdriver, self-locking tweezers, Phillips # 0 screwdriver, tweezers, precision 4 pc (2 slotted / 2 Phillips) screwdriver set, inspection mirror, driver handle, penlight, # 2 Phillips / slotted ¼" screwdriver bits, 6" adjustable wrench, # T-10 Torx / T-15 Torx screwdriver bits, 4 ½" mini-diagonal, ¼" nut driver, 5" mini-long nose, 3/16" nut driver, anti-static wrist strap, 5" hemostat, part storage tube, IC Extractor. (Note: Meter not included) As low as $36.95

Sonic Rover SE-1029

The Rover is an exciting hands-on electronics project, providing an easy way to learn basic transistor, amplifier and switching circuitry. It teaches the fundamentals of sound detection and amplification, as well as switching circuits, DC motors and gear ratios. The front-mounted microphone sensor can be activated by a touch or noise. When the sensor encounters an object, or hears a loud voice command, it will automatically stop, back up, turn to the left 90 degrees, and then resume its forward motion. A dual-colored LED switches between Green and Red to indicate forward and reverse motion. The 48-page manual details breadboarding explorations and circuit construction for this 9-transistor project. As low as $13.95.

Power Supply SE-1014

A project that teaches half-wave, full-wave, and full-wave, and full-wave bridge rectification. When finished, it's a usable power supply featuring four d.c. output voltage selections. An isolation transformer is included and is enclosed in a durable case for safety. The manual has 32 pages of information. As low as $9.95

Analog Multimeter SE-1028

The Analog Multimeter teaches the importance of electronic "basics". This project functions as an AC/DC meter and is designed to cover all aspects of meter theory including diode rectification and protection...and how resistors are used to limit current and drop voltage. This kit is first breadboarded and tested in a series of informative circuits and explorations, which are detailed in the 48-page instruction manual. As low as $26.95.

ORDERING INFORMATION

School Purchase orders: Terms are net 30 days.
Direct Student orders: Must be accompanied by check, money order, credit card or shipped C.O.D. Shipping Charge: $5.00 per kit to cover shipping and handling charges, for C.O.D. orders add $5.50.

QUANTITY DISCOUNT PRICE LIST

Model	Description	1-4	5-9	10-99	100+
SE-1014	Power Supply	12.95	11.95	10.95	9.95
SE-1028	Analog Multimeter	32.95	30.95	28.95	26.95
SE-1029	Sonic Rover	17.95	16.95	14.95	13.95
SE-1030	R/C Race3 Car	42.95	40.95	37.95	36.95
IC-345	Deluxe Tech Tool Kit	39.95	38.95	37.95	36.95

Order Toll Free
1-800-441-6006

MARCRAFT

Marcraft International Corporation
100 N. Morain - 302, Kennewick, WA 99336

MARCRAFT
Your IT Training Provider
(800) 441-6006

A+ Certification

This book provides you with training necessary for the A+ Certification testing program that certifies the competency of entry-level (6 months experience) computer service technicians. The A+ test contains situational, traditional, and identification types of questions. All of the questions are multiple choice with only one correct answer for each question. The test covers a broad range of hardware and software technologies, but is not bound to any vendor-specific products.

The program is backed by major computer hardware and software vendors, distributors, and resellers. A+ certification signifies that the certified individual possesses the knowledge and skills essential for a successful entry-level (6 months experience) computer service technician, as defined by experts from companies across the industry.

Network+ Certification

Network+ is a CompTIA vendor-neutral certification that measures the technical knowledge of networking professionals with 18-24 months of experience in the IT industry. The test is administered by NCS/VUE and Prometric™. Discount exam vouchers can be purchased from Marcraft.

Earning the Network+ certification indicates that the candidate possesses the knowledge needed to configure and install the TCP/IP client. This exam covers a wide range of vendor and product neutral networking technologies that can also serve as a prerequisite for vendor-specific IT certifications. Network+ has been accepted by the **leading networking vendors** and included in many of their training curricula. The skills and knowledge measured by the certification examination are derived from industry-wide job task analyses and validated through an industry wide survey. The objectives for the certification examination are divided in two distinct groups, Knowledge of Networking Technology and Knowledge of Networking Practices.

i-Net+ Certification

The i-Net+ certification program is designed specifically for any individual interested in demonstrating baseline technical knowledge that would allow him or her to pursue a variety of Internet-related careers. i-Net+ is a vendor-neutral, entry-level Internet certification program that tests baseline technical knowledge of Internet, Intranet and Extranet technologies, independent of specific Internet-related career roles. Learning objectives and domains examined include Internet basics, Internet clients, development, networking, security and business concepts.

Certification not only helps individuals enter the Internet industry, but also helps managers determine a prospective employee's knowledge and skill level.

Linux+ Certification

The Linux+ certification measures vendor-neutral Linux knowledge and skills for an individual with at least 6 months practical experience. Linux+ Potential Job Roles: Entry Level Helpdesk, Technical Sales/Marketing, Entry Level Service Technician, Technical Writers, Resellers, Application Developers, Application Customer Service Reps.

Linux+ Exam Objectives Outline: User administration, Connecting to the network, Package Management, Security Concept, Shell Scripting, Networking, Apache web server application, Drivers (installation, updating, removing), Kernel (what it does, why to rebuild), Basic printing, Basic troubleshooting.

Server+ Certification

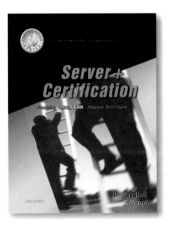

Server+ certification deals with advanced hardware issues such as RAID, SCSI, multiple CPUs, SANs and more. This is vendor-neutral with a broad range of support, including core support by 3Com, Adaptec, Compaq, Hewlett-Packard, IBM, Intel, EDS Innovations Canada, Innovative Productivity, and Marcraft.

This book focuses on complex activities and solving complex problems to ensure servers are functional and applications are available. It provides an in-depth understanding of the planning, installing, configuring, and maintaining servers, including knowledge of server-level hardware implementations, data storage subsystems, data recovery, and I/O subsystems.

Data Cabling Installer Certification

The Data Cabling Installer Certification provides the IT industry with an introductory, vendor-neutral certification for skilled personnel that install Category 5 copper data cabling.

The Marcraft *Enhanced Data Cabling Installer Certification Training Guide* provides students with the knowledge and skills required to pass the Data Cabling Installer Certification exam and become a certified cable installer. The DCIC is recognized nationwide and is the hiring criterion used by major communication companies. Therefore, becoming a certified data cable installer will enhance your job opportunities and career advancement potential.

Fiber Optic Cabling Certification

There is a growing demand for qualified cable installers who understand and can implement fiber optic technologies. These technologies cover terminology, techniques, tools and other products in the fiber optic industry. This text/lab book covers basics of fiber optic design discipline, installations, pulling and prepping cables, terminations, testing and safety considerations. Labs will cover ST-compatible and SC connector types, both multimedia and single mode cables and connectors. Learn about insertion loss, optical time domain reflectometry, and reflectance. Cover mechanical and fusion splices and troubleshooting cable systems. This Text/Lab covers the theory and hands-on skills needed to prepare you for fiber optic entry-level certification.